Sacred Space and Structural Style

RELIGIONS AND BELIEFS SERIES

The series includes books bearing on the religions of the Americas, the Bible in its relationship to cultures, and on ethics in relation to religion. The series welcomes manuscripts written in either English or French.

In the Same Series

Pauline Côté, *Les Transactions politiques des croyants: Charismatiques et Témoins de Jéhovah dans le Québec des années 1970 et 1980,* 1993.

Adolf Ens, *Subjects or Citizens?: The Mennonite Experience in Canada, 1870–1925,* 1994.

Robert Choquette, *The Oblate Assault on Canada's Northwest,* 1995.

Jennifer Reid, *Myth, Symbol, and Colonial Encounter: British and Mi'kmaq in Acadia, 1700–1867,* 1995.

M. D. Faber, *New Age Thinking: A Psychoanalytic Critique,* 1996.

André Guindon, *L'Habillé et le Nu: Pour une éthique du vêtir et du dénuder,* 1997.

RELIGIONS AND BELIEFS SERIES, NO. 7

Sacred Space and Structural Style

The Embodiment of Socio-religious Ideology

VICKI BENNETT

University of Ottawa Press

This book has been published with the help of a grant from the Canadian Federation for the Humanities, using funds provided by the Social Sciences and Humanities Research Council of Canada.

University of Ottawa Press gratefully acknowledges the support extended to its publishing programme by the Canada Council, the Department of Canadian Heritage, and the University of Ottawa.

CANADIAN CATALOGUING IN PUBLICATION DATA

Bennett, Vicki

Sacred Space and Structural Style: The Embodiment of Socio-religious Ideology

(Religions and Beliefs series; no. 7)

Includes bibliographical references and index.
ISBN 0-7766-0440-6

1. Church architecture—Ottawa River Valley (Quebec and Ont.)—History—19th century. 2. Architecture, Gothic—Ottawa River Valley (Quebec and Ont.)—History—19th century. 3. Church buildings—Ottawa River Valley (Quebec and Ont.)—History—19th century. I. Title. II. Series.

NA5246.O8B45 1997 726.5'09713'809034 C97-901267-8

Cover photo: Alain Erdmer
Cover: Robert Dolbec
Typesetting: Danielle Péret

ISBN 0-7766-0440-6

542 King Edward, Ottawa (Ont.), Canada K1N 6N5
press@ uottawa.ca http://www.uopress.uottawa.ca

Printed and bound in Canada

For Alain and Xavier,
whose love sustains and inspires me.

ACKNOWLEDGMENTS

While I must take sole responsibility for any imperfections in this work, the same is not true where credit is due. This book began as my doctoral dissertation and many individuals and organizations helped along the way. I am indebted to my director, Norman Pagé, and to Elisabeth J. Lacelle. This book has profited from the sage critique of John Webster Grant. I would especially like to thank Robert Choquette for reading various versions of this work and generously offering the guidance necessary to bring this book to press.

My research has been generously funded by a Social Sciences and Humanities Research Council doctoral fellowship, a research scholarship from the School of Graduate Studies of the University of Ottawa, a post-doctoral fellowship from Fondation UQAM, and a Concordia University faculty grant. I am most grateful for this funding, which has greatly facilitated my work.

This book has been published with the help of a grant from the Humanities and Social Sciences Federation of Canada, using funds provided by the Social Sciences and Humanities Research Council of Canada.

I would like to thank the archival staff of the Public Archives of Canada and the National Library of Canada; Soeur Marcelle Gratton of the Archives of the Archdiocese (Roman Catholic) of Ottawa, and the late Dr. Shirley Spragg of the Queen's University Archives, in

Kingston. Thanks is also due to the staff of the Ottawa City Archives who went beyond the call of duty to facilitate my research, as well as to Jack Francis and Fred Neal of the Archives of the Archdiocese (Anglican) of Ottawa, who shared both their expertise and their friendship. My on-site research was greatly facilitated by innumerable ladies and gentlemen, who in their capacity as pastor, parishioner, custodian or local historian, gave freely of their time to find keys, light switches and draw my attention to architectural anomalies. Their efforts are, in many ways, epitomized in the kindness of Mr. S. McGregor of Lochwinnoch.

I would like to recognize with gratitude the fellowship of my colleagues Louis Rousseau, Martin Kilmer, Toby Gelfand, Michel Despland, Frank Remiggi, Jean Guy Laundry, Frédéric Castel, and Guy Mongrain. I am most grateful for the interest and comments of many Concordia students, especially Lana Wilhem, Chris Helland, Jane Greening, Uriah Collins, Jesse Katz, Melany Cooney, Kriss Belliard, Mara Cherchover, and Tina Di Rado.

I would like to acknowledge the interest and encouragement of family and friends: Catherine Billington, Beth and Nick Ediger, Wilf and Connie Wight, S.A.T., Sonya Lipsett-Rivera, Glenn Lockwood, and Marcel Erdmer. I am especially grateful to my parents, Patricia and Berard Bennett, whose encouragement during all my studies is very much appreciated.

I am deeply indebted to Alain Erdmer, not only for his professional advice in architectural matters, but for the many years during which he gave so generously of his time, energy, and love. It is to Alain and our son Xavier that I owe my greatest debt.

Ottawa, Ontario, 1997

CONTENTS

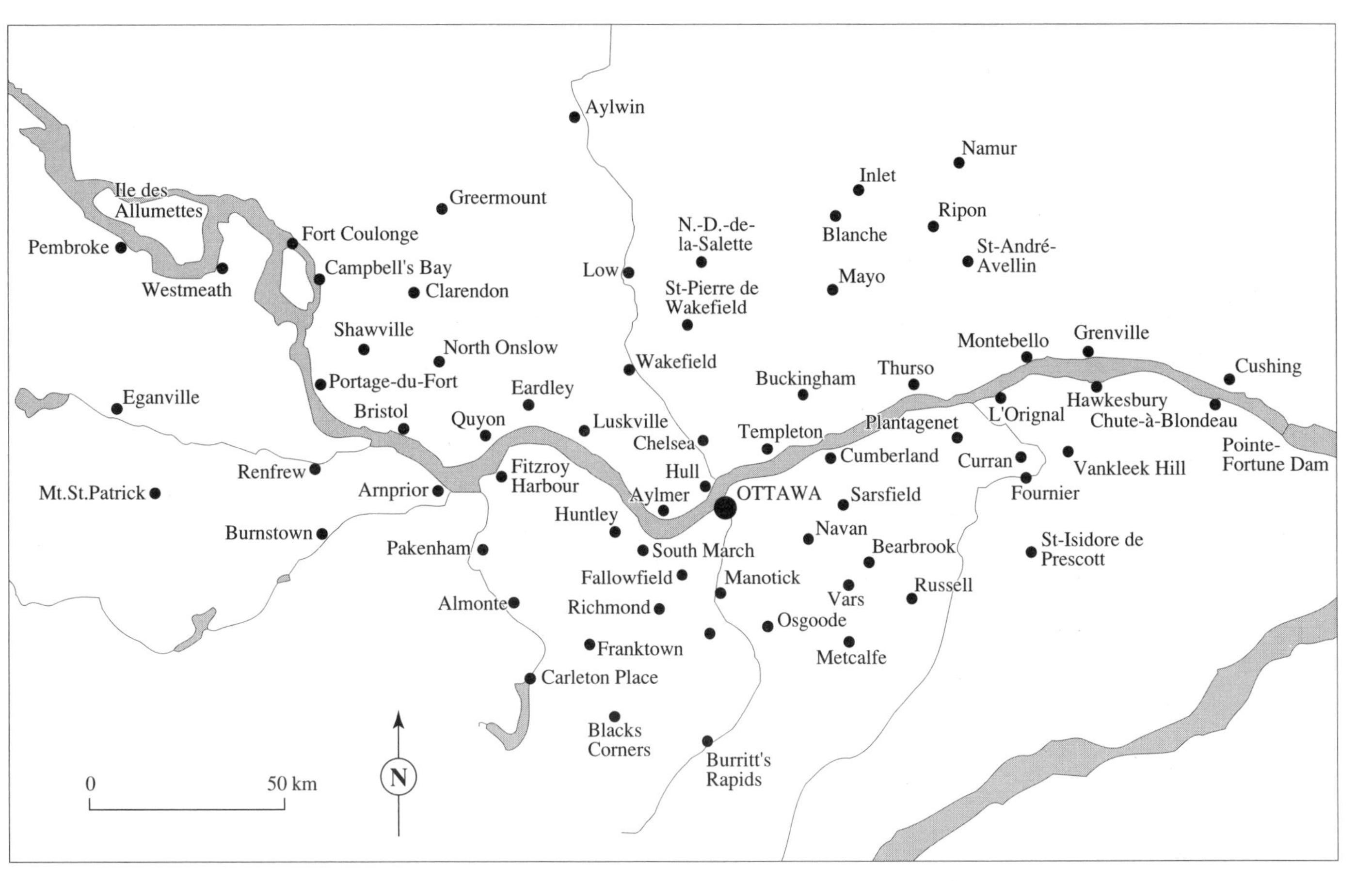

THE OTTAWA VALLEY

INTRODUCTION

The past decade has seen the publication of a wide range of studies that explore numerous and diverse aspects of religion in nineteenth-century Canada. While few researchers would deny that most nineteenth-century congregations who gathered to worship as a community preferred to do so in a space built specifically for this purpose, the architecture engendered by these communities remains largely unexplored. Architectural historians have traditionally concentrated their research on the morphological dimensions of tangible fabric. Nineteenth-century church building is often studied in terms of stylistic categories that are applied more aptly to institutional or domestic architecture, while its religious *raison d'être* enjoys only the most superficial acknowledgment.

In an article written for the *Anglo-American* in 1853, architect W. Hay[1] declared that "Christian architecture is the name given to that peculiar style of building commonly called Gothic. . . . It derived its origin from the efforts of Christians of preceding ages to embody the principles and characteristics of their faith in the structures that they reared for the services of their religion."[2] Hay's thinking on this subject echoes a broadly held contemporary understanding that religious beliefs could—and indeed should—be incorporated in the tangible fabric of a church building. During the nineteenth century, the Gothic style was thought by many to have a unique advantage over other architectural styles because it had never been used for pagan constructions. Instead, it had been invented by Christians specifically for the construction of Christian churches and was, therefore, believed best suited for the embodiment of Christian principles. One consequence of this thinking was the widespread abandonment of classical components by church builders and a renewed interest in medieval prototypes. By the middle decades of the nineteenth century, most Christian denominations in Central Canada built some reference to the Gothic style into their place of worship. This book explores the nineteenth-century association of Gothic architecture with Christian church building as manifest in eastern Ontario and western Quebec.

While many nineteenth-century Christians may have agreed that "Gothic architecture" was synonymous with "Christian architecture," it is less likely that they were in agreement as to what precisely constituted a good "Christian." Christianity was neither interpreted nor practised in a uniform manner during the nineteenth century, and it would not seem unreasonable to expect that an architectural style held to embody the principles of such a multiform faith might reflect a similar degree of diversity. Church builders were certainly not immune to the changing tastes of secular fashion and contemporary style; still, there is worthy evidence to suggest that, when used in a religious context, nineteenth-century interpretations of Gothic might be as diverse as, and, more importantly, closely linked to nineteenth-century interpretations of Christianity.

This widespread interest in Gothic shown by Christians of Central Canada raises several questions: First, what exactly is Gothic? Second, how did a style that was both European and medieval become so widely used in Central Canada? There is no short answer to either question. What is commonly known today as Gothic appeared in its embryonic phase in the *Île de France* during the early twelfth century. Advocates of English nationalism will occasionally claim that Durham Cathedral (c.1093), with its slightly pointed arches, proves the English origins of the Gothic style, although most scholars agree that a Gothic classification of Durham is erroneous. Nearly a century separates the construction of Durham and the construction of Canterbury—the first English church that is undeniably Gothic.[3]

The use of Gothic was not restricted to France or England and, from an early date, spread to Ireland through Scandinavia and the territories of the Holy Roman Empire, as well as Bohemia, Poland, Hungary, and the Baltic. Variants of the Gothic style also appeared in

Italy, the Adriatic, Greece, and Asia Minor. Crusaders brought it with them to Cyprus and the Holy Lands. The Spanish and the Portuguese both developed their own unique interpretation. A striking aspect of medieval Gothic was its adaptability. This is manifest not only in its espousal of a variety of indigenous traditions, but also in its ability to accommodate widely divergent social and economic climates.

Despite the expansiveness of the Gothic tradition, the origins of the term itself remain obscure. The oldest documented use of the term "Gothic" dates not from the Middle Ages but from sixteenth-century Italy, where it was used with injurious intent. Giorgio Vasari, architect of the de Medici family and designer of the Uffizi Museum of Florence, is most commonly credited with having committed "the historical enormity of dragging the word Gothic six centuries out of its proper location and use."[4] Previous writers such as Raphael, Filarete, and Cesar Cesariano did use the term "Gothic" but did so concerning much earlier work and do not appear to have in any way intended the term to include that form of medieval building that now bears the name. Some scholars have suggested *opus francigneum* as an alternative term, although, given the diversity of what is now called Gothic, this would be equally misleading. In a treatise on architecture and techniques published in 1550, Vasari's association of the word "Gothic" with what is commonly referred to today as Gothic is as undeniable as his distaste for Gothic. The style, he warns, is not used by properly trained architects; he begged that "God protect every country from such ideas and style of building. They are such deformities. . . . "[5] While people may address many unusual requests to their God, this may be one of the few requests for the entire world to be protected from a specific architectural style. Vasari's prayers went unanswered and the Gothic style enjoyed a strong European revival that spread rapidly during the nineteenth century through many previously uninfected lands.

Owing to the immensity of the geographical and chronological span covered by medieval Gothic, fixing an end date is difficult. This is especially true in England where Gothic continued to be used in the construction of country churches long after it had been abandoned by the builders of fashionable urban churches. Gothic reappeared as a fashionable architectural style once again during the late seventeenth and eighteenth century in England, but more in terms of a decorative montage than as a logical architectural assemblage. Sir Christopher Wren had made competent use of Gothic for several of his projects, including Westminster Abbey; however, his preference for classical restraint is evident. During the middle years of the seventeenth century, rococo Gothic as typified by the work of B. Langley, enjoyed an increased popularity. However, Langley's *Gothic Architecture Improved by Rules of Proportions* (1742) betrays his understanding of Gothic as something as equally well suited to garden pavilions as to churches. Although scholars are divided on its merits, Horace Walpole's work on the Strawberry Hill Estate (1749-1779), is frequently acknowledged as an important watershed in the revived interest in medieval Gothic. However, the execution of Strawberry Hill is as picturesque as its context is secular. Throughout the eighteenth century, neo-medieval estates bedecked with picturesque Gothic detailing were popular, but traditionally lacked the structural integration and rationalism of medieval Gothic.

By the early nineteenth century, Gothic was increasingly associated with church architecture. Although English Ecclesiologists are often credited with the re-appropriation of Gothic as an essentially ecclesiastical form of architectural expression, the architects of the Commissioners Churches had been using Gothic well before the initial intervention of the Ecclesiologists during the late 1830s and early 1840s. While Gothic may have appeared frequently in these churches, it was not a Gothic noted for its archaeological fidelity. For this reason, the Commissioners Churches were frequently the targets of wrathful criticism from vocal advocates of archaeological correctness, especially after the mid 1830s. One of the earlier and better known advocates of archaeological fidelity in the revived medieval style was A. W. Pugin. In 1836, Pugin published *Contrasts: or, A Parallel Between the Noble Edifices of the Fourteenth and Fifteenth Centuries and Similar Buildings of the Present Day; Showing the Present Decay of Taste,* in which he condemned not only the untutored use of Gothic architecture in the construction of the Commissioners Churches, but the principle of government grants with which they were built.

Many of Pugin's ideas are paralleled in the writings of the Ecclesiologists, although they themselves would have denied any link with Pugin. Begun as The Cambridge Camden Society in 1838 by Rev. Benjamin Webb and Rev. John Mason Neale, while they were undergraduates at Trinity College, Cambridge, English Ecclesiologists were to mount an aggressive campaign of architectural advocacy. Through their extensive writings, they inspired battalions of divinity students and amateur antiquarians to study and record the medieval churches of the British Isles.[6] They published manuals on how churches should be built, dictated what materials should be used, and even ventured to make recommendations concerning the personal piety of the architect. Ecclesiologists did not confine their interests to the architectural well-being of the British Isles, but also went to considerable pains to spread their ideas throughout the colonies and former colonies of the British Empire.

Gradually, clergymen and architects alike brought these new architectural ideals to some of the most distant corners of the Empire, and Central Canada was no exception. However, it is important to remember that while their architectural ideals may have been widely held, they were not universally held. French church architects and scholars, such as Viollet-le-Duc, were also exploring their architectural heritage from the Middle Ages. Although the revival of Gothic in French circles was never to attain the quasi-sacred status it enjoyed among its English advocates, it was a significant and distinctly continental materialization of a revived medieval style. This diversity raises a number of questions. How does an architectural style embody principles of religion? To what extent did nineteenth-century Christians living in Central Canada hold this to be true, and to what extent were they in agreement as to how this should be done? Once again the diversity of Gothic expression raises a number of questions. Were some groups of Christians more likely to use it than others? If the denominations that used Gothic did not use it in a like manner, how were denominational differences translated into a varied architectural expression?

The architectural production of a community is the result of many considerations. Church-building tradition is shaped by both architectural and liturgical observance as well as by the interaction of religious life with the realities of the secular world. One challenge facing those interested in the study of Gothic is adequately defining the term itself. While Gothic was subject to numerous chronological and regional variations, it was and still is most commonly associated with the use of pointed arches, such as the equilateral and lancet arches, the complex ogee arch and trefoil or cinquefoil arch, and occasionally the late four-centred arch. The pointed arch came so much to be associated with the Gothic or "Christian style" that some nineteenth-century writers, including Pugin, preferred to call Gothic architecture: "pointed architecture."[7] In its fullest expression as a visual manifestation of religious belief, Gothic is a complex and sophisticated integration of architectonic volumes that must also be understood in terms of spirit, logic, space, and lighting.[8] In the context of this discussion, it is the element most commonly associated with Gothic, the pointed arch, that will be the criterion used to identify a reference to the Gothic style.

British architectural historian John Summerson once stated: "The places of nonconformist worship have a much more expansive and complicated history—a history, however, of shelter rather than architecture."[9] From the strict perspective of architectural style, the same case can easily be made for, and indeed often is, applied to a great percentage of early Canadian church buildings. As a result, many plainer structures have been the object of little research attention. However, when these same structures are reconsidered in conjunction with congregational opinion and with their role within the community of worship, it is soon evident that their history is a history that transcends the parameters of mere shelter and architectural style. It is precisely this nineteenth-century perception of Gothic as the system of architectural expression best suited to the embodiment of Christian principles and Christian faith that demands an investigation of the subject also from the socio-religious perspective.

Although there are numerous regions that might profit from a greater investigation of this subject, a geographically and historically significant area would be more appropriate to a project of this nature. The Ottawa Valley is particularly well suited to meet these criteria. Straddling the provinces of Ontario and Quebec, the region hosts a diversity of religious, ethnic, and linguistic communities and offers a generous sampling of nineteenth-century religious architecture.[10] W. Westfall has noted that during the thirty-year period between 1851 and 1881, the Anglicans, Presbyterians, and Baptists of Ontario "trebled the number of their churches. The Methodists were even more prolific builders . . . the number of their churches increased by a factor of five."[11] While Westfall's work focuses primarily on south-central Ontario, similar trends can be identified in eastern Ontario and in parts of western Quebec. This trend is particularly evident in the Ottawa Valley, where over the course of the nineteenth century, several hundred places of worship were built. Although many of these buildings were modest log cabins, destined to be used for only a few years, they nevertheless represented considerable financial sacrifice on the part of those who built them. A survey of surviving churches in the Ottawa Valley indicates that a significant number of Christian communities chose to use "Christian" or "Gothic" elements of architecture in the construction of their place of worship. Despite the abundance of religious architecture in the Ottawa Valley, much of it remains unexplored. The area referred to in this book as the Ottawa Valley will include the counties on both the northern and southern shores of the river, beginning in the east with the counties of Prescott and Argenteuil (west of the Pointe-Fortune Dam) and running up river to the western tip of Allumette Island. The Lanark

County Townships of Pakenham, Ramsay, Darling, and Beckwith are also included. All architectural samplings were be taken from this region, although textual evidence, such as denominational guidelines and architectural treatises, are necessarily drawn from a larger field. This book is not intended to provide a detailed biography of all or any one building, but rather to identify stylistic trends and morphological analogies in the architectonic renderings of external and internal space. As none of the denominations included in this study existed in isolation from others of the same persuasion, textual evidence plays an essential part in situating the preoccupations of individual communities within the broader concerns of their denominations.

Too often, our understanding of church building traditions is dictated not by the type of building most common to a given period, but rather by those buildings that have survived physically. Typically, it is the rarer stone churches that survive longer and enjoy better documentation than the much more modest, but far more common, wooden churches. Furthermore, some ministers were more diligent than others in recording or preserving the transcripts and records of the material activities of their charges. Fires, negligence, and general household cleaning have taken a serious toll on the quantity of material that has survived. The unfortunate result being a somewhat skewed perception of early architectural trends.

This book is based on a study that recorded all cult places known to have been built during the course of the nineteenth century in the Ottawa Valley. Material was considered in terms of site selection, external structures, stylistic features and interior design, as well as liturgical requirements and focal points. Consideration of the site choice and orientation helped situate churches within their geographical, social, and architectural context. Often this revealed much about denominational attitudes towards the use of built space for collective worship. The external features of church buildings, especially the façade, were frequently privileged in terms of the materialization of architectural symbolism, architectural detailing, and building material. Examination of the façades invited not only an analysis of the micro-environment through which the faithful passed before entering into the cult space, but also allowed for an analysis of the image parishioners presented to the outside world. In the context of this book, "nave" refers to what in the study of Paleo-Christian and Proto-Byzantine church architecture is commonly called the *quadratum populi* and is devoid of structural implications. Regardless of the architectural format, it is the area where the faithful gathered. An examination of the interior helped identify relations between the lay person and the cult act, gender segregation and the social stratification of its members during worship. The physical layout of cult space varied substantially in accordance to denominational interpretation of sacramental priority. An investigation of cult requirements and liturgical focal points was fundamental to the examination of the spatial interpretation of belief. Decorative programs were noted in terms of their iconographic content rather than their esthetic value.

In order to determine what proportion of Ottawa Valley churches used elements of Gothic in their construction, it was necessary to first consider church building as a whole. To achieve this end, all buildings—regardless of size, material or style—were identified, recorded and cross referenced in a computerized architectural inventory designed for this study (see Appendix I). An investigation of this sort, however, is not without its limitations, and there are inevitably some questions that remain unanswered. Data was gathered from various denominational archives, public archives, missionary reports, denominational publications, denominational and secular journals, nineteenth century directories and atlases as well as from the most important source of primary information, the buildings themselves. Building on these findings, *Sacred Space and Structural Style* explores how various nineteenth-century Christian communities used architectural symbolism, not simply in relation to the material world in which they lived, but in relation to the spiritual world they hoped to attain.

Notes

1. At the time he wrote this article, Hay had been practising architecture in Toronto for several years. For further discussion of his work prior to this, see Chapter Four.

2. W. Hay, "The Late Mr. Pugin and the Revival of Christian Architecture," *Anglo-American Magazine* (1853), 2: 70.

3. Canterbury should, however, not be seen as Gothic's unique point of entry into England. Early examples can also be seen at Roche Abbey (c. 1175) in southwest England and at Worcester Cathedral (1175-1180). Both were probably the result of contact with French Cistercians.

4. The term is generally thought to have been coined in Italy during the Renaissance, and a variety of writers, including Raphael, Filarete, and Cesariano, have been credited with the dubious honour. In each instance there is reasonable evidence to suggest that while the term "Gothic" was used in relation to the early Middle Ages, it was not intended to include those later structures now commonly called Gothic. For further discussion of this subject, see B. Brown, *Vasari on Technique* (New York: Dover, 1960), 135.

5. Brown, *Vasari*, 84.

6. To insure that the churches were properly investigated, members of the Cambridge Camden Society provided a recording sheet in *Report of the Cambridge Camden Society for MDCCCXLI.*

7. A. Pugin, *True Principles of Pointed or Christian Architecture* (London: J. Weale, 1841).

8. Gothic as a holistic reflection of interconnected spatial, architectural, and intellectual contemplation is discussed by E. Panofsky in *Gothic Architecture and Scholasticism*, 44-45.

9. J. Summerson, *Georgian London* (Harmondsworth: Penguin Books, 1978), 231.

10. Furthermore, as R. Choquette observed, "Aux points de vue social et économique, la vallée de l'Outaouais constitue donc une entité homogène centrée sur la rivière des Outaouais; dans leurs activités commerciales et économiques, ses premiers habitants se fichent éperdument de la frontière politique qui doit les diviser." *L'Église catholique dans l'Ontario français du dix-neuvième siècle* (Ottawa: Les Éditions de l'Université d'Ottawa, 1984), 59.

11. W. Westfall, *Two Worlds: The Protestant Culture of Nineteenth-Century Ontario* (Montreal and Kingston: McGill-Queen's University Press, 1989), 129.

CHAPTER ONE

THE IMPLANTATION OF DIVERSE DENOMINATIONS
and Church-building Traditions in the Ottawa Valley, 1820s-1840s

The rich natural resources of the Ottawa River Valley have attracted people to its shores for thousands of years. With the exception of a few rapids, the Ottawa River offered a direct route deep into the heart of North America. With the coming of the Europeans, French voyageurs had been quick to follow their native mentors who traded on the Ottawa River, using it as a highway to and from the interior of the continent. In 1784, a small fortification was built at Fort Coulonge to serve as a stopover and trading post. Some time later a modest chapel was built inside the fort; however, unlike many other trading forts with similarly modest beginnings, Fort Coulonge attracted little in the way of stable settlers. By the final decade of the century a few small and isolated settlements appeared along the banks of the Ottawa River. These first settlers often came to the valley with the hopes of trading and supplying those who continued to travel the river en route to and from the inner lands. Little became of most of these early efforts and most were eventually abandoned. There was very little permanent inhabitation prior to the opening decades of the nineteenth century. By this time the Ottawa Valley had passed into British hands.

During the third quarter of the eighteenth century, with the loss of the thirteen American Colonies after the American War of Independence, British landholdings in North America were dramatically reduced. Much of what Britain did retain was territory that it had recently seized from France, resulting in a somewhat paradoxical situation in which much of what was now British North America was rather more French and Catholic than English and Protestant. This situation was not an entirely new one for the British; they had encountered similar problems several years earlier when they had seized the Rock of Gibraltar from the Spanish,[1] although *cujus regio ejus religio* was now much more theoretical than practical. While the Canadian situation undeniably presented British administrators with a challenge, it was one that they faced with a zeal and determination that was typical of the British where colonial matters were concerned. In 1768, the Governor of Quebec, Sir Guy Carleton, was elevated to the rank of Lord Dorchester and appointed by the Colonial Secretary as Governor General of British North America. This appointment was significant because many interpreted it to be indicative of British stability and permanency. This perception was especially important among those inhabitants of the former Thirteen Colonies who were unsure as to where democratic experiments in the newly united Colonies might lead. A direct consequence of this can be seen in the influx of settlers from the former colonies during the years that followed the American War of Independence. Many immigrants were unquestionably political refugees, others were what might more likely be classified by Canadian immigration officials in the late twentieth century as "economic refugees." Regardless of their motive, most were prepared to swear allegiance to King George III and the Crown of England in exchange for generous grants of land.

Despite the presence of an Anglo-Protestant government, many United Empire Loyalists soon protested that the retention of certain French customs was not really what they had expected to find in a British North America. The decision was eventually taken in 1791 to divide the vast territory of Quebec into two separate provinces, Lower Canada and Upper Canada. Although the city of Quebec remained the seat of the British colonial government for many years, Lower Canada retained much of its French culture, language and Roman Catholic affiliations. In contrast, the newly formed province of Upper Canada was to gradually define an identity that was, if not exclusively, at least predominantly English and Protestant. Much of the border between the two provinces runs down the middle of the Ottawa River; however, both shores of the river were settled by Anglo-Protestants as well as French-Canadian and Irish Catholics.

The first lieutenant-governor of the newly formed province was John Graves Simcoe (1752-1806), who had seen action during the American War of Independence, and, like a number of his contemporaries, felt that if British institutions had been properly established and generously supported, the American Colonies might never have revolted.[2] To avoid repeating these same errors in the new province under his charge, Simcoe worked hard to establish several good examples of British institutional superiority. The effects of these efforts were felt throughout much of the province, including the Ottawa Valley. High on Simcoe's list of truly superior British institutions was the United Church of England and Ireland. Given contemporary concerns that the lack of established religion had facilitated the rebellion in the American colonies, the British government was not eager to see more of this, especially as they watched with horror the democratic experiments of the French revolution. To encourage the prosperity of this fine British institution, provision was made in the Constitutional Act of 1791 for the support and maintenance of a "Protestant clergy."[3] Simcoe undoubtedly had a precise understanding, in his own mind, that the "Protestant Clergy" which the Constitutional Act referred to, meant the clergy of the United Church of England and Ireland, and no one else. Simcoe, however, neglected to ensure the translation of this precision to legal record and it was to be a source of considerable grief and division in later years as more denominations laid claim to these privileges.[4] In an effort to people his new province with "the right individuals," Simcoe encouraged settlement in his new province by late Loyalists, apparently in the belief that they would be not only devout subjects of King George III, but equally devout members of the United Church of England and Ireland, of which King George III was the head.

Many Loyalists were first drawn to the southern parts of the province, but a number chose the shores of the Rideau River, and settlement gradually edged its way towards the Ottawa Valley. In keeping with the ambitions of British emigration policymakers, various tracts of land in this area had been surveyed for settlement during the late eighteenth and very early nineteenth century. This land had initially tended to attracted a greater abundance of speculators than committed settlers. As a result, settlement in the Ottawa Valley continued to be slow for many years and it was only after 1815 and during the 1820s that settlement began to gain some momentum. One notable exception to this early lack of interest in the isolated shores of the Ottawa River was Philemon Wright. The Episcopalian merchant arrived from Massachusetts in 1800 with the intention of identifying exploitable tracts of land. He returned a few years later with his family, workers, livestock, and a collection of tools necessary for clearing land, farming, and lumbering. During the decades that followed, Wright established a small community he called Hull. From there, he began to exploit the rich timber resources that were to play a dominant role in much of the Ottawa Valley's nineteenth century history. The first place of worship, a modest wooden cabin, was not built until 1819. A small stone church was built in 1823 (fig. 1.1).

Fig. 1.1. St. James (Anglican), Hull, 1823.

St. James, with its high walls, squat roof, and small bell tower set slightly in retreat of the axial entry is characteristic of this era (Photo courtesy: Anglican Diocesan Archives, Ottawa).

Lumbering operations were to play an important role not only in opening up the Ottawa Valley for larger commercial exploitation and settlement. They indirectly (but rarely intentionally) brought religion and church building to some of the most isolated forests of the Ottawa Valley. From an early date, great fortunes were made and lost in the lumber trade of the Ottawa Valley. Throughout the nineteenth century, the exploitation of this rich natural resource was to become, for some, a source of significant business interest. Others perceived lumbering operations to be a source of considerable spiritual concern. While the harvesting of timber led to the financial ruin of some, others firmly believed that elements of the industry led to the spiritual ruin of many more. The Methodist preacher W. Sanderson echoed the concerns of decades of other priests and ministers when he cautioned that the lumbering trade impaired spiritual development by isolating people from the stabilizing influences of their families and churches, a problem that was not helped by the irreverent character of many lumbermen. Still, the remote villages and lumber camps could be fertile ground for harvesting souls as well as timber. With this goal in mind, the priest and preachers of numerous denominations journeyed to remote corners of the Ottawa Valley to bring spiritual comfort to isolated camps of loggers and to establish, in their midst, a house of God.

As the clergy struggled to cover the enormous distances of their missions,[5] late Loyalists (and some were, by any standard, very late) continued to trickle northward to the Ottawa Valley. These Loyalists were not all members of the Church of England. Many were Methodists, and Methodism itself was far from homogenous. Although a number of different traditions were active in Central Canada at this time, the Methodist population of the Ottawa Valley remained almost exclusively Episcopal or Wesleyan though also included Baptists and Congregationalists.[6] Significant numbers of Roman Catholic settlers began to appear in the Ottawa Valley during the 1820s and 1830s in places where some degree of religious and linguistic continuity could be assured.[7]

American immigration continued until the War of 1812, after which there was a significant rethinking of British immigration policies. It was felt that many who had been quick to declare their loyalty to the Crown in return for large tracts of land had been reluctant to show the same degree of enthusiasm in repelling expansionist raids from their former neighbours. Suggestions were made that "loyalist settlers" might have been less devoted to the interests of the British Crown than their popular appellation actually suggested. In certain instances they were believed to have actively encouraged invading American troops. In light of this uncertainty the British government thought it prudent to encourage settlement by people from the British Isles. British soldiers, demobilized after the Napoleonic Wars, soon became the preferred recipients of land grants. When a number of disbanded troops settled together, provision was also made for land grants to the established churches. In doing so, the British army was generally inclined to accept a slightly broader definition of the term "established church" than the secular government. While the majority of officers were members of the Church of England, the religious affiliations of the troops tended to be somewhat less homogeneous. There were members of the Church of Scotland, Irish Roman Catholics, and a number of dissenters. The Church of England, the Church of Scotland, and the Church of Rome were recognized by the British army. This was more a consequence of the denominational affiliations of dependable troops than a reflection of an avant-garde spirit of ecumenical advocacy. Land grants to the churches usually consisted of two acres for a rectory, four acres for a church, and six acres for a cemetery. This same spirit of largesse, however, was not extended to all. Various confessions were prohibited by law from holding land for church-building purposes prior to 1828, although they could be built on the privately owned land of a church member.

Military men were not the only supporters of the Crown to be rewarded with generous land grants for their services after the Napoleonic Wars. Notable among those supporters who came to the Ottawa Valley was Hamnett Pinhey. A merchant by trade, he had distinguished himself as a successful runner of naval blockades set up by the French navy. Pinhey's efforts were rewarded with a land grant of one thousand acres in the Township of March. Running inland from the shores of the Ottawa River and a well-protected harbour, Pinhey's land, though only marginally fertile, was prestigiously located, commanding a masterful view of the river and the Gatineau hills. Like Simcoe, Pinhey was eager to maintain the institutions of the British establishment, and was himself prepared to step into the role of a new generation of landed gentry (fig. 1.2).

By the early 1820s, Pinhey was busy re-creating a small settlement in the image of an English gentleman's country estate, on the shores of the Ottawa River. In addition to the main residence, a stable, a mill, barns, and a peacock garden, there was a church devoted exclusively to the Church of England. While the church might invite

Fig. 1.2. St. Mary (Anglican), Pinhey's Point, 1828.
This nineteenth-century illustration by Mary Anne Pinhey Hill depicts the church of St. Mary much as Hamnett Pinhey had intended it to be seen. It stands with understated, but unquestioned authority as an integral (if not necessarily intimate) part of a flourishing country estate (Photo courtesy: National Archives of Canada).

discussion of Pinhey's personal piety, it left little question about his opinions concerning church establishment. Pinhey made his views clear in a rather prophetic letter written on November 26, 1826, to the Bishop of Quebec:

> . . . the church of Stone, a durable chaste and not inelegant structure of Gothic Architecture with its Tower, is built . . . and tho' . . . this Edifice may become a modern ruin, its walls will stand for ages a lasting monument of the efforts of its founders and of the veneration in which they held the Ecclesiastical Establishment of Old England.[8]

For many of those who remained in the British Isles, the economic slump that followed the Napoleonic Wars became a source of increasing hardship, and by the early 1820s the British government began to encourage Irish emigration to British North America. This was not simply a benevolent gesture to alleviate the financial distress of the Irish proletariat, but was primarily intended to defuse the climate of religious and political unrest that had become increasingly volatile. Early Irish settlers found their way to Central Canada and, by the mid 1820s, were settling in the Ottawa Valley, bringing with them their political and religious predispositions.[9] These first waves of immigration were to lay the foundation for much of the religious and ethnic composition of the Ottawa Valley for the better part of the nineteenth century.

Some scholars have suggested that, prior to the 1850s, as much as 90 percent of the population in the Ottawa Valley belonged to either the Church of England, the Church of Scotland or the Church of Rome.[10] By the 1840s, however, the numerical strength of the Methodist population was increasing at an unprecedented rate. Many new settlers from the British Isles were Wesleyan Methodists. While their religious affiliations may not have been the British government's first choice, they were tacitly considered to be more desirable than Episcopal Methodists. The differences were more political than religious as both Wesleyan and Episcopal Methodists traced their origins to the teachings of John Wesley (1703-1791) and his brother Charles (1707-1788). During the early decades of the nineteenth century, Wesleyan Methodists turned generally to England for spiritual guidance while Episcopal Methodists usually looked south of the border for their leadership and preachers.

As a consequence of this continued affiliation with their counterparts in the United States, Episcopal Methodists were regularly considered to be of dubious political persuasion. This conviction was particularly strong among veterans of the Napoleonic Wars, who were all too aware that the United States had chosen to give its support to their enemy, France. This anti-American sentiment was effectively exploited, frequently by members of the Church of England, as a convenient justification for their general anti-Methodist sentiment. Leaders of the would-be established church, such as the Rev. John Strachan of York, nagged on for quite some time that, during the War of 1812, Methodist loyalty was less than perfect. Cleverly reasoned rebuttals by the young Methodist preacher Egerton Ryerson, whose family's loyalties to the British Crown were well known and beyond reproach, did much to help the prestige of the Methodist cause, and its population continued to flourish. Despite this, divisions between Wesleyan Methodists and Episcopal Methodists lasted far beyond the relevance of political preoccupations and dated border disputes of the early nineteenth century. This divisiveness seriously affected church-building projects for many decades. It was only in 1884, when the Wesleyan Methodists and the Episcopal Methodists finally decided to join forces as the Methodist Church, that this ceased to be a factor that impeded architectural progress.

In the early decades of the 1800s, continued concerns that the Americans might again try to invade Canada led to the construction of the Rideau Canal after 1827. The canal was to run between Kingston through the Rideau lakes, along the Rideau River, and to empty into the Ottawa River at Bytown. From here, the waters of the Ottawa River flow downstream to the Lac des Deux Montagnes and southeast to Montreal. The canal was intended to allow the safe movement of troops and supplies without subjecting them to unwelcome surveillance or attack from hostile American forces on the southern shores of the St. Lawrence River. Despite the vast expense entailed in the construction of the canal, the feared invasion never came. This future turn of events was in no way evident during the early decades of the 1800s, and construction of the Rideau Canal proceeded under the leadership of Colonel By amid many great hardships, including epidemics of malaria and financial overrun. A building project of this dimension served to increase the population of an area, attracting large numbers of labourers and skilled individuals into the Ottawa Valley. The increased population was to eventually contribute to the formation of several small congregations and the building of the first churches in Bytown. A modest Methodist chapel built during the fall of 1827 is generally considered to have been the first building raised exclusively for religious worship in what is now Ottawa. This first Methodist chapel was destroyed by fire a short time after its completion.[11] Unfortunately, as is the case with so many early places of worship, little more is known about the construction of this chapel.

Of greater duration and considerably better documentation than the first Methodist chapel was the original St. Andrew, Church of Scotland. When operations on the Rideau Canal stalled in 1828, Thomas McKay put his Scottish stone masons to work building St. Andrew's Church, the first Presbyterian congregation in Ottawa.[12] Solid and austere, St. Andrew's echoed the strong Calvinistic heritage of its congregation, and would probably have continued to do so for many years had it been able to satisfy the demands of an increasingly affluent congregation. Ultimately, St. Andrew's was more a victim of High Victorian taste than of failing masonry or dramatic changes in the practice of worship (fig. 1.3).

The Roman Catholics, who had a variety of building projects underway at several points along the Ottawa River, also undertook the construction of a place of worship in Bytown during the fall of 1828. Their church building project was less ambitious than that of

Fig. 1.3. St. Andrew (Church of Scotland), Ottawa, 1828.
For many years St. Andrew's (shown after the enlargement of 1854) was the oldest surviving Protestant church building in Ottawa. The building is well proportioned with tall walls and a roof that is not excessively squat. The façade, with the central portion in slight relief, anticipates the addition of a tower. The tower was never finalized before the church was dismantled (Photo courtesy: National Archives of Canada).

the more affluent Presbyterian congregation, but the unpretentious wooden chapel established a visible Roman Catholic presence in what was progressively emerging as one of the major centres in the Ottawa Valley. Not to be outdone by Dissenters, Presbyterians, or Romanists, the Anglicans of Bytown embarked on a church-building project of their own in the early 1830s. Although these Ottawa churches figure among some of the earliest religious buildings along the Ottawa River, they were not the first. Similar patterns of church building can be seen throughout the Ottawa Valley near promising commercial centres, such as Hull, or military operations, such as the canal-building activities in Grenville.

As a result of various immigration policies, settlement projects, the lumbering industry, defense strategy, and trading routes, the Ottawa Valley was settled from an early date by a great variety of people. They brought with them diverse linguistic, cultural, and religious traditions as well as their own collection of political quarrels and sectarian prejudices. Included amongst this formidable array of cultural baggage was a great diversity of opinion and concerns related to the manner and practice of church building. Their understanding of the merits of built space for public worship and how it should be organized and funded was often equally varied. Although many Christian denominations came to the Ottawa Valley, the population was thinly spread over a vast territory, and few congregations were served on a regular basis. In most new settlements, regardless of opinion concerning merit or procedure, church building got off to a painfully slow start. While many new settlers may have thought that building a church within their community was a worthy undertaking, getting the necessary resources together to build even the smallest chapel was not easy. This was particularly true in the Ottawa Valley during the first half of the nineteenth century when modest log structures were built to jointly serve as community halls, schools and churches. An entry in Belden's *Historical Atlas of Carleton County* notes that the squared, hewed log structure built at the Cats by Mr. Sheriff in 1832 was not only the first schoolhouse to be built in the township of Fitzroy, but was also the first church in the township.[13] Mr. Sheriff's combined church and schoolhouse was reported to have been "common property for all religious denominations."[14] The realities of pioneer life could provide, or often demand, an occasion for compromise and co-operation between various individual congregations who, for reasons of denominational mistrust or prejudice, might in other circumstances have chosen to have little to do with each other. In fact, the history of church building in the Ottawa Valley offers numerous examples of interdenominational co-operation on church building projects, a phenomenon almost unheard of on the other side of the Atlantic. There were, nevertheless, limits on the extent to which necessity could induce a spirit of ecumenical teamwork. Still, the desire to gather together as a community for joint worship in a place devoted (if only on Sundays) to Christian worship was strong, and though restricted both in terms of number and wealth, small clusters of settlers would pool their finite resources to build a modest house of prayer. Usually this first house of prayer was little more than a bare log cabin and was to be used by the denominations whose members had contributed to its erection and upkeep. Known as "Union Chapels," these small practical buildings were widely used in the Ottawa Valley, especially during the first half of the nineteenth century. They continued to be used well into the second half of the nineteenth century, but gradually faded from clerical and then popular acceptance.

The architectural shell of a Union chapel or church was not the only unifying factor for many of these early places of community worship. Because of the general lack of funds, most Union churches were so stark that they were incapable of offense by simplicity alone. This is not to suggest that all went smoothly. Disputes were frequent, often bitter and ranged from the theological to the janitorial. In spite of their former abundance, most Union churches have since disappeared, leaving only the faintest archival traces.[15] Denominational archives indicate that traditionally most confessions would retain their share in a Union church only until the members of their local community could gather the necessary resources to build a place of worship for their exclusive use. The planning of these early churches, union and uni-denominational, could be organized in a variety of ways. Structurally, they were very simple. When built with wood, their construction was usually a community affair. Once the site was decided upon, the local people would pool their resources, often contributing hard labour or material resources in lieu of cash. Over the course of the winter, logs, stones, and other necessary building material would be dragged to the church site. With the arrival of spring, most of the material was ready at the site. Contributing members would gather to "raise" the church much as one "raised" a barn.[16] If the church building was to be of stone, calls to tender were usually published in the local newspapers. Contracts were usually awarded to local builders. Most of the earliest chapels were built of roughly hewn logs, not stone. As with the Union chapels, little remains of these early places of worship. Their scarcity is due in part to the nature of the structures themselves, which were extremely rustic and subject to rot, uneven settling, and fire. Many chapels that did not simply deteriorate beyond repair were dismantled, and salvageable material was reused for other purposes.

Despite their extreme simplicity and undisguised paucity, these modest buildings served as a focal point for a widely scattered population. Often used during the week as schoolhouses or, when necessary, places of public assembly, the unassuming church offered a hope of community commitment, survival and even possible prosperity for the settlement. In his recent book, *The Upper Ottawa Valley to 1855,* Richard Reid noted that Anglican, Presbyterian, and Roman Catholics in the Ottawa Valley could draw on outside resources for the staffing and construction of their churches. While there is no question that, in these early years, all denominations had to look to external sources for their priests, ministers and preachers, these resources were not always readily available.[17] Clerical manpower was hard to come by and was often surpassed in scarcity only by the availability of building funds. While it may be true that Anglicans, Presbyterians, and Roman Catholics profited more than Baptists, Congregationalists, or Methodists, because they were part of a larger denominational organization and had members who were not infrequently in a position of some political consequence, the Ottawa Valley did not appear to figure prominently as a frequent recipient of external funds for church building. In theory, the "established" Church—the United Church of England and Ireland—was to be provided with funds from the clergy reserves, Crown rectories, such as Beckwith rectory (Franktown), and land in military settlements, such as Richmond. There were also several sources in England that provided funds for the church building in the Colonies, although most communities appeared to have raised the better part of their funds themselves. The scarcity of external funds is clearly illustrated by the experiences of the Anglican merchants of Bytown who formed a committee to plan the construction of a separate Anglican church. When they apprised their bishop of their intent, they were told that while the bishop was pleased to hear of their project, there were nevertheless several rules and regulations of mandatory compliance. The building committee was somewhat disappointed to discover that, while the bishop's approval was necessary, he could, as indeed he did, decline to participate financially.

The bishop's office instructed the committee for the construction of Ottawa's first Anglican church to prepare a financial study and estimate of the projected building as well as an appraisal of the land value and a deed for the site. Work on the proposed church could not begin until a working plan was approved by the bishop. The committee was also informed that all projected spending should be as restrained as possible as the bishop was in no position to offer pecuniary relief of any sort. Disappointed by the lack of help from within their own denomination, the Anglicans of Bytown nevertheless gathered their resources and put out their calls for tender to build a church thirty by fifty feet (interior measurements) in the "Gothick" style.[18] By 1833, the building committee was short £198.17.4 on the £531.7.00 debt it had incurred and there was still considerable work left to be done on the church. Church wardens petitioned the government for financial relief,[19] but government funds did not appear to have been forthcoming. Complaints were voiced in the Canadian Anglican journal, *The Church*, concerning the poor treatment that the Anglican church suffered at the hands of the provincial government. By early 1834, Anglican indignation was echoed in the *Bytown Gazette* in which local editors reprinted complaints first aired in *The Church*.[20]

Church-building funds may have been more a hoped-for possibility than a practical reality, especially when prominent members of the parish were American ex-patriots, but there are several notable exceptions, in the earliest decades, for example, members of the Church of Scotland received modest church-building grants on several occasions.

While there is little evidence to suggest that Ottawa Valley communities were frequent recipients of important church-building grants, the priests and ministers of certain denominations, most notably of the English, Roman, and Scottish churches, appear to have held relatively clear ideas concerning the propriety of church building once the necessary funds were raised. These three denominations could all draw on a long tradition of church building. Despite their occasionally tumultuous history, both the English and Scottish churches bequeathed a legacy of several tried and well-proven church-building types, all well-adapted to the needs of reformed worship.[21] Church building immediately after the English Reformation had been strongly influenced by government interests,[22] but had been later tempered by the Laudian reforms of the mid-seventeenth century. Discussion by Sir Christopher Wren (1632-1723) concerning the architectural requirements of reformed worship that was to be of particular consequence can be traced well into the nineteenth century. In addition, the late eighteenth and early nineteenth centuries had been a time of intense church-building activity in Great Britain and in many of her colonies.

In response to the growing problems stemming from the outdated structure of the English parish system that left large segments of the population without church accommodation, the British Parliament voted a grant of £1,000,000 in 1819 to assist in the construction of new churches. A special commission was established to oversee the awarding of funds, planning, design, and construction of the new churches. Several years later, in 1829, funds were again released to the commission for a second phase of church building. Known as the "Commissioners Churches," they were often most prominently associated with the actual building of a church in the memory of many English immigrants to the Ottawa Valley. The aim of the Commissioners was to produce buildings that were distinctly Anglican. However, this important prerequisite does not appear to have provoked a detailed discussion of what specifically constituted a distinctly Anglican church.

Crown architect J. Soane lay down a number of practical guidelines concerning the building of churches. In terms of architectural style, however, many were of the opinion that Grecian or Gothic could be used interchangeably.[23] Recipients of the first Parliamentary grant tended to prefer the use of the Grecian style in the city and reserve the use of the Gothic style for the construction of country churches. Some church builders, however, were overtly hostile to any use of Gothic, which they referred to as "licentious."[24] However, with increased demands on their limited resources and continued calls for cost-cutting measures, it became progressively more difficult to perpetuate the use of the Grecian style of churches. The mandatory elegant stone porticoes were expensive to build, and towers, which helped distinguish established churches from the meeting houses of dissenters, were notorious for swallowing up very large sums of money. Gothic, on the other hand, "could scrape by with a bell-turret."[25] But it was precisely this scraping by, in order to work within the limits imposed by mandatory cost cuts, that was later to leave the Gothic of the Commissioners Churches open to much criticism from architectural purists.[26]

Interestingly and despite cutbacks, the second phase of church building reflected a renewed preference for Gothic style. Increasingly, younger architects began associating Gothic with sentiments of architectural patriotism and referred to it as the "national style." Although much of the Gothic they used in the construction of the Commissioners Churches still tended to be a rather boxy interpretation of the style, many changes generally attributed to medieval revivalists may have had the ground prepared for them—though cautiously and with much restraint—by the builders of Commissioners Churches. While they did not reflect unwavering fidelity to medieval prototypes, they can be credited with doing much to rekindle a renewed interest in the Gothic style of architecture, especially for the elevation of religious buildings. By the early middle decades of the nineteenth century, the Gothic of Commission Churches was considered *dépassé,* not only by Anglican Ecclesiologists, but by other vocal Gothic purists, such as Pugin. The churches were denounced not only for the shortcomings of their stylistic execution, but also for the economic means by which they were financed.

Roman Catholics held the oldest and most diversified tradition of church building, but another advantage came from nearly three centuries of church-building experience in New France.[27] Roman Catholic church builders were well experienced in dealing with climatic, monetary, architectural, and demographic problems, the extent of which many of their Protestant counterparts were only beginning to realize. Furthermore, rules and regulations concerning the proper execution of cult practice were explicitly set out in seminary manuals, and student priests were often introduced to a variety of acceptable architectural options.[28] Although Catholic church building had continued to evolve in France and her colonies, Catholicism in the British Isles had been in a difficult position from the time of the Protestant Reformation until Emancipation in 1829. Consequently, many of the Irish Catholics who arrived in the Ottawa Valley during the early decades of the nineteenth century had no strong tradition of recent church building. They brought with them memories of overcrowded, aged, and poorly preserved churches

Other denominations such as Baptists, Congregationalists, and Methodists were much less dependent on a denominationally sanctioned architectural trend. In many ways they were still relative neophytes in the field. They were, in terms of their church architecture and, indeed, in most of their church affairs, much more congregationally self-reliant. This was a product not only of the hierarchical structuring of their church government, but also, like the Roman Catholics, of their recent history in the British Isles. As non-conformist denominations, Baptists, Congregationalists, Methodists, Roman Catholics, and others, were legally denied the architectural freedom enjoyed by the Church of England.[29] Even when the building of dissenting churches was not illegal, English law prohibited the construction of steeples and towers, and even bells could not be used by non-conformists. Legal restrictions impaired the growth of church-building traditions among non-conformists for many years.

Congregations not belonging to the Church of England were not free to build their churches as architectural compeers of the established church but were geographically marginalized and banished to architectural obscurity.

Non-conforming denominations coped with architectural restrictions in different ways, many of which are identifiable in the early churches of the Ottawa Valley. One element common to all denominations was the clear desire to gather together for joint prayer in a place of worship built specifically for that purpose. This desire eventually led many struggling communities to gather their resources and build a house of prayer.

Deciding to Build

Despite the importance of a chapel that doubled as a school or a union chapel, the use of such buildings was recognized from an early date as a less than ideal solution. The construction of an edifice built specifically as a church was considered not simply a sign of progress and prosperity within a community, but a sign of that community's ability to "rise above" the trials and drudgery of pioneer life.[30] Church-building projects excited considerable interest in the secular press. In October 1837, the building committee of Christ Church (Huntley) posted notice in the *Bytown Gazette* that they would be accepting tenders for the construction of a church, the plans and specifications of which could be seen in a local store.[31] The building committee did not elaborate or offer any more information on the subject. A much more informative discussion of the project appeared in the same issue of the *Bytown Gazette* in which journalists announced: "it always affords us pleasure to record any circumstance indicative of the improvement and growing prosperity of any part of the country,"[32] and proceeded to give a detailed account of the project, the call to tender, the meeting location, the identity of the committee chair, the projected dimensions and materials.[33]

It was with that same sense of purpose that, in July 1829, the inhabitants of the townships of Marlborough and Oxford assembled together in the Marlborough township schoolhouse with the expressed purpose of making arrangements for the erection of a house of public worship. Stephen Burritt chaired the meeting and Edward Mix acted as secretary, and it was decided by the settlers of Marlborough and Oxford that they should undertake the construction of a church reserved for the exclusive use of the United Church

Fig. 1.4. Christ Church (Anglican), Burritt's Rapids, 1831.
Despite the Gothic references, the classical profile of this church is accentuated by the wooden quoins and the sharp returns of the eaves. The entryway and the lancet windows are elements of survival Gothic, while the elongated finials reflect a use of picturesque Gothic that is comparatively rare in the Ottawa Valley (Photo: A. Erdmer).

of England and Ireland. The projected church was to be built of stone and measure no less than thirty by forty feet, but not more than thirty-five by forty-five feet.[34] In typical church-building fashion of the early 1800s, nothing more had been decided by the late fall of that same year other than to give the building committee the authority to extend the projected length of the as yet unstarted church by five feet. By the following spring, construction was unanimously postponed until the following season. Despite the delays, it appears that the question of what material should be used for the construction of the church was a source of ongoing discussion. A meeting was eventually held specifically to resolve this question.[35] Twelve voted to build a wooden church, while only five continued to support the use of stone as originally projected. A wooden church was eventually completed and opened for service in 1831. Although it has undergone several modifications, the original church has remained in use for the last century and a half and is one of the oldest wooden churches still standing in the Ottawa Valley (fig. 1.4).

Much less is known about the planning and organization of most of the earliest churches. Few of these buildings remain standing today and, of those that do, only a handful are preserved in an environment that would be even remotely reminiscent of the original site layout. Still, it is possible to identify some common characteristics associated with the choice of site, the style and arrangement of the exterior, the internal arrangements, and the architectural furnishings of the sanctuaries.

Site Choice and Surroundings

A significant obstacle encountered early on in many church building projects was the delicate question of choosing the construction site. A suitable site could not appear to favour any particular cluster of families, nor could it be too inconvenient for the majority of the population to reach. Settling this question could be a challenge; distances were great, the population sparse and scattered, and the few roads that did exist were often impassable. Many denominations felt that a church should mark the centre of their community, although this could be interpreted in different ways. Members of the Church of England, the Church of Scotland, and Roman Catholics generally selected sites that were suggestive of a preference for a conspicuous location near the centre of daily activity. By contrast, Methodist site choice often hints of a preference for sites that afforded a more introspective setting. This could mean a site was required to have enough room to hold camp meetings. These criteria alone suggest that these sites were more secluded. Baptists were less likely to gravitate too far inland as they habitually practised baptism by immersion. For a site to accommodate their sacramental priorities, it was necessarily near a decent source of water. Although Baptists were present in the Ottawa Valley from a very early date, they were not involved in significant building activities prior to the second half of the nineteenth century.[36] In other instances, and this was particularly true during the first half of the century, it was not always obvious to any denomination precisely where the future village would develop. In the absence of other clues, the church building itself was considered the most reliable indication of future growth, a fact not missed by would-be entrepreneurs.

Donations of land by individuals or families appear to have been one of the most common sources of land. While many were surely motivated by piety, it is worth noting (without questioning the generosity of any donor) that the value of land often grew proportionately to its proximity to a church and that donations of land were not always from members of the denomination undertaking the construction of the church. In Renfrew, Ontario, Xavier Plant gave land not only to his fellow Roman Catholics, but also to the Anglicans, the Episcopal Methodists, and the Presbyterians. In Aylmer, Quebec, Charles Symmes gave land to both the Anglicans and the Roman Catholics, though he himself was a Presbyterian.[37] Still, generous offers of land were not always graciously accepted. The *Dominion Churchman* pointed out one such case, St. Mark's, in Pakenham, where a well-suited and centrally located site was declined because the parishioners were not in accordance with the religious inclination of the would-be donor.[38] Given the factors at play, it comes as no surprise that choosing the best site for a church building could be fraught with disaster.

In 1839, local Roman Catholics built a small wooden chapel on the site of what is now the Plantagenet cemetery. The original chapel was reputed to have been a curious structure perched on top of wooden stilts. Parishioners had promised to build a modest room for the missionary beneath the chapel; however, the projected *pied-à-terre* was never completed and the chapel remained for some time an architectural anomaly. This rather unique arrangement was not considered by the bishop to be one of the most dignified dispositions for a place of Catholic worship, and several attempts were made to have the local population finish the building. Stalling and squabbling continued until finally an exasperated Mgr. Guigues, their bishop, sent a carpenter out from Bytown to saw down the tall poles and to slide the chapel down a ramp to ground level. Once on *terra firma*, there were other problems. Parishioners had built the chapel without obtaining legal ownership of the land and the deed for the site was still held by Mr. McMartin, a local mill owner. The bishop was unwilling to have a church standing on land for which they did not hold the legal deed, and McMartin refused to sell the property to the diocese. Mgr. Guigues ordered the chapel dismantled and relocated.

The projected relocation of the chapel, far from alleviating problems, only served to present new ones, resulting in considerable animosity among inhabitants, who were of different opinion concerning the merit of the various sites. Eventually the chapel was dismantled and transported to an episcopally approved site under the direction of Étienne Châtelin. Stone was purchased to ensure a structurally sound foundation for the new chapel. The foundation stones were in turn reputed to have been stolen by those opposed to the new location, and it was many years and several churches later before the majority of Catholics in the region felt their architectural requirements were properly addressed. While the whole affair is admittedly not a shining example of Christian co-operation, it is a good demonstration of the extent to which the material church was linked with social stability and rural development.

In other instances, the building of early churches owed much to the driving force of a single individual. Hamnett Pinhey was one such individual, donating not only his own land, but also personal funds to the construction of a stone church which he named in honour of his wife Mary's patron saint (fig. 1.5).

Pinhey was a scrupulous record keeper, and the construction of this church is unusually well documented.[39] When the *Bytown Gazette* erroneously reported that this church had been built with the aid of funds from overseas, notably £300 from the Countess of Ross, Pinhey forced the paper to print a retraction.[40] Many more settlers undoubtedly possessed the personal energy needed for such a project, but very few had at their disposal the personal ways or means of Hamnett Pinhey. Church-building funds were, more often than not, raised from the modest resources of a struggling community. More typical of a church built by community effort is St. John, South March (1838) (fig. 1.6).

The church of St. John had been built specifically to counterbalance Hamnett Pinhey's church of St. Mary. The Anglican bishop in Quebec, C.J. Stewart, had been concerned that the church of St. Mary

Fig. 1.5. St. Mary (Anglican), Pinhey's Point, 1828.

The church of St. Mary is seen here in days of lesser glory. The building had been abandoned following charges of structural insecurity and dynamited. Despite this rather violent affront to its structural integrity, the shell of the church, most notably the eastern wall of the nave, the tower and the opposing end wall of the sanctuary have shown remarkable tenacity (Photo: V. Bennett).

catered to a wealthier segment of the population who held large tracts of land along the banks of the Ottawa River. The Pinhey church was not easily accessible to many of the poorer settlers who held farms farther inland, and, in order to insure a more equitable distribution of spiritual resources, the bishop declined to authorize the consecration of St. Mary's until St. John was built in South March. A similar example of a collective community project can be seen with the construction of the Huntley Church (1837),[41] and in the construction of a modest Methodist stone chapel in Aylmer.[42]

Regardless of their denominational affiliation, most of these early church buildings were set towards the front end of their lots and squared to the property line.[43] Secular surveying thus provided the main frame of reference, although churches built near the banks of the Ottawa River, such as the Pinhey church, frequently faced the river.[44] Despite the actual orientation of a building, churches were frequently discussed in terms of east and west, with the east corresponding to the portion of the church that housed the sanctuary and the west corresponding to the main entry. This practice was especially common among Anglicans. Whether the terms east and west corresponded to geographic reality or not was irrelevant. In this spirit, what has always been referred to as the "tower . . . at the west end"[45] of Christ Church in Ottawa was built to face the Ottawa River and is almost due north while the west end of St. James Anglican, Hull (1823), faced almost due south.

Many of the earliest Ottawa Valley churches stood near the graveyards that were associated with them. Contrary to late twentieth century practices, parishes frequently surrounded not only their burial grounds but also their church buildings with fences. In a questionnaire circulated in 1833 by the Anglican Bishop, each parish

Fig. 1.6. St. John (Anglican), South March, 1838.

St. John's is typical of many rural churches from this era. Skilfully built of coursed rubble masonry, and free from any external adornment, and, like the people who built it, without pretension and discreet in social affectation. Large windows occupy a significant proportion of the lateral walls. The single axial "Eastern" window would have opened immediately above the Eucharistic table (Photo: A. Erdmer).

priest was asked: "Are your burial grounds well and sufficiently fenced in? Have they been duly consecrated? Are pigs or cattle admitted therein?"[46] The Rev. Richard Harte reported to his bishop that in Beckwith the grounds were fenced but not consecrated. To the third question he replied "No pigs—there may be a few sheep."[47] In the township of March, Hamnett Pinhey reported cultivating both corn and potatoes in the churchyard until the death of his wife, Mary, in 1852. After her burial, he grew flowers and flowering shrubs, and lined the churchyard with trees.

External Structures and Adornments

As noted earlier, the great majority of churches raised during the first decades of the nineteenth century were built with wood. Wood was comparatively easy to transport, simple to work and abundantly available in the Ottawa Valley. It, however, was also prone to rot and was notoriously unresisting in the face of fire. Most surviving churches are made of stone. A notable exception is Christ's Church in Burritt's Rapids (fig. 1.7).

Bricks were not used in the construction of earlier churches primarily because they were not readily available. Stone was widely considered to create a sense of endurance and permanence and was usually the preferred building material; however, stone churches were expensive. In their humblest forms, many of these early churches had little if any external arrangements or embellishments. Most Protestant denominations would not tolerate the use of crosses even to distinguish their churches from domestic log cabins. Their entries were usually understated and frequently in the lateral or side wall of the building. When those responsible for the construction of a new church wished to make a bolder statement of religious purpose, they almost invariably (but not exclusively) required their building to be fitted with some reference to the Gothic style.[48] Although a stone structure was beyond the means of many church builders, some still felt compelled to move beyond the roughly hewed or squared timber of a log cabin. A simple frame church was the most common solution. In addition to being relatively inexpensive to finance and expeditious to build, they easily accommodated a restrained Gothic reference, which was important because, during these early years, the inclusion of Gothic elements was widely considered to distinguish the new chapel from common meeting houses and to mark it as a place of Christian worship.

Fig. 1.7. Christ Church (Anglican) Burritt's Rapids, 1831.
The tall lateral walls and squatness of the roof are typical of churches from this era. Less typical are the very narrow windows in the nave. The axis of this church runs east–west, with the entry at the eastern end. The small chancel at the western end was a much later addition (Photo: A. Erdmer).

In their simplest forms, these early churches were entered by a single axial door. The façade was often devoid of any embellishment. The unique reference to Gothic was the small pointed segment of the window above the door and its delicate intersecting tracery. To this most austere arrangement, an innumerable collection of variations could be added. Among the most common and simplest variations was the addition of a tall Gothic lancet on either side of the axial entry. Surviving examples of this arrangement can still be identified at St. John's (Anglican), South March (see fig. 1.6) and Christ Church (Anglican), Huntley, although the façades of both churches have been subject to some later modifications.[49] The Gothic windows in the façade of the Huntley church, which in many ways typifies this manner of building, measure five feet wide across and twelve feet to the apex. In other instances an axial entry is flanked to either side by a Gothic bay and a small light is opened in the apex of the gable. St. Andrew's Presbyterian Church, Ramsay Township (8th Line), had Gothic windows that were both long and wide (fig. 1.8). Built in 1836 of local stone, St. Andrew's had high walls and a squat roof common to churches built during and prior to the 1840s. Despite the use of roughly coursed local field stone, this church was not destitute of elegance.

In other instances, a principal axial entry is flanked to either side by two lesser doorways. One of the best surviving examples of a monumental tripartite entry can be seen on the façade of the Roman Catholic Cathedral of Notre Dame in Ottawa. The original plans, based on Thomas Baillairgé's neoclassic church of St. Patrick in Quebec City, were subject to extensive modifications resulting in a predominantly Gothic façade. The number and placement of the door cases themselves reflect the original plans of 1839. A tripartite entryway was, however, not as much a trait of larger urban churches as it was of Roman Catholic churches themselves. Although builders of Roman Catholic churches containing only a single aisle were encouraged to make do with a correspondingly singular entry, tripartite entries were commonplace on Catholic churches of varying sizes from an early date. It was occasionally suggested (usually by enthusiasts of more esoteric interpretations of architectural symbolism) that the triple doors served as a reference to the Trinity.[50] In their original state the principal entry of

Fig. 1.8. St. Andrew (Church of Scotland), Ramsay, 1836.

In keeping with contemporary church-building customs, the walls are tall and the roof comparatively squat. Restrained classical references can be seen in the treatment of the eaves and eave returns. The windows, with their sober tracery, occupy a significant proportion of the vertical surface (Photo: A. Erdmer).

Fig. 1.9. Christ Church (Anglican), Ottawa, 1832.

Pencil sketch of projected tower added to the vestry minutes of 15 December 1841.

The original building program provided for the tower to be built only to the height of the ridge pole (Photo courtesy: Anglican Diocesan Archives, Ottawa).

many early churches opened directly into the main body of the church. It was rare to find a narthex or vestibule between the church interior and the outside doors. With the passage of time, however, the realities of Ottawa Valley winters usually encouraged the construction of wooden porches immediately in front of many principal entries. Occasionally, as seen on the Huntley church, wooden towers were added, although in this case much later.

A strong axial tower was the defining feature of many early Anglican churches. Serving no liturgical function, the presence of a bold tower had nevertheless come in many ways to be emblematic of confessional sympathy for church establishment, or at the very least, of a sentiment that all involved would benefit from a strong church-state relationship. The extent to which central towers were a deliberate statement on the part of various individual church builders, and to what extent they simply represent remembered tradition, is difficult to determine with precision. Nevertheless, when considered in a confessional context, the presence of towers can ultimately be interpreted as something that goes far beyond a simple desire to emphasize or privilege the façade. Thus, while towers appear on some of the earliest churches built in the Ottawa Valley, they are traditionally confined to those buildings erected by congregations belonging to the United Church of England and Ireland or to the Church of Scotland. Invariably, towers associated with early church buildings were axially aligned and in partial or full relief of the façade. In this manner the base of the tower also served as a small porch or vestibule to the main doorway of the church, which was in turn centred on the longitudinal axis of the church. The original plans for Christ Church, Bytown

(1832), included a central tower with embattled parapets to stand in full relief of the main façade. Due to financial constrictions, however, when the contract was finally drawn up in 1832, it was clearly stipulated "that a tower be erected at the west end of said church to the height of the ridge pole."[51] It was not until a decade later, in 1842, that the superstructure of the tower was completed according to a pencil sketch in the vestry minutes of December 1841 (fig. 1.9, fig. 1.10).[52]

The tower's additional story was intended to house the church bells and was opened on each face by a long Gothic arch filled with wooded louvers. When completed, the tower was crowned with a crenelated parapet, a particularly effective formula when church builders sought solid monumentality. There was no spire, nor were the corners accentuated with pinnacles, an arrangement that seems to have been fairly common among earlier churches. Spires were less important than the massive towers from which they rose. The deliberate use of frontal towers to achieve an effect of monumentality is clearly demonstrated through the persistent inclusion of architectural features that are visually striking. Pinnacles, quoins, as well as embattlements and crenelated parapets, which are of a strictly military utility, figure prominently in this category.[53] Typical of this type of arrangement is Christ Church in Burritt's Rapids (fig. 1.4, fig. 1.7). Here a central tower is crested with embattled parapets. The four corners of the tower are surmounted by wooden Gothic pinnacles while the corners of its clapboard tower are equipped with wooden quoins. While both are structurally useful and harmonious when used as an integral part of stone masonry, the pinnacles and wooden quoins are structurally insignificant and rather unlikely ornaments when placed on a wooden frame construction. A more harmonious and structurally effective use of accentuated quoins can be seen on the tower of St. Mungo's Presbyterian Church in Cushing (fig. 1.11). Here, in keeping with the church building tradition of rural Scotland, a massive stone tower precedes a comparatively modest stone church.

The extra attention given to the masonry work on the quoin stones of the tower is further emphasized by the use of a darker stone, a motif repeated in the arch stones of the churches various windows. The summit of the tower corners are marked by four small turrets. In other instances, as illustrated with the original St. Andrew's Church of Scotland, Bytown (1829), an axial tower was planned but never finished. The base of the tower stood only in partial relief of the façade, and the planned superstructure was never completed above

Fig. 1.10. Christ Church (Anglican), Ottawa, after addition of transepts, 1841.

This woodcut illustrates the nave and western transept (1841). The transformation of the ground plan from rectangular to cruciform by the addition of transepts to the original building during the early 1840s was simply out of the necessity to accommodate a greater number of people and was not linked to later interests in architectural symbolism. This illustration appeared in 1872, just prior to the demolition of the original church (Source: *Canadian Illustrated News*, 13 April 1872).

the roof line of the main body of the church. Termination of the projected tower continued to be a topic of discussion and concern for several decades. Plans for its completion were drawn up as late as 1864.[54] By 1870, the women of St. Andrew's congregation had raised in excess of $1,550.00 for the construction of a steeple.[55] Despite this commitment to the tower project, the proposed structure was never completed. The original church was demolished only two years later in favour of a larger and more fashionable structure.

Even in their simplest form, the towers associated with most of these early churches contained some allusion to Gothic.[56] The most frequent reference was made by framing the axial entry with a Gothic arch. Further stylistic emphasis was achieved through the inclusion of windows or belfry openings with pointed arch heads or through the use of pointed half rounds, and intersecting window tracery. As with simpler towerless churches, the gable wall against which a tower stood could be devoid of any other opening. St. Mungo (Church of Scotland), in Cushing, the nearby Anglican church of St. Matthew in Grenville, and the Pinhey church are all good surviving examples of this arrange-

Fig. 1.11. St. Mungo (Presbyterian), Cushing, 1836.

Presbyterian churches differed little from contemporary Anglican structures. When Scottish builders chose to front their churches with an axial tower, the resulting structure was frequently in fuller relief than the frontal towers of English churches. Lateral walls were also tall and contained long wide windows. It was not uncommon for the lateral windows of Presbyterian churches to open from a slightly lower course and to be slightly wider than those on Anglican churches (Photo: Xavier Erdmer).

ment. As with towerless churches, the doorway in the gable wall of the church could be flanked to either side by lancet windows, as seen on St. Andrew's Church (1828) and Christ Church (1832), in Ottawa.

When towers were wanted, but were beyond the means of a congregation, small bell turrets offered a popular compromise. Usually set to straddle the roof ridge and in slight retreat of the main façade, they appeared on some of the earliest churches, notably on the Anglican Church of St. James in Hull (fig. 1.1), but enjoyed particular success among Roman Catholic church builders. In elevating structures of this nature, Roman Catholic builders were able to draw freely on Québécois prototypes, lending a distinct flavour to many Ottawa Valley churches. Bells were considered to play an important role in the practice of early nineteenth century Catholic culture, and no church was considered complete without them. Considerable efforts were made by individual priests and parishioners to acquire bells. When the physical or financial structure of a local church could not support a bell tower or turret, bells would occasionally be placed in a small tower of wooden scaffolding, in the manner of a rustic campanile, beside the façade of the church itself. This practice continued well into the second half of the nineteenth century.

When early church builders wished to accentuate frontal monumentality, both Gothic and neoclassic elements could be used in the same building. Combinations of this nature were not common during the late eighteenth and early nineteenth centuries. This unlikely stylistic combination was not perceived by nineteenth century church builders to be as contradictory as it often is to the late twentieth century eye. Perhaps the most valiant attempt to create an architectural presence can be seen in the original church of St. James (Anglican), in Carleton Place (fig. 1.12). While the old church of St. James is sometimes mentioned in connection with the activities of the parish, even the correspondents for the *Canadian Churchman,* who were not known for their restrained architectural opinions, did not attempt a description.[57]

Originally built as a modest frame structure in 1834, the church of St. James eventually acquired a well-proportioned pediment and Doric entablature, supported in turn by four Doric columns.[58] A photograph taken just prior to its demolition shows a building which is (with a little imagination and some good will) vaguely reminiscent of a protostyle temple. A collection of gentlemen are gathered on the deep front porch of St. James under the pediment supported by what appears to be four Doric columns. In keeping with Vitruvius' canons

Fig. 1.12. St. James (Anglican), Carleton Place, 1834.
Despite the stylistic contrast between the classical façade and the Gothic windows, a certain degree of architectural unity is achieved primarily through the omnipresent sobriety of the structure. This earlier nineteenth century use of survival Gothic offers a marked contrast to the light and highly decorative quality of the Victorian barge-boards of the private home beside the church. This photograph was taken shortly before the church was dismantled in the early 1880s (Photo courtesy: Anglican Diocesan Archives, Ottawa).

for the Doric order, the columns rest immediately on the floor of the church porch. Each fluted column is composed of three drums.[59] The Doric entablature is simple, well proportioned, and undecorated. There is no frieze; the horizontal cornice of the pediment rests immediately upon the architrave. The tympanum, like the entablature, is undecorated. The white paint only helps to reinforce the impression of a Greek temple. A square tower sits heavily above the pediment, looking more like an awkward afterthought than an integral part of the structure. This rural and distant reference can nevertheless trace its architectural ancestry to James Gibbs' much copied façade for St. Martin-in-the-Fields, London (1721-1726). Somewhat closer to the Ottawa Valley, Holy Trinity, the Anglican Cathedral in Quebec City (1800-1804), was also copied from Gibbs' St. Martin, although economic and climatic conditions had already necessitated some major structural modifications.[60] At this point, the similarities with classical architecture stop. The grandiose references to classical and neoclassic architecture are in fact simply a preface to a modest vernacular Gothic structure. St. James Church is entered through a large pointed doorway, flanked to either side by large Gothic windows. The unadorned lateral walls of the nave present a striking contrast to the forceful embellishments of the neoclassic façade.

While Anglicans may have attempted to refer to denominationally significant edifices in the construction of rural and colonial churches, similar trends cannot be identified among Ottawa Valley Methodists. Despite the precedent set by Wesley's City Road Chapel, London (1777), itself a porticoed hall, and Wesley's own partiality to Thomas Ivory's Octagon Chapel in Norwhich, Methodist church building was long marked by austere simplicity. Towers and prestigious façades were not a primary concern, and this is clearly reflected in the building of the Ottawa Valley's first Methodist churches. A deeper examination of the role these buildings played for those who built them suggests, however, that these modest structures fulfilled a need that extended far beyond pedestrian demands for shelter and the materialistic constraints of mere architecture.

Interior Design and Arrangements

Although the external structures of some churches from this era have survived relatively unaltered, the same cannot be said for most interiors. Among the few surviving sources for this under-documented subject are floor plans drawn up for the purpose of pew rental. These plans are particularly useful in that they provide a relatively clear ground plan of the church and principal internal features. Pews, pulpits, sanctuaries, and stoves are usually included as they often affected the price. In some instances the names of parishioners and the prices they paid for their pews are noted on the plan. When rental rates are included, they consistently reflect the fact that proximity to the cult act was dictated by financial ability. Larger and more expensive pews flanked the lateral walls of the nave, where the lighting was better, and clustered immediately around the pulpit and reading desk, where the acoustics were better. The Eucharistic table was very much isolated from the majority of the faithful, partly because of its location behind the pulpit, immediately against the western wall.

Regardless of their denominational affiliation, the nave occupied the largest percentage of the building mass in all of these early churches though few early churches could boast spacious interiors. Still, despite their diminutive proportions and general lack of adornment, the importance of the nave should not be undervalued and can contribute much to our understanding of religious practice during the early nineteenth century. The arrangement of the nave plays an important part in determining the relative positioning of the faithful to the cult act. The small size of the nave was due in part, but by no means solely, to the original population base of many early congregations. Several congregations in rapidly expanding settlements were obliged to enlarge their churches only a few years after the original construction.[61] This was particularly true among Anglo-Protestant congregations whose churches were traditionally sized conservatively, especially when compared to the churches of similarly populated Roman Catholic congregations. A distaste for oversized churches was firmly entrenched in the minds of many Anglo-Protestants and the roots of this antipathy can be traced back to the early days of the Protestant Reformation and the restructuring of the English church during the sixteenth century. At this time large portions of many big and now liturgically redundant medieval churches were closed off so as to create a more intimate place of worship. The need for all to see and hear became a fundamental requisite of all Reformed architecture. Given the abundance of pre-Reformation medieval churches available, it was some time before Protestants were in need of new church buildings and thus some time before they were forced to elaborate on the architectural needs of reformed worship. One of the earlier, and certainly one of the more celebrated Protestant architects to do so, was Sir Christopher Wren, who noted:

> it should seem vain to make a *Parish Church* larger than that all who are present can both hear and see. The *Romanist,* indeed, may build larger churches, it is enough if they hear the Murmur of the Mass and see the Elevation of the Host, but ours are to be fitted for Auditors.[62]

Although the introduction of the Auditory or Room Church antedated Wren's career by several years, the expansion of this type owed a great deal to his influence. Much of the success of Wren's plans was due to his thoughtful study of the needs and functions of a Protestant church building. Wren had insisted that parish churches must reflect the new liturgical simplicity but still not fail to visually underscore the importance of sacramental unity. From this simple yet fundamental criterion was to emerge one of Wren's most influential church types. Based on a simple rectangular floor plan that formed a single room, there was no structural distinction between the nave and sanctuary. The only concession to privileged space was a small area at

Fig. 1.13. St. Mary (Anglican), Pinhey's Point, 1828.

The ogee arch of the sanctuary wall is significantly larger than the windows of the nave, that measure five feet at the base. Originally, the Eucharistic table would have stood immediately beneath this window. The squat and comparatively crude doorway immediately east of the sanctuary was opened when a vestry was added. Now in ruins, the interior of the church is used as a burial ground (Photo: V. Bennett).

the western end of the church where the floor might be raised and possibly enclosed with a small railing.

The influence of Wren's approach to Protestant church building is evident in numerous early churches in the Ottawa Valley, most notably among those buildings belonging to the United Church of England and Ireland.[63] The influence of this approach can be traced well into the nineteenth century, especially among rural buildings. Even during the latter decades of the nineteenth century, Canadian Anglo-Protestants who rejected the use of a revived medieval Gothic "often advocated the continued use of church designs that drew their inspiration from the work of Sir Christopher Wren.[64] In contrast to their Protestant counterparts, early Roman Catholic churches in the Ottawa Valley tended to be both wider and more elongated. Longer churches were indeed better suited to ceremonial needs of Roman Catholic worship. The new stone church begun in 1841 to replace Ottawa's first Roman Catholic church, a decrepit and decaying wooden structure, remains today as one of the largest and oldest churches still standing in the Ottawa Valley.[65]

With few exceptions (usually when round-headed windows were used),[66] the naves of these early churches were lit by large

Gothic windows. Stylistically, these window types could range from the very simple mitred arches of Christ Church, Burritt's Rapids (fig. 1.4, fig. 1.7), to the technically complex ogee arches of St. Mary's, Pinhey (fig. 1.13).[67]

By far the most common window type was a long, relatively broad bay with an equilateral or drop arch-head. Windows opening into the nave were filled with clear glazing, which allowed for the admission of great quantities of unaltered daylight, while at the same time reducing the need for artificial lighting (fig. 1.14).

Candles were not only an expensive fire hazard, but were occasionally considered by some Protestants to be "Romish." Many of the few early churches that have survived to the latter decades of the twentieth century now display richly stained glass in the sashes of their windows. It must be remembered that the presence of coloured glass is the result of later modifications. Very few early church builders, especially Protestant church builders, would have filled their windows with coloured glass of any sort, and few would have, even if it had been easily available. The stained glass seen in some of

Fig. 1.14. Christ Church (Anglican), Huntley, 1839.

An altar is now built against the eastern wall where a Eucharistic table would have stood. The wooden reredos is a late addition. Above the altar a Gothic window is set slightly higher than the windows in the nave. Stained glass has replaced earlier plain glass. The sanctuary was raised three steps above the nave. Immediately east of the rood screen is the choir. The organ and choir seats are placed parallel to the central axis of the church rather than perpendicular, as were those of the nave. This would not have been the original seating plan (Photo: V. Bennett).

these churches of this period is invariably a later addition. The impact of this change should not be underestimated as the internal atmosphere of a church is drastically altered by the introduction of coloured glass. Early nineteenth-century Protestant worship demanded a clear, bright interior. Contemporary Roman Catholic thought on this matter, on the other hand, suggested that it was inappropriate for the inside of churches to be too bright.[68] However, regardless of how Catholic church builders in the Ottawa Valley may have felt about the use of stained glass, the question was essentially academic. During the early decades of the nineteenth century, there simply was not much stained glass available. Catholic churches, initially at least, were obliged to make due with a more austere solution than they might normally have preferred, and their churches remained fairly well lit, owing primarily to the general expense and scarcity of coloured glass. The clear glazing of the windows, combined with their size and the whitewashed walls, made for interiors that were both bright and austere. This was particularly well suited to Anglo-Protestant denominations whose worship priorities focused on reading and preaching the Word of God. The Word of God was to be seen and heard by all, and some congregations deliberately scheduled services to be held at such a time that no artificial lighting would be required, while others were somewhat more flexible on this subject. As early as 1842, the nave of Christ Church, Bytown, was lit by gas lamps; however, the congregation had to settle for lamp shades with a thistle on them instead of the tulip-shaped shades they had originally hoped for.[69]

It was in the profound simplicity of the nave that a number of complex relationships were defined. The physical arrangements of the nave offered a telling cross-section of religious and social stratigraphy. This is particularly evident in congregations belonging to the Church of England, the Church of Scotland, and the Church of Rome. The phenomenon occurs not only in terms of relationships between the faithful themselves, who sat in box pews or benches stratified according to their financial worthiness, but also in terms of the faithful's collective place before the sacred. Less distinguished parishioners were relegated to the back of the church or to benches in small galleries that clung above entries and occasionally to the side walls, while those of social standing enjoyed ring-side seats.[70] Box pews appear on the floor plans of many of the early churches, while benches were used in poorer parishes. Regardless of the quality of the seating, its rental was a subject of considerable concern and the quantity of documentation devoted to the subject of pew rental by Anglicans and Presbyterians and Catholics is substantial. In contrast, Methodists generally did not like to charge for seating, although they

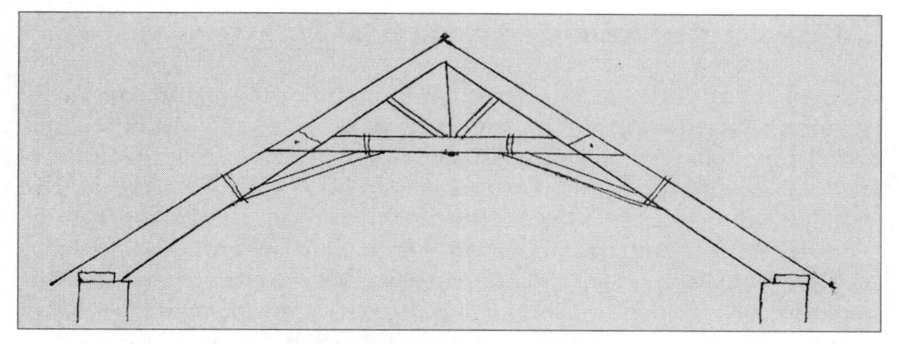

Fig. 1.15. Christ Church (Anglican), Ottawa, 1832.
Tie beams and trusses were typical of the roofing used to cover many of the early church buildings, as illustrated in this letter from Alex Christie to the Christ Church Building Committee, Bytown, 8 June 1841. During the first half of the nineteenth century, these ceilings were usually ceiled with plaster or wooden paneling (Photo courtesy: Anglican Diocesan Archives, Ottawa).

occasionally practised gender segregation during worship.[71] While gender apartheid may have been practised at different times by various congregations, there is little architectural evidence to suggest that the practice was common in Ottawa Valley churches. Overhead, ceilings were often little more than the underside of the roof (fig. 1.15), which was, contrary to later developments within certain denominations, more a consequence of poverty than a preferred solution.

When funds were available, ceilings were frequently finished with some form of vaulting. Barrel vaults or elegant semi-elliptical vaults were popular solutions, and these vaults could be covered with plain plaster ceilings or boarded. Occasionally, as in the original church of St. Andrew (Presbyterian) in Ottawa, a horizontal cornice ran immediately below the spring of the plastered ceiling vault. Another arrangement typical of this era can still be seen inside Christ Church in Huntley (fig. 1.16).

The basket-handle vault of the ceiling is composed of twenty-four wooden panels that run parallel to the longitudinal axis of the building. These panels are underscored at regular intervals by horizontal banding. The vault springs from the side walls of the church at a height of nineteen feet and reaches approximately twenty-three feet at the intrados face of the crown. In most churches from this period the ceiling was uniform throughout the church with no change over the sanctuary area (fig. 1.17).

Liturgical Requirements and Focal Points

The liturgical centres of most churches built in the Ottawa Valley during the first half of the century were very simple. It was in fact this initial simplicity that occasionally allowed several different denominations to collaborate in the construction and use of union chapels. The extent of this austerity is especially evident in the arrangement and furnishing of the sanctuaries. Surviving floor plans suggest that the sanctuaries in churches of all denominations were very modestly sized, as is particularly evident on the seating plan from the church of St. Mary (Anglican) at Pinhey's Point; although Roman Catholic sanctuaries were comparatively more spacious than those of comparably populated Protestant congregations. Very few churches built during this period had architecturally distinct chancels, and even the plans for the Roman Catholics' most ambitious church-building project in the Ottawa Valley, the new stone church of Notre-Dame in Bytown, did not include an architecturally distinct chancel.

One of the most consequential factors in determining the architectural differences between Catholic and Protestant sanctuaries was the liturgical requirements of the Roman Catholic Mass. The Roman

Fig. 1.16. Christ Church (Anglican), Huntley, 1839.

Most windows are now decorated with figural imagery. The original mullions and transoms would have been filled with small panes of clear glass. The varied tones and fluid lead lines of the subsequent glass work create a sense of mobility that would not have been achieved with the original glazing. A single window in the northern wall retains a style of glazing much closer to the original style. Light levels around this window are significantly higher (Photo: A. Erdmer).

Fig. 1.17. Christ Church (Anglican), Huntley, 1839.
Christ Church has remained in constant use since it was officially opened in 1839. Its roughly east–west orientation is the result of conformity to secular surveying. The stone walls are two feet thick. The neatly cut, regular courses are broken only by the arch-stones of the windows. There are no buttresses and no other form of external adornment. The tower is a later addition (Photo V. Bennett).

Catholic liturgy focused on the weekly or, when possible, daily offering of the Eucharist. The celebration of the Mass culminated with the transubstantiation of the bread and wine and its distribution to the laity.[72] This understanding of the Lord's Supper was contrary to contemporary Protestant tradition in a number of ways. Most importantly, nineteenth century Protestants universally rejected the doctrine of transubstantiation. Protestants did not accept, as did Roman Catholics, that during the celebration of the Eucharist, Christ was substantially present through the consecration of the bread and wine.[73] Though united in their rejection of transubstantiation, the various Protestant denominations did not share a united view on the nature and role of the Christian Eucharist. The position of Presbyterians and members of other Reformed churches on the question of the Eucharist was primarily influenced by the teachings of John Calvin. The Lord's Supper was to be a great source of spiritual nourishment, and, while Christ was believed to be present during the celebrations, this was strictly a spiritual and not a substantial presence.[74] The position of the Reformed churches on this question differed from both the Lutherans and Baptists. While denying transubstantiation, Lutherans did accept consubstantiation. In this doctrine, which is in many ways closest to the Roman Catholic position, Christ was held to be present not simply in the substance of the elements, but also with the substance of the elements.[75] The Lutheran position in turn differed from Baptist thought which, under the influence of Ulrich Zwingli, had come to understand the Lord's Supper as a strictly commemorative event. Both the spiritual and literal presence of Christ in the Eucharistic elements were denied; however, through the commemorative act of the Eucharist, a participant was reminded of the benefits of salvation. Although Anglicans frequently speak of themselves as members of a "Reformed Church,"[76] their position, especially on the matter of Eucharistic doctrine, was frequently at variance with other Reformed churches. The Anglican position, as set out in Archbishop Thomas Cranmer's *Book of Common Prayer* (1562) and *The Thirty-Nine Articles* (1563),[77] allowed for considerable flexibility, accommodating both the Low and High churches.

The Roman Catholic understanding of the sacrificial dimension of the Eucharist was suited to celebrate this sacrament on a fixed or built altar. As all other cult activity was subordinate to the Mass, the Eucharist, as focal point of the Mass was by extension to be the focal point of the place of cult. The frequency, primacy, and substance of the Roman Catholic Eucharistic celebration justified the dedication of significant architectural space to this purpose, which is again in contrast to contemporary Protestant practice in which, despite considerable doctrinal diversities, the Eucharistic celebrations of all denominations were held infrequently. In many Protestant communities, the Eucharist was celebrated only several times a year at most. Much more significance was attached to preaching and the reading of Scripture. Furthermore, as a commemorative re-enactment of the Last

Supper, the use of a large immobile sacrificial-style altar was considered to be most inappropriate, and, for this reason communion tables and not altars were used in Protestant congregations. Owing to the infrequency of Eucharistic celebrations, and coupled with the portable nature of a communion table, most Protestant congregations had little need or even justification to reserve a large portion of the church building for Eucharistic celebrations. In many Protestant churches of this era, the privileged position of axial centrality was frequently occupied by a large, frequently oversized pulpit, a reading desk or a three decker. In certain instances, when the communion table did occupy a position of axial centrality, it was usually an understated furnishing, placed against the end wall of the church, very much overshadowed by the pulpit and reading desk. In further contrast to the Roman Catholic tradition that preferred to reserve a generous and reverential space around the central altar, there was very little space between the pulpit and the first row of worshippers.[78]

Permanent baptismal fonts were very rare in the early Ottawa Valley churches, regardless of their denominational affiliation. Protestant congregations that were fortunate to have in their possession something more substantial and decidedly more dignified than a utilitarian basin usually placed it along the central axis of the church building and at the very front of the church. The proximity to the pulpit and communion table was a deliberate reflection of Calvinistic thought in which the importance of visual sacramental unity is stressed. The degree to which Calvinistic thought was influential on this question varied between the various Protestant denominations. A notable exception were the Baptists, who practised total immersion in the administration of this sacrament. The importance of a highly unifocal sacramental arrangement was a recurrent liturgical theme among many nineteenth century Protestants. This concern stemmed from a rejection of the multiplication and diversity of special devotions that had gained in popularity during the late Middle Ages. Leaders of the Protestant Reformation felt that the fragmentation of devotional centres would ultimately fracture the attention of the laity. Those gathered in a house of Christian prayer were not to be distracted from the primary of devotional activity which centred on the Word of God.

In this same spirit, Protestant congregations active in the Ottawa Valley during the first quarter of the nineteenth century, unlike Roman Catholics, rejected nearly all expression of visual embellishment. Iconic symbolism was rarely used and the employment of figural imagery in religious paintings or sculpture was inconceivable. Although many Protestant denominations eventually relaxed their aversion to decorative embellishments, some harboured strong feelings against the use of decoration, which lingered well into the latter decades of the nineteenth century. Some Protestants even occasionally avoided practical objects such as candles for fear that they would create an atmosphere of "Romish superstition." To avoid this and still allow the minister to read on an overcast day, lancet windows were frequently practised at either end of the sanctuary wall in Presbyterian and Methodist churches.[79]

Despite the modesty of their material surroundings, early nineteenth century church builders were clearly very much aware that it was the atmosphere and mind set in which worship was conducted that ultimately must remain faithful to their interpretation of the Gospels. During the fall of 1839, the *Canadian Christian Examiner and Presbyterian Magazine* published "What is Popery?"[80] It was a brief article dedicated to enumerating what the author perceived to be the most evident faults in the practice of the Roman Catholic worship. Readers were informed that as far as religion was concerned: "You want plain, sober, calm, clear evidence of truth."[81] While the article was not intended to address the topic of church building, the author's guidelines for religious practice in many ways offer a concise description of all Christian churches built in the Ottawa Valley during the early decades of the nineteenth century.

Notes

1. The British were also obliged to make concessions to obtain some degree of co-operation from a population that neither spoke their language nor shared their understanding of Christianity. The seizure of Gibraltar remains to this day a point of controversy between the British and the Spanish.

2. S. R. Mealing, "The Enthusiasms of John Graves Simcoe," *Canadian Historical Association Report*, 1958.

3. The Constitutional Act of 1791 reserved one seventh of all public lands for the support and maintenance of a "Protestant clergy." A. Wilson, *The Clergy Reserves of Upper Canada: A Canadian Mortmain* (Toronto: University of Toronto Press, 1968).

4. For a typical discussion of the subject see: "How ought the Clergy Reserve question be settled?" *Canadian Christian Examiner and Presbyterian Magazine,* 3, 9 (September 1839): 269; see also: W. Bettridge, *A Brief History of the Church in Upper Canada: Containing the Acts of Parliament, Imperial and Provincial, Royal Instructions, Proceedings of the Deputation: Correspondence with the Government: Clergy Reserves Question* (London: W. E. Painter, 1838).

5. . . . Clarendon Mission—This mission is about 100 miles north of Brockville, on the north side of the Ottawa river, opposite the Bonchere river, on the Upper Canada side. The mission embraces the Township of Clarendon and Bristol. There are six appointments for preaching besides several prayer meetings. There are four classes and 47

members in the society. A Temperance Society has been formed on the plan of entire abstinence—it now numbers 50. It is about six years since this settlement commenced. The emigrants are mostly from Ireland and Scotland. . . . *8th Annual Report of the Missionary Society of the Wesleyan Methodist Church in British North America 1833*, 6-7.

6. The names of some Methodist groups changed slightly from year to year, and there were numerous mergers. In the early 1830s, the Canada Conference became the Wesleyan Methodist Church in British North America. In 1835 it became the Wesleyan Methodist Church in Canada in Connexion [*sic*] with the English Conference and retained that name until 1874, after which it united with several other Methodist groups to become the Methodist Church of Canada. In 1884, this union joined the Methodist Episcopal Church in Canada, the Primitive Methodist Church in Canada, and the Bible Christian Church to become The Methodist Church.

7. For a complete discussion of demographics of early French settlement in the Ottawa Valley, see R. Choquette, *L'Église catholique dans l'Ontario français du dix-neuvième siècle* (Ottawa: Éditions de l'Université d'Ottawa, 1984) 59-89.

8. Hamnett Pinhey to the Lord Bishop of Quebec, 26 November 1826. The church still stands on the banks of the Ottawa River, though, as predicted by Pinhey, a modern ruin. Nevertheless, it is a lasting monument to the efforts of its founders. I am grateful to Dr. B. Elliot for sharing this quotation with me.

9. See D. Akenson, *The Irish in Ontario: A Study of Rural History* (Montreal and Kingston, McGill-Queen's University Press, 1984); B. Elliot, "The Northern Tipperary Protestants in the Canadas: A study of migration, 1815-1880" (Ph.D. diss., Carleton University, 1984); and G. Lockwood, *Montague: A Social History of an Irish Ontario Township* (Smiths Falls: Corporation of the Township of Montague, 1980).

10. Richard M. Reid, *The Upper Ottawa Valley to 1855*, (Ottawa: Carleton University Press, 1989) xxix.

11. Archives of Queen's University, *Papers of the Presbyterian Church in Connection with the Church of Scotland*, Collection 2263, Box 1, file 1, 1831. Postscript dated 24 November on a letter to Rev. Robert McGill from John Cruickshank: "To the Methodists belongs the credit of having erected the first place of public worship in Bytown. This was in the fall of 1827."

12. This general term will include the various Presbyterian church divisions and unions (such as the Church of Scotland, Auld Kirk, Free Kirk and Session) as well as the numerous variations and associations of Presbyteries (such as The Presbytery of the Canadas, The Missionary Presbytery of the Canadas in Connection with the United Associate Secession Church in Scotland), and Synods (such as the Synod of the Presbyterian Church of Canada in Connection with the Church of Scotland and the Synod of the Free Presbyterian Church of Canada). This group will be referred to hereafter as Presbyterians unless a more specific designation is necessary.

13. H. Belden, *Historical Atlas of Carleton County, Ontario—Illustrated 1879* (Toronto: H. Belden, & Co., 1879), xliv. The Cats is now known as Fitzroy Harbour. According to local tradition, the name dates to the time of Champlain when early explorers mistook the large number of raccoons in the area for some kind of cat. Unlikely as this may be, the name remained in use well into the nineteenth century.

14. Belden, *Carleton,* xliv.

15. A notable exception is the "Union Chapel" built of stone at Bell's Corners. Erected in 1853, this was a much later structure. Though no longer standing, the Bell's Corners Union Chapel is exceptional in that there is a detailed, if unfavourable, description of the interior dating from 1864. See *Canadian Churchman,* 6 April 1864; and the accompanying excellent photograph of the exterior dating from the late 1890s. The

history of the denominations that contributed to the construction of this Union Chapel is discussed in some detail in Bruce S. Elliot, *The City Beyond: A History of Nepean, Birthplace of Canada's Capital 1792-1990* (Nepean: City of Nepean, 1991), 64.

16. The Rev. R. H. Naylor explains that on March 24 and 25, 1868, "'bees' were held to make logs for the church . . . and that two weeks later, on April 7th, . . . twenty-six men assembled and raised the building, which has ever since been known as St. Luke's Caldwell." *The Church in Clarendon* (St. John's: E.R. Smith Co., 1919), 45.

17. Archives of Queen's University, *Papers of the Presbyterian Church in Connection with the Church of Scotland*, Collection 2263, Box 1, file 2. In a letter dated 25 September 1831, from William Mitler to the Rev. R. A. McGill, Mitler mentions that part of the minister's stipend was provided for by the Glasgow Colonial Society. Between 1821 and 1843, Scottish Presbyterians were served by the Society for Promoting the Religious Interests of Scottish Settlers in British North America, which was also known as the Glasgow Colonial Society. In 1836, the General Assembly of the Church of Scotland established the Committee for Promoting the Religious Interests of Scottish Presbyterians in the British Colonies, which became the Colonial Commission in 1856. For Anglicans, in addition to assistance from the provincial government, there was also the Society for the Propagation of the Gospel and the Society for Promoting Christian Knowledge. Roman Catholic priests came to the Ottawa Valley from Quebec, Ireland, and France. The French Oblates made considerable contributions to the progress of Catholicism in the Ottawa Valley and provided the Diocese of Ottawa with its first bishop. Considerable contributions to Catholic education and public health were also made by the Soeurs Grises, who established a community in Ottawa in 1845.

18. Although officially called the United Church of England and Ireland, the addressing of bids tendered for the construction of the new church indicate that "The English Church" or "The Episcopal Church" were more common terms in popular parlance. See the Anglican Diocesan Archives, Ottawa, Box 6-O-3C1-1.

19. the Congregation of necessity attend divine service in the Church in said unfinished state, the Pulpit such as it may be called/ and seats being of temporary plank, the walls not plastered and no ceiling. The only article of furniture hitherto obtained has been one stove. . . .

Letter of 9 August 1833 to "His Excellency Sir John Colbourn, Knight Commander of the Bath, Lieutenant Governor of the Province of Upper Canada and Major General commanding Her Majesty's Forces therein," church wardens A. Bruwrele, G. W. Baker and Geo. Patterson, Anglican Diocesan Archives, Ottawa, Box 6-O-3C1-1-74.

20. " The Churches in this mission are neat stone edifices—that at Bytown being recently built at the sole expense of the congregation on a site given by Nicholas Sparks Esq. It is calculated to contain about 300 persons and is usually well filled . . . the church is used as a military chapel, and a minister is called to officiate to the troops. The objection to assist this mission on the part of the Government either with land or salary appears the more extraordinary and unjust from the circumstance of its lending aid to every other denomination in the place *but the Establishment*, and from the Scotch Church having both a valuable Clergy reserve and a Salary for its minister. . . ." "Church Statistics and Intelligence—Mission of Bytown in Upper and Lower Canada," reprinted from *The Church* in the *Bytown Gazette*, 16 January 1834.

21. On the final day of the General Assembly of the Church of Scotland held in Edinburgh during the spring of 1835, delegates addressed the issue of "Overture on New Churches." The outcome of this discussion was published in *The Principal Acts of the General Assembly of the Church of Scotland,* section XX, and forwarded to church members in Canada:

I. That the Act of Assembly 1789 amendment, the erection of Chapels of Ease be rescinded.

II. That Presbyteries shall have the power of granting constitutions to new churches, under the control, and liable to the review, of the general assembly.

III. That when a Petition shall be presented to them for a new erection, they shall strictly observe the following rules:

1*st* They shall cause to be cited in the usual form all parties having interest, —namely the Minister and Kirk—Session of the Parish in which the new church is to be built, the Heritors of the Parish, etc. . . .

2*dly* In every petition for a new erection, the petitioners shall be required to state explicitly and minutely the number of persons who may be accommodated in the intended church, the sum subscribed for its erection, the person or corporate body in whom it is proposed to invest the property, the wished-for mode of electing a minister and other office bearers, the provision made for keeping the church in repair, for defraying the expense of common elements, and all the other circumstances with which the Presbytery may deem it necessary for them to be acquainted; and the constitution shall contain regulations as to these matters, and shall prescribe the bounds of the parish to be erected, the Presbytery abstaining carefully from giving decree for a new erection when there is not a reasonable prospect of the church being permanent.

3*dly* . . . in all cases . . . by the title-deeds, the church shall be inalienably mortified as a church in connection with the Church of Scotland, and the building and ground shall not be subject to be made liable for the debts of the church or chapel . . . .

6*thly* No constitution shall be granted till two-thirds of the expense incurred in purchasing ground and building the church shall have been liquidated . . . .

Despite the above-mentioned specifications, there were few precise architectonic prescriptions. To this day, religious architecture flowing from the Scottish tradition remains somewhat understudied even in Scotland itself. This need for further work is especially evident when compared with the abundance of literature that is readily available on the history of English religious architecture.

22. Most notably under Henry VIII (1540, six articles of the Westminster Parliament), Edward VI, and Elizabeth I.

23. ". . . we may have either a Greek dress of the parallelogram or a Gothic dress, and we may adopt either the one or the other. . . ." Archdeacon Wollaston to Mr. Jenner, 23 August 1819, quoted in M. H. Port, *Six-Hundred New Churches* (London: S.P.C.K., 1961), 52-3.

24. Port, *Six-Hundred*, 49.

25. Port, *Six-Hundred*, 61.

26. As Port points out, "the delight of medieval Gothic, and the charm of the slender and delicate forms of eighteenth century rococo Gothic were alike absent . . . the play of light and shadow, the depth and variety of the moldings that are much of the delight of Gothic" were abandoned. Instead, architects were now obliged to "reconcile the Gothic style not merely to the Protestant preaching-box element, but also an increasingly strict financial control which deprived them of ornament. . . . The result was a box-like building with a few windows with pointed heads," Port, *Six-Hundred*, 57.

27. A sampling of the diversity of work done on this subject can be seen in *Album des églises de la province de Québec*, vols. 1-7 (Montréal: Compagnie Canadienne Nationale de Publication, 1928); M. Brosseau, *Le style néo-gothique dans l'architecture au*

Canada (Ottawa: Centre d'édition du Gouvernement du Canada, 1980); A. Gowans, *Church architecture in New France* (Toronto: University Press, 1955); G. Morisset, *l'Architecture en Nouvelle-France* (Québec: Charrier et Dugal, 1949); G. Morisset, *Les églises et le trésor de Lotbinière* (Québec: G. Morisset, 1953); G. Morisset, *Les églises et le trésor de Varennes* (Québec: s.n., 1952); Luc Noppen, *Les églises du Québec (1600-1850)* (Quebec: Éditeur Officiel du Québec/Fides, 1977); L. Noppen, *Notre-Dame de Québec* (Québec: Éditions du Pélican, 1974); L. Noppen et al, *Québec, trois siècles d'architecture* (Québec: Libre Expression, 1979); P.G. Roy, *Les vieilles églises de la province de Québec, 1647-1800* (Québec: Imprimeur du Roy, 1925); F.K.B.S. Toker, *The Church of Notre-Dame in Montreal* (Montreal and Kingston: McGill-Queen's University Press, 1970); R. Traquair, *The Old Architecture of Quebec* (Toronto: Macmillan Co. of Canada, 1947); M. Trudel, "Les églises ont-elles souffert de la conquête?" *Revue d'histoire de l'Amérique française*, (June 1954): 25-71; L. Voyer, *Églises disparues* (Québec: Libre Expression, 1981); D. Tremblay, "Caractères et tendances de l'architecture religieuse dans le Québec," *Journal of the Royal Architectural Institute of Canada* 323 (June 1952): 228-230.

28. See R. Bordeaux, *Traité de la réparation des églises: principes d'archéologie pratique* (Évreux: A. Hérissey, 1862); A.-R. Devie, *Manuel de connaissances utiles aux ecclésiastiques sur divers objets d'art notamment sur l'architecture des édifices religieux anciens et modernes, et sur les constructions et réparations d'églises—Avec plans et dessins lithographiés* (Lyon: L. Lesne, 1843); M. Schmidt, *Manuel de l'architecture des monuments ou Traité d'application pratique de l'archéologie chrétienne à la construction, à l'entretien, à la restauration et à la décoration des églises* (Paris: Roret, 1845).

29. B. Little, *Catholic Churches Since 1623: A Study of Roman Catholic Churches in England and Wales from Penal Times to the Present Decade* (London: Robert Hale, 1966), 38.

30. As reported in an early history, the village of L'Orignal "boasted no church till 1836, when the Presbyterians rose above the necessity of holding their meetings in the school by erecting a place of worship of their own." H. Belden, *Historical Atlas of Prescott & Russell, Stormont, Dundas & Glengarry Counties, Ontario* (Toronto: H. Belden & Co., 1881), 60.

31. *Bytown Gazette*, 25 October 1837.

32. Ibid.

33. Ibid.

34. The Archives of the Diocese of Ontario (Anglican), Kingston, Vestry Book-Burritt's Rapids, Merrikville Parish, Marlbourough Township, 1829-1893-document 5MM1 state:

> Res'd 1st—By the majority of those present that they will exert themselves for the purpose of erecting a house of public worship for the established church of England exclusively.
> 2'd—That the aforesaid church shall be erected at or near the burying ground Lot 8-25 in the first concession of the aforesaid Township of Marlborough.
>
> 3'd—That the materials for erecting the walls of the aforesaid church should consist of stone, lime and sand.
>
> 4th—That the dimensions of the aforesaid church shall be left to the discretion of the building committee with these exceptions, that is to say that it shall not exceed 35 by 45 nor shall it be less than 30 by 40 ft.
>
> 5th—That the building committee shall consist of George L. Bassitt, Henry Burritt and Stephen Hurd Esquires.
>
> 6th—That the committee shall neither of them be contractors for the erection of the aforesaid church or any part thereof. . . .

35. See Archives of the Diocese of Ontario (Anglican), Kingston, Vestry Book —Burritt's Rapids, Merrikville Parish, Marlbourough Township, 1829-1893—document 5MM1.

36. Baptists had been in the Ottawa Valley since the 1820s. Lutherans did not appear in any number prior to organized German immigration in the second half of the nineteenth century. See P. Hessel, *Destination Ottawa Valley* (Ottawa: Runge Press Ltd., 1984).

37. R. Jefferson, *Faith of our Fathers: The Story of the Diocese of Ottawa* (Ottawa: The Anglican Book Society, 1956), 158; C. Bennett, *The Story of Renfrew* (Renfrew: Juniper Books, 1984), 180-189.

38. "The ground [for the first church] had been selected somewhere about the time of the rebellion, in preference to a splendid lot in the village, generously offered by Mr. Dickson, simply we understand, because the loyal Churchmen of the parish would not be indebted for the site of their Church to a reformer! Laudable and natural as the feeling may have been at the time the result has worked untold evil," *Dominion Churchman,* 10 August 1876.

39. Although the church itself is now in ruins, Pinhey himself was a keen writer and in addition to keeping the Bishop well informed about the project, kept a set of daily accounts concerning work and progress on the construction site. His daughter, an accomplished artist, illustrated the façade and northwestern exterior of the side of the building. A photo of the southeastern flank survives, taken in the early twentieth century just before the church was dynamited. There are regretfully no photographs or illustrations of the interior but an early floor plan drawn up for the purpose of pew rental has survived. There is also enough of the church preserved to confirm this fact. I am grateful to Dr. B. Elliot, Head of the Pinhey's Point Foundation, for bringing Pinhey's writings on this subject to my attention.

40. "We are requested by the gentleman who built the church to state that the building was commenced in the Spring of 1825, was completed at Christmas of 1828; and no subscription from that noble lady nor any contribution neither in England or Ireland has ever been received or solicited towards it," *Bytown Gazette*, 13 June 1839.

41. The vestibule that precedes St. John's church, South March, and the axial tower of Christ Church, Huntley, are both later additions.

42. Although this chapel has subsequently undergone numerous alterations, it is one of the few surviving Methodist structures from this era.

43. St. James, Franktown, 1822; Christ Church, Burritt's Rapids, 1831; St. Matthew's, Grenville, 1832; and Christ Church, Huntley, 1839, are good examples and are all still standing. St. James, Hull, 1823 (now lost), may have been an exception.

44. The original Christ Church in Ottawa was built facing the river and, therefore, also lies along a north-south axis. When the new church and present cathedral was built, in 1872, this orientation was retained.

45. Anglican Diocesan Archives, Ottawa, Box 6-0-3; C-1:1, no. 46.

46. Archives of the Diocese of Ontario (Anglican), Kingston, Box 6-L, file 2-1.

47. Ibid.

48. Several early exceptions include St. James Anglican in Franktown (1822), the Methodist chapel in Aylmer (1828), and the Scottish Kirk in Beckwith (1834).

49. A small porch has been built against the façade of the South March church, while the central entry of the Huntley church is now preceded by an axial tower.

50. X. Barbier de Montault, *Traité pratique de la construction et de la décoration des églises selon les règles canoniques et les traditions romaines* (Paris: P. Louis Vivès, 1878), 44.

51. Anglican Diocesan Archives, Ottawa, Box 6-O-3; C-1: 1, no. 46.

52. Select Vestry Minutes, 15 December 1841, Anglican Diocesan Archives, Ottawa, Box 6-O-3, file 1.2.F1, no. 136-8.

53. A good example was the façade of the original St. Stephen's church in Buckingham, 1845, which had four wall buttresses with pinnacles and elongated finials. An embattled parapet ran between the two central pinnacles. See *St. Stephen's Anglican Church, Buckingham & Saint Thomas Church, Lochaber, Quebec, 1845-1945*, Quebec, 8.

54. Public Archives of Canada, MG9 D7-35, vol. 23, part 1. Minutes of the Temporal Committee Meeting, 4 October 1864.

55. J. MacPhail, *St. Andrew's Church—Ottawa: The First Hundred Years, 1828-1928* (Ottawa: Dadson-Merrill Press Ltd., 1931), 20.

56. One of the few exceptions to this general rule is the Anglican church of St. James' in Franktown (1822).

57. In 1863, a correspondent for the *Canadian Churchman* (18 June 1863) who accompanied the bishop to Carleton Place on a confirmation tour, noted: "The exterior of the church has lately been repainted and it would add very much to its appearance if the interior were renovated in a like manner."

58. Anglican Diocesan Archives, Ottawa, Box 6-L-C1.

59. It is not possible to tell if there are actually twenty flutes as recommended by Vitruvius (III:9); however, on the original photograph, the shadowing is strong and well balanced, and the conventions of the more ornate orders are clearly not used.

60. For further discussion of the Holy Trinity Cathedral in Quebec City, see Luc Noppen & Lucie K. Morisset, *La présence Anglicane à Québec* (Sillery: Les éditions du Septentrion, 1995), a well documented and generously illustrated discussion of the architectural history of Quebec City.

61 Less than ten years after it was built, the Congregation of Christ Church, Bytown, was obliged to add transepts and galleries to its church, and a few years later, the neighbouring Presbyterian Congregation of St. Andrew's church lengthened its church on Wellington Street.

62. C. Wren, *Parentalia: or Memoirs of the Family of the Wrens; viz of Matthew Bishop of Ely, Christopher, Dean of Windsor, etc., but chiefly of Sir C. Wren; in which is contained, besides his works, a great number of Original Papers and Records . . . Compiled by his son Christopher . . . Published by S. Wren with the Care of J. Ames* (London: T. Osborne & R. Dodsley, 1750), 320.

63. Historian of church architecture, J. White considers Wren to have exercised the single most important influence on Anglican church building prior to the changes introduced by the Ecclesiologists and ritualists during the early Victorian Era. J. White, *The Cambridge Movement: The Ecclesiologists and the Gothic Revival* (Cambridge: Cambridge University Press, 1962), 2.

64. Although Wren himself occasionally used Gothic (most notably when he worked on Westminster), it is a competent but dry technical execution that bespeaks no love or affinity for the style.

65. The interior measurements of the nave are 20.12 m x 39 m. See N. Pagé, *La Cathédrale Notre-Dame d'Ottawa* (Ottawa: Presses de l'Université d'Ottawa, 1988), 129.

66. St. James, Beckwith, is one of the better preserved examples.

67. In a letter dated 10 January 1827, Pinhey provides his builder with a drawing of ogee-arched windows. While Pinhey was flexible concerning the exact dimensions of these windows (about 5 feet), his plans clearly called for an ogee-arch head. See Public Archives of Canada, Ottawa, Hill Collection, MG .2646, vol. 19.

68. "Il n'est pas à propos qu'une église soit trop éclairée; une mystérieuse obscurité invite au recueillement. C'est pour cela que nos ancêtres mettaient aux fenêtres des vitraux peints qui affaiblissaient la lumière et la faisaient arriver aux yeux toute imprégnée de sujets de méditation." See A. R. Devie, *Manuel de connaissances utiles aux ecclésiastiques sur divers objets d'art notamment sur l'architecture des édifices religieux anciens et modernes, et sur les constructions et réparations d'églises—Avec plans et dessins lithographiés* (Lyon: L. Lesne, 1843), 317.

69. Correspondence from Thomas Lang of Montreal to Rev. S. S. Strong, 1842. The letter includes statements of price for 22 lampshades, six spare chimneys and two gross of lamp wicks. Considerable correspondence concerning lamps and lamp repair follows. See Anglican Diocesan Archives, Ottawa, Box 6-O-3, C-1-2 File 2, document 170.

70. See Thomas Bedford-Jones, "How St. Alban's Church and Parish had their Beginning under the First Rector," *Journal of Canadian Church History* (May 1957).

71. See *Canada Christian Advocate* (January 1846).

72. The doctrine of transubstantiation was first articulated at the Fourth Latran Council in 1215.

73. Decrees of the Council of Trent (1545-1563) further clarified the position of the Roman Catholic church on the question of transubstantiation.

74. See *The Westminster Confession* (1647), as well as the *Second Helvetic Confession,* written in 1561 and made publicly available in 1566.

75. Luther outlined his position on this question in the *Augsburg Confession* of 1555.

76. Notably as in the previously mentioned writings of Sir Christopher Wren.

77. Bishop Cranmer's *Book of Common Prayer* was revised in 1552. Cranmer was also responsible for the doctrinal position as outlined in *The Forty-Two Articles* of 1552. This latter work formed the basis for *The Thirty-nine Articles* (1563), which appeared several years after Cranmer's death in 1556.

78. There are a few rare photographs of church interiors; however, these photographs date at best to the latter decades of the nineteenth century by which time the original disposition had usually been altered or added to. Nevertheless, the original arrangements can still be identified.

79. In Ottawa, as late as the 1850s when the Rev. M. Spence wished to hold evening services on the Sabbath, he was obliged to apply to the Temporal Committee, "for the means necessary to light the church." Eventually the Committee "having taken the same into consideration, agree[d] to provide Branch Candlesticks for the Pulpit and for the Presenter's Desk." St. Andrew's Temporal Committee Meeting, 23 May 1853. Public Archives of Canada, MG 9 D7-35 vol. 23, part 1.

80. The *Canadian Christian Examiner and Presbyterian Magazine* was at this point in connection with the Church of Scotland.

81. "What Is Popery?" *Canadian Christian Examiner and Presbyterian Magazine* 3, 10 (October 1839), 293.

CHAPTER TWO

THE ROLE OF THE CHURCH EDIFICE IN DEVELOPING SETTLEMENTS: Permanence and Commitment

During the second quarter of the nineteenth century, church architecture held increasing interest among inhabitants of Central Canada. As local newspapers and city directories enjoyed a growing readership and augmented circulation, editors rarely missed an occasion to note, along with the factories, post office, mills, and other commercial enterprises, the number of churches any one town or village might have had to its credit. Expanded steam and rail travel, more roads, and even the greater availability of newspapers all gradually contributed to an erosion of a once prevalent sense of isolation. The expanded availability of printed news occurred not only in the context of secular journals, but was also gaining new ground as an important vehicle for the dissemination of confessional news.[1] Unlike (but not necessarily contrary to) the presence of industrial establishments, the presence of church buildings was increasingly depicted as integrally related to the state of both sacred and secular affairs.

When church-building projects were evaluated in the press (secular or confessional), site, location, and structural quality all figured prominently. The emphasis placed on these features cannot be dismissed as journalistic fodder. It is instead reflective of the complex nature of the universe as understood in nineteenth century Central Canada. In this intricate world vision, the sacred and the secular, while remaining two distinct entities, were inextricably intertwined. The condition of church buildings was perceived to reflect the virtues (or vices) of the community as a whole. How a community cared for their place of worship was considered to be a reliable reflection on the state of most other affairs. Attention given to the material maintenance of church architecture was seen to proclaim not only the moral fabric of a community but also its work ethic. Oblique references to this idea were common, although direct ones were not unusual. In November of 1846, the *Christian Guardian* noted that members of communities possessing a sincere interest in Christianity usually assumed the responsibility for the construction of church buildings. This facilitated the worship of God, which was in and of itself a commendable undertaking. Through the construction of suitable church buildings the "worth and stability" of a congregation was openly and demonstratively stated. A community's attitudes towards the upkeep and maintenance of its religious edifices were viewed as detectable aspects of daily life.[2]

From a secular perspective, the geographic location of a church building was often considered to reflect the merit of the denomination to which it belonged, while the physical condition of the building reflected the commitment of the denomination to the community in which it stood. The clergy was well aware of the potential that this line of thinking might have in aiding the expansion and the recruitment of new members. Increased attention was transferred to publicly announcing the construction, renovations, or opening services of chapels in secular journals. Correspondents from confessional journals and authors of missionary reports rarely let slip an occasion to comment on the improvement of their own public image. This image, however, was rarely monolithic. It could vary not only between the various Christian confessions, but also within a denomination and even within a given congregation. The same building could be discussed from several very different perspectives, as the image any one group wished to present to the secular world was not necessarily identical to what was presented to religious rivals, potential converts, or even their own members.

An important prerequisite for any denomination hoping to successfully introduce itself into a community was to rid themselves of any mark of transience. This was especially important in areas that had only recently begun to establish permanent settlements. Creating a reassuring sense of permanence was not always easy—particularly at a time when all brave new endeavours were not automatically rewarded with unqualified success. Priests, ministers, and self-taught preachers were still a rare commodity. Members of the clergy who did venture to labour in the Ottawa Valley were responsible for enormous tracts. A preacher for the Missionary Society of the Wesleyan Methodist Church on the missions in the Eastern Districts reported that the Ottawa Valley was "a 'region of the valley and shadow of death' until visited by our Missionaries."[3] While no one else appears to have equated the Ottawa Valley with the valley of death, many other ministers were responsible for equally large tracts of land. In 1844, Rev. William Morton reported that the Wesleyan Methodist Mission of Clarendon in western Quebec covered the townships of Litchfield, Clarendon, Bristol, and Onslow.[4] Morton's successor, Rev. W. Pattyson, reported in 1852 that Thorn and part of Aidly Township had been added to the mission.[5] The resulting charge was an area of over four hundred square miles, which was not exceptional. The Wesleyan Methodist Mission of Buckingham, also in western Quebec, included the Papineau Seignory, the townships of Herrington, Augmentation, Lochaber, and Buckingham as well as the township of Cumberland on the Ontario side of the Ottawa River.[6]

Further west and upriver on the Ontario side, the Wesleyan's Bonnechère Mission included the townships of Admaston, Bromley, Horton, McNab, Stafford, and a large expanse of previously unsurveyed land. In 1849, the Rev. Wilson suggested that the mission be divided since the seventy-mile length of his charge was too large for a single individual.[7] Wilson's point was certainly valid as travel was not easy, and many missions were visited a few times a year at most.[8] The infrequence of clerical visitation did not facilitate or enhance either an air of permanence or a sense of commitment. The clergy's arduous task was further complicated by the fact that, for many settlers, the line between certain denominations was rather fluid. Defection by the laity from one denomination to another was not uncommon.[9] Settlers often attended the services of whatever minister was available. This was particularly common where there were no church buildings. It was also more common between certain denominations than others. Anglicans were often reluctant to worship with dissenters, and Roman Catholics were on the whole more likely to take their chances of salvation on their own rather than risk perdition by frequenting the religious edifices of Protestants. Those denominations that could assure the construction of a small building were more likely to attract the greater following. It was not unusual for a minister to complain that a loyal parishioner had departed suddenly when a rival denomination built a church. Within Methodism, the presence of two rival branches divided the resources of both communities, and ultimately hurt the Methodist cause more than anything else. The loss of a church building, however modest, was considered a major setback to any community (fig. 2.1).[10]

Fig. 2.1. Union Chapel, Bell's Corners, 1853.

This solid stone structure was a collective effort of local Methodists, Anglicans, and Presbyterians. In 1864, it was publicly ridiculed in the Anglican Press by correspondents favourable to the revival of medieval tradition (Photo courtesy: Anglican Diocesan Archives, Ottawa).

Church leaders from all denominations soon realized that the construction of a church, no matter how modest it might be, stood as a constant and tangible witness to their commitment and intent of permanency. In popular perception a denomination that invested resources in the construction of a church building was more inclined to remain or at least return to the community and would probably be more inclined to provide stable spiritual service. By the same token, however, church buildings could be the focal point of vandalism if the denomination to whom it belonged was not perceived to be a welcome addition to the community. The vandalism of churches was not generally viewed in a very positive light. When the Roman Catholic Church in Fitzroy Harbour was destroyed by an arsonist, the *Ottawa Tribune* noted: "There is one all seeing eye from which the darkness of the night has not concealed the unhallowed perpetrator of this act, an Omnipotent Being, and he has said vengeance is mine, and I will repay."[11] Over the course of the nineteenth century, Catholic church buildings were vandalized on a number of different occasions. The fact that Protestant churches did not appear to be similarly afflicted should not necessarily be seen as a meritorious reflection of the local Roman Catholic population, as Orange Lodges appear to have been particularly prone to misfortune.[12]

Given these circumstances, it was not unusual that when a missionary or priest traveling through an area identified the need to regroup a community, he would suggest and often organize the building of a small church. The construction of a church building thus served as a visible and physical rallying point that both motivated and united a community in the furtherance of a common religious cause. A Roman Catholic priest working in the Ottawa Valley suggested that construction of a small church building was a useful tool in the struggle against heresy and a potent antidote to the efforts and soul pilfering of Protestant missionaries. In 1854, church authorities were concerned when they discovered French-speaking Swiss Protestants working among the parishioners of l'Ange-Gardien in Angers.[13] In that same year, construction of a chapel was begun. The intention of the church-building project was to gather local Roman Catholics and concentrate their energies on a project that would supply a visual sense of progress. Once completed the church was to be a source of unity and a focal point for the community. Regretfully, this particular project fell somewhat short of these good intentions. The site chosen for the construction of the new chapel was not considered central enough for significant portions of the community, and soon parishioners were squabbling among themselves. Although not stated openly, it appears that despite this disappointment, church leaders considered the souls of their flock to be in much less peril fighting over the location of a Catholic church than worshipping in a Protestant one. By contrast, in communities where there was a strong Roman Catholic presence and numbers were sufficient to warrant requesting the services of a full-time priest, parishioners were usually told they must first build a church (fig. 2.2).

During the middle years of the nineteenth century, the population of the Ottawa Valley expanded both in number and in prosperity. Anglicans, Roman Catholics, and Presbyterians, all of whom had a strong presence since the implantation of the first settlements, continued to increase in numbers. This was also true of several other denominations such as the Methodists and Baptists, who had also been in the Ottawa Valley from a very early date, but had been numerically weak and architecturally inactive. The Baptists were beginning to make serious inroads for the first time although there had been Baptists in the Ottawa Valley from a very early date. It was only during the 1850s that they became stronger and flourished, leading one Wesleyan minister to complain about the increased activities of the "Immersionists." All this had considerable effect on architectural projects and the race to build. Increasingly, this new material prosperity and confessional expansion was presented, especially by

Fig. 2.2. Anglican Chapel, Deux Rivières.
Though built in the northern reaches of the Ottawa Valley and a somewhat later structure, this church is typical of the numerous modest chapels built during the first half of the nineteenth century. Few have survived; still they must be acknowledged as a significant factor in the overall study of church-building trends (Photo courtesy: Anglican Diocesan Archives, Ottawa).

the clergy, as a gift from God. It was felt to be only natural that this sign of divine favour be duly recognized. While prayers of thanksgiving were always recommended, there was an increasing conviction that gratitude for material prosperity should also be given a visible and more specifically material expression. Within a Roman Catholic community, options through which a material expression of gratitude might be demonstrated were diverse. Religious imagery and devotional statuary had long played an important role in the practice of Roman Catholic piety. The same, however, was not true of contemporary Protestant communities. Many Protestant traditions were solidly grounded in aniconic doctrine[14] that on occasion, in more extreme cases, listed towards iconoclasm.[15]

While the discussion of this topic is traditionally associated with the formative years of Protestant thought, it should not be dismissed as overly retrospective or irrelevant to the study of nineteenth century church building in Central Canada. An ongoing preoccupation with this subject was prevalent among Protestant leaders well into the nineteenth century. Incessant discussion of the visual atmosphere in which people lived, worked, and worshipped reflected a very real concern that negligence in this matter could occasion a fall from grace, which would lead a person away from the Word of God and, in especially regrettable cases, into the shadowy world of Roman superstition and idolatry. The *Christian Guardian* made it quite clear to the Methodist population of Central Canada that, while Christian charity might dictate the tolerance of Catholic churches, it was decidedly unProtestant to assist in their construction.[16] Similar attitudes formed a recurrent theme in contemporary Protestant writing. The distrust for any environment that did not conform to the ideal, plain, well-lit neatness that so many Protestant churches embodied was pervasive. Much of this thinking spread into the secular spheres of life and is reflective of the complexities of nineteenth century cosmology in which two worlds, that of the sacred and that of the secular, were intertwined.[17] The perception of two worlds substantially different, but co-existent and in constant company, was reinforced by discussions of the physical environment that appeared in portions of confessional journals reserved for scientific matters. Typical of this conviction is an article published in 1847 in the science column of the *Christian Guardian:*

> Dark and somber dwellings and streets are the well known resort of the most depraved classes in all cities and towns. . . . Darkness provides a carelessness and depression of mind, and the whole nervous system, especially if conjoined with idleness, its almost necessary companion. A dark house. . . is generally a dirty house if such dwellings were exposed to the light of day a sense of shame would often induce a superior degree of cleanliness: and the cheerfulness of mind which a light house tends to foster would be productive of still greater advantages.[18]

Much of the contrast drawn between the benefits of brightness, the ills of darkness, and the various effects of each on the well-being of human beings is extended into the discussion of religious practice. During the middle years of the nineteenth century, Roman Catholics are continuously depicted by Protestants as being gloomy, dark, and unhealthy. The evils of Roman Catholicism and the unenlightened superstitious practices it was considered to foster were the subject of frequent and lengthy discussions in the Protestant press. Authors took particular pleasure in denouncing shortcomings of Roman Catholic rituals and enumerating their faults, frequently equating the Church of Rome with darkness,[19] fear,[20] excessive clerical propinquity,[21] and uncleanness.[22] There is, however, little evidence to suggest that these writings were based on first-hand personal observations. Still, in keeping with these concerns, nineteenth century Protestant writers frequently sought to reaffirm their rejection of the visual expressions of Roman Catholicism. In doing so, they ratified many declarations originally avowed by the patriarchs of Protestant thought. Consistent with this tradition is Nathan Bangs' discussion of the visual dimension of Christian worship, although his critique of Catholic doctrine suggests that he may not have been sufficiently conversant with a number of subtle but very crucial nuances.[23]

Restricted in terms of options available for the material declaration of spiritual sentiment, many Protestant congregations turned to the building of churches as a heresy-free alternative. In this context, the construction of a small church building, again no matter how modest it might be, must also be seen as an embodiment of belief and a tactile witness of spiritual devotion. As such, the building of a church then became much more than the promise of an improved settlement, but emblematic of commitment to a higher cause. Despite the prevalence of a new zeal for church building, it is important to remember that among more conservative elements, an attitude of caution towards this subject remained well into the 1840s. One Methodist declared that, owing to the omnipresence of God, he had to question the wisdom of throwing too much of one's energy into the building of churches.[24] While they continued to exist for some time, concerns of this sort were becoming progressively less prevalent, which is not to suggest that the role and image of the church edifice was becoming any less complex. Instead, as one moves from the public discussion of the church edifice to a confessional or congregational one, the abstraction and complexity of symbolic content increases. It becomes not merely a neat symbol of Christian industry, but rather a quasi-mystical focal point of the faithful.

When discussed in a secular context, the outward appearance of a church building retained its importance as general reflection of the congregation's role in society as a whole. The oversight of a church-building project by the local press was not something to be indulged. In 1847, the staff of the *Bytown Packet* was taken to task for not reporting the church-building efforts of the Congregationalists who had established themselves in the town the previous year. In an effort to amend this *faux pas*, the paper apologized for the oversight and, after first noting the merits of the site and its location, proceeded to give a detailed report of the Congregationalist's building activities.[25] When discussed from a confessional perspective several additional factors figured into the equation. One consideration of particular importance was the method by which the church would be financed. As in most things related to the construction of a nineteenth-century church building, this was not a straightforward unidimensional issue.

Instead, the financing of church-building projects was part and parcel of how a denomination understood its own role in the doing of God's work, its relation with the material world, and its dealings with secular governments. The United Church of England and Ireland felt that, as the official church of England, it should receive state assistance for its church-building projects. Assistance in the construction of churches was seen as being an integral duty of Christian government, and many of its demands for government funding was based on its claims to church establishment.

Anglicans were not alone in this claim; the Church of Scotland also considered itself an established church. In 1840, the unification of the Presbyterian churches was brought about in part as a means of obtaining greater access to funds and more government aid. This union was short lived; the "Disruption" of 1843 caused a deep division between the Auld Kirk and the Free Church in Scotland that reached the parishes of Central Canada in a matter of months. The division of congregations into Auld Kirk or Free Kirk supporters soon appeared in the Ottawa Valley and were especially manifest in the expansion of the Free Kirk, or Free Church, support.[26] Here, the division was often manifest through a secondary split that tended to run along urban/rural lines. In the farming communities of the Fitzroy Harbour, Huntley, and Thorbolton areas, a number of wealthy rural families chose to join the Free Church while those who elected to remain with the Auld Kirk found themselves increasingly isolated. The Auld Kirk was left much smaller and as a predominantly urban church with little interest in rural concerns.

In the Ottawa Valley, the legacy of the Scottish rift is apparent through a great attachment to the Presbyterian practice of church government, a more pronounced leaning towards Calvinistic doctrine, and the expansion of an Evangelical spirit.[27] Even so, within individual congregations, there was rarely a unified commitment to one faction. Parishioners fought over the funding of missionaries, the division of parishes, and property claims. The resulting animosity was often so great that the two factions were often in a state of such disagreement that they were unable to use the same church building. The most visible outcome of this problem was the construction of new churches; however, there was more to the Scottish rift than a need for new buildings. Devotees of the Free Church cause held very firm views on how the building of churches should be financed. Funds were to be raised from within the community itself. The emergence of Free Church as an energetic and vital force leant considerable weight to the voluntarist cause.

Voluntarism had been gaining momentum for some time among several other Christian denominations, especially among Baptists and Methodists. In 1847, the Episcopal Methodist journal, the *Canada Christian Advocate*, denounced the government funding of churches, and called state-paid churches a "source of incalculable evil."[28] Over the course of the next few years the voluntarist position was to make extraordinary gains in strength and popularity. This growth was to come at the expense of the established churches. The voluntarist position, as its name implies, called for each denomination to raise its own church-building funds; however, despite their strong stand concerning the origins of funds and the high value placed on the building of churches, voluntarists had no philosophical affinity to any particular building style. Most of the denominations that espoused voluntarist principles were very slow to officially advocate architecturally specific criteria for their churches. Nor was there agreement among voluntarists as to the role played by a church building in either a religious or secular context. Given the divergence of denominational perspective, there was a remarkable visual similarity between many of their churches. At the same time, among non-voluntarist denominations, a stricter adherence to certain architectural standards was increasingly encouraged, a tendency that grew during the nineteenth century. Owing to the more conspicuous nature of buildings raised by the Church of England, the Church of Scotland, and the Church of Rome, greater attention is frequently given to their development both in terms of architectonic presence and cultural significance. Of equal importance for our understanding of religion during the nineteenth century is the increased discussion of the need and importance of church building among dissenting denominations.[29]

Enterprising Friends of the Methodistic Zion

In 1844, the Rev. N. Bangs published a two-volume history of the Methodist Church.[30] Although his writings were directed primarily at an American audience and dealt essentially with Episcopal Methodism in the United States, the editorial staff of the *Canada Christian Advocate* judged his opinions to be of timely relevance to their Canadian readers, and Bangs' writings on a number of topics concerning Methodist history and ritual appeared in the paper. His discussion concerning the importance of church buildings was reprinted in its entirety. Bangs expressed concern that in recent years the Episcopal Methodist Church had lost a significant number of potential converts and even members to other denominations. This loss was not attributed to any lack of spiritual zeal or devotion on the part of Episcopal Methodist preachers, but rather to their negligence in providing effective leadership on the matter of church building. Bangs explained that far too many communities had ignored the need to build suitable places for worship. They had been content to gather in the modest manner of earlier times which meant religious services were still being held in farmers' barns and isolated stands of trees. While this manner of worship had been popular during the frontier days, it was rapidly losing much of its appeal as villages and towns developed. As other denominations built churches that were proper and conveniently situated, many Episcopal Methodist leaders were alarmed to discover that the desire to worship in a building dedicated specifically to this purpose was so strong that many parishioners were prepared to change their denominational alliances to do this. Bangs stated openly that he believed that the Methodist Episcopal church had suffered a significant numerical setback as a direct consequence of the neglect to build churches.[31] To maximize ministerial efforts and combat numerical decline, Bangs proposed radical architectural remedies. He insisted that for Episcopal Methodism to enjoy success, it was necessary to build churches not only in every town and village but also in every neighbourhood of reasonable size.[32] On this point he was very clear that not just any sort of rustic shack was acceptable as the effectiveness of ministerial work was significantly diminished when the building was shabby and unpleasant to frequent. The condition of the church building was presented as being directly related to the size, consistency, and moral standing of those who frequented it. Readers were informed that people would not be attracted to a denomination that did not provide a suitable place of worship. "The Building of churches," declared Bangs emphatically, "gives permanency to the cause."[33]

This new preoccupation with church building was in no way an exclusively Episcopal Methodist phenomenon. In November 1846, the Wesleyan Methodist journal *Christian Guardian* reprinted an article on church building in Canada that had recently appeared in the *Genesee Evangelist*.[34] The *Christian Guardian* added to the position outlined in the *Genesee Evangelist* by suggesting that rundown churches never did much to inspire confidence in a cause and that people were generally inclined to avoid religious services held in buildings that were less than pleasant. Although superficially the structure may appear linked to material advancement, it is important to avoid over-emphasizing this aspect of the question as the building of suitable churches ultimately related with the furtherance of a higher cause (fig. 2.3).

Fig. 2.3. Wesleyan Methodist Church of Bytown, 1853.

This austere expression of survival Gothic was the urban counterpart of many smaller rural churches. It is especially representative of Methodist architecture during the middle decades of the nineteenth century. Monumental, yet devoid of frivolity, this solid stone church stood as a sober embodiment of Methodist principle. It was demolished in 1875 to make way for a larger and more fashionable church (Photo courtesy: National Archives of Canada).

The *Christian Guardian* called the construction of churches "pleasing evidence of the progress and triumph of True religion."[35] The equation of church buildings with "the triumph of True religion" suggests that a much greater significance was being attached to even the smallest and most modest church building than has been traditionally allowed for in contemporary scholarship. Compelling evidence exists to suggest that the construction of church buildings was seen to play an important part in accomplishing one's Christian duties and to be an integral component of leading an exemplary Christian life.[36] Increasingly, the building of churches came to be seen not only as a wise thing to do in terms of the prosperity of one's chosen denomination, but also as partial fulfillment of one's duties before God. Absorption with this augmented role of the church building became increasingly evident in the confessional press. Typical of this trend was an article that appeared in 1847 in the *Christian Guardian* in which the reader was asked: "if God who has crowned our labours and increased our resources be not honoured by us in the erection of temples for his worship, if we build houses for ourselves, adorn and embellish them, while the house of the Lord is not built, can we reasonably expect that God will honour and bless us?"[37] The correspondent continued ominously to tell readers that those communities that failed to honour God through the construction of churches that were of equal value to their own homes and their own temporal well-being would be punished.

It is perhaps needless to stress that decently fulfilling God's covenant was unequivocally and, in and of itself, a formidable endeavour. Furthermore, the understanding of how an individual was to discharge this duty was to become successively more complicated. In many instances the heterogeneous nature of the discussion that surrounded this issue coincided with the increasing prosperity of many congregations. The connection between the augmented material affluence of the laity, the construction of churches and prosperous religion is an important one. Among Methodists, discussions of church building reveal not simply an advocacy of prolific architectural activity, but much soul-searching. A sincere and anguished debate emerged as Methodists wrestled to articulate a position on church building that fulfilled a complex and often contradictory set of criteria. Less than two decades before, a Methodist congregation wishing to build a church was obliged to do so on land belonging to one of their own members, but now, with the legal right to hold land, Methodism had acquired a sense of permanence they had long been denied. This period also coincided with an increasing popularity of Methodism and a growing prosperity among Methodists in their secular affairs. Methodists took this to be a sign of divine favour. God had openly and visibly blessed their work, and Methodists were eager to give a tangible expression of their recognition and gratitude to God. In the context of the day, this was best proven through the building of churches or, as one correspondent to the *Christian Guardian* put it, the construction of a suitable place of worship "gives ocular demonstration of a noble and generous people."[38]

This bond or link between good work and divine favour soon became emblematic of much more than a denominational attainment of social standing, assuming a new role that surpassed individual expressions of gratitude. Increasingly, church building was equated to an instrument through which Christians could spread the word of God's salvation. It was suggested that a lack of adequate church accommodation could result directly in the loss of souls. This added a new tone of urgency to the subject of church building.[39] More than ever, the church building was portrayed as a valuable tool for the evangelization of the general population. The

Christian Guardian explained that if the lukewarm and the uncommitted could be enticed to enter a church, they would be more receptive to "the graces necessary for the transformation of their lives."[40] This does not mean that Methodists believed God to be particularly present within a specific and tangible locus of the building. Instead, the church was progressively perceived as channeling agent for the grace of God.

While there lurked a strong fear of souls being lost for the want of decent accommodation, church buildings themselves tended to remain architecturally unambitious. It is perhaps due in part to this continued plainness that architectural historians often overlook much of the debate that surrounded these buildings. This leaves an important source of nineteenth century religious thought largely untapped. Much of the discussion concerning the role of the church building came at a time when Methodists were seeking to reconcile the values of older traditions and a modest lifestyle with the reality of an augmented popularity and greater access to material prosperity. As an increasing number of sturdy church buildings began to appear, the romantic image of the simple but rugged preacher praying in the fields to the gathered multitude of simple folk began to fade from popularity.

Much of this came at a time when both Episcopal and Wesleyan Methodists were trying to establish a stronger presence along the shores of the Ottawa Valley. During the early 1840s, "The Bytown Circuit" of the Episcopal Methodist Church was placed under the charge of Rev. J. Gardener. He was responsible for evangelization not only in the small settlement clustered at the junction of the Rideau and the Ottawa rivers, but also for a vast tract of land that extended westward along the southern shore of the Ottawa River, as well as along the northern shore to include Hull and its surrounding areas in the province of Quebec. The circuit was alternatively and perhaps more appropriately known as the Nepean and Hull Circuit. Although Methodist preachers were still few and far between, Gardener was dismayed to discover that his ministerial efforts were not always courteously received. He had been particularly affronted by the inhospitable reception he received from a cluster of Methodist families settled several kilometres west of Bytown in the Nepean area and published his disappointment in the *Canada Christian Advocate.*[41] Gardener explained that although ten members had settled in the Nepean area, they would have nothing to do with him. He had left them to their own resources, declaring, "I entered Bytown as Paul entered into Corinth."[42]

What is of particular interest in Gardener's story is not that members of his own denomination were unreceptive, but rather the manner in which he continued to demonstrate how his efforts were soon to bear visible signs of fruition. Like Paul, Gardener was neither easily discouraged nor destined for complete failure. Once in Bytown he gathered together a small group of about thirty people who were more sympathetic to his efforts. The new congregation rented a small schoolroom, which they outgrew after only a short time, and soon made plans to replace the rented schoolroom with a building erected specifically for worship. Gardener explained: "we deemed it necessary and prudential in fear of God to undertake the erection of a Chapel. Knowing that 'except the Lord build the house, they labour in vain that build.'"[43] He described the new chapel as a simple rectangular structure, optimistically noting that there was enough room for a gallery should the need arise. It is the reasons given by Gardener for the construction of the Bytown chapel that are of particular interest. His description of construction motivated by a sense of prudence and a fear of God are suggestive of concerns that go far beyond a preoccupation with convenience, centrality, and the ability to attract a congregation. The small and unassuming building was clearly linked to loftier concerns.

The idea of retribution for architectural omissions was not unique to Rev. Gardener and was explicitly detailed in the Methodist press.[44] When the Methodist Episcopal Church in Bytown was officially opened on December 15, 1844, thanks largely to Gardener's Pauline spirit of perseverance, the occasion was discussed by Gideon Shepherd in a report to the *Canada Christian Advocate*. Shepherd gave a brief description of the building, which echoed much of what Gardener had already noted. More importantly, Shepherd also mentioned that one of the sermons preached that day was on verses 20-22 of Saint Paul's letter to the Ephesians.[45] Although the sermon is not preserved, the selection of this passage is significant. The letter speaks in several ways to issues that were of concern to Methodists at this time. In this scriptural passage, an undesirable sense of transience is replaced by a new sense of permanence, stability, and belonging. More importantly, this new status is linked with a multiform exploitation of architectural symbolism. This attention to the scriptural use of architectural symbolism is indicative of a strong interconnection seen by Methodists between a church building, permanence, and prosperity. It provides a justification of their insistence on the need to provide a tangible presence and to be a viable, visible, and integral part of society. The prevalence of this attitude among Methodists in the Ottawa Valley is evident in much of their discussion of local church-building initiatives. The building of churches was presented as a moral duty, symbolic of a sacred bond between God and his people. In his annual account for 1853, Rev. W. M. Pattyson reported that Methodists of the Osgoode Mission, whom he referred to as the "enterprising friends of the Methodistic Zion,"[46] were currently involved in the construction of four separate churches. Two years later, he reported that the year had been blessed with signs of divine pleasure, and five churches were completed.[47]

The association of church building with spiritual prosperity became more pronounced over the course of the next few years. During the early 1850s, the Wesleyan Methodist minister for the Gatineau Mission complained of the great difficulties in maintaining a high spiritual standard among his parishioners.[48] Rev. John Armstrong grieved that his mission was plagued with "back sliding" and "loss of grace," especially during the winter months.[49] Less than four years later, many of these dilemmas had been effectively eliminated. Armstrong noted in his annual report for 1856: "Churches are rising and what is best of all souls are being saved . . . Their attention has been directed towards the construction of a suitable place of worship . . . ."[50] This connection was not a fanciful invention of Armstrong, but was echoed by numerous other preachers.[51]

During the 1840s and 1850s an interesting pattern began to emerge in the Ottawa Valley between religious revivals and church-building projects. The acknowledgment of divine favour in the context of a religious revival was often followed by the construction of a church. The link between revivals and church building is particularly evident among Methodists. Frequently the report of a successful revival in a missionary society or a confessional journal was followed several weeks later by a second report announcing that a building project was being planned, if not already underway. Recurrent evidence suggests that it was often during the emotional climax of a revival meeting, when an increased sense of religious fervour and devotion was prevalent, that a congregation identified the need to build a church.

During the late summer and early fall of 1846, revivals were experienced in a number of Ottawa Valley communities. Typical of this phenomenon were reports of increased religious activity and sentiment. Wesleyan Methodists in the Bytown District reported to the *Christian Guardian* that "the Head of the Church is graciously visiting his people in this and the adjoining district."[52] This was confirmed in the same issue of the *Christian Guardian*, when Wesleyans from the nearby community of Goulbourn reported "a cloud of mercy has for some time been hanging over this circuit and has distilled its blessings upon the people . . . evening after evening individuals were found at the altar of prayer imploring mercy."[53] From across the Ottawa River, the minister in charge of the Gatineau Circuit noticed a similar occurrence. He reported that "the Good Lord has been visiting us with an outpouring of his Holy Spirit."[54] Increasingly, Methodists in the Ottawa Valley responded to such signs of God's favour by expressing their gratitude and commitment to continued devotion through the construction of churches. This can be seen in the considerable church-building activity reported by Methodists shortly after the Ottawa Valley revivals of 1846. Editors of the *Christian Guardian* were notified that new Methodist chapels were being built in Goulbourn, Huntley, and Richmond, and the editor noted that these reports were all published "with great pleasure," adding that it was their hope that such excellent examples of Christian industry would be a good example to those circuits "that have hitherto been backwards. . . ." [55] Methodists from the Richmond Circuit reported that they, too, were prepared to celebrate God's attention in architectural terms:

> Within the last two years we have erected and have now underway of erection no less than five new chapels, three of which are commodious being 40' X 30' each . . . I do pray that these chapels may present a scene similar to the temple of Jerusalem in its best days, "Whither the tribes go up, the tribes of the Lord, unto the testimony of Israel, to give thanks unto the name of the Lord".
> . . . We are looking and believing for a great gathering of souls.[56]

When the purpose of a modest wooden chapel is equated with the Temple of Jerusalem, it becomes clear that the symbolic function of these chapels far exceeded the measures of traditional architectural critique. This report demonstrates the projection of highly complex religious ideals onto unpretentious structures. The modest building was clearly used to give visual expression to a recondite and remarkably symbolic world vision. It reveals a perception of church space as something much more than a physical rallying point, something linked instead to a unique understanding of God's movement through time. When examined from this particular perspective, the building of Methodist churches can be seen as an architectonic recognition of God's favour as manifest in the expansion of God's grace.

The Church of England and "Things Necessary for the Becoming Performance of Divine Service"

As some denominations enjoyed unprecedented growth, others were rocked by internal and external strife. The Anglican Church in particular was to feel these pressures. Although their traditional position of social and financial privilege was increasingly called into question, this did not divert Anglicans from questioning the visual dimension of worship practices. A spreading anxiety that the neglect to build suitable places for worship might have more serious consequences than previously conceived had also been spreading among members of the United Church of England and Ireland. In 1849, the Venerable A. N. Bethune, Archdeacon of York, published an open letter to the clergy in which he suggested that in addition to their ministering to the spiritual church, the clergy also had very real obligations concerning the well-being of the material church. Bethune's subsequent discussion of the question synthesizes a variety of contemporary concepts and concerns. Bethune's understanding of what constituted the material church embraced an assortment of subjects and reflected a growing Anglican concern that it was not only crucial for worship to be performed correctly, but that it should be performed within an environment that conformed to the requisites of Anglican correctness. In keeping with this objective, Bethune attended to a wide range of topics, including "The providing of things necessary for the becoming performance of Divine Service," "The enlargement of churches when necessary," "Church revenue," "Parsonage Houses," "Church Yards" and "Insurance of Churches and parsonages." He began his list of charges, however, with "The Building of Churches."[57]

Bethune began cautiously by stressing that he did recognize that many new communities were fortunate to have the use of schoolhouses as temporary places for Sunday worship. He then emphasized that schoolhouses should be recognized for precisely what they were: temporary and secular.[58] By the "Building of Churches," the archdeacon did not mean the construction of anonymous community halls or meeting places used as schoolhouses during the week. He acknowledged that in most newly settled communities both financial and material resources were limited. The challenges of simply surviving from one season to the next often siphoned away any plethoric resources. He recognized that settlers could not build their homes, clear their lands, plant, harvest, and market crops, and finance the construction of a suitably distinguished church all at the same time, but cautioned that it was not advisable to put off the necessity of church construction indefinitely. New communities were counseled to build at the earliest opportunity. The church was to serve only as a place of worship and, as such, it should be in a place that was truly set apart, a place consecrated uniquely for the purpose of religion. Bethune explained to his readers that it was not collective prayer alone that fulfilled the requirements of sacred worship, but the whole environment in which religious acts were performed. The atmosphere that encompassed the act of worship was to be one of hallowed reverence that reinforced the sacredness of purpose.[59] It is unlikely, however, that he would have approved of the parishioners of St. John the Evangelist, in Richmond, who allowed their church to be used as a drill hall by the Queen's Consort's 60th rifles.

Bethune's discussion of the need to build churches reflects a growing opinion that newly found prosperity in the emerging towns and villages of Central Canada was part of God's divine plan. He considered it natural and, in fact, even prudent to suggest that the same zeal that was so manifest in the construction of worldly housing be also directed towards the adequate housing of a place of prayer. Although he may not have agreed, his arguments were very close to those of many contemporary Methodists.

> Persons have only, as a community, to exert the skill and industry which they usually employ, as individuals, in securing to themselves a comfortable residence. . . . Let the same feeling, deepened and sanctified, animate Christians in contemplating their obligation to erect and adorn the house of God. Let the "children of light," in this instance, exhibit the prudence and zeal which characterize the "children of the world." If this were done, we should have fewer complaints of the difficulty, much less of the impossibility, of erecting a becoming edifice of prayer: what one, for individual satisfaction or comfort, is enabled to effect for himself, a whole community, without any extraordinary self-denial or serious self-deprivation, can surely accomplish. In this way, in the prosperous and populous city, in the rising town or village, we should discern the sanctuary of God, standing out, in its proportions and adornments, pre-eminent amongst the mere structures of the world.[60]

Although Bethune did not insist on any radical departures from previous church-building traditions, his discussion was important because it was one of the earliest public calls for a re-evaluation of the role that a church building should play in a community from within the Anglican community in Central Canada. This discussion of the role of the visual church within the community came at a significant point in the history of Anglican church building in Central Canada. While the image of a religious edifice standing out in a place of preeminence had long been a characteristic one of Anglican churches, Bethune's insistence on the need for a clearer distinction between sacred and secular uses had not been a prevailing concern. Despite the judicious tone of his remarks, the public call for a new and reverential treatment of the church edifice anticipated much of the radical restructuring of Anglican architecture that was to characterize the following decades.

Architectural Forms and Liturgical Functions

The decision to build a space in which to worship was a significant event in the lives of most nineteenth century Ottawa Valley communities. Once the decision had been taken and the site chosen, it became a rallying point for the congregation. Roman Catholic parishioners often marked the site of their future church with a cross, while Protestant congregations often gathered to hear preaching or for the singing of hymns. The first major public ceremony held in connection with the site of a new church was usually the laying of the cornerstone. When the original cornerstone was placed for St. John's Church (Anglican) in Richmond in 1823, Masonic symbols were engraved on either side of the date.[61]

In the remote areas many communities built their first place of worship with logs.[62] For Roman Catholics, log chapels were generally intended as temporary structures. In contrast, Methodists used a great number of these buildings, but were less inclined to encourage rapid replacement. Some well-intended projects, despite their modest ambition, were sabotaged for lack of funds. Almost ten years elapsed between 1846 when the first logs were positioned for Rosebank Methodist Church and the time it was properly shingled. Most of the churches erected in the Ottawa Valley during the 1840s and 1850s continued the traditions of earlier years. They were small, neat, and functional. In 1840, Rev. S. S. Strong organized the construction of a small church for his Anglican parishioners in Clarendon Center, Quebec (now Shawville). The church itself, a small frame structure, was forty feet long and thirty feet wide. It had been built by two local tradesmen, George Hodgins and Thomas Wilson. This church was still in use when Rev. W. H. Naylor arrived to take charge of the parish in July 1876. Naylor described the original church as "a plain, unadorned, clapboard frame building, with great Gothic arched windows, a gallery across the West end . . . and a tower at the West end through which the entry was made."[63] This description could be applied to a significant number of church buildings from this period and, with the elimination of the tower, could be applied to many more.

Site Choice and Surroundings

Churches were habitually set back a small distance from village streets. Occasionally, later modifications altered this arrangement as, for example, in the case of the Mellvile Presbyterian Church built in Ashton in 1852. When the church was renovated in 1879, it was enlarged through the façade, which, in turn, created an impression of the whole church being nearer to the roadway. In the country, where more land was available, churches were commonly further withdrawn from the roadways. The orientation of nearly all churches was routinely dictated by secular surveying, and most churches, regardless of their distance from it, continued to face the front property line.

Church architecture continued to be seen as an indicator of where the centre of activity was to be. The location of a church building continued to have an important effect on defining where the centre of newly settled communities would be. For this reason, great importance was still attached to the church site, even before the building itself was begun. Once chosen, it was very difficult to change the site without provoking considerable controversy. The Roman Catholic bishop, Mgr. Guigues, discovered this first-hand when he changed the projected location of the Plantagenet township church from the village of Curran to the village of Plantagenet. The bishop had decided to change sites because the people of Curran did not appear to have been particularly zealous in raising the necessary funds. If the citizens of Curran had not been sufficiently aroused to promptly fulfil their church-building commitments, the relocation of the township church stirred up a considerable and immediate response. Irate residents accused the French-born bishop of being anti-French and anti-Catholic![64]

During the second quarter of the nineteenth century, the worship practices of some Methodist communities continued to include the gathering of large numbers of people for a period of several days at camp meetings. The site criteria required to accommodate camp meetings were very different from the site requirements of a church that hoped to be at the heart of a thriving new village. For a property to provide adequately for camp meetings, the site needed to be both wide, deep, and preferably with a sufficient number of trees to afford a certain degree of privacy. The use of a site for camp meetings did not necessarily exclude the construction of a church. When the same site served both requirements, the campground was traditionally located at the rear of the property while the church building was nearer to the public roadway. In 1846, under the direction of Rev. Benjamin Nakeville, Wesleyan Methodists built a small chapel on the 10th line of Goulbourn Township. It was described a year later as "a neat little white church" behind which was a campground.[65] Influenced by John Wesley's decision to preach in open fields, the mere existence of a place to gather had been enough for some older Methodists; however, with increased settlement, expanded prosperity and even despite the continued survival of camp meetings, the preferred setting progressively shifted to church buildings. At a time when fewer Methodist services were being held outside, the image of Wesley preaching in the fields to the poor and unchurched progressively captured popular imagination. For a number of years, lithographed impressions of this important event were offered for sale through the Methodist Press, occupying to some extent the role of an icon of Methodism.

External Structures and Stylistic Features

A number of church-building traditions first introduced into the Ottawa Valley during the 1820s and 1830s continued to be used during the second quarter of the nineteenth century. Some were to be of considerable duration, appearing with only minor variations over the course of several more decades; others were by now in their terminal phases. Among the endangered species of religious architecture were neoclassic churches or those churches with neoclassic façades and Gothic naves.

In 1839 the Roman Catholics of Bytown decided the time had come to replace their original and very modest wooden chapel. Although construction did not begin until 1841, it was decided that the new church, Notre-Dame, should be built in stone, a more prestigious and decidedly more permanent material, and be the largest in the Ottawa Valley. The original builders sought inspiration from the neoclassic design of St. Patrick's Church in Quebec,[66] which had been built only a few years earlier in 1831 in compliance to plans prepared by architect Thomas Baillairgé.[67] This new church, which eventually became the Roman Catholic Cathedral of Ottawa, was subjected to considerable stylistic and structural modifications over

Fig. 2.4. Notre-Dame d'Ottawa (Roman Catholic), Ottawa, 1841.

Traces of the original church can be seen on the ground floor. Tuscan doorways with unadorned pilasters impose a mood of solidity and abstemious sobriety anchoring the façade solidly to the ground. This imposes a horizontality that no subsequent elevation could negate. The doors are spanned by round-headed arches and restrained archivolts. Above the principal entry is an enormous window arch formed by a Gothic drop arch. The drip stone, however, conforms to the tracing of an ogee arch. This motif is repeated in the tracery of the triplets. The major force of continuity between the ground floor and the coping of the towers are the reticulated quoins. The belfries and spires were added much later (Photo: V. Bennett).

the course of the nineteenth century. Despite these alterations, much of the original plan can still be easily identifiable, most notably in the treatment of the main entries (fig. 2.4).

Very different in scale, but typical of a church with a neoclassic façade and Gothic nave was a small church built in Ottawa after the fragmentation of St. Andrew's parish (Church of Scotland) in the wake of the Scottish disruption.[68] Known as Knox Free Presbyterian Church, Ottawa, the new congregation built a small white wooden church in 1845.

The façade was framed to either side with Doric pilasters, and a second set flanked the unique and axial doorway. The central entry was flanked to either side by large rectangular windows. A similar, but slightly smaller, window was centred above the entry. The pilasters were surmounted by an understated entablature. The architrave and cornice were unadorned, and the frieze was interrupted only by four monotone triglyphs. The gable end of the roof and the raking cornices were arranged in the manner of a classical pediment. The tympanum was devoid of all decoration and was opened by a central oculus.

Other types of church buildings, while maintaining a stylistic consistency, at least in general terms, continued to be used but were also fading in popularity. This is evident in the decreasing popularity of decorative Gothic façades. The façade of the original Anglican church of St. Stephen in Buckingham, Quebec, was representative of a picturesque interpretation of Gothic that was widespread during the eighteenth century and that had survived into the early middle decades of the nineteenth century.

The plain, high-walled church had simple Gothic windows and a relatively squat roof embellished only on the façade by wall buttresses and pinnacles. The central portion of the façade was emboldened by the addition of a crenelated parapet. The use of redundant external structures was primarily for visual effect and was frequently reflective of only superficial stylistic affiliations, their overall presentation being more theatrical than archaeological. Among the most common additions were pinnacles, buttresses, quoins and elongated finials, frequently of wood. Towers, steeples, and bell turrets were also used for effect, but predominantly by those denominations that favoured a strong church-state relation. As these external structures represented an additional cost that was not necessary to the initial construction of the church building, they were frequently added

Fig. 2.5. Knox Free Church (Presbyterian), Black's Corners, 1845.

The rich colour and texture of the local stone is counterbalanced by the stark white sashes of the window, and intersecting tracery. Tall walls and a comparatively modest pitch of the roof again reflect residual elements of Georgian tradition. The Gothic tracery of the window sashes is repeated in the treatment of the door frame and the lateral windows (Photo: A. Erdmer).

Fig. 2.6. St-Bernard (Roman Catholic), Fournier, 1859.
Though details are scant, this dark diminutive daguerreotype still offers a rare view of wooden Catholic churches from this era. The façade is not unlike those found on many Protestant counterparts, although the overall length is greater. The church has a well-proportioned belfry and elongated steeple set just in retreat of the main façade (Photo courtesy: Archdiocesan Archives [R. C.], Ottawa).

some time after the original construction. One of the most common building types to be continued from the early decades of the 1800s and well into the second half of that century was the plain rectangular frame structure with a single axial entry.[69] The exterior of these churches was destitute of all adornment, and a stylistic affiliation with Gothic was achieved solely through the arch heads of the entry and nave windows. As before, the pointed segments of these arches were frequently filled with a fragile intersecting tracery.

A very typical façade of this era can be seen on Knox Free Church (Presbyterian) in Black's Corners (fig. 2.5). Like the congregation of Knox Free Church in Ottawa, the congregation in Black's Corners had emerged as a result of the rift in the Scottish church. When they built their church in 1845, they did so, as their name implies, with volunteer labour. The church was built with stone quarried nearby and transported to the building site by members of the community. The treatment of the Black's Corners façade is, in many ways, representational of church façades from this period. Here, as in many other churches, an axial entry is flanked to either side by long

Fig. 2.7. St-Pierre-Célestin (Roman Catholic), Pakenham, 1852.

With its use of survival Gothic and the trace elements of classical influence in the treatment of the façade, this church could belong to any one of many early nineteenth-century denominations. The axial belfry and stout steeple set just slightly in retreat of the main façade, suggest that this church belonged to one of the three "Establishment" churches. The steeple cross identifies the building as Roman Catholic (Photo courtesy: Archdiocesan Archives [R. C.], Ottawa).

Gothic windows. The vertical ascension of the window arches usually peaked at a slightly higher point than the apex of the door arch. The lack of structural embellishment is increasingly evident in the treatment of the lateral walls. The quoins are not accentuated and, here again, only the voussoirs of the window arches interrupt the coursing of the masonry. There is, however, a slight difference in the finishing of the masonry work. Here, the rougher random rubble coursing contrasts with the slightly more attentive treatment of the square rubble coursing on the façade.

Gables could end abruptly, as they do at Black's Corners, and on the church of St-Bernard (Roman Catholic), Fournier (fig. 2.6), or return inward, modestly alluding to the more forceful pediments of classical frontons as can be seen on the façade of St-Pierre-Célestin (Roman Catholic), Pakenham (fig. 2.7). Typically the greater percentage of the building's verticality is achieved in the height of the walls, while the pitch of the gable is comparatively modest.

In South Gloucester, the monumental and gothic façade of Our Lady of the Visitation, with a length of one hundred feet, foreshadowed church-building trends that were to enjoy increased popularity during the second half of the century (fig. 2.8). Contemporary Protestant congregations of comparable size would have built a much more compact structure. Roughly contemporary to the Ottawa

Cathedral, the shell of this rural church was also built in a restrained Gothic style, though many rural Catholic churches of this era are characterized by their stark simplicity (fig. 2.9). The equilateral arch heads of the entries are marked only by the patterning of the voussoirs.

Much of the monumentality of the South Gloucester church was achieved through the height and emphasis of the end wall. Although vertically integral, the gable is not a continuous extension of the main façade. Instead, its upper portion corresponds to the roof of a blind triforium that extends above the central nave. The central axis of the church was further emphasized by a large and elongated Gothic window immediately above the central doorway; it was embellished by only the most frugal use of mullions and transoms. A small and slightly squat ogee niche is perched immediately above the window, centred on, but well below the apex of the gable wall. Above

Fig. 2.8. Our Lady of the Visitation (Roman Catholic), South Gloucester, 1849.

The blind triforium is somewhat of an architectural anomaly. The belfry and steeple are late additions (Photo: V. Bennett).

Fig. 2.9. St-Jean-Baptiste (Roman Catholic), L'Orignal, 1853.

The façade of St-Jean-Baptiste was marked by its stark simplicity. Embellishments appear only in the contrasting colour of the reticulated stone quoins, voussoirs and in the keystones of the door arches. Used in this manner, the contrasting stone contributed to the structural permanence of the church, and also served to visually establish an image of solidity and stability. An axial rose window is located above the keystone of the principal entry, but well beneath the apex of the gable. A solid tower was built in slight retreat of the main façade, and was capped with an unceremoniously squat belfry (Photo courtesy: Archdiocesan Archives [R. C.], Ottawa).

the stone façade is a steeple. The lower portion is a belfry articulated with six open gables, which, in turn, is surmounted by a slender spire. The climax of the whole structure is a cross.

Internal Designs and Adornments

While the façades of some churches continued to sport gratuitous and occasionally grandiose appendages, the interior design continued to present a stark contrast devoid of all architectural affectations. The ground plan of most churches was rectangular, with those belonging to Roman Catholics slightly more elongated than those of their Protestant counterparts. In terms of internal design, there was very little variation from the architectural and liturgical organization of the preceding decades. The primary improvement was in the quality of simple furnishings: in general, benches replaced rough planks and interiors were plastered with greater frequency. Roman Catholics also differed from their Protestant neighbours in that an effort was usually made to acquire a suitable statue of the parish's patron saint. The installation of the fourteen stations of the cross was also considered to be an important step towards finishing the interior of a Roman Catholic church.[70]

Even with the addition of visual imagery and religious statuary, most Roman Catholic churches continued to be austere, especially when contrasted with contemporary constructions in more cosmopolitan centres or with local constructions in the later decades of the century. Most Ottawa Valley churches from this era continued to distinguish themselves with functional practicality. Despite their utilitarian confines, the naves of Protestant buildings were not the reflection of an economically dictated reductivist monotony, but reflected a continued preoccupation with seeing and hearing the Word of God. The diminutive size of many surviving churches, such as Christ Church (Anglican) in Ashton, is echoed in the descriptions of many other churches built at this time, but now lost. The Wesleyan Methodist missionary in Osgoode reported: "There is but one small chapel on the Mission. The place has become too straight: a few spirited friends have put up a frame 40 x 30' this spring and expect to get it covered-in this summer."[71] In continued contrast, Roman Catholic churches are proportionately larger and longer. The clapboard church of St. Mary's in Almonte was sixty feet long and forty feet wide,[72] the wooden church of St. Bernard in Fournier was seventy feet long and thirty-six feet wide.[73] Even larger, measuring over one hundred feet in length, forty-five feet in width and with walls thirty feet high, was the new stone church at South Gloucester.[74]

For many Ottawa Valley communities, the 1840s and 1850s were a time of rapid growth and expansion, and galleries offered a very practical solution to a real need. These small balconies ran along the lateral walls of the nave and often across the inner face of the main entry. They were widely used by many congregations of varying denominational affiliation, but were rarely part of the original building. During the construction of several Ottawa congregations, it was reported that the installation of galleries was not yet necessary; however, with the growing importance of Ottawa, they felt that there would likely be a need for galleries in the near future. In a spirit of foresightedness, the walls of these churches were specifically built to accommodate the construction of a gallery. Galleries were added on several occasions to Christ Church, Ottawa, first to the nave in 1841, and then to the transepts in 1855 (fig. 2.10).[75] In 1849, the seating capacity of Knox Presbyterian Church, Ottawa, was increased by a gallery.[76] Other congregations such as the York Street Methodist Episcopal Church saw galleries as something to be planned for, if not necessarily built immediately. In 1845, Rev. Gardener wrote to the

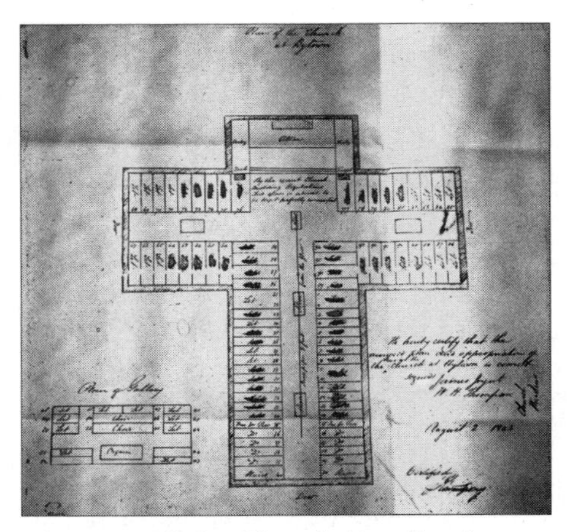

Fig. 2.10. Christ Church (Anglican), Ottawa, after addition of transepts in 1841.

Dated August 2, 1842, this was used to record pew rental in the modified church. In addition to listing the new sittings in the transepts, it includes those in the gallery built above the main entry in 1839. The plan notes the position of the altar, desk, pulpit, and vestries. The text in front of the sanctuary reads: "By the recent Church Building Regulations this space is advised to be kept perfectly unoccupied" (Photo courtesy: National Archives of Canada, NMC 5184).

Canada Christian Advocate to inform his fellow Methodists that "we then proceeded to erect a house 36' by 42' of sufficient height to admit a gallery."[77] None of these churches have been preserved.

Several surviving churches are believed to have once had galleries that were later removed. The Anglican St. James Church (Franktown) is reputed to have been able to accommodate 250-350 people.[78] Were it not for a gallery, although none has survived, this would seem highly optimistic. Likewise, the second church of St. John (Anglican) in Richmond had an overflow gallery at one time, but no mention is made of it beyond 1878.[79] One of the few surviving churches with a well-documented gallery is the Anglican church of St. John's in Kars (fig. 2.11). Here the galleries run the entire length of the lateral walls of the nave. More unusually, they are continued over the sanctuary to abut against the end wall of the church.

In terms of seating arrangements, little had changed. The Church of England, the Church of Scotland, and the Church of Rome continued to rent out seats, usually on an annual basis. Seats in the galleries were always considerably less desirable than those near the front of the church. The Roman Catholic church of St. Victor, built in St. Albert in 1855, was originally a rough log structure only 25 feet x 25 feet[80] and fitted with rough plank galleries. These galleries were a source of chagrin, not so much for the impecunious occupants of the galleries themselves, but for those in the more costly seats below. During the winter months, snow from the boots of those

Fig. 2.11. St. John (Anglican), Kars, 1850.
Galleries can be seen running the full length of the northern and southern walls, which would have allowed some of the parishioners to perch directly above the pulpit and communion table. A rather common arrangement during the first half of the century, this arrangement fell into disrepute and most galleries were eventually removed (Photo courtesy: Anglican Diocesan Archives, Ottawa).

in the galleries would melt and drip through the floor boards onto the heads of the more prosperous parishioners seated on the main floor of the church. This indignity was considered especially intolerable as it was of greatest inconvenience to those who had paid the higher price for their seating.[81]

Liturgical Requirements and Focal Points

During the second quarter of the nineteenth century, the liturgical requirements of most denominations active in the Ottawa Valley did not change significantly from practices of the first quarter of the century. Roman Catholics sustained a fundamental dedication to the Eucharistic celebrations, while Protestant denominations collectively continued emphasis on the reading and preaching of the Word of God. No sanctuaries have survived unmodified from this time, and written accounts rarely note the specific amount of interior space reserved for the sanctuary. As in the preceding period, however, the overall dimensions of most churches precluded overly spacious sanctuaries. The changes that did occur during this period came about primarily as a result of the parishioners' increased ability to finance preferred church furnishings. In this manner a greater number of Roman Catholic churches were able to acquire altars of a quality better suited to their sacred purpose. Well-built communion rails were less scarce, and many parishes were able to fit their churches with stations of the cross and devotional statuary.

In Protestant churches of all denominations, the pulpit and reading desk continued to occupy a position of preference. In many churches there was still very little space between the pulpit and the

Fig. 2.12. St. Andrew (Church of Scotland), Ottawa, built 1828, enlarged 1854.

Though devoid of gratuitous embellishments, St. Andrew's was less austere than its Free Church neighbour. The pulpit was elevated well above the pews and was accessible by freestanding stairs. The pulpit was covered with understated paneling, but the abat-voix was comparatively ornate. A tall candlestick was placed to either side of a central lectern. These were strictly for reading and were not associated with any religious symbolism. The whole construction is framed by a Gothic arch. The arch itself is traced with molding and applied to the end wall of the church. To either side of the pulpit is a large Gothic window. There is no architectural distinction between the nave and the sanctuary. An elliptical plaster vault covers the whole church. The cumbersome heating pipes were common features in contemporary churches (Photo courtesy: National Archives of Canada).

first row of pews. Despite this there was a degree of separation between the preaching of the Word and the parishioner. The sanctuary of St. Paul's, an Anglican church built in Shawville, Quebec, in 1842, was described by Rev. Naylor as having "no East window, a corner at the east end partitioned off for a vestry, a somewhat lofty pulpit, entered from the vestry . . . ."[82] Indeed, if there is any newness in Protestant sanctuaries of this era, it is the increased abundance of the "somewhat lofty pulpit." With enhanced financial circumstances many Protestant communities, like their Roman Catholic counterparts, were now able to provide more becoming furnishings for the focal point of their devotions. In the Ottawa Valley, most Protestant services remained centred on the pulpit well into the late 1850s. A report written in 1845 on the condition of religion in the Ottawa Valley spoke favourably of the raised pulpits that were beginning to appear in Episcopal Methodist churches.[83]

The use of elevated pulpits became especially pronounced in Presbyterian churches. In 1854, the Temporal Committee of the church of St. Andrew (Church of Scotland), Ottawa, decided to increase the length of the church by thirty-two feet (fig. 2.12). The contract was awarded to a Mr. McIntosh, who was also retained for the "alteration of the pews and aisles."[84] The proposed changes evidently caused great concern among those parishioners who had paid significant sums of money to occupy pews in close proximity of the pulpit. Within three months the Temporal Committee was obliged to issue a statement assuring the patrons of preferential pews that "those holding purchased pews in the church be allowed to locate themselves at the nearest relative position from the Pulpit to that which they formerly occupied."[85] Far from reflecting pettiness or trifling concerns, the experience at the church of St. Andrew is a graphic demonstration of the importance given to the Word during religious services.

In Presbyterian churches, the pulpit was frequently placed along the central axis of the church (fig. 2.13). The importance of the pulpit is further underlined by the frequent use of two side aisles instead of a single central aisle. In this way a greater number of people could be seated directly in front of the object of attention. The end wall of the church behind the pulpit was frequently opened on either side of the pulpit by Gothic lancets which allowed generous quantities of light to enter the sanctuary and reduced the necessity for artificial lighting. Similar arrangements could also be found in Methodist churches, although they were somewhat less common.

Fig. 2.13. Fitzroy Presbyterian Church (Presbyterian), Fitzroy Harbour, 1858.

This external view of a modest rural church demonstrates the common practice of placing windows at opposing ends of the sanctuary. Inside, a pulpit would have stood between the windows. The church is built with roughly coursed random rubble, but while the corners do have reinforcing quoins, these have not been accentuated (Photo: V. Bennett).

Although a significant part of Anglican worship during this era was focused on the addresses issued from "lofty pulpits," the Anglican pulpit was not as frequently aligned with the central axis of the building as was the Presbyterian or Methodist pulpit (fig. 2.14, fig. 2.15). Instead, the Communion Table, though traditionally understated, often enjoyed a position of axial centrality. The reading desk and pulpit were placed to either side of the Communion Table and, in more prosperous parishes, could take on monumental proportions. When fitted with architectural detailing, ornate sounding boards, and prominent canopies, pulpits and reading desks could assert a significant structural presence. There were rarely pairs of elongated windows in the end wall of an Anglican sanctuary. Instead, if the end wall was not left blank, a single great window opened the end wall above the Communion Table. This same central axis was used to align the baptismal font in those parishes fortunate to afford one. During the first half of the nineteenth century, the baptismal font was placed at the front of the church immediately before the sanctuary, often in the central aisle. Like the walls of the nave, the sanctuary walls of these early churches remained free from figural imagery.

Fig. 2.14.
Christ Church (Anglican), Ottawa, after the 1841 modifications.

Photographed just prior to demolition in 1872. The sanctuary of Christ Church was marked by a shallow apse closed with a low altar rail. Although common to many churches of this era, the set of text panels seen here was a later addition, as indicated by the decorative use of ornate Gothic tracery. The sounding boards and canopies of the reading desk and pulpit echo the embattled crenelations of the frontal tower (Photo courtesy: Anglican Diocesan Archives, Ottawa).

Fig. 2.15.
St. Stephen (Anglican), Buckingham, 1852.

The first row of pews clusters immediately against the sanctuary. There is no central aisle. The Ten Commandments are painted on the end wall and centred on the axis of the church. To the parishioners' left is a painted text of the Lord's Prayer and to their right, the Apostles Creed. Above, the words "God" and "Love" are framed by an arched moulding. Below is the Communion Table. Though centred on the axis of the church, it does not enjoy the same prominence as the texts. Primacy of the Word is further stressed by the conspicuous pulpit and reading desk. In this photograph, the church is draped in black for the funeral of Rev. W. D. Evans, who was killed in a canoeing accident in 1889, three days after preaching a sermon on the text "Behold I die" (Photo courtesy: Anglican Diocesan Archives, Ottawa).

Notes

1. One Methodist preacher questioned whether some ministers of the word might not be spending too much time with their correspondences and not enough saving souls. Ironically, and so this concern could be shared with the largest number of individuals, the question "Is it the duty of Christian Ministers to disseminate religious intelligence thro' the press?" was addressed in a letter to the *Canada Christian Advocate,* January 1845. B. Nakeville, a colleague working on the Richmond circuit in the Ottawa Valley, replied: "It is a matter of thankfulness that the communion of saints is not confined to the limited circle of private acquaintance, but may be extended over a great part of the visible church by means of written communication. . . . Certainly the revival of the work of God and the gathering of sinners to the fold of Christ ought to be as faithfully and circumstantially recorded as the more inferior transactions of either nations or individuals which only relate to this present life. . . ." "Revival Intelligence," *Christian Guardian*, October 1846, 2.

2. ". . . it will generally be found where religion is prosperous an effort is made to erect churches for the accommodation of the worshipers of Israel's God. We are happy to know that much more is being done by Methodists at the present day in Canada than at any former period, and with the sentiments expressed by the last *Genesee Evangelist,* we heartily concur: This is creditable to the taste and respect of the people and manifests a high sense of appreciation for the worth and stability of our religious institutions, and a desire to render them commodious and even imposing." "Building and Improvement of Churches," *Christian Guardian,* 18 November 1846, 18.

3. The missionary was referring specifically to the Clarendon, Plantagenet, Bonchere, and Pembroke Missions, and noted: "individuals were known to travel upwards of one hundred miles in order to hear the preached word and receive the Lord's Supper." See *16th Annual Report of the Missionary Society of the Wesleyan Methodist Church in Canada 1840-41*, 24-91.

4. *Annual Report of the Missionary Society of the Wesleyan Methodist Church in Canada—1844*, XXXVI.

5. *Annual Report of the Missionary Society of the Wesleyan Methodist Church in Canada—1852*, XLVII.

6. *Annual Report of the Missionary Society of the Wesleyan Methodist Church in Canada—1845*, XXXIV-XXXV.

7. *Annual Report of the Missionary Society of the Wesleyan Methodist Church in Canada in Connexion with the English Conference—1849*, XXX.

8. "In some seasons of the year from the overflowing of the rivers and streams, and the absence of passable roads, the difficulties of traveling are almost insuperable." See *16th Annual Report of the Missionary Society of the Wesleyan Methodist Church in Canada 1840-41*, 24-91.

9. Although this occurs most frequently between Protestant denominations, and appears to have been more common between the Methodists and Presbyterians, the practice was not exclusive to them. Rev. W. Morton from the Wesleyan Methodist's Clarendon Mission reported: "This place had long been a barren desert . . . but at length the Lord visited it with the out pouring of his Spirit, and many were brought to God—among the rest some French Canadians who in broken English give a pleasing account of their conversion." See *Annual Report of the Missionary Society of the Wesleyan Methodist Church in Canada—1844*, XXXVI.

10. Letter to the Editor, *Christian Guardian*, 19 May 1830.

11. *Ottawa Tribune*, 15 September 1854.

12. Disaffection between Roman Catholics and members of Orange Lodges cannot have been helped by the "Prospectus of the *Orange Lily*," that was published in Bytown in June 1849, which declared that "the *Orange Lily* will be devoted to the advocacy of the Protestant Faith, British principles, and British connection, general intelligence, and at all times it will be the unprejudiced, firm, and uncompromising champion of the LOYAL ORANGE INSTITUTION." This declaration immediately followed an article denouncing Popery as "a hindrance to national prosperity." See *Orange Lily*, June 1849, 24.

13. ". . . un certain bourgeois de chantier 'suisse,' du nom de Sicard, avait entraîné dans son apostasie un petit nombre de familles ignorantes que la misère mettait à sa merci. En 1854, M. Michel, vicaire de Buckingham vint prêcher contre l'hérésie. . . ." H. Legros and Sr. Paul-Émile, *Le Diocèse d'Ottawa, 1847-1948* (Ottawa: Le Droit, 1949), 227.

14. Luther's position on the use of visual imagery was perhaps the most tolerant of Protestant reformers. He recognized the role of the visual in assisting the recall of, and reflection on, doctrine and had a true pedagogical value. C. Christensen, in *Art and the Reformation in Germany*, quotes Luther: "Ordinary people are caught more easily by analogies and illustrations than by difficult and subtle discussions; they would rather look at a well drawn picture than a well written book" (60). Luther was also well aware, as demonstrated through his accomplished exploitation of this domain, that religious imagery could be easily manipulated to strengthen one's own position. Others, such as Andreas Von Karlstadt, Ulrich Zwingli, Heinrich Bullinger, and Martin Bucer all depicted religious imagery as a source of ill in society and an occasion for sin. It was, however, the writings of John Calvin that were to be especially influential among Protestants in the British Isles. Calvin stressed the primacy of spiritual worship, denying the use or validity of any form of visual symbolism in the act of worship In Scotland, many of Calvin's ideas were taken much further by John Knox, whose theology and reform was to form the stylobate of the Scottish Church. See C. Eire, *War Against the Idols: The Reformation of Worship from Erasmus to Calvin* (Cambridge University Press, 1989) for one of the most recent and useful discussions of Reformation theology and the religious and social implications of aniconic, iconophobic, and iconoclastic thought..

15. Again Luther was a voice of moderation. He was against violent acts of iconoclasm, especially when it was an extension of mob violence, for as he explained, again quoted in Christensen, *Act,* "the devil does not care about image breaking He only wants to get his foot in the door so that he can cause shedding of blood and murder in the world" (50).

16. *Christian Guardian,* July 1830, 219.

17. "The physical and the spiritual worlds are in perpetual connection and all our true interests are essentially religious; therefore to separate true knowledge from mere feeling is to divide what God has joined together and thus produce a profane severance like that of faith from love which as it begins in distrust must end in malevolence." *Christian Guardian,* January 1848, 45.

18. "Moral Effects of Light," *Christian Guardian,* March 1847, 86.

19. In 1849, a Methodist missionary, based in Buckingham, Quebec, reported: "All is not gloom and darkness. There are some within our bounds who have been brought to a knowledge of salvation by the remission of sins, who were once the slaves of vicious indulgence, and others were subject to the delusive and destructive error of Popery." See *The Annual Report to the Missionary Society of the Wesleyan Methodist Church in Canada in Connexion with the English Conference*, 1849.

20. "An attempt was also made this year (1806) to establish a mission for the benefit of the French Catholic population in Lower Canada, and W. Snyder, who understood and could preach in the French language, was appointed to this service. He entered

upon his work in a French settlement, in the vicinity of the Ottawa River, and for a time was cordially received and listened to with much attention, so that great hopes were entertained of a successful issue of his labours. Having occasion, however, to be absent from his field of labour for a few weeks, the parish priest took the opportunity to go among the people and warn them of the danger of hearing the "Protestant heretic," threatening them with excommunication—which, in their estimation, was a sure prelude to damnation—if they did not desist. This so wrought upon their fears, that, upon the return of brother Snyder, not a soul dared hear him or to receive him into his house. He was, therefore, reluctantly compelled to abandon the enterprise in despair, nor has any thing [*sic*] been done effectually for those people since. The charms of Roman Catholicism still hold them in bondage to their priests." N. Bangs, *A History of the Methodist Episcopal Church, Vol. II. From the year 1793 to the Year 1818,* 3rd ed., (New York: Carleton and Phillips, 1853), 182-183.

21. "Rome is a city of priests . . . they cluster the streets like mosquitoes," *Christian Guardian*, February 1848, 69.

22. Typical of this attitude is a discussion that appeared in *Young Churchman: A Literary Magazine*, May 1851, which declared itself to be "designed chiefly for the youth of the Church of England in the Province of Canada": "*Romanist:* Where was your religion before Luther? *Protestant:* Did you wash your face this morning? *Romanist:* Yes. *Protestant*: Where was your face before you washed it?" (70).

23. "The visible church of Christ is a congregation of faithful men in which the pure word of God is preached, and the sacraments duly administered according to Christ's ordinance. . . . The Romish doctrine concerning purgatory, pardon, worshipping and adoration, as well as of images as of relics and also invocation of saints, is a fond thing, vainly invented. . . . " N. Bangs, *A History of the Methodist Episcopal Church, Vol. 1: From 1766 to 1792* (New York: G. Lane & Stanfore, 1844), 171.

24. "It is a philosophy and narrow religion which does not recognize God as all in all. Every moment of our lives we breathe, stand or move in the temple of the most high; for the whole universe is a temple. . . . How then can we speak of that presence as peculiarly in the sanctuary which is abroad through all space and time?" "The Omnipresence of God," *Christian Guardian,* 28 October 1846, 1.

25. "We apologize for not having noted here the neat substantial building intended as a Congregational church, lately erected on the rising ground between the Upper and Lower Town, a little south of the Sappers' Bridge, one of the best situations for such a purpose. The building is fifty feet in length and thirty-six feet in breath. The lower part of the basement in stone, is twelve feet in height and is intended to be available for all purposes consistent with the upper part being used as a church. The body of the church is a frame building and is twenty feet in height but is not intended to be finished this season. There is also a tower or steeple of the building which, when finished, will be about 70 feet in height in which it is in contemplation to have a town or public clock and with a bell sufficiently weighty to be heard in all parts of the town. . . . " *Bytown Packet,* 23 October 1847.

26. See R. W. Vaudry, *The Free Church in Victorian Canada 1844-1861* (Waterloo: Wilfrid Laurier Press, 1989) and G. C. Lucas, "Presbyterianism in Carleton County to 1867" (M. A. diss., Carleton University, 1973).

27. Vaudry, *The Free church*, XIV.

28. *Canada Christian Advocate,* December 1847, 171.

29. This does not include radical Reformers such as Brethren or Mennonites, whose presence in the Ottawa Valley during the nineteenth century was minimal.

30. See Dr. N. Bangs, *History of the Methodist Episcopal Church* (New York: Lane & Stanford, 1844), vols. 1 & 2.

31. Bangs, *History*, vol. 2, 293-294.

32. N. Bangs, quoted in the *Canada Christian Advocate*, 1, 4 (23 January 1845), states:

> No doubt our readers will have observed that where comfortable houses of worship have been erected for the comfort and accommodation of those who desire to hear the glad tidings of Salvation by our ministry, the Congregations are large, respectable and *permanent*. On the other hand, where we have no places of worship, or those which are inferior or uncomfortable, our hearers have generally dwindled down to be few more than the society and consequently, we have not the same opportunity for being useful.

33. *Canada Christian Advocate*, 1, 4 (23 January 1845).

34. The article from *Christian Guardian*, November 1846, reprinted from the *Genesee Evangelist* states: "... it will generally be found where religion is prosperous an effort is made to erect churches for the accommodation of the worshipers of Israel's God. We are happy to know that much more is being done by Methodists at the present day in Canada than at any former period. . . . "(18).

35. *Genesee Evangelist*, reprinted in *Christian Guardian*, November 1846, 18.

36. "Every member of the Church, rich or poor, has a duty to perform according to the means God has given him, in this as well as in every other Christian enterprise ... These remarks apply with almost equal force to every other vicinity of the province where churches are being erected." *Canada Christian Advocate*, 1,4 (23 January 1845).

37. *Christian Guardian,* 10 March 1847, 82.

38. *Christian Guardian*, 27 July 1847, 82.

39. "... unless suitable accommodation be provided, hundreds will find a home elsewhere... and it is to be feared that numbers attend nowhere on the Lord's day because there is no suitable place in which the service is held in their neighborhood." *Christian Guardian*, 10 March 1847, 82.

40. *Christian Guardian*, 10 March 1847, 82.

41. Rev. J. Gardener, "Historical Sketch of the Bytown Circuit," *Canada Christian Advocate*, 1, 3 (9 January 1845).

42. Ibid.

43. *Canada Christian Advocate,* 1, 3 (9 January 1845). Gardener also adds that in addition, "our brethren and friends have contributed to the erection of two other churches and are now engaged to bear their part in enclosing a burying ground, which it has pleased Her Majesty's Honorable Board of Ordinance to bestow upon the Methodist Churches."

44. "There can be no question but the Divine Being will properly rebuke us by honoring us just in proportion as we honor Him: and we regret that ... to more than one spot could we point where once a flourishing society, by which a laudable effort was made to erect a rude log chapel, in days of comparative poverty. . . . Years rolled on; the hand of Providence poured out blessings; the weak became strong, and the poor became rich. But the house of God became dilapidated, no effort was made to erect a building in which to worship God ... in accordance with his own declarations, Jehovah "lightly esteemed" the ungrateful ones; a spiritual dearth ensued; and now hardly a wreck is visible of a society which once promised much for the future." *Christian Guardian,* 10 March 1847, 82.

45. Gideon Shepherd, "State of Religion: The Ottawa Valley," *Canada Christian Advocate*, 30 January 1845.

46. *Annual Report of the Missionary Society of the Wesleyan Methodist Church of Canada—1853*, XLV.

47. "No year has transpired without divinely accredited seals of a Wesleyan instrumentality; and none has been so prolific as in the closing in the spiritual, numerical and financial departments. We make progress, except in quarter age, which we attribute to the building of five churches. . . . "*Annual Report of the Missionary Society of the Wesleyan Methodist Church of Canada—1856.*

48. Gatineau was another large mission typical of Ottawa Valley appointments: "This mission is in Canada East, and extends about forty miles up the Gatineau River from Bytown. It comprehends a part of four townships viz.: Templeton, Hull, Wakefield, Masham and also extends into unsurveyed lands. There are seven regular appointments and some occasional ones. . . . " Rev. W. Morton, *Annual Report of the Missionary Society of the Wesleyan Methodist Church in Canada—1847*, XXIX.

49. *Annual Report of the Missionary Society of the Wesleyan Methodist Church of Canada—1852,* XXV.

50. *Annual Report of the Missionary Society of the Wesleyan Methodist Church of Canada—1856*, LXIV.

51. Several years earlier, Richard Wilson, a Methodist minister working on the Bonnechère circuit, equated the lack of church buildings in the "townships of McNab, Horton, Admaston, Bromley, Stafford and some unsurveyed lands" not merely to a situation that was unfavourable, but to one that was evil. "The want of chapels has hitherto been greatly against our interests," explained Wilson, before adding hopefully "but there is a prospect to this evil being speedily removed." See *Annual Report of the Missionary Society of the Wesleyan Methodist Church in Canada in Connexion with the English Conference—1850*, XXXIV.

52. *Christian Guardian*, October 1846, 2.

53. Ibid.

54. Ibid.

55. *Christian Guardian*, November 1846, 2

56. *Christian Guardian*, February 1848, 66.

57. Ven. A. N. Bethune, "A charge addressed to the clergy of the Archdeanery of York," *The Church,* 13, 14 (1 November 1849).

58. " . . . in a new country, we avail ourselves of school-houses for Divine service: in our necessity we should be thankful for this resource, but it is one which . . . should be regarded only as temporary." Bethune, "A Charge."

59. There is something congenial to the religious mind in this special consecration, and something very abhorrent to it in the occasional employment for holy purposes of that which is perhaps habitually allotted to common uses. The tone of reverential feeling is, of necessity, much impaired by the absence of its appropriate symbols; and though the fervor of genuine devotion may be felt in a school-house or private abode, the proprieties of public worship cannot be so easily maintained in a common or unconsecrated edifice." Bethune, "A Charge."

60. Bethune, "A Charge."

61. This stone has been incorporated into the structure of the present St. John's Church (1859). Masonic participation in cornerstone ceremonies has been recorded for a number of churches including St. John, Richmond, 1823; Holy Trinity, Hawkesbury, 1844; and St. James, Carleton Place in 1881.

62. This is a trend that was to continue well into the third quarter of the nineteenth century. Rev. W. H. Naylor explained in his memoirs entitled *The Church in*

Clarendon (St John's: E.R. Smith Co., 1919), that on March 24th and 25th, 1868: "'bees' were held to make logs for the church . . . and that two weeks later, on April 7th . . . twenty-six men assembled and raised the building, which has ever since been known as St. Luke's, Caldwell." (45).

63. The original church of St. Paul's was used for the last time in January of 1878 and was dismantled in April of 1880. In his memoirs, *The Church in Clarendon,* Naylor mentions: "Should any of the younger generation wish to know the site of the old church, they may take the Hugh Eliot family monument and measure forty feet east for the length of the church and 30 feet north and south for its width. This will give almost the exact site of the old St. Paul's. The entrance was in the West End." (10).

64. Letter from P. Gareau to Mgr. Guigues, 14 October 1858, Archdiocesan Archives (R. C.), Ottawa, Curran files, 1-1(1)-1. This was not the first time the inhabitants of Curran/Plantagenet had become embroiled in a controversy over the location of their place of worship See also A. de Barbezieux, *Histoire de la Province Ecclésiastique d'Ottawa et de la Colonisation dans la Vallée de l'Ottawa* (Ottawa: La Cie d'imprimerie d'Ottawa, 1897), vol. 1, 334-335, and V. Bennett, "Early Catholic Church Architecture in the Ottawa Valley: An initial investigation of nineteenth-century parish churches," *CCHA Historical Studies* 60 (1993-1994), 24.

65. Rev. J. Courlay, quoted in Lucas, *St. Paul's*, 41-45.

66. See N. Pagé, *La Cathédrale Notre-Dame d'Ottawa* (Ottawa: Les Presses de l'Université d'Ottawa, 1988), 22-24.

67. M. O'Gallagher, *Saint Patrick's, Quebec: The building of a church and of a parish 1827-1833* (Quebec: Carraig Books, 1981), 16-39.

68. Anon., *Knox Presbyterian Church, Ottawa, 1844-1948* (n.p., n.d.).

69. See Chapter Five.

70. Letter of 17 October 1855 to Mgr. Guigues, concerning the installation of the Stations of the Cross. Archdiocesan Archives (R.C.), Ottawa, South Gloucester Collection, 5-1.

71. Report by H. Shaler in *Annual Report of the Missionary Society of the Wesleyan Methodist Church of Canada—1850*, xxxv.

72. Archdiocesan Archives (R.C.), Ottawa, Almonte Collection, F6-2-1, 1-2-13.

73. *Annual Report for 1878*, Archdiocesan Archives (R.C.), Ottawa, Fournier Collection, 1-5-1, 1.

74. *Rapport Annuel, 1866,* Archdiocesan Archives (R.C.), Ottawa, South Gloucester Collection, 5-1.

75. Notes by Rev. S.S. Strong, second rector of Christ Church, Ottawa, Anglican Diocesan Archives, Ottawa, box 6-0-3, file C-1:1 no. 28.

76. N. Fee, *Knox Presbyterian Church Centenary* (Ottawa: Mortimer Ltd., 1944), 28.

77. *Canada Christian Advocate*, 23 June 1845.

78. *150th Anniversary of St. James' Anglican Church Franktown*, n., n.d.

79. Anglican Diocesan Archives, Ottawa, 6C-1 R-4.

80. It was elongated by fifteen feet in 1860. See Barbezieux, *Histoire,* vol. 1, 340.

81. L. Brault, *Histoire des Comtés unis de Prescott et de Russell* (L'Orignal, 1965), 193.

82. Naylor, *The Church*, 10.

83. Gideon Shepherd, "State of Religion: The Ottawa Valley," in *Canada Christian Advocate*, 30 January 1845.

84. Minutes of the Temporal Committee meeting, 19 April 1854, Public Archives of Canada, MG-9 D7-35, vol. 23, part 1.

85. Minutes of the Temporal Committee meeting, 24 November 1854, Public Archives of Canada, MG-9 D7-35, vol. 23, part 1.

CHAPTER THREE

RESTRUCTURING IDEOLOGIES: Church-building during the Middle Decades of the Nineteenth Century

"What is meant by a suitable place of worship?"[1]

In the years leading up to Confederation, the presence of the church edifice played an ever-augmenting role in projecting an image of permanence for each individual denomination. Increasingly, Canadian Christians were convinced that if their community wished to maintain an unfettered control over its own activities and needs of worship, they would have to secure for themselves a structure over which they could maintain exclusive control. As one Methodist minister observed: "It is desirable that in all principal societies and neighbourhoods, we should have churches as far as possible. If we occupy schoolhouses we have to take our turn with whatever comes along."[2]

This belief in the virtues and necessities of securing a place of worship devoted exclusively to one's own confessional requirements also contributed to an already animated field of architectural activity. The realization of these projects was helped in part by the increased population itself which provided the organizers of church-building projects with a greater pool of human and fiscal resources to draw upon.[3]

While there is little question that the mid-nineteenth century was a period of extensive church-building activity, it was also an era when the building of churches became the object of much ethical, theological, and occasionally purely intellectual debate. Increasingly, church leaders and church builders were looking to define a system of architectural expression that would do much more than simply fulfil the need for a gathering place and a visual presence in the community. For many, previously acceptable church-building formulas were no longer adequate. What was required in a church building was a structural and stylistic expression that would not only be understood as an architectonic embodiment of Christian principles, but one that would express Christian principles in accordance with their own specific confessional interpretation. In conjunction with this, many Christian church builders were searching to define a new system of architectural expression that would also reflect their understanding of their role in society and their relation with the divine. The expanded discussion of this subject frequently coincided with one or more significant shifts in the liturgical focus or ritual practices of their denomination. Therefore, while there was little doubt that any congregation would be "justified in throwing the fullness of our architectural skill into edifices which are raised in his honour," just how God, "the adorable Architect of the universe,"[4] was best honoured by the architectural offerings of humanity was another question altogether. It was, however, a question that was being asked with more and more frequency.

Increasingly, the Christian population of nineteenth century Canada was no longer questioning the need to build churches, but rather how to build churches. The relevance of many older church-building habits was being challenged. The reasons for this new skepticism varied; there were a multitude of determinants active on both a confessional and local level. Within each denomination a vicissitude of considerations—from new liturgical trends to schisms, and from confessional fragmentation to contemporary fashion—combine to contribute to the final product. Other factors such as political patronage, social issues, and increased personal prosperity were issues never far removed from the religious concerns of many nineteenth century minds. They contributed to the shaping and defining of confessional cosmology and could have a very direct effect on architectural choices. It was within this complex world vision that the church edifice was called upon to serve as the point of liaison between the seen and the unseen, the secular world and the sacred world.

An ever-flourishing number of ministers and interested lay members were beginning to feel that traditional architectural customs were no longer able to furnish a distinct association with their own denomination—a concern especially prevalent among Anglicans. More importantly, however, many felt that older building traditions were no longer adequately fitted to fulfil the spiritual need and embody the theological tenets of their confession. Consequently, the discussion of church architecture became progressively more frequent, intense, and urgent. The confessional and the secular press both tackled the topic with unprecedented zeal, although the latter was more inclined to avoid questions of doctrine. As individual Christian communities looked for direction or guidelines in order to best fulfil their architectural obligations, the guidance which they received from their respective denominational authorities varied greatly.

Parting of Church and State

As people began questioning their old church-building habits from within their own denomination, changes were occurring in the secular world that would have far-reaching repercussions on the church-building concerns of several denominations. The intrusion of secular developments was particularly evident among Anglican congregations, but was in no way exclusive to them. Despite the hopes of Lt. Gov. Simcoe, "loyalist" immigration from the United States had produced a large influx of people who felt no particular attachment to the United Church of England and Ireland. Instead, many of these former American colonists belonged to voluntarist denominations.

Furthermore, by the 1830s and 1840s, they had gained, along with voluntarists of British origin, considerable numerical significance in Central Canada, and were becoming increasingly active in provincial politics. An early outcome of this was the emergence of political priorities and religious beliefs that were frequently at variance with the preoccupations of the Church of England. These differences were especially manifest in the confrontational, and often vitriolic, assaults voiced against the Clergy Reserves. Controversy over the land set aside by Simcoe for the support of a "Protestant clergy" had been simmering for some time. The Church of Scotland had petitioned the government for grants from the reserves on the grounds that they were not only "Protestant," but they were also an Established Church.[5] Other denominations, such as certain groups of Wesleyan Methodists, were more or less inclined to accept government funds when and if they were offered them, and saw no reason why preferential treatment should be awarded to the United Church of England and Ireland. Strict voluntarists, especially Free Kirk Presbyterians and Baptists, argued that not only would they never accept state funds, but that nobody else should either.

Voluntarist thought soon spread beyond its traditional confines of confessional affiliation to gain increased popularity with a wider segment of the population. Developments of this sort were not welcomed by the Anglicans of eastern Ontario and western Quebec, who were becoming increasingly fearful that the privileged position to which they had always aspired, but never quite fully secured, was now in greater peril of eluding their grasp than it had ever been before.[6]

In the fall of 1850, the Bishop of Quebec decided that the time to address this problem was long overdue. Although his remarks were officially directed at the Anglican clergy in the diocese of Quebec,[7] the bishop did not correspond directly with his priests and missionaries, but published his opinion in an open letter to the *Canadian Ecclesiastical Gazette*. The decision to discuss the question in a public (albeit confessional) forum suggests that the bishop was in fact targeting a much larger and not exclusively clerical audience. The bishop's opening tone was a combination of righteous indignation and impending doom:

> A proceeding has been witnessed in one of the branches of our Provincial Legislature, affecting the interests of the Church of God which is fraught with alarming presage, and warns us that so far from looking for countenance and support from that body, in furthering the cause committed to our hands, we must anticipate from its interference, only what is disastrous and destructive. I refer, it must be needless to say, to the address of the Legislative Assembly praying for the alienation of the Clergy Reserves from Religious and the appropriation of them to secular uses.[8]

Though verbose, this text offers a profitable insight into the convictions and preoccupation's of Anglican Church officials. In the eyes of the bishop, the Legislative Assembly's increasingly favourable disposition towards a voluntarist position was nothing short of unreserved hostility. It was a betrayal of the treaty of mutual support that was long held (especially by members of the Church) to exist between the government of Great Britain and the Church of England.[9] With a transgression of such magnitude, the bishop suggested in less than subtle terms that it was one's moral obligation to put up some active resistance:

> It cannot however, be our duty before God or man, to acquiesce unresistingly in the policy which not only is opposed to all provision by civil authority for the maintenance of pure and sound religion and declares war against the very remnant of any connection between professed Christian governments and Christianity.[10]

For the pessimistic, the skeptical, and the non-Anglican, there remained perhaps several delicate questions, the most obvious being how God could allow such a calamity to befall His chosen people. The bishop anticipated the possibility of a cynical discussion of this problem, and realized full well that any morbid rhetoric of this nature would be less than encouraging to his already battle-weary flock. With this goal in mind, he sought to defuse any potential problem concerning God's refusal to resolve the Clergy Reserves question in favour of the Anglican Church before the concern was voiced aloud. Mountain suggested that the trials and tribulations of the present day should not be perceived as a secularly generated pestilence, but rather understood as a test from God of His beloved,

> . . . if it now be the will of God to permit that after a series of measures injurious to our interests, which will be matter of History hereafter, our very patrimony, small as it is, should be violently wrested out of our hands, we must only submit in faith and patience so as to serve a dispensation of his Providence and look through all the darkness of our prospects to the promise that the gates of Hell shall not prevail against the Church. We must endeavour, in such a case, as a Church *to take joyfully the spoliation of our goods. . . .*"[11]

However, if the bishop might have been prepared to accept trials from the Divine, he was not prepared to turn the other cheek to the slings and arrows of his mortal detractors. On this point, he appears to have been more inclined to suggest that God would come to the help of those who made a resourceful attempt to help themselves. Thus, while noting that "the motto of some of our adversaries in their proceedings towards the church appears to be nothing short of *Delenda est Carthago*," he did not feel any reason to concede defeat.[12] Nevertheless, it is clearly evident that Mountain had seen the writing on the wall. He was all too aware that the ecclesiastical establishment was not to be. Furthermore, he made it his own obligation and duty to ensure that all members of the Anglican Church in both Upper and Lower Canada, not only the clergy directly under his charge, were equally aware of this predicament.[13] If the days of the ecclesiastical establishment, of which Hamnett Pinhey had spoken so warmly in 1826, were clearly numbered, the same was also true for church architecture as Pinhey knew it;[14] however, this latter point was undoubtedly less clear to most in 1850.

Four short but tumultuous years after Mountain's letter appeared in the *Canadian Ecclesiastical Gazette*, the Clergy Reserves question closed with the secularization of the land. This single event, more than any other, served to focus the reality of disestablishment for many Anglicans as they unwittingly became voluntarists. Interestingly, some of the most intense and substantially significant discussion on the subject of church building coincided with a time when the Anglican Church in Canada was passing through one of the most turbulent periods in its history. C. Fahey has suggested that, in reaction to these changes, the Anglican Church was to "withdraw into itself, turn its back on the social and political activities that had previously occupied so much of its time and to act as a beacon of purity in the midst of a corrupt society."[15] Although the withdrawal of government involvement in church affairs was an undeniably significant event in the history of the Anglican Church in Canada, it is important that Fahey's observations not be taken out of context or oversimplified. The introspection of the Anglican Church after the secularization of the Clergy Reserves should neither be conceived as a rejection of the state in a way that could even remotely suggest that the Anglican community as a whole was becoming unpatriotic, nor as an implication Anglicans were beginning to reject their duties of Christian charity or Protestant good works. Anglican contemplation and introspection of this era was highly complex and eminently nuanced. The Anglican Church did not seek a facile solution by simply and ruefully capitulating to assume the role of the wronged party in the divorce of church and state. It sought, instead, to reaffirm its own position as a vital and venerable institution, rooted in apostolic tradition and preserved through apostolic succession, which meant, to a large extent, that the Anglican cosmos was gradually being redefined through a restored interest in its own history as a constant and visual presence within Christendom, as well as through its undefiled link to Christian cosmogony. This re-evaluation of its own past was to produce, within the Anglican Church, some of the most significant and far-reaching changes since the days of the Reformation. The renewed interest in ancient liturgical observances and a greater attention to the complexities of ritual tradition were to achieve their most imposing manifestation in the structures raised to serve and promote a collective participation in these customs.

The Oxford Movement

Needless to say, it was not the secularization of the Clergy Reserves alone that brought about the manifold transformations within the Anglican Church. There is, however, reasonable evidence to suggest that the turmoil resulting from the related quarrels left many church members more receptive to a wave of new ideas that were, in turn, to act as the agents of this transformation. At the same time that relations between the secular government and the Anglican Church in Central Canada were deteriorating, a number of intellectuals in the British Isles were calling into question the validity of the existing church-state relations. Although motive, scope, and intensity of intellectual articulation varied considerably from one school of thought to another, many key figures were also open advocates of very specific expressions of ecclesiastical architecture. In almost every instance, the character of preference was overwhelmingly Gothic.

Among the most prominent critics of state interference in church affairs were members of the Oxford Movement. The movement originated during the 1830s with a small group of Oxford professors, John Keble, E. B. Pusey, and John Henry Newman, all ordained ministers in the United Church of England and Ireland. The Oxonians used the suppression by the British Parliament of several sparsely populated Irish bishoprics as a pretext to publicly question the right of state to dictate church affairs. They maintained that, as the British Parliament presently enjoyed considerable power over the Church of England, the decision of 1828 that allowed dissenters not only to vote but also to sit in Parliament could place their church in a most disadvantageous position. This situation had only been aggravated in 1829 by the extension of these same privileges to Jews and Roman Catholics. The professors argued that if the church was not free to determine its own destiny, the day could theoretically come when the Church of England would be controlled by parliamentarians of a dissenting religious affiliation.[16] Between 1831 and 1841, Keble, Pusey and Newman collaborated in the preparation of a series of lectures published under the title *Tracts for the Times*,[17] in which they set forth their opinions on a number of points about church-state relations and worship patterns.

Although the origins of the Oxford Movement, or Tractarianism, was linked to public opposition to state interference in Church affairs, this was only one dimension of their concern. Their systemic approach to religion and liturgical reform was considerably more complex, reaching far beyond secular or administrative interests; their primary concerns were theological. Tractarianism placed a renewed emphasis on clerical privilege, which stemmed primarily from its conviction that the English Church had maintained an unbroken line of apostolic succession. It placed a high value on its belief in baptismal regeneration, the Sacrament and the ministry. Most importantly, it accepted the Eucharist not simply as a commemorative event, but as the real presence of Christ's body and blood, a radical departure from earlier trends. Under its influence, the Eucharistic celebration was increasingly valued as the high point or climax of liturgical observance. This was to have a dramatic impact on the hierarchical structuring of Anglican Church architecture.

As early as 1840, Pusey wrote that Tractarianism occupied itself not uniquely with abstract theology, but also with "the visible part of devotion, such as the decoration of the House of God."[18] Although the Tractarians did not officially advocate specific architectural or stylistic arrangements, their rethinking of liturgical priorities left an open invitation for a re-evaluation of "the visible part of devotion." With the transferal of the liturgical focus from the pulpit to the communion table, the architectural requirements of a church building changed substantially. There was no longer any reason to build churches that were architecturally focused on a pulpit once the liturgical focus had gravitated to the communion table.

Despite the open flow of ideas known to have existed between Canada and the British Isles, the extent to which people in Central Canada were intimately familiar with *Tracts for the Times* remains today a matter for some discussion. J. Kenyon has noted that although *The Church* maintained that the *Tracts for the Times* were not read very often, Bishop Strachan claimed they commanded a wide interest.[19] In the case of Strachan, this might in fact have meant that he personally found the *Tracts* interesting and, therefore, felt that they ought to be widely read. Whether the original texts of the *Tracts for the Times* were widely read or not, they were most certainly widely discussed. Their various merits and shortcomings were debated not only in the Anglican press, but also in the denominational journals of other Christian confessions, as well as in the secular press. Opinion on the subject was very diverse. Some factions were eager to identify with the validation of a church tradition that antedated and was independent of secular authority, while others still considered that much of the church's authority was based on its recognition by the state. Opinion on both the worth and the repercussions of Tractarianism, however, was divided not only during the mid-nineteenth century. Late-twentieth-century scholars also approach the topic with some division. As J. W. Grant has pointed out, interest in the Oxford ideas lead to the fear among some Protestants in Canada that "continued State support for the church of England would perpetuate injustice and subsidize perversion of Protestant Principles."[20] P. Stanton, on the other hand, considers the Oxford Movement to have been "a rejection of Protestant denomination over the Church in the nineteenth century."[21]

The Tractarians or members of the Oxford Movement were not alone in their quest to re-evaluate the traditional role of the United Church of England and Ireland in nineteenth century society, nor was Pusey alone in his concern for the "visual parts of worship." The study of traditional liturgies, ancient English architecture, and medieval ritual was soon pursued with augmented interest by ritualists, the Ecclesiologists of the Cambridge Camden Society,[22] and other High Church Anglicans. It is difficult to ascertain the precise extent to which much of this interest grew out of the Oxford Movement or was a synchronous development. Establishing a clear distinction between followers of the Oxford camp and Cambridge camp can be exceptionally arduous. There was much cross-fertilization between the two groups; some Anglicans were active members in both spheres. Although specific architectural concerns were pursued with greater conviction by some than by others, all involved were very much concerned by the environment in which worship took place. Ritualists took particular interest in visual ceremony, moving from an expanded use of Eucharistic celebrations to include a revived interest in vestments, crucifixes, incense, lighting effects, music, surpliced choirs, and eventually even such physically demonstrative acts of pre-Reformation as genuflection. Although the influence of the Ecclesiologists or the Cambridge Camden Society is most frequently associated with the revival of medieval Gothic, they, like the members of the Oxford Movement, also advocated the removal of the state from church affairs. Interestingly, while the Oxford group may have refused to affiliate themselves with any particular architectural style, preferring instead to concentrate on theological pursuits, prominent Oxonians occasionally converted to Rome, something that almost never happened among Cambridge Ecclesiologists.[23] It was, however, the refusal of the Oxford group to recognize Gothic as "the one Christian style, to the exclusion of all others," that remained a fundamental difference between Cambridge and Oxford.[24]

The Puginesque School of Gothic Architecture

For the architectural activities of the Cambridge Ecclesiologists to be fully appreciated, it is first essential to situate the intellectual and architectural activities of A. W. Pugin. While his name is now one of those most intimately associated with the revival of archaeological Gothic, during his lifetime much of his work was shunned by mainstream Anglican revivalists and architectural elitists such as the Cambridge Camden Society. Both Cambridge Ecclesiologists and Pugin were emphatic that Gothic was a uniquely Christian style, and insisted that it was only through the use of Gothic that Christian architecture could achieve its fullest expression. Although Cambridge Ecclesiologists and Pugin held many similar architectural principles, Pugin's Roman Catholicism and his vitriolic Protestant rhetoric discharged any possibility of collaboration. The importance of his work was only beginning to gain wider interest towards the end of his life, and it was only posthumously that the magnitude of his contributions were recognized. Notwithstanding the belated acknowledgments, Pugin's labours were particularly important in that they addressed a population which, for the first time in several centuries, was free to build churches as they saw fit. Furthermore, although Pugin shared a great many stylistic and philosophical ideals with members of the Cambridge Camden Society, his material interpretation of the Gothic style is not shared. A very conspicuous difference exists between the architectural legacies of the Ecclesiologists and the Puginesque school of church building.

In his own writings, Pugin maintained that it was only in Gothic architecture, which he referred to more commonly as "Pointed" or "Christian" architecture, that the principles of the Christian faith were properly embodied and justly illustrated. He lashed out against the use of neoclassic elements in church architecture on the grounds that their origin was linked to paganism. He condemned any use of sham Gothic that was not grounded in archaeological tradition,[25] and in so doing categorically rejected the romanticized and picturesque interpretations of Gothic that had characterized many of the late-eighteenth and early-nineteenth century interpretations of this style. Pugin also harshly condemned the Gothic of the Commissioners Churches, as well as the principle of government assisted financing by which they were built.[26] As far as Pugin's church-building values were concerned, there were two crucial dicta that could not be neglected in the quest for architectural excellence:

> 1st, that there should be no features about a building which are not necessary for convenience, construction and propriety. 2nd, that all ornament should consist of enrichment of the essential construction of the building.[27]

Pugin was firmly convinced that church builders were much better off to raise churches that were within their means, honestly built, and sealed by a modest dignity. To aspire to public displays of pomposity with hollow or pretentious structures was unbecoming.[28] If church builders were to have the appropriate fiscal resources at their disposal, however, Pugin was not at a loss for advice and held very clear ideas as to precisely what was needed in a Catholic church. He set forth with great confidence where and why each item in the church should be positioned in relation to other elements:

> A Catholic Church, not only requires pillars, arches, windows, screens and niches, but it requires to be disposed according to a certain traditional form; it demands a chancel set apart for sacrifice, and screened off from the people; it requires a stone altar, a *sacranium sedilia* for the officiating priests, and an elevated rood loft from whence the Holy Gospel may be chanted to the assembled faithful; it requires chapels for penance and prayer, a sacristy to contain the sacred vessels, a font for the holy sacrament of baptism, a southern porch for penitents and Catechumens, a stoup for hallowed water, and a tower for bells and unless a building destined for a church possesses all these requisites, however correctly its details may be copied from ancient authorities, it is a mere modern conventicle, and cannot by any means be accounted a revival of Catholic Art.[29]

Pugin's discourse on the subject of revived Catholic art was explicitly clear. A true revival of the long suppressed tradition could not be achieved simply by adherence to technical excellence. While he allowed that a few contemporary designers had grasped the principles and architectural technicalities of medieval Gothic, he felt that the majority had not.[30] According to Pugin, the one thing that was consistently conspicuous by its absence in all modern works was the deep sense of spirit or even soul that he believed to be present in so many of the medieval Gothic churches. Pugin maintained that this profound spiritual essence could not be achieved in a modern church unless the ancient beliefs and devotional practices that had contributed to the spiritual sum and substance of the ancient churches could also be reclaimed.[31]

For Pugin, Christian architecture was necessarily dependent on and grounded in Christian doctrine. The form, spatial function, numerical canon, and structural elevation of all architectural elements in a church were to be reflective of and built upon Christian doctrine: "The three great doctrines: of redemption of man by the sacrifice of our Lord on the Cross, the three equal persons united in one

Fig. 3.1. Ste-Chapelle (Roman Catholic), Paris, 1248.

While Camdanian Ecclesiologists took their cues from the prototypes of medieval England, Pugin turned to medieval France for his inspiration. The dramatic upward momentum as seen in this XIXth engraving of the Ste-Chapelle is echoed in much of Pugin's work (Source: *London Illustrated News*, 8 March 1856).

Godhead and the resurrection of the dead, are the foundation of Christian Architecture."[32] When faithfully discharged, Gothic was the architectural embodiment of Christian doctrine and was to be visibly manifest throughout and interfused into every dimension of the church (fig. 3.1).[33]

Pugin's understanding of the material church was thus deeply rooted in his vision of the spiritual church. Architecture was not independent of doctrine. Just as every teaching of the spiritual church was part of a greater reality, yet individually distinct, so too should each element of the material church be of individual merit, yet harmoniously integrated into the greater structure. Furthermore, Pugin felt that it was the role of the material church to incarnate and impart to the faithful a sense of this greater reality that was the spiritual church. A mission of this magnitude could not be accomplished in a building that was "debased and hideous,"[34] or in a church that was marred by "pagan emblems and theatrical trumpery."[35] Nor could it be accomplished with parishioners crowded around and peering directly into the sanctuary. A hierarchical ordering of longitudinal space was necessary to underscore the "mystical separation between the people and the sacrifice."[36]

Churches that were called to embody great doctrines were also called upon to have an element of greatness about them. Pugin insisted that church buildings that were structurally diminutive could not provide the spatial freedom necessary to create an atmosphere of grandeur and majesty. In his estimation, generous dimensions were essential to achieve the powerful architectural effect necessary for creating an environment worthy of Christian worship. Such environmental vastness, however, was not one that could be achieved simply through the augmentation of scale. For Pugin, there was an important distinction to be made between the architectural canons of Gothic or Christian architecture, and classical or "Pagan architecture" as he called it. In Gothic structures, the multiplication of architectural components was increased proportionately with the scale of the building, while the canons of classical architecture required only that structural components be augmented, not multiplied.[37] On this point he was uncompromising, and he made no effort to conceal his dislike of St. Peter's Church in Rome. Pugin felt that the exaggerated scale of the individual structural elements, notably the use of neoclassic column bases that were beyond human proportion and scale, was quite simply an unqualified perversion.[38]

Pugin felt that structural height should be celebrated as an important feature of Catholic church architecture, and offered several reasons. First, a vast internal height lent itself particularly well to the creation of an atmosphere of grandeur and greatness and was well suited to the embodiment of uplifting meditations. Second, external manifestations of height served a practical purpose but should also serve to reinforce Christian belief. The strong material presence of a tower and the slender spire tapering into the skies recalled the sacred mysteries of the Resurrection and Ascension into heaven: "Every tower built during the pure style of pointed architecture either was or was intended to be surmounted by a spire. . . . When towers were erected with flat embattled tops, Christian architecture was in decline."[39] Pugin explained that square-topped embattled towers were never terminated with spires, but had a very different function: the upward sweep of the spires, on the other hand, was specifically associated with ecclesiastical architecture.

Pugin also considered the celebration of its structural substance to be a distinguishing feature of Gothic architecture, observing that "pointed architecture does not conceal her construction but beautifies it."[40] To this end, he expounded upon the virtues of flying buttresses and pinnacles. Although the structural necessity of flying buttresses might be evident to Pugin, he warned his public against dismissing pinnacles as simply decorative:

> They should be regarded as answering a double intention, both mystical and natural; their mystical intention is, like other vertical lines and terminations of Christian architecture, to represent emblems of the Resurrection; their natural intention is that of an upper weathering to throw off rain.[41]

Despite Pugin's enthusiasm on this subject, it should be remembered that while flying buttresses played a very conspicuous role in the High Gothic of medieval France,[42] they enjoyed only a very limited usage throughout the course of medieval English Gothic.[43] His insistence on vertical ascension and interior vastness is an important feature of Puginesque Gothic. It reflects a preference for a specific French formula that embodies one of the most obvious differences between French Gothic and English Gothic. English churches are of a significantly lesser height and, hence, have only an occasional need for, and then make a very restrained use of flying buttresses. Despite this fact, Pugin believed that the architectural traditions of a nation should be cultivated for the better interests of that country.[44]

> In general our English churches are deficient in internal height . . . . I think the internal vastness of Amiens, Beauvais, Chartres and other French Churches, should serve as useful examples to us in this respect in the revival of Pointed and Christian Architecture. Nothing can be conceived more majestic than those successions of arches, divided by light and elegant clusters of shafts running up to an amazing height and then branching over into beautiful intersecting ribs, suspending a canopy of stone at the enormous height of not infrequently one hundred and fifty feet. Internal altitude is a feature which would add greatly to the effect of many of our fine English churches, and I shall ever advocate its introduction as it is a characteristic of foreign pointed architecture of which we can avail ourselves without violating the principles of our own peculiar style of English Christian architecture, from which I would not depart in this country on any account.[45]

Here again, Pugin reaffirms his position that spiritual greatness and doctrinal greatness are most suitably embodied through architectural greatness. In fact, in Pugin's thinking, Gothic architecture was so much a logical outcome of Catholic doctrine that he actually questioned the right of those outside the Church of Rome to make use of Gothic elements in the construction of their churches. "It is a great profanation," declared Pugin, "to deck out Protestant monstrosities in the garb of Catholic Antiquity. . . ."[46]

As an architect, Pugin was a man of considerable talent. He was, however, diminished in the eyes of many of his contemporaries, not solely because of his affiliation with the church of Rome, but also to a considerable degree by his reputedly unpleasant personality. His lack of tact was legendary and is characteristically evident in much of the anti-Protestant slander that peppers his architectural writing. When he published the first edition of *Contrasts: Or A Parallel Between the Noble Edifices of the Fourteenth and Fifteenth Centuries, and Similar Buildings of the Present Day Shewing the Present Decay of Taste: Accompanied by Appropriate Text*, a number of his statements about Protestants were generally considered so offensive that he was eventually obliged to provide some form of retraction. This he did in the preface to the second edition of the book, although his general reluctance and lack of repentance was only thinly veiled. Pugin admitted that while he may not have been perfectly correct in accusing Protestantism of destroying Catholic architecture, he reaffirmed that he was "perfectly correct in the abstract facts that pointed architecture was produced by the Catholic faith." He also reiterated that this architectural idiom, so well suited to the expression of Catholic faith, was ravaged in the British Isles "by the ascendancy of Protestantism." He did, however, admit that he may have been erroneous in regarding Protestantism itself as the nucleus of this destruction. Instead, he suggested that Protestantism was in reality the "effect of some other more powerful agency," claiming that "the real origin of both the revived Pagan and Protestant principles is to be traced to the decayed state of faith throughout Europe in the fifteenth century."[47] His retraction could hardly have been expected to produce a spirit of reconciliation, or encourage interdenominational discourse on the subject of religious architecture.

The Cambridge Camden Society

At the same time Pugin was denouncing the ill effects of the Protestant Reformation on Catholic architecture, members of the Cambridge Camden Society were embarking on an architectural mission of their own. Part of this mission was to reinstate much of the visual dimension of worship that had been rejected during the English Reformation. They set about to do this with much of the zeal and ideological flexibility characteristic of a religious crusade. Although members of the society sought to restore many of the same visual elements as Pugin, they were not prepared to allow him much credit in this undertaking. In 1843, they soberly announced in a statement clearly aimed at Pugin that "no architect has as yet arisen, who appears destined to be the reviver of Christian art."[48] They rejected Pugin's claim that Gothic was a Roman Catholic expression, insisting instead that it was, in fact, linked to the Church of England. They maintained that the single most important feature of a church was that "it be built in such a way that the rubrics and canons of the Church of England be constantly observed and the sacraments rubrically and decently administered."[49]

As the Ecclesiologists were unable to identify a single champion for their cause, they set about to remedy the situation themselves. Their aim was to put forth as clearly as possible what precisely was needed to achieve "rubrical" correctness. The outcome of this undertaking was a proliferation of publications dedicated to the study, analysis, restoration, and construction of church architecture. No other denomination can even approach the quantity of material written and circulated by Anglicans on the subject of church building during the nineteenth century. The impact of their work was such that various merits or shortcomings of church architecture became a subject of current discussion, not only in Anglican and architectural circles, but also, with increased regularity, in the denominational journals of other Protestant confessions, as well as in the secular press.

Their public program of Gothic advocacy began in 1841 with *A Few Words to Church Builders*,[50] in which they set forth their primary preoccupations:

> Our three leading principles have been:
> –Reality,
> –The absolute necessity of a distinct and spacious chancel and,
> –The absolute inadmissibility of Pues [*sic*] and Galleries in any shape whatever.[51]

To these three basic points they added a great many other suggestions and requirements. In that same year, they also published the first edition of their journal, the *Ecclesiologist*, although it did not become a scholarly publication until after 1845.[52] Their single most important publication, *The Symbolism of Churches and Church Ornaments: A translation of the First Book of the Rationale Divinorum Officiorum written by William Durandus sometime Bishop of Mende*, was produced by Rev. B. Webb and Rev. J. Neale, and appeared in 1843. The translation of the original thirteenth-century Latin text was prefixed by a lengthy introductory essay, which the translators used as a vehicle for their own architectural agenda.[53]

The effects of this publication were to have repercussions on church building in some of the remotest corners of the British Empire. The impact on church building in Canada is arguably without parallel.[54] The translation also had the less fortunate effect of resulting, all too often, in a "wholesale adoption of medieval symbolism, even when it was no longer relevant or when the original significance was strictly functional."[55] In fairness to the translators, it should be remembered that Durandus himself was occasionally inclined to push his use of symbolism far beyond what might have been considered acceptable by even some of the more open-minded enthusiasts of architectural symbolism. His use of feminine symbolism to interpret the role of the church is a clear example of this. Many of the symbols he discussed, such as the Bride of Christ, the *Ecclesia Mater,* the good daughter and the pious widow, had been used since antiquity with little objection. However, his equation of the Christian church to a harlot "because She is called out on many nations, and because She closeth not Her bosom against any that return to Her . . . "[56] would have appealed to only a very limited following. There is certainly no evidence that this zealous application of architectural symbolism had even the smallest following among the Christians of nineteenth century Canada.

In their introductory essay *The Symbolism of Churches and Church Ornaments*, Neale and Webb propounded a complex correlation between theological abstraction and visual materialization. Gothic was presented as a logical progression in the history of religious architecture and "was the necessary result of the teaching of the Church, as being the only legitimate expression of uprisingness and verticality."[57] They also claimed that the breaking of the traditional round-headed arches found in the Norman churches marked a definitive break with architectural formulas that had perpetuated the embodiment of pagan traditions.[58] Furthermore, Neale and Webb maintained that the evolution of architectural symbolism was directly linked to an increased understanding of theological complexities. Their already enigmatic understanding of church architecture was further complicated by their views on church-state relations. They maintained that the distancing of the state from church affairs would subsequently and most naturally be followed by better church architecture. They demonstrated this theory by linking what they estimated to be the hallmarks of architectural progression with policies that favoured the English Church: "Contemporary with the appearance of Early-English [Gothic],[59] was the great victory of the Church over Erastianism, by the martyrdom of S. Thomas of Canterbury, and the abrogation of the Constitutions of Clarendon."[60] Conversely, they determined that increased state involvement had a direct and detrimental effect on church architecture: "But, hardly had Early English finished its course of splendor, when, while traces of rare glory were developing daily, the Statue of Mortmain began to tell upon the church."[61]

Neale and Webb also insisted that with increased state interference, the church was denied independence of symbolic and material expression, resulting in the loss of the symbolic meaning of many ancient architectural traditions.[62] Church architecture continued to decline until the restrictions and obstructions imposed on the church under Edward IV resulted in the Perpendicular perversion of the Gothic style. For the Cambridge Ecclesiologists, churches built in the Perpendicular style embodied these restrictions and the disempowerment of the church. Furthermore, they maintained that Perpendicular Gothic was a stylistic interpretation of secular origin and, thus, not truly suited for Christian churches.[63] Relief from these distressing circumstances was not forthcoming. Instead, with the introduction of the Tudor style, English Church architecture reached a new low. The depressed arches of the Tudor style also reflected the prevalence of spiritual deprivation, which, Neale and Webb were quick to point out, was not a misfortune confined to the British Isles. The French Church had also suffered similar indignities:

> The state gradually interfered with it, embraced it with its dangerous friendship, made its observances meaningless while sustaining their splendor, secularized its abbeys, by appropriating them to political ends, made statesmen of its bishops, gave it outside show, while eating out its heart.[64]

In France, this interference on the part of the secular government was clearly evident to the Cambridge Ecclesiologists in the introduction of flamboyant Gothic.[65]

In Italy, where the church was not considered to have suffered from an undue amount of state interference, the lack of a great Gothic tradition was attributed to residual pagan influences. Like Pugin, the Cambridge Ecclesiologists were convinced that, along with state interference, the other great antagonist of fine ecclesiastical architecture was paganism. They noted that, originally, English Protestantism had retained the use of some important elements of Trinitarian symbolism, such as trefoils and devices with equilateral triangles; however, this was all to change after the "Revolution when those faint traces of symbolism died away into that *nec plus ultra* of wretchedness, the Georgian style."[66] The neoclassic elements characteristic of the Georgian style that had, until recently, been used in the construction of so many English churches was considered not their only disfigurement. Cambridge Ecclesiologists state their own position vis-à-vis ultra-Protestantism, and state-sponsored church building in a damning denunciation of the "PUE-RENTED EPISCOPAL CHAPEL" in which "the Royal Arms occupy a conspicuous position for it is a chapel of the ESTABLISHMENT."[67] The shortcomings of the Protestant preaching chapel are contrasted with a commendatory and impassioned discourse on the superiority of the structures and symbols of a "Catholick Church." By "Catholick," Cambridge Ecclesiologists meant the Church of England, not the Church of Rome. Cambridge Ecclesiologists proceeded to set forth the merits and necessities of a "Catholick" church.

For them, unlike Protestant chapels that were crowded among shops and chimneys, the spire of a "Catholick" church should be visible from a great distance, rising above the commotion's and disharmony of secular life, and alluding to the omnipresence of a higher being. The church itself should be arranged so that all elements of faith and doctrine are embodied in its fabric from the ground up, and there to be externally as well as internally manifest. The very structure of the church should declare the merits of Christian faith to all who passed. The cruciform ground plan, as expressed in the transepts, recalled the underlying importance of the Atonement for the salvation of all. Apsidioles and lateral chapels recall the Communion of saints and those who had rallied around the church. On the spire, the weather cock urged prayerful vigilance, while the repulsive and displeasing presence of the gargoyles were to incarnate the wretchedness of souls lost. Like Pugin, Cambridge Ecclesiologists denounced the horizontally and earthliness of the crenelated parapets, praising instead the uplifting constitution of buttresses, pinnacles, and recognized words of sacred wisdom in the tracery of the window. Trinitarian symbolism dictated the division of the nave into a central nave flanked to either side by two aisles. The length of the church, when divided into nave, transepts, and choir, also recalled the Three Persons as did the tripartite elevation of the church through the pier, triforium, and clerestory window. The timelessness of Christ's supramundane nature was held to be symbolically incorporated into the layout of the church: "Him First in the two-fold western door; Him Last in the distant Altar; Him Midst in the great Rood; Him Without End in the monogram carved on boss and corbel."[68]

Baptismal fonts stood at the entry of the church and were to be deep, as Neale and Webb explained, "for we are buried in Baptism with Christ." The prophets and saints were symbolized in the piers and columns of the church, while the sculpted foliage of their capitals recalled the abundance and integrity of their achievements. The lofty nobility of saintly achievement symbolized in the structural elevations of the nave was used to underline the sharp contrast with the menial virtues and ultimate fragility of secular figures: "Beneath our feet are the badges of worldly pomp and glory, the charges of Kings and Nobles and Knights: all in the Presence of God as dross and worthlessness."[69]

By contrast, high above the funeral dalles of the church floor were the open timbers and hammer beams sculpted with the Heavenly Hosts. Between the depths of the earthly graves and the heights of the rafters with its immortal population of cherubs, seraphs, thrones, principalities and powers, were the church windows, in which the lives of great devotion to the church were commemorated. To teach and inspire, they are memorialized in glass, enlightening, both literally and symbolically, those inside the church. All this was, however, overshadowed by the magnificence of the rood screen.

Symbolic of the death through which all humanity must pass, the rood screen separated the church militant from the glories of the church triumphant. As it symbolized a passage through death, it was to bear the triumphal cross of Christ, who by rising from his own death was the first to overcome death. Collectively, these formed the necessities of a "Catholick" church. Church builders were not to simply pick out a few elements that they found interesting or inexpensive to build. Neale and Webb stressed the importance of the structural and symbolic unity in a church. In concluding their discourse, they note: "Verily, as we think on the oneness of its design, we may say: *Jerusalem aedificatur ut civitas cujus participatio ejus in idipsum.*"[70]

Although books devoted to the discussion of English church architecture[71] and symbolism had been in circulation prior to the formation of the Cambridge Camden Society, they were to enjoy a new demand and popularity after the publication of *The Symbolism of Churches and Church Ornaments*. Many of these new books were written by people in sympathy with, but not necessarily members of, the Cambridge Camden Society. George Ayliffe Poole's widely read and influential little manual, *Churches: Their Structure, Arrangement, and Decoration*,[72] was clear evidence that the Cambridge Camden Society held no monopoly on the subject of church symbolism.[73] Poole was another avid Gothic advocate and did not refrain from criticizing the work of that most celebrated and very Protestant of architects, Sir Christopher Wren. In particular, Poole denounced Wren's lack of appreciation for Gothic. Like Pugin and the Cambridge Ecclesiologists, Poole considered the whole upwards movement of the Gothic church to materialize the Christian hope of resurrection (fig. 3.2).[74] Cambridge Ecclesiologists were familiar with the earlier work of Poole and referred to it in some of their own publications; however, they judged Poole to be a bit too concerned with the "symbolism of details rather than any general principle."[75]

In 1847, the Cambridge Camden Society, now known as the Ecclesiological Late Cambridge Camden Society, published *Instrumenta Ecclesiastica*,[76] in collaboration with the architect William Butterfield (fig. 3.3). The book enjoyed a wide circulation, and a second edition was published in 1856. This manual was essentially a pattern book assembled for easy use by artisans and craftsmen. There is clear evidence of its influence on Canadian church architecture from the late 1840s onwards.[77] The Cambridge Ecclesiologists produced two other important publications in 1848: *A*

Hand-Book of English Ecclesiology, [78] and *Hierurgia Anglicana or Documents and Extracts Illustrative of the Ritual of the Church in England after the Reformation.*[79] They continued to publish a variety of papers and reports throughout the 1850s and during the early 1860s. By the time their final publication appeared in 1868, Gothic church building and the use of architectural symbolism had become a widely accepted practice; however, the closure of the Ecclesiological Society did not leave a literary void. Even before the Ecclesiologists retired their journal, a whole new generation of writers and practitioners, inspired by their work, were flooding Britain and British colonies with their own interpretation of Gothic style.

Fig. 3.2. Bishop Strachan Memorial Church (Anglican), Cornwall.

This building is a near perfect example of Ecclesiology correct Camdanian Gothic (Source: *Canadian Illustrated News*, 11 December 1875).

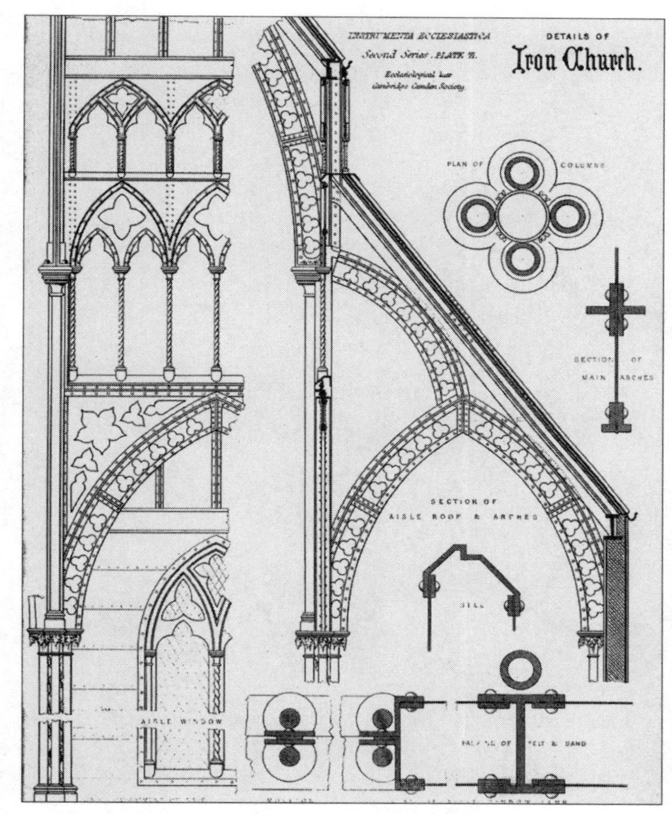

Fig. 3.3. Illustration from Butterfield's *Instrumenta Ecclesiastica*, 1847.

The interest in the revival of medieval style was not confined to architectural projects (William Butterfield, *Instrumenta Ecclesiastica*, 1847).

Colonial Gothic and Ecclesiology in the North American Context

American architects had been toying with elements of Gothic since the late eighteen and early nineteen hundreds. Their employment of Gothic had, however, not been marked by much fidelity to medieval prototypes and had only the most superficial nexus to Christian doctrine. Most early churches were essentially simple rectangular structures on to which a delusive Gothic rigging was applied. This manner of a romanticized and picturesque exploitation of Gothic was typified by the decorative influence of Batty Langley that had not yet yielded to a scientific and structural understanding of the style (fig. 3.4).[80]

Fig. 3.4. Batty Langley, "Gothick Temple," 1742.

Gothic purists denounced the work of Langley as stiff and insensitive to the true religious vocabulary of the style (Butty Langley Engraving, 1742).

During the first decades of the 1900s, this approach to Gothic church building was particularly evident in the work of Charles Bulfinch and John Holden Green.[81] A greater understanding of Gothic is evident in the work of Maximilian Godefroy[82] and Benjamin Latrobe,[83] although neither of these architects, despite their French origins, ever worked to closely emulate medieval prototypes. Nevertheless, and in spite of its classical influence and the dry stiff articulations of its orders, St. Mary's Chapel, designed by Godefroy in 1806 for the Roman Catholic Seminary in Baltimore, is considered by some scholars to be the first building in North America that could be legitimately called neo-Gothic.[84] This approximation of Gothic continued to be used well into the second quarter of the century by architects such as Josiah R. Brady, John Leach, William Passman, and L. S. Punderson; however, by the second half of the 1830s, a new and very different form of Gothic expression was beginning to attract interest.

The ideas concerning the Christian worth of medieval Gothic that had been circulating in Europe and the British Isles wasted little time in crossing the Atlantic Ocean. The Oxonian *Tracts*, Pugin's demand for medieval perfection, and the Gothic advocacy of the Cambridge Ecclesiologists were exciting considerable interest among clergy, architects, and a certain portion of the educated public.[85] As early as 1839, the Right Reverend J. Inglis, formerly of New York and first Anglican bishop of Nova Scotia, became a patron member of the Cambridge Camden Society. Two years later, in 1841, he was joined by the Right Reverend G. W. Doane, Bishop of New Jersey. By 1843, one of America's most influential architects, Richard Upjohn, had in his personal library a complete set of John Britton's *Architectural Antiquities*, J. M. Neale and J. Le Keux's *Views of the Most Interesting Collegiate and Parochial Churches in Great Britain*, several issues of *The Ecclesiologist*, as well as J. Neale and B. Webb's translation of *Rationale divinorum officiorum*, and Pugin's *True Principles of Pointed or Christian Architecture*.[86] Upjohn wasted little time in translating his literary acquisitions into architectural realities. By the time Upjohn completed Holy Trinity Church (Episcopal), New York, in 1846, it resembled so closely the "Ideal Church" published in Pugin's *True Principles,* that one is more inclined to think in terms of architectural plagiarism than stylistic coincidence. Likewise, James Renwick's Grace Church, (begun in 1843), also in New York, had decidedly Puginesque undertones.

By the mid-1840s, the Cambridge Camden Society was actively seeking to extend its sphere of influence into the "colonies." Their ideas were met with considerable, but not universal, success. They were especially prosperous among Episcopalians in the regions around Baltimore, New York, and Philadelphia. In 1846, plans were ordered directly from the Cambridge Camden Society for the construction of St. James-the-Less in Philadelphia. The church was completed in 1848 and, far from raising fears of English architectural imperialism, St. James occasioned a wider interest in Gothic architecture that was in keeping with Camdanian interpretation. As W. Pierson has justly noted, however, St. James-the-Less was "not an American Gothic Revival church; it was rather a transplantation of an English parish church."[87] Nevertheless, interest in English Ecclesiology had become so consequential that in April 1848, the New York Ecclesiastical Society was formed. Six months later, their journal, the *New York Ecclesiologist*, appeared. Contrary to the construction of St. James, this journal was not, as P. Stanton pointed out, "a pallid imitation of the *Ecclesiologist,*" but rather "the first

American journal devoted solely to architecture, and it possessed character, individuality and independence of mind."[88]

The extent to which this new approach to Gothic church building had aroused the interest of American churchgoers is apparent in the commissions of Frank Wills,[89] Henry Dudley, John Notman, and J. W. Priest. Richard Upjohn, however, was to become the one widely recognized as the single most important architect of Ecclesiastical Gothic in the United States. Although he was not always in a state of unqualified agreement with the English Ecclesiologists, by the mid-1840s, Upjohn had abandoned the Puginesque interpretation of revived Gothic. His architectural inspiration was now drawn from the type of rural English parish church of which the Cambridge Ecclesiologists were so fond. But it was through his adaptation of this rural English prototype to the realities of North American life that Upjohn was to play a major role in the emergence of a distinctly American interpretation of Gothic. The legacy of Upjohn's work is especially evident in the numerous small scale churches designed by Upjohn himself or inspired by his book, *Upjohn's Rural Architecture, Designs, Working Drawings and Specifications for a Wooden Church and other Rural Structures.* This manual was written by Upjohn and published in 1852 specifically to meet the increased demand for his church designs.[90]

Not all American architects working in the revived Gothic style chose to follow the same route as Richard Upjohn. One notable exception was James Renwick. Renwick did not transfer his interests to rural Ecclesiology, but remained allegiant to the Puginesque school of Gothic revival. In keeping with this spirit, Renwick was persuaded that the material church should convey to the faithful an appreciation for the greater vitality of the spiritual church. To achieve this, Renwick, like Pugin, used structural height as an essential component of church building. He skilfully articulated vast internal heights to produce an atmosphere of resplendence and eminence while successfully exploiting elements of outward elevation. Externally, Renwick used pinnacled buttresses, elongated finials and slender spires to achieve a forceful sense of vertical ascension. In doing so, he echoed Pugin's insistence that spiritual greatness was most suitably externalized through architectural greatness.

When the Roman Catholic diocese of New York was elevated to the rank of archdiocese in 1850, the new archbishop, John Hughes, was determined to use all the resources at his disposal to elevate the social prestige of Roman Catholicism. This was not an easy undertaking. Strong anti-Catholic sentiment had long been widespread in the United States. The Catholic Church in the Thirteen Colonies had not enjoyed many of the privileges that the French bishops had skilfully extracted from the British after they overran Quebec. In New York, the new archbishop was mindful of both the resources at his disposal and challenges he faced. In particular, Bishop Hughes was eminently aware that if cleverly managed, church architecture could contribute significantly to his agenda. A carefully designed new cathedral could be a conspicuous and enduring monument to the social prestige of American Catholicism. With this in mind, Hughes set out "to build a church which in size and splendor alone would outstrip any other church in the nation. . . . "[91] Given the character of his mission, it was perhaps not unanticipated that Bishop Hughes turned not to Richard Upjohn but to James Renwick to furnish the plans for St. Patrick's Cathedral in New York City. In his turn, Renwick looked to the great Roman Catholic cathedrals of medieval Europe for his inspiration.[92]

When St. Patrick's was finally finished in 1879, nearly three decades had elapsed since Bishop Hughes had originally aspired to build a church that would stand "for the glory of God, the exhalation of Our Holy Mother the Church, the honour of the Catholic name in this country and as a monument of which the city of New York, either in its present or its greatness, need never be ashamed."[93] Archbishop Hughes did not live to see the completion of his dream;[94] however, in many ways and despite the numerous modifications to the original plans, St. Patrick's Cathedral met his hopes and aspirations. Indeed, some late-twentieth-century architectural historians see the Roman Catholic cathedral in New York as "one of the major architectural triumphs of the nineteenth century."[95] This statement may be true, at least to some extent. St. Patrick's Cathedral is undeniably a significant and conspicuous example of Gothic in the use of nineteenth century Roman Catholic church building. Furthermore, given its location in the heart of one of the world's busiest cities, St. Patrick's has certainly enjoyed much more attention than many other churches of this same era. This being said, it is, however, important to recognize the place of St. Patrick's in the context and perspective of nineteenth-century Roman Catholic church building in North America. That is to say, although St. Patrick's was undeniably an example and source of inspiration for other church builders and that its size and splendour alone did outperform most other churches of its era, it is not, and never was, the architectonic embodiment of a new approach to church building. The importance of St. Patrick's Cathedral in New York lies not so much in that it is innovative, but rather that it is representative.

Medieval Gothic in a Canadian Context

More than a quarter of a century before Bishop Hughes of New York was openly discussing plans for his new cathedral, construction of North America's first monumental Gothic church was already well underway in Montreal. Though frequently referred to as the Notre-Dame 'cathedral' of Montreal, the church itself was built under the direction of the French Sulpicians as a parish church or, perhaps more appropriately, *the* parish church of Montreal.[96] Having tended to the spiritual needs of Roman Catholics on the island of Montreal since the mid-1600s, the social, religious, and political involvements of the Sulpicians and, by extension, their church-building activities, are a legacy inextricably intertwined with the chronicles of Montreal.[97] While the architecture of Notre-Dame remains in many ways an anomaly, the importance of this church is such that it cannot be completely ignored.

By the early 1820s, the parishioners of Notre-Dame, being both French and Roman Catholic, were increasingly apprehensive of the flourishing and conspicuous Anglo-Protestant presence in Montreal. It was decided that the time was ripe for a salient and tangible expression of French Catholicism's strength, vitality, and eminence. Not lacking in ambition, the *marguilliers* of Notre-Dame were determined that their new church must be, at the very least, an architectural equal of the best American and European churches. To this end, Jean Bouthillier was dispatched to New York during the fall of 1823 and entrusted with the responsibility of securing the services of the best architect available. After what can best, or perhaps only, be described as a *concours de circonstance*, Bouthillier recommended James O'Donnell, an Irish Protestant, who had been living in New York since 1812. He had never before designed a monumental church, nor been commissioned to build a Roman Catholic church.[98] Undaunted by this significant paucity of relevant experience, O'Donnell himself also undertook to enlighten the building committee of Notre-Dame on the subject of his own architectural credentials: "I have studied under some of the first Masters, and have carefully examined some of the best monuments in Europe, France excepted which I have not been in."[99]

O'Donnell's earlier churches, including Christ Church (Anglican), New York, 1823, and The First Presbyterian Church, Rochester, 1824, show little evidence that a careful examination of Europe's best monuments had exercised even the remotest stylistic influence on O'Donnell. Furthermore, the American Presbyterian Church,

Fig. 3.5. Notre-Dame (Roman Catholic), Montreal, 1829.

Perhaps best known, but one of the least imitated Canadian churches, Notre-Dame has a unique Gothic identity. Predating much of the lively debates about the revival of pure archaeological prototypes, this church owes more to the Commissioners Churches of the early-nineteenth century and the imagination of architect James O'Donnell (Source: *Ballou's Drawing Room Companion,* n.d.).

Montreal, designed by O'Donnell in 1826—while Notre-Dame was under construction—offers no documentation to the contrary (fig. 3.5). As for Notre-Dame itself, twentieth-century architectural historians have long been divided on the virtues (or shortcomings) of this church.

Gérard Morisset, a long respected chronicler of historic architecture in Quebec and an ardent architectural *nationalist,* complained that: "c'est à la construction de l'actuelle Notre-Dame de Montréal que cet esprit archéologique apparaît au grand jour." He noted that

Thomas Baillargé had declined to work in Gothic and quotes, with obvious admiration, a letter the architect sent to the building committee of Notre-Dame in 1824:[100] Morisset asks his reader that, if Thomas Baillargé did not feel able to build such an important church in the Gothic style, could one really expect such a charge to be properly executed by James O'Donnell, a Protestant and Irishman? Morisset accused O'Donnell of arbitrarily imposing an architectural style that completely ignored both the local climate and local building traditions. He denounced the church as being "un gothique troubadour d'origine anglaise, de formes sèches et d'une construction irrationnelle."[101] For Morisset, the fallacious temperament of Notre-Dame is manifest throughout:

> L'illogisme ne se manifeste pas seulement à l'intérieur dont le décor est radicalement faux, mais aussi à l'extérieur. Les divisions verticales de la façade ne correspondent pas à la coupe transversale de l'édifice—ce qui explique et la maigreur des tours et le vide désagréable des grandes arcades.[102]

In contrast to Morisset's obvious disgust with the building, Alan Gowans has suggested that it was precisely the Catholicism and Frenchness of the Gothic style that made the church so well suited to the parishioners of Montreal.[103] Ramsay Traquair saw in Notre-Dame a monument that not only went against tradition, but one that symbolized the first serious attack on the architectural traditions of New France.[104] Robert Hubbard, former director of the National Gallery of Canada and biographer of Christ Church, (Anglican), Ottawa, doesn't appear to suffer personally from any great distaste for Notre-Dame. He does, however, see in Notre-Dame a church that is both too English and too Protestant to have any widespread appeal among French Canadian Roman Catholics.[105] More recently, Mathilde Brosseau simply noted that, of all the contemporary critics, Jérôme Demers, Superior of the Séminaire de Québec and author of *Précis d'Architecture*, articulated the most succinct critique. Demers had tersely dismissed the church for its use of Gothic, its Protestant heritage, and its lack of structural cohesiveness.[106] Luc Noppen reserves judgment, but points out that the Gothicness of Notre-Dame is superficial.[107] It would be difficult to argue effectively against this observation, and Morisset's complaint concerning the lack of structural parallel between the façade and the interior are not ungrounded. Indeed, his remarks demonstrate quite clearly that, contrary to his own classification, Notre-Dame in Montreal is not marked by an "esprit archéologique," but rather by a superficial interpretation of Gothic ungrounded in historical precedent.[108] Whether one likes the architecture of Notre-Dame in Montreal or not, it is difficult to deny the church's striking visual and imposing physical presence, even amid the much taller office towers of the late-twentieth century. Furthermore, the important question is, as Franklin Toker has pointed out, not how the building is judged today, but rather how it was perceived at the time of its construction. First, it might be useful to consider the main architectural features of the Notre-Dame.

The façade of Notre-Dame consists of a central portion flanked to either side by a pair of large towers.[109] This tripartite arrangement is not a truthful reflection of the internal arrangements. The ground plan is rectangular. The lowest level of the central portion is opened by three huge arcades that form a sort of porch in front of the entries. The medial section of the façade is anchored on either end by a massive square tower. The entries do not correspond to the interior aisle arrangement as might logically be expected in a design influenced by European prototypes. Instead, all doors open into the central nave. Above each doorway is a large Gothic window. The three massive Gothic arches preceding the entries rise above the level of both the doorways and windows of the inner façade. The porch arches of the exterior façade are surmounted by three exceptionally large Gothic niches; however, there is no visual or architectonic linkage between the great arches of the ground level and the upper levels of the niches. Instead, the powerful upward thrust of the frontal arches is bluntly arrested by a double row of projected banded moulding. This moulding, which contours the towers at regular intervals, also constrains the upward momentum of the triple niches and the Gothic windows in the towers.[110]

The central portion of the façade is crested by decorative stepped embattlements instead of the creneau and merlon composition more common to some medieval English churches.[111] On the corresponding level of the tower is a third set of Gothic arches that share the same base line as the central embattlements, but rise considerably above the crest of the crenelage. These arches are not filled with glass, but with wooden louvers, and are in turn surmounted by oculi which give the appearance of being squeezed tightly between two rows of horizontal banding, resulting in a rather squat presentation. Above each oculus is a final Gothic arch, each reminiscent of the arches below the level of the oculi and also closed by a louver. The towers, like the central portion of the façade, are crested with decorative stepped embattlements. A small sharp turret rises from each of the four angles.

The main body of the church is a simple rectangle. The sanctuary is not architecturally distinct but is contained within the main body of the church. Along the lateral walls of the church are a series of large Gothic windows that open onto the eight bays of the side aisles. Since there is no clerestory—the whole church is covered by the same roof—these windows represent the only source of natural light to the nave. The massive skylights that straddle the roof crest are later additions. Wall buttresses were placed between the windows and capped with turrets that repeat the turrets of the frontal towers. The immense volumes of the vast interior were completed during the final quarter of the nineteenth century.

Though often overlooked by architectural historians working from a continental perspective, Montreal's Notre-Dame must be recognized as one of the earliest monumental Gothic style churches in North America. Still, while it is one of the boldest initiatory attempts of Gothic monumentality, Notre-Dame owes much more to the *appliqué* Gothic of England's Commissioners Churches than it does to medieval prototypes. Despite this fact, Notre-Dame enjoyed widespread approval and admiration during the middle and even latter decades of the nineteenth century. Much of this can be attributed to its great height and imposing internal volumes. The twin towers of the façade were a striking visual presence and unquestionably secured, for the local Roman Catholic population, a much sought-after quality that Malcolm Thurlby has aptly termed "skyline superiority."[112]

With the exception of the protests from several well-known contemporary Roman Catholic architects, such as Thomas Baillargé and Jérôme Demers (who may have had a vested interests in the matter), there appears to have been comparatively little objection from the French Canadian parishioners or even the general public. When Notre-Dame was officially blessed on July 15, 1829, the opening was attended by a great number of Roman Catholics and Protestants alike and received widespread attention in the press. Even the Wesleyan Methodists' *Christian Guardian,* while denouncing Notre-Dame as a "temple of idolatry," had to admit that it was "splendid."[113]

Interestingly, few Roman Catholic churches drew much direct architectural inspiration from Notre-Dame. Those that did were frequently built several decades later. Furthermore, their stylistic fidelity to Notre-Dame was often somewhat superficial and the question of aesthetic merit still another matter.[114] Despite the lack of direct descendants, Notre-Dame in Montreal should be credited with playing a significant role in the introduction of the Gothic style to Catholic church building in Central Canada. Despite the fact that the conception and construction of Notre-Dame predates the first serious use of archaeological Gothic by nearly two decades, Notre-Dame is important in that its eminence and influence as a centre of French Catholicism helped to create a greater openness towards the use of Gothic among the Roman Catholic population of Central Canada.

By the middle decades of the nineteenth century, Catholic church builders were increasingly inclined, not simply to include Gothic features, but also to use Gothic ingredients that were grounded in historical precedent. This more pensive form of Gothic expression was introduced, to a large extent, by French expatriots and is reflective of a considerably more rational and decidedly French interpretation of the style. Typical of this approach to Gothic is St. Patrick in Montreal (fig. 3.6). The church was designed and built between 1843 and 1847 by Félix Martin, a French Jesuit, in collaboration with Pierre-Louis Morin, a French architect. Both men were familiar with the formal principles of Gothic church building, and applied them to their new church with reasonable success.

Fig. 3.6. St. Patrick (Roman Catholic), Montreal, 1843–1847.

Architects Pierre Morin and Félix Martin, demonstrate a skillful mastery of medieval Gothic. The Gothic used here, however, is clearly French and marked by a careful verticality (Source: *Ballou's Drawing Room Companion*, n.d.).

Contrary to O'Donnell's use of twin towers on Notre-Dame, however, Morin and Martin chose to accentuate the vertical ascension of St. Patrick with a single axial tower on the main façade. The tower was set slightly in retreat of the main façade and surmounted by a spire. The tower was flanked to either side by turrets that stood in slight relief of the façade and that were reinforced with angle buttresses. These turrets were, in turn, topped with spires similar to, but lesser than, the central spire. This formula for vertical ascension was again repeated with the elongated finials that top the angle buttresses at either end of the façade. A large rose window was placed above the gable of the principal entry, while elongated windows with pointed arch-heads were placed above the side doors of the main façade.

Unlike Notre-Dame, the horizontal divisions of St. Patrick's façade were effectively negated through the effective use of the turrets and wall buttresses. The lateral walls of St. Patrick are remarkable both in terms of their austerity and effective verticality. Seven elongated Gothic lancets occupy the greater percentage of the vertical height of the lateral walls. They are placed between engaged wall buttresses that repeat the presentation of the various angle buttresses and animate the façade. These buttresses are continued around a semi-circular and architecturally distinct apse. The lancet windows that open into the axial apse of the church are not as tall as those in the lateral walls of the church, but are surmounted by small rose windows. The whole composition is marked by an austere verticality. Furthermore, and again in contrast to Notre-Dame, St. Patrick offered an interpretation of Gothic church building that lent itself with far greater facility to replication on a lesser scale. By the mid-nineteenth century, the Gothic style was enjoying an unprecedented level of acceptance and even popularity among Roman Catholic church builders.

The extent to which Roman Catholic church builders were motivated by a new found affection for the Gothic style is particularly well illustrated by the architectural history of Notre-Dame in Ottawa.[115] In 1839, it was decided that the plain wooden chapel, built only seven years earlier, needed to be replaced by a larger, more dignified, and decidedly more prestigious structure in stone. The new church was to be based on the plans of St. Patrick's Church in Quebec City.[116] This neoclassic church had been built several years earlier to accommodate Quebec City's rapidly augmenting Irish community. The church was designed by Thomas Baillargé, who had found some of his inspiration in the Anglican Cathedral of Quebec City, which was in its turn an adaptation of James Gibbs' St. Martin-in-the-Fields, London, England (1721-1726).[117] After several slight modifications, including the addition of two square towers on the façade and an architecturally distinct sanctuary, construction began on the Ottawa church during the spring of 1841. It was originally intended to be 70 feet wide, 90 feet long, and 40 feet high, but was lengthened in 1843 to attain an overall length of 128 feet. The following year, in 1844, care of the Roman Catholic community in Bytown passed into the hands of French Oblates, who left the completed portions of the lower level *in situ* and finished the church in the Gothic style, noting only that: "C'est sous l'impression de l'enthousiasme général que les missionnaires oblats prirent la résolution, avec l'approbation du public, de terminer l'église dans le style ogival autant qu'il serait possible de suivre ce style."[118]

Anglican Ecclesiology in Canada

French Jesuits, Oblates, and Sulpicians were by no means the only clergy to be preoccupied with a new interest for Gothic church building. During the mid-1840s, a number of individuals, who were to play an influential role in the introduction of Gothic in Anglican church building, arrived in British North America. Of particular importance were two Anglican bishops, Edward Field and John Medley, as well as the architects that accompanied them. In 1845, Bishop Edward Field took charge of the Diocese of Newfoundland, and, in that same year, John Medley became first Bishop of Fredericton. Both had been actively involved in the study and advocacy of revived medieval Gothic in the British Isles. Upon inspecting the state of church architecture in their new dioceses, both bishops were extremely displeased with what they discovered. Indeed, on the occasion of a speech delivered to the Anniversary Meeting of the Ecclesiological Late Cambridge Camden Society, in May 1848, Bishop Medley reported:

> Throughout the whole of North America no correct type of a church was formerly seen. The ordinary type seems to have been borrowed from the buildings erected by the Puritans, and from the different religious bodies who sprang up from time to time, the church having no form of its own, nor apparently any reference to the ancient churches of the mother country. The common plan of a small village church was that of a parallelogram, 40 ft. by 28, sometimes with, often without a small chancel, occasionally apsidal. The roof was very flat and sealed inside, with no timbers appearing. The spire was the favourite termination of the tower, which was poor and thin. There was no central passage to the altar. The pulpit often occupied its place, and always concealed it from view. There was scarcely ever a font. The windows were either entirely square or round-headed, or pointed, with square sash-lights, in portions about 4 ft. by 9. These sash-lights were often covered with green Venetian blinds to keep out light

> and heat. The stoves, of which almost always two and often four, are found in a church, sent their long arms throughout the entire building, meeting in the centre and going through the roof. The pews were commonly square and all sold by auction to the highest bidder. The sacramental plate was of inferior material and most unsightly form.[119]

Bishop Medley, nevertheless, took a positive approach to this unfavourable situation and informed his audience that "Happily the greater part of these edifices were built of wood, and must ere long decay."[120] The poor style and state of pre-existing church buildings was not the only problem to confront the new bishops. Medley and Field were also faced with the prospect of building a cathedral in their new dioceses. Both bishops were determined that if this task was to be properly fulfilled, the new cathedrals must be built according to the dictates of ecclesiastically correct Gothic. Furthermore, as there was not an abundant reserve of local architects schooled in the finer points of medieval Gothic, both bishops turned to the British Isles for architectural assistance.

Fig. 3.7. Cathedral of St. John's (Anglican), Newfoundland, 1848.

Begun in 1848 during the episcopacy of the Rt. Rev. Bishop Field, who held the joint see of Newfoundland and Bermuda, St. John the Baptist was built in accordance with plans by George Gilbert Scott, and under the supervision of William Hay. Much of the original church was destroyed by fire on July 1892. Although somewhat modified, the rebuilt church has retained much of its original character (Source: *London Illustrated News*, 23 June 1849).

Fig. 3.8. Most Holy Trinity (Anglican), Bermuda, 1840s.

Bishop Field also turned to Sir George Gilbert Scott and William Hay for the plans of his original cathedral in Bermuda. This building was gutted by fire in January of 1884. At Field's request, plans for the new cathedral were prepared by William Hay. For this reason, despite its later date, the cathedral offers a particularly accomplished example of revivalist Gothic (Courtesy of the Bermuda Government Archives; photo: Thomas W. Hall).

To ensure stylistic integrity, Bishop Field commissioned a well-regarded architect, George Gilbert Scott, to design the new Cathedral of St. John's (fig. 3.7). At the time of his commission, Scott enjoyed the reputation not only of a fine designer, but also of one of the leading architects of the revived Gothic style.[121] To further guarantee that the plans for the new Gothic Cathedral of St. John's were properly executed, Bishop Field retained the services of William Hay as the on-site architect. Hay had received much of his early architectural training under the tutorship of Scott and was a logical choice for this task. Following the completion of the cathedral in Newfoundland, Hay remained in North America and worked out of Toronto for some time. Later, he again collaborated with Bishop Field in the Gothic construction of Most Holy Trinity, the pro-cathedral in Hamilton, Bermuda (fig. 3.8).[122]

Like his counterpart in Newfoundland, the new bishop of Fredericton, John Medley, was not without opinion on the matter of church building. Prior to his appointment to the newly formed See of New Brunswick, Medley had been closely associated with the intellectual concerns and the architectural activities of both Oxford and Cambridge. He had worked with both John Keble[123] and William Butterfield, the preferred architect of the Cambridge Camden Society.[124] Medley was more than an interested spectator or even casual participant in the revival of archaeologically correct Gothic

Fig. 3.9. Christ Church Cathedral (Anglican), Fredericton, 1853.
A combined effort of architects William Butterfield and Frank Wills, Christ Church cathedral was one of the first major Canadian churches to be so intimately linked with the ideals of Camdanian Ecclesiology (Photo: N.M.E.).

churches. He was well-versed in the historic tradition of English ecclesiastical art and architecture and, at the time of his appointment to the See of New Brunswick, was recognized by many of his contemporaries as a leading expert in the field of revived medieval tradition.[125] It is hardly surprising, then, that a churchman and scholar of John Medley's caliber should choose a like-minded individual to design and supervise the construction of his new cathedral. Medley's architect of choice was William Butterfield and his understudy, Frank Wills. Wills came to New Brunswick with Medley to oversee the construction of the cathedral (fig. 3.9).

While the cathedral was being built (1846-1853), Wills designed for Medley's personal use a small chapel that was consecrated in March of 1847 and dedicated to Saint Ann (fig. 3.10). Later, Wills was to claim that this chapel was "the first ecclesiastical building erected in the British Provinces on which ancient architecture has been attempted to be honestly carried out."[126]

In Canada, during the early decades of the nineteenth century, most Anglican ministers and their church-building committees appear to have proceeded in their undertakings, secure in the knowledge that their church would be built as churches always had been. Gradually, however, many traditional church-building habits were being openly criticized, usually by newcomers from the British Isles. By the middle years of the nineteenth century, a number of potential church builders were beginning to admit that they were no longer as self-assured as they may once have been. Canadian Anglicans began to write to church authorities in unprecedented numbers to request architectural guidance. By the late 1840s, architectural inquiries had become so numerous that Anglican authorities decided the question needed to be addressed publicly. Consequently, church officials circulated a series of articles on the subject of church building throughout the Anglican press. The first major article prepared in Toronto by the Building Committee of the Church Society appeared during the

Fig. 3.10. St. Ann (Anglican), Fredericton, 1847.

Though often imitated but rarely equalled, the chapel of St. Ann is a tribute to Frank Wills' mastery of the Gothic style. The quinqueparti lancets and the triple bell cote are particularly fine (Photo: N.M.E.).

spring of 1850 in vol. XIII, no. 37 and no. 38, of *The Church*. The second major article appeared a year later in the *Canadian Ecclesiastical Gazette* and was authored by Bishop George Jehoshaphat Mountain. Mountain, until his recent promotion to the Episcopal See in Quebec City, had been Bishop of Montreal.

In the first set of recommendations to be issued by the Diocese of Toronto, the Building Committee of the Church Society addressed questions of site, structure, and style. The committee suggested that while churches should be situated so as to be easily accessible to the majority of the population, they should not be too near major roads. Churches were not to be built near factories or in close proximity to any other thing that might disturb church services. Worship was to be conducted in an atmosphere of reverence and tranquillity. Furthermore, the tranquillity that was an essential requisite of Sunday worship was to remain undisturbed even on weekdays:

> The site of the church should be central, but with regard to population rather than to space. It should be accessible by carriage ways, but not so near to principal thoroughfares, foundries, &c., either in towns or villages as to be likely, either immediately or at a distant period to subject the service of the Church, even on week days to be disturbed by noise.[127]

It was also recommended that, whenever possible, sufficient land was to be acquired around the church site so as to permit the eventual construction of a parsonage and a school. The committee did not offer any suggestions as to precisely how the presence of a school might contribute to the serenity of the site. The church building itself was to be "grave and substantial" and "as solid as the nature of the material will readily admit,"[128] and in keeping with "ancient custom," the chancel was to stand at the easternmost end of the building.[129] The committee also suggested that internal decoration ought to be favoured over external decoration. This did not mean that the exterior of the church was to be devoid of Anglican characteristics: "Care should be taken in all churches that their appearance shall indicate the purpose for which they were intended, and if possible distinguish from places of worship of other bodies of professed Christians."[130]

So that there might be no question as to how church builders might elevate a decidedly Anglican structure, the Toronto committee offered (with little room for negotiation) several additional recommendations. All churches were to be built in the Gothic style because Gothic was the most appropriate style for ecclesiastical edifices (although the committee neglected to explain precisely why this might be). The committee was also adamant that the Gothic used must not be a superficial application, as had frequently appeared in earlier buildings. Instead, the Anglican use of Gothic was to be stylistically correct and executed by persons who were well-versed on the subject. Ideally, they explained, the "perfect church" would have a tower or a bell cot, a porch, a baptismal font carved in stone, a nave, a chancel, and a separate vestry. Larger churches might even have transepts. The overall length of a church was to be three times its width. Vestries, for those seeking architectural perfection, were to be placed on the northern side of the church, but could be placed along the southern wall, due to the prevailing winds and the severity of Canadian winters. Claiming similar climatic concerns, the committee told church builders not to place the main entrance in the western façade, but rather on the leeward side of the church.[131]

The foundations of a church were to be solidly built, preferably of stone or concrete, and well drained. Additional drainage in the form of open paved drains was also recommended for brick or stone churches, as were basements. Both kept the church drier, thus enhancing its structural integrity. The walls of brick churches were to be at least fourteen inches thick, while the walls of stone churches were to measure a minimum of eighteen inches. Buttresses could be used to strengthen a wall, but were not to be used simply for decorative purposes. Inside, the church was to be well ventilated and the floors paved with stones or tiles, especially under fonts and stoves. Chimneys from the stoves could be brought up above the roof line in buttresses, but were under no circumstances to be disguised as pinnacles or decorated with crosses.[132] The roof of the church was to have a pitch sufficiently steep so as to allow the rapid evacuation of rain and snow. Battlements were to be avoided, as they tended to retain rain and snow. The roof of a church was, at the very least, to be equal in height to 75 per cent of the external width of the building. The committee did point out, however, that "the most esteemed English architects" were building churches with roofs that were equilateral triangles, based on the external width of the building.[133]

In April 1850, the Building Committee of the Church Society of Toronto published the second installation of its recommendations. Having previously noted that in Anglican churches, reverential attention was to be fastidiously accorded to the area where Holy Communion was celebrated,[134] the committee now outlined how privilege was to be supplied to any area set aside for the practice of divine service. These internal arrangements were presented as mandatory for a practice of Anglican worship. Sanctuaries, for example, had to be equipped with an altar table that should not be less than four feet by two and a half and should stand at least three feet and three inches high. The committee also provided specifications for the proper arrangements for chancel doors, choirs, pulpits, and reading desks. A number of practical recommendations concerning the maintenance of fonts, the construction of vestries, porches and towers, the ringing of bells, the management of drafts, and the upkeep of churchyards were also included.[135] Interestingly, there was never even the faintest reference to Oxford Tractarianism or the architectural studies of the Camdanians; however, the influence of English ecclesiology was blatant in all the recommendations made by the Building Committee.[136]

In January 1851, the Anglican Bishop of Quebec, G. J. Mountain, announced that he had recently received so many requests for guidance on the question of church building that he was "prompted to put in print, once and for all (without thinking it necessary to guard against any imputation of giving importance to the material to the prejudice of the spiritual edifice), a statement of some few standing rules and general principles upon this subject. . . ."[137] His advice was published in two consecutive issues of *The Canadian Ecclesiastical Gazette.*[138] In his opening remarks, Mountain referred his readers to the above-mentioned article published a year earlier in *The Church*,[139] pointing out that not only were the recommendations most beneficial, but that a committee similar to the one that had prepared the article was presently at work in the Diocese of Quebec. Mountain reiterated much of what had originally appeared in *The Church;* however, it is very clear that he was not simply repeating what had been said earlier. Mountain was evidently well versed in contemporary church-building literature. He assured his readers that the church-building committee of his own diocese was currently preparing a set of plans in consultation with "an accomplished English architect." The architect in question was Frank Wills, the same architect who had been brought to Fredericton by Bishop Medley for the construction of his new cathedral. Wills had in the interim been designing proper Gothic churches in the eastern United States. While Bishop Mountain did not enjoy Bishop Medley's reputation as an authority on ecclesiastical art, his choice of Frank Wills as architectural adviser for his diocese could hardly have been uninformed. Instead, the engagement of Wills as the consulting architect was in itself indicative of the rapidity with which an interest for medieval Gothic churches was spreading throughout the Anglican population of Canada. Furthermore, Mountain's choice of architect, as well as his discussion of style, structure, and resource material, was strongly suggestive of someone who was well aware of and in agreement with much of what the Camdanians had been advocating.

Bishop Mountain clearly stated that regardless of how modest a church building might be, it was absolutely essential that both the interior and the exterior instantly identify it as a "House of God." Potential church builders were then promptly advised that marking an edifice as a "House of God" would be best achieved through the use of Gothic. Gothic, Mountain explained, was "incomparably the preferable style for Church-architecture."[140] He was very clear, however, as to what type of Gothic was to be used. By Gothic he did not mean the use of "false and fantastic ornament" or other "peculiar features of what is commonly called Gothic," and church builders would be well advised to know a little bit about what they were doing. He specifically stated that the interpretation of Gothic to which he referred was "so unlike what men have been accustomed to see in Canada, that it requires time even to reconcile their minds to that which, with longer experience, they find to be essential to correct taste and to architectural propriety."[141] Mountain insisted that stylistic fidelity to the ancient traditions of Gothic church building was absolutely essential. He also stated quite emphatically that if the earlier use of superficial or sham Gothic was not abandoned, it would not be long before church building in the Central Canada would become an object of contempt and scorn.[142]

As there were few examples of medieval style Gothic churches on the western side of the Atlantic, and fewer still in Central Canada, Mountain suggested that local architects might seek inspiration or further knowledge on the subject by reading an architectural guide by Matthew Bloxam. Bloxam had written the small but very influential book several years earlier for the Society for Promoting Christian Knowledge.[143] Like Field and Medley, Bloxam himself was not entirely without a stylistic agenda. He had been a prolific writer on the subject of church architecture and was an honourary member of the Cambridge Camden Society. He shared his interest in religious art and architecture with his brother, John Rouse Bloxam, who was a personal friend of both John Henry Newman and A. W. Pugin.[144] After clearly establishing that Anglican churches were to be built in the Gothic style, Mountain instructed builders to orient their churches so that the sanctuary marked the easternmost end of the structure. In terms of building materials, he gave preference to durable materials such as stone and brick, pointing out that "One of our Bishops in

Australia has made it a rule to decline to consecrate wooden Churches, regarding them as mere temporary structures."[145] The authors of the recommendations published in *The Church* had also favoured the use of stone, but they were inclined to be a bit more flexible concerning the use of wood, especially in its advice to new communities.[146]

Once again the size and proportion of an Anglican church were to be carefully balanced. The overall recommended dimensions were that the length of a church be three times its width.[147] Mountain also discussed the various merits of towers, steeples, and bell cots. While agreeing that there should be some form of external elevation, the size and structure was to be dependent on the overall composition of the church. The roofs of churches were to be steeply pitched, and rafters could be opened to the inside if they were presentable. Mountain specifically stressed that flat ceilings were to be avoided, as were "battlements and all ornate appendages in architecture."[148] He also recommended that southern porches be used in favour of axial entries in the western façade. He claimed that this arrangement was better adapted to local climatic conditions. Throughout the church, lancet windows were preferred.[149] In the sanctuary, at the eastern end of the church, lancet windows could be closely grouped together in a set of three. If this arrangement was used, all windows were to have the same base line; however, the head of the central light could be taller.

In his second article, Mountain detailed the rules concerning church furnishing and the necessary levels of lighting. Church builders were instructed on the importance and relative positioning of communion tables, pulpits, reading desks, communion rails, altar linens, kneelers, and choir seats.[150] Each item was clearly described and defined. In little more than a year, the Anglican population of Central Canada had been exposed to a significant quantity of very precise and highly detailed church-building advice. Anglican church builders were clearly aware of these recommendations. Structural changes were occasionally introduced with restraint, resulting more from architectural caution rather than ecclesiological conservatism.

As Anglicans were discussing the moral merits of various architectural styles and distinct Anglican features, other Anglo-Protestants had been watching with a mixture of cautious interest and alarm. This was particularly true of the various Methodist denominations. Although Methodists had rejected the emotionless rationalism of the eighteenth-century Anglican Church, they were not prepared to throw themselves wholeheartedly behind the restoration of pre-

Reformation ritualism. Readers of the *Christian Guardian* were cautioned not to be swept along in the current of Anglican architectural reform: "The Church of England has long been known to tolerate within her pale the widest diversity of opinion and to include among her clergy men of every shade, from the half-popish Puseyite down to the half-political half-infidel man of the Broad Church."[151]

Nevertheless, by the middle years of the nineteenth century, the matter of better-looking churches had became an object of much questioning and in certain instances, moral dilemma. More conservative elements in some Methodist communities were persistently reluctant to assign God to a place built by human hands. Others worried that without church buildings, Methodism could not survive.[152] Still others feared that, although churches should be built, they should be neither too elegant nor stylish for this would in some way be sinful.

Presbyterians wasted little time in noticing the changes that were beginning to appear in Anglican church building. They immediately identified the changes occurring within the Anglican church as far from superficial. It was quickly understood that it was no coincidence that significant modifications to the visual dimension of Anglican worship were occurring at the same time as dramatic changes to liturgical and doctrinal emphasis. As early as 1840, the *Canadian Christian Examiner and Presbyterian Magazine* announced grimly: "Most of our readers are aware that a party in the Church of England, whose Head Quarters are at Oxford, are labouring to introduce popery into the Church, as well as into the country at large under a mask of concern for religion. . . ."[153] In order to clarify precisely how they believed this papal infiltration was occurring, the *Canadian Christian Examiner and Presbyterian Magazine* reprinted an article from the *Edinburgh Christian Instructor* under the heading "The Church of England a Half-Reformed Church." The article attributed the current changes occurring within the Anglican Church as an unfortunate result of incomplete reform: "Nor have we any great cause to wonder at the Popery of the Church of England, in her liturgy, rubrics, canons, vestments, rites, and in what may be termed her *traditional*, as distinguished from her *symbolical*, theology. . . ."[154] Presbyterian church builders saw little need or purpose in even discussing the possibility of venturing beyond the basic dictates of Calvinistic austerity, a position to which their buildings from this era are stark testimony.

Readers of Baptist publications were frequently warned against the dangers of ritualism, and Baptist church builders demonstrated little inclination to undertake any sort of serious architectural innovation. It was not until 1868 that an Ontario Baptist Church Edifice Society was formed and then only as an appendage to a quarterly meeting of the Executive Board of the Baptist Missionary Convention of Ontario. Their stated objective was "to aid Regular Baptist Churches to build or purchase Meeting Houses by loan or grant from its funds."[155] There was no mention of any fixed plans or building criteria.

The Baptist clergy, however, was, with increasing regularity, discussing church architecture in intensely symbolic terms. Typically, this symbolization of church architecture was used as a means to instruct the Baptist faithful on matters of theological concern and usually appeared in the form of short articles or stories in the Baptist press. But, articles with titles such as "Wise Master Builders"[156] and "The Door by Which We Enter the Church,"[157] did not really address the requirements of physical church building at all. "The Building, The Builder and His Works,"[158] an article that appeared in the *Canadian Baptist* during the fall of 1867, was in fact an exegesis of 1 Corinthians 3: 10-15. In a brief article, "The Chapel is in the Heart," published in 1867, Jeremy Taylor advises Baptist readers:

> In your retirement make frequent colloquia, or short discoursing with God and thy own soul. Every return of the heart in these intercourses, is a going to Him, an appearing in his presence and in representing Him present to thy spirit and thy necessity. This was long since called by a spiritual person "a building to God a chapel in our heart." It reconciles Martha's employment with Mary's devotion. For thus in the midst of the works of your trade you may retire into your chapel—the heart—and converse with God by frequent addresses and returns.[159]

Taylor's observations are in many ways representative of Baptist employment of architectural symbolism during this era.

By the middle years of the nineteenth century, the rethinking of church architecture and building priorities was not uncommon among the leaders of various Christian denominations. Depending on the denomination, circumstances or individuals involved, in the discourse could be theoretical, theological, purely symbolic, or could address the material and practical concerns of church building. It is worth noting that the interest in church building was not restricted to the confessional press.

Notes

1. *Christian Guardian*, 10 March 1847, 82.

2. *Christian Guardian*, 19 March 1856, 94.

3. W. Westfall has pointed out that "between 1851 and 1881 all major Protestant denominations either matched or exceeded the rate of increase in the population as a whole, and quite remarkably church building outpaced even the rapid rate of denominational expansion. In this period the Anglicans . . . trebled the number of their churches. The Presbyterians (taken as a whole) and the Baptists . . . trebled the number of their churches. The Methodists were even more prolific builders . . . again taking all the Methodists together, the number of their churches increased by a factor of five." W. Westfall, *Two Worlds: The Protestant Culture of Nineteenth-Century Ontario* (Montreal and Kingston: McGill-Queen's Press, 1989), 129.

4. Ven. A. N. Bethune, "A charge addressed to the clergy of the Archdeanery of York," *The Church* 13, 14 (November 1849).

5. In the archives of Queen's University, the papers of the Presbyterian Church in Connection with the Church of Scotland, Collection of the Presbyterian Church in Canada, No. 2263, box 1, file 2, contain numerous correspondences on the clergy reserve question and the rights of the Presbyterian community.

6. For a fuller discussion of this divisive question, see A. Wilson, *The Clergy Reserves of Upper Canada: A Canadian Mortmain* (Toronto: University of Toronto Press, 1968) and C. Fahey, *In His Name: The Anglican Experience in Upper Canada, 1791-1854* (Ottawa: Carleton University Press, 1991).

7. Son of the Honourable and Right Reverend Jacob Mountain, First Bishop of Quebec, the Right Reverend George Mountain became the First Anglican Bishop of Montreal in 1836. At this time, the Diocese of Montreal extended westward to the northern shore of the Ottawa River. In 1850, he became the third Bishop of Quebec, until his death in 1863.

8. *Canadian Ecclesiastical Gazette* 1, 4 (September 1850), 30.

9. This concept of betrayal is discussed in some detail by Fahey, *In His Name.*

10. *Canadian Ecclesiastical Gazette* 1, 4 (September 1850), 30.

11. Ibid.

12. "We then, while we confide the issue to God, must not be wanting in what He enables us to do for ourselves: there ought to be no apathy, no backwardness, no faint-heartedness in the cause: whatever may be the result, we must not lie under the everlasting reproach of having left undefended the interests of our people and our posterity—and we must enlist in our support, the names of all Churchmen who value their Religion." *Canadian Ecclesiastical Gazette* 1, 4 (September 1850), 30.

13. In the event that there were still some Anglicans who had not yet grasped the full magnitude of the situation, Mountain ended his circular in blunt and unmeasured terms: "the present system of payments from home, in any shape, for the support of the Clergy must be brought to a close, and that the most severe spiritual privation must in many examples, await them and their children after them, if the predatory irruption into the sanctuary which is now threatened, cannot effectively be repelled. . . ."*Canadian Ecclesiastical Gazette* 1, 4 (September 1850), 30.

14. The work and writings of H. Pinhey are discussed in Chapters One and Two.

15. Fahey, *In His Name,* xv.

16. These same rights were extended to Roman Catholics the next year (1829).

17. *Tracts for the Times, by Members of the University of Oxford* (London: J. G. & F. Rivington & F. Parker, 1831-1841).

18. See O. Chadwick, *The Mind of the Oxford Movement* (London: Black, 1960), 51.

19. See J. Kenyon, "The Influence of the Oxford Movement upon the Church of England in Upper Canada," *Ontario History* 51 (1959), 84.

20. John W. Grant, *The Church in the Canadian Era* (Burlington: Welch Publishing Company, 1988), 17.

21. P. Stanton, *The Gothic Revival and American Church Architecture* (Baltimore: John Hopkin's Press, 1968), xix.

22. Formed in May 1839 by B. Webb and J. M. Neale. It was begun as The Cambridge Camden Society, a name that was later changed to The Ecclesiological Late Cambridge Society in 1845, then shortened to the Ecclesiological Society in 1852. Hereafter, the members and associates of this movement will be referred to as Cambridge Ecclesiologists. The terms English Ecclesiologists, Canadian Ecclesiologists, American Ecclesiologists, or simply Ecclesiologists are used to refer to the ever widening number of individuals who took an active interest in the subject, but were not [Cambridge] Ecclesiological Society members.

23. This is possibly due to a widespread acceptance of transubstantiation among Oxonians, something that most Camdanians denied.

24. See *Ecclesiologist* 1, 3 in J. White, *The Cambridge Movement: The Ecclesiologists and the Gothic Revival* (Cambridge: Cambridge University Press, 1962), 43.

25. A. W. Pugin, *Contrasts: Or A Parallel Between the Noble Edifices of the Fourteenth and Fifteenth Centuries, and Similar Buildings of the Present Day; Shewing the Present Decay of Taste: Accompanied by Appropriate Text* (London: A. W. Pugin, 1836), 51-52.

26. Pugin, *Contrasts*, 49.

27. A. W. Pugin, *True Principles of Pointed or Christian Architecture* (London: J. Weale, 1841), 1.

28. "Better is it to do a little substantially and consistently with truth than to produce a great but false show." See Pugin, *True Principles*, 27.

29. Pugin, *Contrasts*, 58.

30. "I must here mention two great defects very common in modern pointed buildings, both of which arise from the great fundamental principle of decorating utility not being understood. In the first place, many architects apply the details and minor features of the pointed style to classic masses and arrangements: they adhere scrupulously to the regularity and symmetry of the latter, while they attempt to disguise it by the mouldings and accessories of the former. They must have two of everything, one on each side: no matter if all the required accommodation is contained in one half of the design." Pugin, *True Principles*, 51-52.

31. "The mechanical part of Gothic architecture is pretty well understood, but it is the principles which influenced the ancient compositions and the soul which appears in all the former works which is so lamentably deficient [in modern works]. Nor . . . can they be regained but by a restoration of ancient feelings and sentiments . . ." Pugin, *Contrasts*, 43.

32. Pugin, *Contrasts*, 2.

33. "The First; the cross is not only the very plan and form of a Catholic Church, but it terminates each spire and gable, and is imprinted as a seal of faith on the

very furniture of the altar. The second is fully developed in the triangular form and arrangements of arches, tracery and even subdivision of the buildings themselves. The third is beautifully exemplified by the great height and vertical lines which have been considered by the Christians from the earliest times as the emblem of the resurrection." Pugin, *Contrasts*, 2-3.

34. Pugin, *Contrasts*, 51.

35. Ibid., 52.

36. Ibid., 56-57.

37. Ibid., 53.

38. Ibid., 54.

39. Ibid., 9-10.

40. Ibid., 3.

41. Ibid., 8.

42. Typical of French Gothic from this era is the cathedral of Notre-Dame in Chartres (1194-1220), where the architect sought to achieve a greater degree of integration among the various spatial divisions while creating a combined effect of monumentality and vertical ascension. This was achieved by carrying the central colonnade boldly upward, suppressing the tribune, and retaining only the triforium as a horizontal spatial division. The horizontal effect of the triforium was in turn negated to a large extent by the new and overwhelming character of the clerestory windows. The disintegration of the wall mass was further advanced through the introduction of a new window arrangement in which two lancets were surmounted by a small rose allowing for an increased opening of the wall. The combined effect urged the eye upwards. It was the suppression of the tribunes that necessitated the addition of flying buttresses to brace the upper wall. Instead of attempting to negate their presence, the architect of Chartres frontalized the buttresses by creating a series of small pinnacled and pinioned niches. Chartrian canons were further refined at Reims (1212-1280), and Amiens (1220-1247), and the flying buttresses of the Early Gothic Notre-Dame in Paris (1225-1230) were, in fact, thirteenth-century additions. The architects of Beauvais (1225-1272), on the other hand, did nothing to advance Gothic construction, either in terms of stylistic symbolism or structural integrity. Instead, preoccupied with vertical ascension, they pushed the building program beyond the limits of contemporary engineering knowledge, ultimately resulting in the collapse of the choir vaults in 1284.

43. The nave and side aisles of medieval English cathedrals were considerably narrower than their Continental counterparts. English Gothic vaults were also traditionally much lower than those in contemporary French constructions, while, at the same time, the individual bays were comparatively wider. This arrangement tended to emphasize the horizontality of each individual spatial unit. The vertical continuity of the nave's elevation was further fragmented by the frequent use of heavy mouldings, prominent consoles and distinctive capitals. When the Perpendicular style (which many revivalists denounced as being debased owing to its secular origins) is used, the paneling fragments and fetters the full effect of vertical ascension.

44. "Another object to Italian architecture is this: we are not Italians we are Englishmen. God in His wisdom has implanted a love of nation and country in every man, and we ought to view the habits and manners of other nations without prejudice, derive improvement from all we observe, but we should never forget our own land." To this he added: "In short, national feelings and national architecture are at so low an ebb, that it becomes an absolute duty in every Englishman to attempt their revival." Pugin, *True Principles*, 47-48.

45. Pugin, *True Principles*, 55.

46. Pugin, *Contrasts*, 57.

47. Pugin, *Contrasts*, 2nd edition (New York: Leicester University Press, 1973), III.

48. J. M. Neale and B. Webb, "Introductory," *Rationale Divinorum Officiorum* (Leeds, 1843), XVIII.

49. See *Ecclesiologist* 1, 10, quoted in White, *The Cambridge Movement*, 92

50. J. M. Neale, ed. *A Few Words to Church Builders* (Cambridge: University Press, 1841). This book was re-edited in 1842 and 1844.

51. Neale, *A Few Words*, 5.

52. According to White in *The Cambridge Movement,* their last issue was published in 1868.

53. In discussing this publication, it is necessary to distinguish between the opinions of the nineteenth-century Anglican translators expressed in the introductory essay and those set forth in the original text by the twelfth-century Roman Catholic bishop. In the interest of clarity and simplicity, references or quotations from the introductory essay will be referred to as *The Symbolism of Churches and Church Ornament*, while those from Durandus's medieval text will be referred to by the original Latin title, *Rationale Divinorum Officiorum.*

54. Some scholars have suggested that the publication "materially changed the course of Ecclesiology," and "marked the real adoption of symbolism as a significant feature of Ecclesiology." White also points out that some modern Catholic scholars are less enthusiastic about the work of Durandus, suggesting that ". . . this kind of fanciful explanation of liturgy attained what we might call a luxurious as well as unhealthy growth." White, *The Cambridge Movement,* 69.

55. J. White, *Protestant Worship and Church Architecture: Theological and Historical Considerations* (New York: Oxford University Press, 1964), 134.

56. Durandus, *Rationale,* 19.

57. J. F. Russell, ed., *A Hand-Book of English Ecclesiology* (London: Joseph Masters, 1848), 16.

58. White, *The Cambridge Movement*, 88.

59. At this point, the Ecclesiologists were maintaining that the most superior expression of the Gothic style was to be found in Early English Gothic architecture.

60. John Mason Neale and Benjamin Webb, introduction to *The Symbolism of Churches and Church Ornaments,* by Guilielmus Durandus (Leeds: T. W. Green, 1843), CXXIII.

61. Neale and Webb, *Symbolism*, CXXIII.

62. In *Symbolism,* Neale and Webb write that the "State interfered more and more with the Church and, not allowed to carry out Her own designs, it is no wonder if the latter quickly began to forget Her own symbolic language." (CCXXIV).

63. Again in *Symbolism,* Neale and Webb ask rhetorically if this undesirable state of affairs is not plainly visible throughout the structure: "Does not its stiffness, its failure in harmony, its want of power and adaptation, its continual introduction of heraldry, its monotony, its breaking up by hard continued lines, its shallowness, its meretriciousness, its display,—set forth what we know to have been the character of the contemporary Church?" (CXXIV).

64. Neale and Webb, *Symbolism*, CXXV.

65. In *Symbolism,* Neale and Webb described flamboyant Gothic as "a vast collection of elegant forms, meaninglessly strung together: richness of ornament, . . . vagaries of tracery, as if the hand possessed of Church Art, were suddenly deprived of

Church feelings: nothing plain, simple, intelligible holy: parts neglected, parts ostentatious . . ." (CXXVI).

66. Neale and Webb, *Symbolism*, CXXVI-CXXVII.

67. Ibid., CXXIX.

68. Ibid., CXXX.

69. Ibid., CXXXI.

70. Ibid., CXXXII.

71. The stylistic terms and chronological divisions, "Early English," "Decorated" and "Perpendicular" under which English Gothic is still studied today were devised and first set forth in 1817 by Thomas Rickman, himself a Quaker.

72. G. A. Poole, *Churches: Their Structure, Arrangement, and Decoration* (London: J. Burns, 1846).

73. In the introduction to his book *Churches,* Poole noted that much of the material used in this book had originally appeared several years prior, when a series of lectures he had delivered to members of the Leeds Church of England Library and Reading-room had been published at their request. The 1846 edition, however, was new and expanded (V).

74. Poole, *Churches,* 63.

75. The Camdanians also claimed that, in his new book, Poole had "adopted several of the symbolic interpretations advanced by the writers of the Cambridge Camden Society." They did, however, concede that to the best of their knowledge, Poole was the first "to reassert that the octagonal form of Fonts was figurative of Regeneration." Neale and Webb, *Symbolism*, XXVIII.

76. W. Butterfield, *Instrumenta Ecclesiastica: A Series of Working Designs for the Furniture, Fittings and Decorations of Churches and their Precincts* (London: John Van Voorst, 1847).

77. *Ecclesiastical Gazette,* December 1858, 93.

78. Ecclesiological Late Cambridge Camden Society, *A Hand-Book of English Ecclesiology* (London: J. Masters, 1848).

79. J. F. Russell, ed., *Hierurgia Anglicana or Documents and Extracts Illustrative of the Ritual of the Church in England after the Reformation* (London: J. G. F. & J. Rivington, 1848).

80. W. H. Pierson, *Technology and the Picturesque: The Corporate and the Early Gothic Styles* (New York & Oxford: Oxford University Press, 1978), 122.

81. John Holden Green's St. John's Episcopal Church in Providence, Rhode Island (1810), is remarkably well preserved and a particularly good example of decorative Gothic.

82. M. Godefroy, a trained architect and former army officer, had come to Baltimore from France to serve as a professor of fine arts. Despite his European origins, Godefroy used Gothic more as an architectural order than an architectonic manifestation of interconnected doctrine.

83. In 1805, Benjamin Latrobe submitted two proposals for the new Roman Catholic cathedral in Baltimore, one using Gothic features, the other drawing on Roman classicism. Although it was the second proposal that was chosen, the Gothic plan has survived and serves as a lucid testimony of the decorative and superficial exploitation of Gothic that was common in this era.

84. Although himself a neoclassicist, Godefroy's use of Gothic in this instance was clearly to satisfy the religious preferences of his employers.

85. Stanton's *Gothic Revival* is widely recognized as the most authoritative discussion of English Ecclesiology and its effects on church architecture in the United States.

86. Stanton, *Gothic Revival*, 60-61.

87. Pierson, *Technology and the Picturesque*, 186.

88. Stanton, *Gothic Revival*, 161.

89. The importance of Frank Wills will be discussed later in this chapter.

90. In 1852, unable to meet all the requests addressed to him for church plans, he published *Upjohn's Rural Architecture, Designs, Working Drawings and Specifications for a Wooden Church and other Rural Structures* (New York: George P. Putman, 1852). In this book, he adapted much of his knowledge of English Ecclesiology and church building into structures that should be easily interpreted into the architectural context of rural America. See also Pierson, "The Board and Batten and the Gothic Revival Church," in *Technology and the Picturesque*, 432-455.

91. Pierson, *Technology and the Picturesque*, 211.

92. While the influence of various European prototypes is detectable, it is plainly evident that Renwick has drawn much of his inspiration from the cathedral of Cologne. This is especially obvious in the treatment of the lateral elevations.

93 . See J. Hughes, letter dated 29 May 1858, in Pierson, *Technology and the Picturesque*, 209.

94. Completion of St. Patrick's Cathedral was seriously delayed by the outbreak of the American Civil War. Archbishop Hughes died in 1864.

95. Pierson, *Technology and the Picturesque*, 269.

96. For this reason, many French Roman Catholic inhabitants of Montreal simply refer to the church as *La Paroisse*.

97. Many points of historical interest concerning the planning and construction of this church have been previously addressed with academic rigour and considerable insight by Franklin K. B. S. Toker, *The Church of Notre-Dame in Montreal: An Architectural History* (Montreal and London: McGill-Queen's University Press, 1970). In this study, I have used the French translation, *L'église Notre-Dame de Montréal : son architecture, son passé* (Quebec: Éditions Hurtubise HMH Limitée, 1981).

98. The events leading up to this choice are fully discussed in Toker, *L'église Notre-Dame de Montréal*, 62-64.

99. See James O'Donnell, letter dated 16 March 1824, to the Building Committee of Notre-Dame, in Toker, *L'église Notre-Dame de Montréal* , 209.

100. "Votre bâtisse devant être gothique et n'ayant étudié que l'architecture grecque et romaine, ce que j'ai cru suffisant pour le pays, je n'ai pris qu'une connaissance superficielle du gothique et je me crois de ce côté au-dessous de cette tâche." Thomas Baillargé quoted in G. Morisset, *L'Architecture en Nouvelle-France* (Quebec: Éditions du Pélican, 1980), 87.

101. Morisset, *L'Architecture*, 87.

102. Ibid.

103. A. Gowans, "Notre-Dame de Montréal," *Journal of the Society of Architectural Historians* 9 (March 1952), 25.

104. R. Traquair, *The Old Architecture of Quebec* (Toronto: Macmillan Co. of Canada, 1947), 2.

105. R. Hubbard, "Canadian Gothic," *Architectural Review* 116 (August 1954), 102-108.

106. M. Brosseau, *Le style néo-gothique dans l'architecture au Canada* (Ottawa: Centre d'édition du Gouvernement du Canada, 1980), 36.

107. L. Noppen, *Les églises du Québec (1600-1850)* (Quebec: Éditeur Officiel du Québec/Fides, 1977), 144.

108. Morisset, *L'Architecture*, 87.

109. The upper levels of the towers were added between 1841 and 1843, after O'Donnell's death in 1830, but with considerable fidelity to his final plans.

110. Similar arrangements of elevated frontal arcades can be seen at Lincoln Cathedral, although here, there are three separate arches. Perhaps the closest to the Montreal solution is the façade of Peterborough Cathedral. The façade of Peterborough is also anchored to either side by square towers. The horizontal dimension of both façades is reinforced by the strong vertical banding which is so characteristic of medieval English Gothic. Lichfield, and especially the Cathedral of Wells, have a strong horizontal presence.

111. The embattlements on the façade of Notre-Dame in Montreal are in some ways reminiscent of those cresting the west front of York Minster Cathedral.

112. M. Thurlby, "nineteenth century Churches in Ontario: A Study in the Meaning of Style," *Historic Kingston,* Kingston Historical Society, January 1987, vol. 35, 100.

113. *Christian Guardian,* 1830, 1 : 28, 219.

114. Perhaps the closest imitation is the parish church of Sainte-Anne-de-la-Pérade, designed by C. Coursol in 1869. There are, however, several other examples, such as the less felicitous façade that was added to the earlier church (1842-1843) of Saint-Michel in Yamaska (c. 1850). The parish church of Saint-Barthélémy, Quebec, designed by Victor Bourgeau in 1868, is clearly an Italianate adaptation of the volumes and spatial distribution of Notre-Dame.

115 . The architectural history of this church has been thoroughly documented by N. Pagé in *La Cathédrale Notre-Dame d'Ottawa* (Ottawa: Les Presses de l'Université d'Ottawa, 1988).

116. Although detailed architectural discussion is limited, M. O'Gallager's *Saint Patrick's, Quebec: The Building of a Church and of a Parish, 1827-1833* (Quebec: Carraig Books, 1981), offers a useful discussion of the planning and organization of this church-building project.

117. See Luc Noppen and Lucie K. Morisset, *La présence Anglicane à Québec* (Sillery: Les éditions du Septentrion, 1995) and Luc Noppen, *Les églises du Québec*, 158-169, 184-187.

118. Quoted in Pagé, *La Cathédrale,* 34.

119. John Medley, "Colonial Church Architecture," communicated by the Lord Bishop of Fredericton; being the substance of his speech delivered at the Anniversary Meeting of the Ecclesiological late Cambridge Camden Society, on Tuesday, 9 May 1848. *Ecclesiologist* (1848), 361.

120. Medley, "Colonial Church Architecture," *Ecclesiologist* (1848), 361.

121. K. Clark, *The Gothic Revival:* An essay in the History of Taste, 3rd ed. (Towbridge, Wiltshire: John Murray, 1983), 175.

122. Bermuda Archives Photo HC 1/87; HC 1/97; HC 1/968 and Bermuda Archives folio 6 Photo HC. Misc. I am grateful to Karla M. Hayward, Assistant Archivist, Bermuda Government Archives, for making this information available to me.

123. J. Medley had contributed to Keble's publication of the *Homilies of Saint John Chrysostom*, as well as to Keble's *Lives of the Fathers*. For further discussion, see Stanton, *Gothic Revival,* 129.

124. William Butterfield was the primary contributor to one of the Ecclesiologists' major publications, *Instrumenta Ecclesiastica* (London: J. Van Voorst, 1847). The publication was essentially a copybook that provided examples of architectural plans and elevations and minute architectural details such as roof crests and iron hinges. There had been a plan at one point to present each colonial bishop with a copy of this book, although it is not clear for how long or to what extent this project was acted upon.

125. This opinion is shared by a number of twentieth-century scholars, including P. Stanton who, in *Gothic Revival,* referred to Bishop Medley as "one of the most knowledgeable of the English clergymen preoccupied with the history of Gothic architecture and its revival in the nineteenth century" (127-128).

126. F. Wills, *Ancient English Ecclesiastical Architecture and its Principles Applied to the Wants of the Church at the Present Day* (New York: Stanford & Swords, 1850), 109-111, quoted in Stanton, *Gothic Revival,* 130. Wills subsequently designed a number of churches that were strongly reminiscent of the St. Anne Chapel, notably St. Michael's Church in Sillery. In doing so, Wills remained faithful to the prescriptions of Camdanian Ecclesiology and his mentor William Butterfield. At no point was his work reflective of Puginesque Gothic as Noppen and Morisset suggest in *La présence Anglicane à Québec,* 170. While both Pugin and the Ecclesiologists advocated a return to medieval Gothic, they sought their inspiration from archaeological prototypes that were, structurally and philosophically, dramatically different. Pugin drew his inspiration from the great churches of medieval France, while the Ecclesiologists sought their prototypes among the small rural churches of medieval England.

127. *The Church* 13, 37 (11 April 1850), 145.

128. Ibid.

129. Ibid.

130. Ibid.

131. Ibid.

132. Ibid., 146.

133. Ibid.

134. Ibid.

135. *The Church* 13, 38 (18 April 1850), 150.

136. *The Church* 13, 38 (18 April 1850), 150 and the *Canadian Ecclesiastical Gazette,* February 1851, 69

137. "Circular to the Clergy . . . ," *Canadian Ecclesiastical Gazette*, 8 January 1851, 64.

138. *The Canadian Ecclesiastical Gazette* served as the diocesan journal for the dioceses of Quebec, Montreal, and Toronto, thus included the Ottawa Valley.

139. *The Church* 13, 37 (11 April 1850) and *The Church* 13, 38 (18 April 1850).

140. *Ecclesiastical Gazette*, 8 January 1851, 64.

141. Ibid.

142. Ibid.

143. Bloxam's book enjoyed numerous new editions. The edition used in this study is M. Bloxam, *The Principles of Gothic Ecclesiastical Architecture with an Explanation of the Technical Terms and a centenary of Ancient terms*, 8th ed. (London: David Bogue, 1846).

144. The bishop also recommended Brandon's works on parish churches and suggested that those less familiar with architectural terminology might wish to acquire the three volumes of *Glossary of terms used in Architecture*. These publications were considered to be well illustrated, although the bishop felt that most examples were too costly for

the majority of new Canadian parishes. Before all else, a church should be "*finished* and *out of debt*, when it is opened for use, and so be ready for Consecration—although it should be necessary in order to gain these objects to make some sacrifice of architectural effect." *Canadian Ecclesiastical Gazette*, 9 January 1851, 64.

145. The bishop does mention that, on this point, "There is, however, authority against me," and refers to an article recently published in England, "Essay on Wooden Churches," by Rev. E. Scott in the *Canadian Ecclesiastical Gazette*. *Canadian Ecclesiastical Gazette,* 9 January 1851, 65.

146. "In new settlements it is often better to build in wood, unless stone is actually as cheap; because it frequently happens that the church first erected is not in the best position for the population, which afterwards grows up and sometimes has to be abandoned; or that the population increases so rapidly, as to require in a few years an all together new structure. It is not desirable to bestow much expenses upon wooden churches, in as much as they are in their nature temporary erections, but they should be substantial and good of their kind." *The Church* 13, 37 (11 April 1850), 146.

147. The Building Committee of *The Church* allowed a ration of one to three and a half, if the measure included the tower. *The Church* 13, 37 (11 April 1850), 146.

148. *Canadian Ecclesiastical Gazette,* 9 January 1851, 64.

149. These were described for the benefit of the reader as "a long and *very* narrow window with a pointed arch at the top," suggesting perhaps that these were as yet so scarce that the bishop had reason to believe a number of church builders would still be unfamiliar with them. See *Canadian Ecclesiastical Gazette,* 9 January 1851, 65.

150. The seating arrangement suggested for the choir was very similar to the one worked out in England by Rev. Hook and Rev. J. Jebb. The discussion was published by Rev. J. Jebb, *The choral service of the United Church of England and Ireland; being an inquiry into the liturgical system of the cathedral and collegiate foundations of the Anglican communion* (London: J. W. Parker, 1843). This solution was endorsed by the Ecclesiologists.

151. *Christian Guardian*, 24 April 1861, 66.

152. *Christian Guardian*, 10 March 1847, 82.

153. *Canadian Christian Examiner and Presbyterian Magazine*, March 1840, 91.

154. "The Church of England a Half-Reformed Church," *Edinburgh Christian Instructor*, as quoted in *Canadian Christian Examiner and Presbyterian Magazine*, March 1840, 91.

155. "Ontario Baptist Church and Edifice Society," *Canadian Baptist,* 8 February 1868, 3.

156. *Canadian Baptist,* 9 February 1871, 2.

157. *Canadian Baptist,* 24 February 1870, 4.

158. This article was a copy of a text read at the Elgin C. Ministerial Conference by the Rev. J. Cooper, London. See *Canadian Baptist*, 5 September 1867, 2.

159. Jeremy Taylor, "The Chapel is in the Heart," *Canadian Baptist*, 28 November 1867, 6.

CHAPTER FOUR

GOTHIC ARCHAEOLOGY AND ECCLESIOLOGY: The Introduction of Revived Medieval Tradition into the Ottawa Valley, 1850s–1870s

Inhabitants of Central Canada who avoided religious circles and declined to browse through the pages of sectarian journals were not immune to the discussion of religious architecture and the Christian merits of Gothic. In 1853, a Canadian literary magazine, the *Anglo-American*, carried an article in which William Hay expounded at length on the great contributions made by Pugin to the convalescence of church building. Hay was a Scottish Episcopalian, not a Roman Catholic, and when he spoke of the "revival of Christian architecture" he meant the revival of an archaeologically correct Gothic.[1] Furthermore, Hay was in a position to offer an informed opinion on this subject, if perhaps not a completely unbiased one.

Sacred Structures and Secular Interest

In Puginesque style, Hay made no effort to be diplomatic. Having informed the Canadian public that Gothic was the only style reflective of Christian thought and that, as such, it was perfectly adapted to the execution of Christian church buildings, he proceeded to denounce the use of every other style he had ever seen:

> For more than two hundred years had English Christianity been made to assume the architectural garb of every known system of Pagan mythology—the heathen temple, the Moorish mosque,

> the Chinese pagoda, or an olla podrida [*sic*] of all, whichever happened to strike the fancy of the architect.[2]

The effects of what Hay saw as two centuries of architectural negligence and abuse had been, in his mind, disastrous. His readers were told that the age-old symbols once used to render visible the elements of Christian faith, were no longer apparent on the very buildings in which Christian faith was practised.[3] Instead, adorned with "the outward marks of heathenism," Christian churches had become a "confused collection of pinnacle and minaret, pier and canopy—suggestive of an assemblage of foreign delegates at a peace convention."[4] While Hay decried the abandonment of Gothic in the construction of Christian churches, however, he made it very clear that he did not advocate the reinstatement of Gothic through an unstudied use of gratuitous or superficial Gothic form. He was specifically intolerant of the "fantastic specimens" and "arborial petrifications" of Batty Langley, claiming that the architectural writings of Langley had only served to pervert good taste. In comparing the writings of Pugin to those of Langley, Hay felt the shortcomings of the latter were painfully evident.

Despite his great admiration for Pugin, Hay nevertheless felt that the Canadian public should be alerted to the fact that occasionally there was "a strange un-English aspect" to some of Pugin's designs.[5] This inconvenience being noted, Hay stressed that all of Pugin's work was grounded in truth. Readers were informed that this truth was an important lesson, for it was on the foundation of one single principle, that of truth, that all good architecture was built. For the benefit of those Canadians who may not have been as intimately familiar with the writings of Pugin, Hay explained how truthfulness was achieved in the work of Pugin.[6] He then reviewed for his readers the architectural principles Pugin considered essential for architectural excellence.[7] His enthusiasm for Pugin's work was blatant. He even offered an excuse for the architect's conversion to Roman Catholicism. He noted that Pugin's conversion occurred at a time when the Catholic Church was devoting considerable effort to the construction of churches, thus implying that Pugin was probably motivated more out of a zeal for good Christian architecture than ideological solidarity with the teachings of the Church of Rome.[8] However, as William Westfall has justly pointed out, in his eagerness to promote Gothic as an architectural style uniquely suited to the embodiment of the Christian faith, Hay "confused architecture and ethics,"[9] thus transgressing one of the most basic rules of contemporary architectural critique. Similar transgressions were not uncommon in the nineteenth century.

Despite his preoccupation with Gothic perfection, Hay did not offer the Canadian public any great quantity of precise architectural instruction. What he did do was openly imply that the choice of any style other than Gothic would not reflect well on church builders' commitment to Christian culture. In 1854, a second article concerning church architecture appeared in the *Anglo-American Magazine.*[10] The author began with an overview of architectural theory, in which he contrasted the "majestic grandeur of the vast cathedral" with the equally valid, but architecturally different, "simple dignity of a village church." The reader was assured that both categories of ecclesiastical architecture, when properly executed, were deserving of admiration. This admiration, however, was earned for markedly different reasons. A cathedral was to incarnate the "sublime canonization of art," while a village church was to appear as if it came about as a "spontaneous creation of nature." To assume that the difference between these two types of ecclesiastical architecture was simply a question of scale and proportion was to completely and utterly misunderstand the most elementary principles of architecture. The author noted that Canadian church builders were particularly guilty of perpetuating this error, and suggested that this problem was so great that nearly every church in Canada was defiled by architectural inadequacies of some sort. There were almost no perfect examples of pure Gothic. He then continued to enumerate the imperfections of Canadian churches and in doing so provides an interesting contemporary perspective on the architectural landscape of nineteenth century Central Canada.[11] His inventory of faults, however, revealed more than a concern for architectural excellence:

> Nothing tends to deform our Canadian churches generally more than the great height of the walls contrasted with the squatness of the roof. . . . A steep roof is the beauty of a Gothic church. In the early English styles, the outline of the roof usually formed the two sides of an equilateral triangle. With a roof of this pitch, or even somewhat less, the walls need not be higher for rural churches than from nine to twelve feet, as the whole space within the roof may be gained by making the external boarding of the roof, also the ceiling of the church.
>
> While advocating the extension of the wooden element, we are not to be supposed as approving its application to illegitimate uses such as the mullions and tracery of the windows of a stone or brick church. The mullions and tracery of pure ecclesiastical edifices are essentially a portion of the wall, and had their origin in thinning and perforating that part for the purpose of admitting light. When circumstances will not admit [the] using of stone, it is better to be content with single perforations for the windows

after the manner of the early English. Nothing is more offensive to good taste than a want of truthfulness in ecclesiastical design.[12]

Despite the secular context, the author betrays himself as someone who is not innocently pursuing architectural perfection. While the tone of the article might be less abrasive than the previous article, the underlying theme is no less dogmatic. This author is clearly advocating a renewed use of medieval Gothic as interpreted by English revivalists; however, while the call for architectural "truthfulness" reflects the architectural theories of both Pugin and Anglican revivalists, the author's discussion of suitable church typology is clearly Camdanian. This is especially evident in the discussion of the vertical distribution of country churches and the superiority of Early English, or Early Pointed Gothic. It is also important to note, while considering this public discussion of sacred architecture, that the magazine in which both articles appeared was a secular publication.

During the winter of 1860, a correspondent for the *Montreal Gazette* identified the current era as an "age of church building" and suggested that readers were possibly interested in a brief update on church buildings in Canada.[13] Assuming that this was the case, the corespondent proceeded to describe, in considerable detail, the perfections of Holy Trinity, a small Anglican church that had recently been the object of extensive renovation (fig. 4.1). In its revised condition, the church was said to be reminiscent of a thirteenth-century English country church. The correspondent also explained that it's Early English interpretation of Gothic was also known as "Early Pointed" and was particularly well suited to the Canadian climate.[14] The reason for this fortunate acclimatization seemed to be linked to the facility with which the steeply sloping roofs shed snow.

A collection of modifications was considered to have contributed greatly to the overall improvement of the church. Each alteration moved the church further away from the plain rectangular ground plan of earlier tradition. Originally accessed by way of an axial door in the base of a frontal tower, the church now had a new entry on the lateral wall that was preceded by a small porch. Inside, but still very near the door, stood a stone baptismal font, imported especially from England to complement the other changes. A tower was completed and embellished by the addition of an elongated spire. The external appearance of the church was considered to have been greatly improved by the addition of various masonry details including drip stones, plinth courses, and buttresses.

Fig. 4.1. Holy Trinity (Anglican), Hawkesbury, after renovations of 1859.

Although a massive axial stone tower still fronts the church, few traces of the original structure are readily evident. It now bears the hallmarks of revived Gothic. These features are especially notable in the stepped-angle buttresses, the elongated broach spire, and the tracery of the large Gothic window. The pitch of the roof has also been significantly increased (Photo courtesy: Anglican Diocesan Archives, Ottawa).

The roof of Holy Trinity had been modified so as to acquire a new and much steeper pitch. Internal roof supports were replaced by Early English style rafters and the timbers of the roof trusses formed equilateral arches, which were in turn supported by wall corbels that were left open to the inside and considerably altered the presentation of the ceiling. Windows throughout the church were transformed into elongated lancets. In a striking departure from earlier tradition, all the windows were filled with stained glass, which included not only Scriptural passages and symbolic devices, but also a large amount of figural imagery depicting the life and works of Christ.

More significantly, the entire structure was considered to have been very much improved by the construction of a small but architecturally distinct chancel and a small vestry at the eastern end of the church. The floor of the chancel, which contained the sanctuary, was raised above the level of the nave and enclosed by a rail. The eastern wall of the sanctuary was opened by an elevated central arch flanked to either side by similar lancets of lesser height. The three divisions of the window were connected by slender shafts. The entire composition was unified by the hood of the dripstones. This arrangement, the reader was told, was similar to the one used at Salisbury Cathedral.[15] The entire church had now achieved the desirable situation of being "most imposing in appearance."[16] The remodeled church was also presented with a new silver communion service, and the correspondent from the *Montreal Gazette* suggested to readers that "such instances of Christian liberality are worthy of public notice because they are worthy of public imitation."[17]

The small Anglican church that received such attention in the secular press of Montreal was not built in Montreal, but in Hawkesbury, on the shores of the Ottawa River. Still preserved in the final decade of the twentieth century, Holy Trinity offers concrete evidence that Anglican church builders in the Ottawa Valley were well aware of the architectural discussions in other parts of the Empire and had been seriously rethinking their church-building traditions.

Construction of the original Holy Trinity Church had begun in 1844.[18] By 1857, the limestone church was judged in need of major renovations. Church wardens retained the services of local contractor John Higginson to build the chancel, porch, and spire, and to refit the interior of the church.[19] In his statement of work for the summer of 1857, Higginson reported that work had begun with the removal of the galleries and stairs. Galleries were considered deformities by most Ecclesiologists and were neither renovated or replaced.[20] The entryway was moved to the north side of the church and the spire completed.[21] Despite their small size, the new chancel and porch were reinforced with buttresses, as were the nave and tower, which had stood without assistance for a good decade and did not appear to have exhibited any signs of structural insecurity.

Structures of Transition

While Holy Trinity in Hawkesbury may have been one of the first Ottawa Valley churches to have significant portions overtly worked in medieval Gothic, it is not the first indication that Ottawa Valley church builders were attuned to the architectural discussions that had been attracting an ever increasing audience in Central Canada. Surviving evidence suggests that several years before revivalist ideals were implemented on a large scale, a number of their ideas had been cautiously seeping into the construction of new churches.

Few churches reflective of early experimentation with elements of revived Gothic have survived. Of those that do remain, either physically or in archival imagery, fewer still are considered to be particularly good examples of any easily identifiable category of Gothic. In truth, many are not, but this does not diminish their importance. It is precisely this understated evidence of a willingness to try, albeit with the greatest of caution, new formulas that move away from decades of architectural practice that renders these churches particularly interesting. Initially, few church builders ventured very far from traditional ground plans. Most Anglican churches built in the Ottawa Valley during the late 1840s and 1850s continued to be small single room structures (fig. 4.2). There appears to have been a certain reluctance to forsake the traditional parallelogram in order to include architecturally distinct chancels or even vestries. Nevertheless, discreet modifications to the superstructure suggest that a greater conformity to the plans and programs discussed in the Anglican press was indeed intended. Many of the earliest changes were introduced with such reserve that they may have passed with relatively little remark (fig. 4.3).

Many traditional arrangements were retained. Axial entries continued to be preferred. In keeping with older traditions, a single central door was usually flanked to either side by a Gothic lancet. When a tower was present, it was invariably central, with the base doubling as entry and vestibule. In churches without towers, a window in the gable end continued to be common, although the opening was often further beneath the apex of the gable than it had been in earlier buildings. Another characteristic of churches built during the transitory phase is the understated lateral wall. Lateral walls were no longer built as high as their counterparts in earlier churches.[22] As church builders did not reduce the height of the gable end, the squatness that characterized the roofs of many earlier churches also began to fade. With the steepening pitch of the roof and the contracted height of the nave walls, the lateral windows were unavoidably affected. Regardless of how parishioners might have felt about the role of reduced lighting in the creation of a prayerful atmosphere, the lack of wall forced the abandonment of the great Gothic windows that were so characteristic of churches built before the 1840s.

Fig. 4.2. St. Augustine (Anglican), Prospect, 1854.

Typical of many Anglican churches from this era, this small rural church is noticeably different from earlier counterparts such as St. John (1838), in South March (fig. 1.6). Both churches are built with local stone, and St. Augustine has retained an axial entry. The spatial distribution differs notably in the redistribution of the wall/roof ratio and in the reduced size of the windows (Photo: A. Erdmer).

Fig. 4.3. St. Augustine (Anglican), Prospect, 1854.

The height of the walls has been dramatically reduced in favour of a larger roof surface. The windows are considerably smaller than those traditionally built into Anglican churches just a few years earlier (Photo: A. Erdmer).

In the village of Richmond, the builders of St. John, 1859, retained an axial entry in the base of a massive central tower, as well as a rectangular floor plan in the nave area. They did not, however, build the lateral walls to their traditional height. The understated height of the nave and increased slope of the roof contrast with the solid monumentality of the tower. More significantly, the sanctuary was housed in an architecturally distinct chancel. Despite the boldness of this move, the chancel itself, in contrast to the frontal tower, is marked by a cautious narrowness. Although the single lancet is asymmetrically placed in the end wall of the chancel, the window is positioned to be aligned with the central axis of the church. An equally diminutive vestry clings the northern flank of the chancel and, contrary to all Ecclesiological laws of dignity and decorum, opens directly into the sanctuary (fig. 4.4).

Fig. 4.4. St. John (Anglican), Richmond, 1859.
Builders of St. John's Church were among the first in the Ottawa Valley to experiment with new architectural ideas, although they did not orient the chancel to the east end. A traditional axial tower was retained on the façade of the church; however, the slope of the roof was much greater than that of many earlier churches, and the height of the lateral walls was much reduced, which, in turn, affected the size of the narrower and necessarily shorter lateral windows (Photo: V. Bennett).

The extent to which a new interest in reshaping places of collective worship is evident even among some of the most modest country churches. Simple wooden churches such as St. Peter (Anglican), Alfred, 1859, and St. Mary (Anglican), Navan, 1862, presage the more dramatic changes that appear during the 1860s.[23] By the late 1850s, the influence of the revived medieval style is increasingly evident, even in very modest rural constructions. While traditional tracery commonly found on survival Gothic churches has been retained above entryways, the general outline of the church reflects an interest in revived Gothic. The slope of the roof is no longer influenced by classical architecture, but reproduces the Early English equilateral triangle, and vertical planking is used to accentuate an upward movement.

English Archaeological Gothic

Although churches representing a subtle transition between the traditional use of Gothic and the new interest in fidelity to medieval prototypes can be recognized, the earliest known example of an overtly Camdanian interpretation of medieval Gothic did not appear in the Ottawa Valley until the late 1850s. It was not until the early 1860s that these architectural changes appeared in the construction of new churches. Typically, church builders used archaeological Gothic to varying degrees, some much more markedly than others, some more successfully than others. In the Ottawa Valley, two churches in particular, St. Paul in Almonte and St. Alban the Martyr in Ottawa, were considered by contemporaries to be near "perfect" examples of archaeologically correct Gothic. Both were built for Anglican congregations and are of particular interest as they were widely discussed at the time of their construction. Furthermore, both are comparatively well documented and have survived into the final decade of the twentieth century with a good portion of their original design still intact.

During the spring of 1862, the parishioners of St. Paul in Almonte decided the time had come to build a church. A committee was formed and members selected. By the time the committee held its first meeting on August 14 of that same year, one zealous member had already acquired the plans that had been used for the construction of the Anglican church in Lynn.[24] At a subsequent meeting held in February 1863, the committee decided to use the specifications of the church in Lynn, although some modifications were later introduced. The St. John the Baptist (Anglican) Church in Lynn had been designed in 1860 by Thomas Fuller, the same architect who was credited with giving the Hawkesbury church its distinctive "early English" flavour. Contrary to the Hawkesbury project where the liberty of design was challenged by the structural residue of an earlier church, Fuller was able to realize his ideas more fully on the new site.[25]

While the church was still under construction, St. Paul (fig. 4.5) drew considerable attention and enthusiastic reviews. The *Canadian Churchman* announced that, of all the churches in the diocese, St. Paul

Fig. 4.5. St. Paul (Anglican), Almonte, 1863.

The principal entry is through a small side porch. Paired lancets in the gable end reflect Christological symbolism. The quatrefoil alludes to the universality of the Gospels. Four was also considered to represent the cardinal directions and God's creative power, as well as the rivers of Paradise. The enclosing circle is again emblematic of totality (Photo: V. Bennett).

was "the most correct, in its ecclesiastical details"[26]—despite the fact that the west end was almost due east. During the Episcopal visit of September 1863, it was reported that the bishop had been extremely pleased with the project and that he had referred to the new church as "a perfect gem."[27] On the occasion of its consecration, St. Paul was admired for the solidity of its stonework and praised for the quality of its Gothic programme. More significant in terms of ecclesiastical architecture, St. Paul, with its cut-stone cornices, mullions and other architectural refinements, was described by contemporaries as being "an ornament not only to the neighbourhood in which it is erected but to the Diocese at large, as it is generally admitted to be the most perfect in ecclesiastical architecture of all the country churches in the Diocese of Ontario."[28]

While St. Paul was intended as the principal Anglican church in Almonte and was built under the direct supervision of several local and wealthy individuals, the situation was very much different with the construction of the other great example of archaeologically correct Gothic in the Ottawa Valley, St. Alban the Martyr. This church was built in Ottawa during the mid-1860s specifically to accommodate the influx of civil servants when the seat of government was transferred from Quebec City.[29] The rector of the new parish, Rev. Thomas Bedford-Jones, had already determined that the new church was to conform both architecturally and liturgically to the revivalist school of thought.[30]

Unlike St. Paul, Almonte, at which one individual had been in effect the driving force of the building committee, the construction committee of St. Alban originally included no less than eighteen individuals.[31] This committee had intended to offer £25 for the best design, but when Thomas Fuller donated a set of plans, the parish gratefully accepted.[32] Despite its promising start, the construction of St. Alban was not destined to be a particularly harmonious project. While St. Alban and St. Paul figure among the most comprehensive and clearly the most faithful constructions of archaeologically inspired Gothic in the Ottawa Valley, they were in no way the only examples.

Surroundings

During the middle decades of the 1900s, land was still plentiful and affordable in much of the Ottawa Valley. Few parishes had difficulty in securing sites that conformed to the seclusion from the noises

Fig. 4.6. St. Luke (Anglican), Eardley, 1864.

The interest in the revival of a medieval-style Gothic church building was felt even on simple log structures. Here, the original log church, with vertical planking on the upper portion of the gable ends, can be seen from the sanctuary end. A vestry and side porch were built against the side wall of the church (Photo courtesy: Anglican Diocesan Archives, Ottawa).

of mills and factories and the traffic of everyday activity recommended by many Anglican Church officials. This is especially evident in the site choices of rural or small village churches, where noise and traffic would not have posed a significant challenge to the choice of any site.

Preservation of this original environment can be seen at St. Thomas Church in Bristol (1875) and in the archival documentation of the Church of the Good Shepherd (now lost) in Plantagenet. While the preference for seclusion is reflected in the choice of many Anglican church sites, it was not always possible to secure such sites in rapidly growing towns. Limited by their financial resources, the parishioners of St. Alban in Ottawa bought only a very modest piece of land for their new church. The site was so small that, once completed, only the northern flank of the church did not abut the property line. Although the site itself was to impose innumerable hardships on the parish, the building of St. Alban affords an excellent example of the Gothic adaptability in the face of adversity.[33] Serious geological restrictions contributed to and were aggravated by a constant shortage of monetary resources and necessitated frequent and major revisions to the original plan.[34]

Gothic revivalists had not been content to merely address the placement and positioning of a church building. They also offered church builders precise instructions concerning the most desirable arrangement for all other features that could or, in their minds, should be associated with a church site. It was considered that along with a properly aligned cemetery,[35] a well-designed site plan should also make provision for a rectory. While same-site cemeteries were common in the Ottawa Valley, rectories were frequently off-site but close at hand. When rectories were on-site, they were representative of contemporary domestic architecture. Only in rare instances were rectories designed to have stylistic and architectural continuity with the church. Perhaps the most successful example of this can be seen at St. Paul, Almonte (fig 4.5). Here, material and a certain degree of stylistic continuity is evident in the masonry, treatment of gables, as well as in the sequencing and proportioning of the roof line. The windows, however, unlike those of the church, are simple rectangles. Gothic is used to distinguish the house of the God from the house of the rector.[36]

Although the interpretation and implementation of Ecclesiastical recommendations varied, most parishes were increasingly attentive to the maintenance and upkeep of their church site. The grazing of sheep and cattle on the church grounds was no longer tolerated. Instead, Ottawa Valley Anglicans began to place a new importance on church buildings surrounded by tidy, well-kept grounds. This could be achieved in a number of ways. In certain instances it meant establishing fixed regulations relating to burial practice. This concern for the immediate environment is also evident in parishes where the actual church building dates from an earlier era. In 1857, it was decided at a vestry meeting of Christ Church, Huntley, that intramural burial would be forbidden and that no new graves be placed within ten, but preferably twenty feet of the church walls.[37] Although the Huntley regulations may have been more representative of contemporary trends, the rules and regulations determining burial practices in and around Anglican church buildings did vary. In Portage-du-Fort, both Mary Seaton (d. 1862) and her husband, George William Usborne (d. 1886) were buried beneath the nave of St. George's Church.[38] This practice was neither encouraged or discouraged with any vigour by Ecclesiologists; however, in the Ottawa Valley, intramural burial remained very rare.

A characteristic of many Ottawa Valley church sites that is frequently overlooked is the horse shed. Although few have survived, horse sheds appeared on church sites with increasing regularity during the third and fourth quarter of the nineteenth century. This useful but decidedly unecclesiastical feature does not appear to have ever been discussed by English Ecclesiologists; even in condemnation, their presence cannot be simply dismissed as irrelevant. Horse sheds were in no way an exclusively Anglican phenomenon and occupied both a significant and conspicuous portion of many church sites. They were discussed with regularity in parish minutes and vestry notes, and were usually hailed as a sign of progress.

Orientation

With the new interest in medieval Gothic came an increased tendency for Ottawa Valley Anglicans to build their churches so that the longitudinal axis of the central nave ran east-west. In keeping with revivalist thinking, the sanctuary, or when possible a chancel, was placed at the easternmost end of many churches.[39] The concern for literal orientation was common but not universal in the Ottawa Valley. This is well illustrated by St. Paul, Almonte (fig. 4.7). Despite the reputation of this church for Gothic perfection and its architecturally distinct chancel, the sanctuary is not oriented. Although the longitudinal axis of St. Paul runs roughly east-west, the sanctuary is at the westernmost end. Anomalies of orientation aside, this arrangement arguably allowed for a better adaptation of the church to the site. St. Bartholomew in the Ottawa neighbourhood of New Edinburgh is oriented north-south with a sanctuary at the southern most end. The church is, nevertheless, set as far back from the street as the modest lot would permit, and much of its environmental integrity is assured by its immediate proximity to the grounds of Rideau Hall.

Entries

By the second half of the nineteenth century, few Anglicans were willing to have their churches directly accessible to the secular world. Coinciding with this concern was a marked shift away from the bold façades and axial entries that had previously dominated Anglican church architecture. The entry into many churches built during this era was no longer through the gable end or front of the church, but through a small side door. This entry was usually preceded by an understated porch, an arrangement particularly useful in the construction of very small churches.[40] By means of a single and structurally simple modification, the focus of the entry was reoriented.

The sanctuary was no longer directly accessible, either in physical or visible terms. Regardless of the size of the church building or the affluence of a congregation, the side entry was to become a standard feature of the final quarter of this century.[41]

Fig. 4.7. St. Paul (Anglican), Almonte, 1863.
A double battened door is placed beneath an arched hood mould and a relieving arch. Both arches are Gothic and spring from a point level with the lower end of the porch gable. Ecclesiologists considered this simple arrangement to be proof of the superiority of English over French architecture as it symbolized the two natures of Christ joined in one person (Photo: A. Erdmer).

Towers and Bell-gables

Despite the move away from the architecturally bold façade and entryway, towers that had figured so prominently in earlier constructions were not abandoned. Ottawa Valley church builders now preferred towers placed along the lateral wall of the church nave. The tower base commonly doubled as the porch for the side entry or the vestry. Towers had been a conspicuous part of the original building plans for both St. Paul, Almonte (fig. 4.8), and St. Alban, Ottawa, although neither was ever built.[42] Had either of these towers been completed as planned, they would have offered an important display

Fig. 4.8. St. Paul (Anglican), Almonte, 1888.
The church is depicted with a tower which was never built (Source: *Canadian Architect and Builder*, 1, 8, September 1888).

of Gothic refinement. Less ambitious tower-building projects were planned and completed, although rarely without difficulty or delay. At many sites where less ambitious towers had been planned, their construction was frequently delayed or abandoned altogether in times of fiscal restraint.[43]

Church bells continued to be highly valued by many Anglicans during the nineteenth century. The importance of church bells as an integral part of Christian practice as well as their history, "mystical signification," and practicality had been set forth for public enlightenment by the Ecclesiologists.[44] Although various points of historical distinction were addressed, significant portions of the discussion were marred by an unbridled use of exaggerated and occasionally gratuitous symbolism. This unfortunate indulgence, frequently accompanied by the advocacy of androcratic symbolism detracted from the substance of concurrent scholarship.[45] Much of this discussion, including serious applications, such as the tolling (rather than the chiming) of bells during the Quadragesima and Septuagesima and the role of bells in the marking of canonical hours, went well beyond the practice or interest of most Ottawa Valley Anglicans. Still, few Ottawa Valley parishes were willing to do without bells as they were considered by many to be an integral and important feature of the church building. Even when monetary hardship did not allow for the construction of suitable towers, many parishioners demonstrated that they were not willing to forego the use of bells for want of a decent tower. Years earlier, this might have been difficult to resolve while still maintaining stylistic continuity and structural integrity; there was now, however, a solution suggested by the promoters of medieval Gothic that was both archaeologically and ecclesiologically correct: the bell-gable. Indeed, George Ayliffe Poole noted in *Churches their structure, arrangement and decoration* that "a good bell-gable is ten times more beautiful than a wretched steeple. . . ."[46] For Anglican church builders in the Ottawa Valley bell-gables or bell-cotes proved to be an enduring and eminently practical solution. They appeared on many small churches and continued to offer a gracious face-saving solution, especially when monetary restrictions forced the abandonment of more ambitious tower-building programmes (fig. 4.9).

A tower had also been planned for the church of St. Alban the Martyr, in Ottawa, but it too fell victim to structural modifications and eventually had to be abandoned due to instability of the soil on the site (fig. 4.10). At St. Alban, a bell-gable was placed to mark the transition between the nave and the chancel and doubles as a sanctecote. The door by which one actually entered the church also now enjoyed a very great increase in symbolic importance. Ecclesiologists used the Gospel of John 10:9—"I Am the Door: by Me if any man enter in, he shall be saved"[47]—to justify Christological symbolism at the entryways of churches.[48] Despite the growing tendency to move the principal entry from an axial position on the western façade to a smaller side porch, the western end, although in some ways understated, was not destined to remain blank. Windows, usually elongated Gothic lancets, were opened in the western gable end of the church. This afforded some compensation for the loss of window space that had occurred with the reduction of the lateral walls. Anglican architectural specialists maintained that Trinitarian symbolism was inappropriate at the western end of a church, owing to its very specific affiliation with Christ and the door. Christ was thought to be best represented by couplets so as to symbolize the duality (human/divine) of His nature.

Fig. 4.9. St. Paul (Anglican), Fitzroy Township, 1887.
This small country church is entered by an axial tower on the main façade. It is carefully oriented with the sanctuary to the east. The tower is gradually staged back in the manner of Early English buttress building and topped by a bell cote. This arrangement allowed both considerable stylistic continuity and economy (Photo: A. Erdmer).

Fig. 4.10. St. Alban (Anglican), Ottawa, 1866.
This nineteenth-century illustration gives a better perspective than is possible today. The roof descends to within a few feet of the ground leaving only limited space for windows which remain subordinate. Externally, the transition between the nave and chancel is marked by a sanctecote and chancel walls that are significantly taller than those of the nave. This illustration also depicts the original eastern window. The architect used an Early English formula, flanking an elongated lancet with two of lesser height. The three windows were unified by a single-hood moulding (Photo courtesy: Anglican Diocesan Archives, Ottawa).

With the removal of the central doorways, the western end of the church was now fully exploitable in symbolic terms. Pairs of elongated windows were installed and devoted to the memory of Christ's ministry on Earth and the salvation He offered.[49] In doing this, the western end of the church came to be symbolic of Christ, the mystical door, the only door through which one could truly enter the church. The spiritual significance of this passage from the profane to the sacred was again underscored by the new location of the baptismal font. Many Anglican parishes now moved their font from the sanctuary to a new position near the main entry where it served to remind all who entered of their own spiritual entry into the church through the sacrament of baptism. The font was also used to reinforce the fact that the physical church was in its own way a sacred space, a space set apart for the initiated.

During the first half of the nineteenth century, very few parishes had proper baptismal fonts. It was much more common to have a small basin set aside for administration of this sacrament. Many poorer parishes simply used whatever was available when the need arose. During the second half of the nineteenth century, Anglicans were increasingly looking to offer tangible reverence to this sacrament. A stone font was presented to Holy Trinity, Hawkesbury, in 1857.[50] It had been ordered directly from a firm in Exeter, England, at a time when production of such liturgical objects was still rare in Central Canada.[51] In December 1865, a stone baptismal font was presented to St. Alban by two parishioners who worked locally as professional stonecutters.[52] The St. Alban's font, like the font imported to Hawkesbury from England, was octagonal.[53] Both fonts are representative of a renewed and heightened use of symbolism. The octagon though long associated with the baptismal doctrine of regeneration, had slipped out of current usage among many Anglicans. Ecclesiologists understood the octagon as a composite of seven, symbolizing perfection, plus one, thus symbolizing continuity. [54]

Fig. 4.11. St. Bartholomew (Anglican), Ottawa, 1868.
The sanctuary was distinguished only by internal finishing and the eastern window. The sanctuary floor was elevated three steps above the floor of the nave. The baptismal font can be seen immediately in front of the principal side entry (Photo courtesy: Anglican Diocesan Archives, Ottawa).

Nave

Despite its prominence near the entry of the church, the new position of the baptismal font was not the only modification readily apparent. The church interior was no longer bright or austere. Instead, those entering were now enveloped by soft lighting. Lower levels of light were no longer feared as an entry for superstition, but were increasingly considered to be conducive to a quiet and prayerful state.[55] This semi-obscurity contributed to an atmosphere of sacred mystery. It was necessary to pause a moment while the eyes refocused on the opposing wall of the nave, and visitors were prevented from intruding without ceremony into the church.[56]

Initially, the most striking feature of these walls was their height. They were no longer tall or important, but had been reduced to a human scale. Yet these new churches were neither squat nor low,[57] for the vertical height lost by the walls was taken up by the roof. The increased height of the roof and the reduction in the height of the walls had a very direct result on the lighting in this part of the church. Gone were the great wide windows with their clear glazing that admitted volumes of unaltered daylight. The new low walls simply did not allow for the larger windows that were in many ways the hallmarks of earlier construction. Strict Ecclesiologists would have preferred to see every iota of church fabric gravid with Ecclesiological symbolism;[58] however, during the third quarter of the nineteenth century, church builders in the Ottawa Valley preferred to retain a relatively simple and unified spatial elevation in the nave. The triforium and clerestory appear only rarely in Anglican churches of the Ottawa Valley, Christ Church Cathedral, Ottawa, being a notable exception. In some instances, the height of the lateral wall dropped until the lateral walls were very low and, with neither clerestory or triforium, the traditional systems for lighting elongated churches were very much reduced. Occasionally it was necessary to break the lateral eaves with gabled windows. In other instances, small dormers or "chien-assis" are opened in the slope of the roof.

The church of the Good Shepherd, Plantagenet, was typical of churches from this era that sought to replicate medieval Gothic with very low walls, significantly pitched roofs and correspondingly small windows (fig 4.12).[59] It was also recommended that windows be smaller and less common than was previously traditional. This would have apparently reduced the glare of the summer sun and the glare of the winter snow.[60] It is not clear, however, as to why these climatic conditions did not cause an equivalent level of concern among other denominations.

Fig. 4.12. Good Shepherd (Anglican), Plantagenet, 1875.
Within the Anglican Church, the influence of Camdanian Ecclesiology was eventually to be felt through the whole range of church building. In Plantagenet, the church of the Good Shepherd achieves much of its vertical height through the steep pitch of the roof. The lateral walls are not much taller than the three small boys that stand in front of the church (Photo courtesy: Anglican Diocesan Archives, Ottawa).

Contracted dimensions of the windows naturally restricted the amount of daylight that was allowed to enter the church; these already-reduced quantities of light were further diminished by the introduction of coloured glass. The design used for the window glass could be either figural or geometric, and painted Scriptural texts continued to be popular. Although simple geometric motifs had been used as edge-work in older churches, simple geometric motifs were now not as much of a reflection of conservative parishes as a reflection of modest means (fig. 4.13).

Figural imagery was a new feature and represented a significant departure from earlier convention. This new acceptance of the use of figural imagery in a religious context must be seen as a significant break with earlier tradition. The same stained glass that manipulated and transformed the daylight into Scriptural texts and imagery also played an important part in establishing and maintaining the aura of dignity and prayer inside a parish church. One of the earliest and

Fig. 4.13. St. Paul (Anglican), Almonte, 1863.

The stark elegance of the lateral windows reflects skilful use of Early English styling. The window gables break the roof line to achieve the height necessary to efficiently light the nave. The tracery of the window echoes the Christological and evangelical symbolism of the main façade. Each gable is set with two lancets surmounted by a quatrefoil. The three separate windows are unified by a drip stone moulding that follows the intrados face of the voussoirs (Photo: A. Erdmer).

most expansive iconographic programs appeared during the makeover of Holy Trinity, Hawkesbury. At the time of their installation, the windows attracted considerable interest and demonstrated the extent to which the church builders were influenced by developments in the British Isles.[61]

Although walls were frequently understated, the opposite was true of ceilings. In lieu of plastered surfaces or false ceilings, the roof timbers were allowed to appear internally. The advocates of a return to medieval Gothic were very much against the use of ornate plastered ceilings.[62] Many Anglican congregations in the Ottawa Valley now gathered beneath open timbers of unceiled roofs that rose high above them. Rafters, tie-beams, roof trusses, and struts were all stained with dark oils. This inexpensive and very effective combination of open timbers and dark stain allowed even very small churches to create the impression of a great space.[63] It was a solution particularly well suited to the many congregations in the Ottawa Valley where money was scarce and good timber was abundant.

Much in keeping with earlier habit, the floors of the nave continued to be very plain. The occasional embellishment rarely consisted of more than a simple geometric motif painted on the floor boards. Ecclesiologists had warned that crosses were not to be used on the floor,[64] although heraldic devices were acceptable.[65] On this point, revivalists were not offering anything new. Christological reference using floor-level imagery had been frowned upon since late antiquity, and church patrons in the Ottawa Valley rarely came from families in which the heraldic devices were figures of prominent relevance. What did concern many parishioners was the leasing or ownership of prestigiously located pews. The well-placed pew had long been an icon of social standing. Furthermore, in newly settled areas such as the Ottawa Valley, the pew had been a tangible symbol of success that members of an increasingly affluent middle class could acquire even without ties to the upper echelons of a highly stratified British class system. However, closely associated with the renewed interest in medieval Gothic was an increasingly prevalent intolerance of the traditional box pew, the ornate pew, and the personal pew.

Since the early 1850s, Anglican Church officials in Central Canada had been actively working to regulate the pew trade. In 1850, *The Church* advised builders that all pews in the nave were to face the chancel and were to be doorless.[66] They could be equipped with kneelers, but were to remain unlined, though cushions were permitted. Church builders were now recommended to strive for a greater visual unity and social equality within the church by furnishing it throughout with a single pew type. Pews were to be solid but visually understated; it was considered unnecessary for the backs of pews to exceed a height of three feet.[67] During his tour of Central Canada in 1859, the Bishop of London, England, addressed Canadian members of the Church of England in a series of visitation lectures. A recurrent theme in these lectures was the shortcomings of the pew system.[68] The text of these lectures was published in the *Canadian Ecclesiastical Gazette* and was, thus, made much more accessible to the general public than the bishop himself. By the 1860s, concern among Ottawa Valley Anglicans about the merits of pew rental was growing. Experiments with "free" sittings were introduced in several parishes, notably at St. Paul, Almonte, and St. Alban, Ottawa (fig. 4.14).

These attempts at a more democratic approach to the distribution of church seats met with varying degrees of success. Pew rental was avoided at St. Paul, Almonte, from the time of construction until 1878 when it was introduced to avert impending financial disaster. At St. Alban, Ottawa, the abolition of pew rental was an integral part of the founding principles of the church. The rector of the newly formed parish noted that the old practice of pew rental resulted in a financially-based social stratification.[69] The *Canadian Churchman*

Fig. 4.14. St. Alban (Anglican), Ottawa, 1866.

The eastern window in the chancel has been changed and is now a tripartite but single window. Below it is an ornate Gothic reredos and altar. Large organ pipes can be seen against the northern and eastern walls of the sanctuary, immediately behind the chancel arch. The ceilings of both the chancel and the nave have been covered with wood paneling. The small mitred archway immediately south of the chancel leads to a vestry (Photo courtesy: Anglican Diocesan Archives, Ottawa).

announced to the rest of country that St. Alban was "to be a FREE CHURCH, ever open to Christian Worshippers, and its ministers are to be wholly maintained (if possible) by weekly offerings of grateful hearts. . . ."[70] While coronary appreciation can be difficult to quantify in mercantile terms, fiscal realities were such that the Rev. Bedford-Jones was obliged to solicit funds from outside the local community. In doing so, the absence of pew fees was not presented essentially as the primary reason for the shortage of funds, but as a point of merit that distinguished the parish as a deserving recipient of any charitable donation.[71] One very tangible outcome of all these efforts was a greater attempt at the uniform construction of understated, open-ended pews, an arrangement preferred by English revivalists, who also felt that uniform seating would help draw the eye towards the altar.[72]

During the course of this visual journey towards the altar, it becomes increasingly evident that the introduction of a revived medieval Gothic coincided not only with a significant restructuring of the sanctuary area, but also with new concern for the visual primacy of the Eucharistic celebration. Canadian church authorities were now recommending that a central passage no less than four feet

Fig. 4.15. St. John (Anglican), Richmond, 1859.
The altar has retained its traditional position beneath an axial eastern window, but is styled more closely to a sacrificial altar than to the traditional Eucharistic table. Arched panels on the front of the altar are inscribed with an alpha, a superimposed IHS, and an omega. The choir seats are placed parallel to the central axis of the church. The text above the chancel reads: "My house shall be called a house of prayer" (Photo courtesy: Anglican Diocesan Archives, Ottawa).

wide should run through the main body of the church to the sanctuary.[73] The very fact that the altar had replaced the pulpit as the primary focal point at this end of the church was indicative of a significant repositioning of liturgical priorities.

Over the course of the third quarter of the nineteenth century, the growing influence of Camdanian Ecclesiology became increasingly evident in the Anglican architecture of the Ottawa Valley. Under their influence, a much greater emphasis was placed on the sacrament of the Eucharist, and in contrast with earlier practice, Holy Communion was now received by more people and with greater frequency. Although there initially had been some concern that the Eucharist, if received too frequently, would lose much of the sense of privilege with which it was associated, the contrary proved true. The builders of Gothic churches saw to that.

In contrast to earlier arrangements where the financially privileged were in immediate proximity to the centre of cult activity, churches built in the revived Gothic style exacted a greater measure between laity and liturgy. No longer was it considered appropriate to allow the first row of worshippers to press against and peer directly into the sanctuary. Arrangements of this sort were considered to lack a certain dignity and clearly did not contribute to an atmosphere of sacred mystery. Older church buildings, such as Pinhey's church of St. Mary, were now criticized for their lack of sanctuary space.[74] What church builders now needed was a space that would both emphasize and set apart the Eucharist while still surrounding it with a sense of awe and privilege. Several steps could be taken to remedy this problem, and, once again Ottawa Valley church builders were drawn to Camdanian solutions.

Unquestionably, the construction of an architecturally distinct chancel was the preferred solution. The chancel had the greatest visual impact, both in terms of setting Eucharistic ritual apart and for surrounding it with a sense of awe and mystery. Anglican church leaders in Central Canada had been advocating the construction of chancels and referring church builders to Canadian treatises for some time. In keeping with English tradition, chancels built in Ottawa Valley churches during this period were flat ended. Frequently, but not exclusively, they were architecturally distinct from the main body of the church. The roof line was often, but not invariably, lower than that of the main body of the church. Privilege inside the chancel area was emphasized physically, symbolically, and decoratively. The chancel was to be both narrower and of a lesser height than the main body of the church, and the intersection of the two areas defined by a chancel arch.[75] Entry into the chancel sanctuary was restricted by the footings of the chancel arch and was further reduced by the presence of chancel rails. Inside, the sanctuary floor was elevated above the floor level of the nave. When finances permitted, walls were often painted in privileged colours traditionally reserved for royalty, such as cobalt and royal blues, deep purples, and gold.[76] The finest stained glass was usually placed in the eastern window of the chancel where the iconographic programme alluded frequently, but not exclusively, to the mystical dimensions of the Trinity. This was most frequently achieved by the use of triplets. However, despite the equality of the Trinity, the eastern lights were often composed of an elongated central lancet flanked to either side by similar lancets of a lesser height (fig. 4.16).

The focal point of the chancel, the altar table, stood immediately beneath the windows of the eastern wall. It was to be placed on a raised platform and preferably enclosed with a rail. The table and surrounding railing were, in keeping with the ordinances of the church

Fig. 4.16. Holy Trinity (Anglican), Hawkesbury, after internal renovations of 1859.

The eastern windows of the chancel were arranged to echo one of the most distinctive features of Early English Gothic, an elongated lancet flanked by identical lancets of lesser height. Externally, these windows were joined by arched shafts and covered by a single arched drip stone (Photo courtesy: Anglican Diocesan Archives, Ottawa).

edifice itself, to be solid and substantial.[77] Those adhering to strict Camdanian Ecclesiology used wooden communion tables; others suggested that the use of stone altars was equally acceptable.[78] In the Ottawa Valley, wood remained the preferred material, but probably due primarily to availability and cost. The pulpit was to be placed at the northwestern angle of the chancel and the reading desk at the southwestern angle. Neither the pulpit nor the reading desk was to be placed along the central axis of the church, as this would block the view of the altar table.[79] Acts of worship should be focused towards the east.[80] The pulpit was also to remain at the eastern end of the church.[81] The reading desk was usually placed within the sanctuary rails, but not too far from them. In this manner the clergyman could be distinctly leading the people yet still be among them.[82] Most pulpits and lecterns used in the Ottawa Valley during this period were wooden constructions.[83]

Fig. 4.17. St. Luke (Anglican), Eardley, 1864.

During the 1870s, the original logs were covered with planking, and a substantial tower was built above the vestry. The church is seen here undergoing renovations during the summer of 1990. Human scale, provided by the person painting the tower, serves to illustrate the narrowness of the original structure and the steep angle of the roof (Photo: V. Bennett).

The vestry itself was becoming increasingly common during this period; however, under no condition was the door from the vestry to open into the enclosed portion of the sanctuary. With a growing importance given to the clergy, it was no longer acceptable to have a small section of the church curtained off. Increasingly, new vestries were architecturally distinct, often forming a counterbalance to the side porch. If space allowed, it was permissible to have an area reserved for the choir and its accompanying organ at the westernmost end of the chancel. A space at least five feet wide was to be left open between the easternmost row of seats and the chancel.[84] While sanctuaries were housed in architecturally distinct chancels and, by the second half of the nineteenth century, this had become a preferred solution, not all Anglican parishes in the Ottawa Valley were in a financial position to build one. Several solutions were commonly adopted. By far the simplest way to distance the laity from the place of cult was increasing the area closed off by chancel rails and raising the floor level of the sanctuary. This solution also had the further advantage of being both simple and economical and was adopted in varying degrees by a number of parishes. It was also popular in that this arrangement could be built into earlier churches and, thus, providing a liturgical update at little expense. In very small churches, however, this arrangement had the definite disadvantage of monopolizing space that was already at a premium.

A second solution, one also offered by Ecclesiologists, had originated in England in response to a specific problem. Some pre-

Reformation churches now in the possession of certain congregations, had been built not as parish churches, but for monastic ritual. The adaptation of the elongated monastic chancel had proven particularly cumbersome to contemporary Anglican practice. During the early 1840s, Rev. John Jebb and Rev. Walter Farquhar Hook devised a solution by which the parish choir could occupy the area once reserved for the monks. These seats were inside the chancel and were placed parallel to the central axis of the church, rather than perpendicular as were those of the nave.[85] This formula, by which oversized English churches were adapted to the contemporary needs of smaller parishes, was also used by Ottawa Valley church builders to adapt early and undersized churches to the needs of an expanding, but not necessarily wealthy, population. This was done by simply reorienting the space immediately in front of the sanctuary. The choir was thus used to create a distinct and transitional space between the laity and the cult act.[86]

Fig. 4.18. St. James (Anglican), Hull, 1866.

The use of the equilateral triangle in defining the roof line is especially evident in this late-nineteenth-century photograph of St. James (now lost). Despite the presence of several Early English features, St. James lacked much of the stylistic purity and strength that distinguished St. Paul, Almonte, and St. Alban, Ottawa. The unambitious ascension of the triplets was negated by the horizontal banding beneath the oculus. The bell turret was uninspired and stylistically only marginally compatible (Photo courtesy: Anglican Diocesan Archives, Ottawa).

The liturgical implications of the architectural modifications introduced during this period were reinforced through the introduction of small scale liturgical objects. This phenomenon is well illustrated by a Communion service presented to Holy Trinity, Hawkesbury, in memory of George Hamilton by employees of his lumbering firm.[87] Prior to the presentation, the service had been shown at the Provincial Exhibition in Toronto, and its silversmith, W. C. Morrison, had won first prize. The prize was for the quality and the excellence of his work as a metal smith, for, although Morrison was the silversmith, he had not designed the Communion service. Still, the production of the Communion service attracted considerable interest, even among the secular press. The Toronto *Colonist* published a detailed description that was, in turn, reprinted in the Anglican *Ecclesiastical Gazette*.[88] The article offers a number of useful insights into the interests of the day, demonstrating clearly the significance attached by contemporaries to the manufacture of liturgical objects of high quality and sophisticated design in Central Canada. The article also provides clear evidence that Latin was steadily moving back into the Anglican church. Although the correspondent for the Toronto *Colonist* attributed these to "John Butterfield, the well-known architect of City Road, London,"[89] (a point that the editors

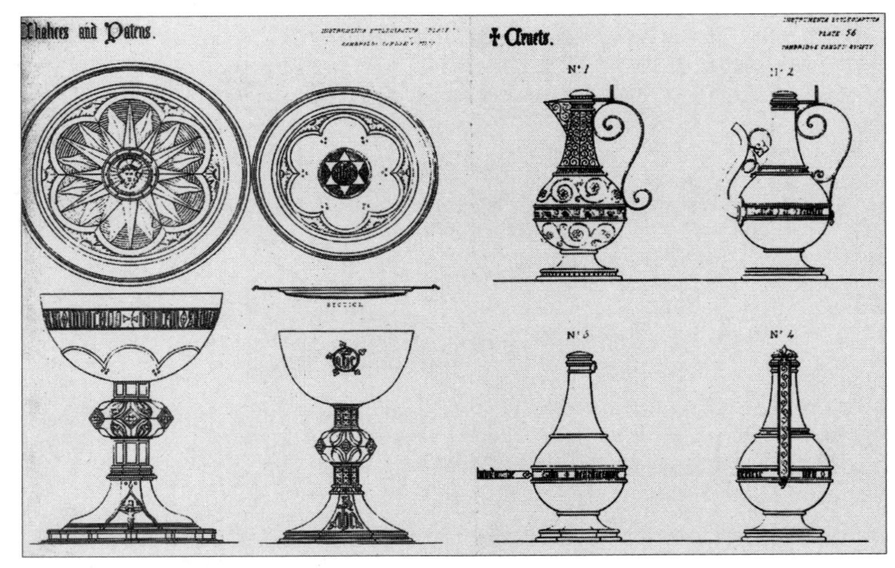

Fig. 4.19. Plates 55 and 56 from *Instrumenta Ecclesiastica*, 1847.

of the *Ecclesiastical Gazette* do not appear to query), it is more likely that the correspondent was referring to the work of William, not John, Butterfield. William Butterfield, in addition to being the author of St. Clement, City Road, was a major contributor to *Instrumenta Ecclesiastica*. Plates 55 and 56 (fig. 4.19) in the first volume of this pattern book illustrate "Chalices and Patens" and "Cruets and Flagons" corresponding to the description of the Hawkesbury service.[90]

Notes

1. W. Hay, "The Late Mr. Pugin and the Revival of Christian Architecture," *Anglo-American Magazine*, 1853, 70-73.

2. Ibid., 70-71.

3. This hostility towards the use of neoclassic elements in the construction of churches was common among many Gothic enthusiasts of the day. G. A. Poole, forcefully denounces the use of the pagan style in his architectural writings, stating that a "Gothic church, in its perfection, is an exposition of the distinctive doctrines of Christianity, clothed upon with a material form; and is, as Coleridge has more forcibly expressed it, 'the petrifaction of our religion.'" G. A. Poole, *Churches: their structure, arrangement and decoration* (London: J. Burns, 1846), 24 -25.

4. Hay, "The Late Mr. Pugin," 71.

5. This was attributed to Pugin's "earlier association with the pointed architecture of Normandy." Hay, "The Late Mr. Pugin," 73.

6. "He set forth the consistent canons of ancient design, and furnished the means of testing architectural excellence apart from mere fancy. He demonstrated that 'the laws of Architectural composition are based on equally sound principles as those of Harmony or Grammar, and, that they can be violated with greater impunity is simply owing to their being less understood.'" Hay, "The Late Mr. Pugin," 72.

7. "1. That all the ornaments of pure pointed edifices were merely introduced as decorations to the essential construction of those buildings. 2. That the construction of pointed architecture was varied to accord with *the properties of the various materials employed*. 3. That no features were introduced in the ancient pointed edifices which were not *essential either to convenience or propriety*. 4. That pointed architecture is most consistent as it decorates the useful portions of buildings instead of concealing or disguising them. 5. That true principles of architectural proportion are only found in pointed edifices. 6. That the defects of modern architecture are principally owing to *the departure from ancient* consistent principles." Hay, "The Late Mr. Pugin," 72.

8. Ibid., 73.

9. W. Westfall, *Two Worlds: The Protestant Culture of Nineteenth-Century Ontario,* (Montreal & Kingston: McGill-Queen's University Press, 1989), 135.

10. The article, though not signed, is attributed to William Hay, "Ecclesiastical Architecture," *Anglo-American Magazine*, Toronto, 1854, 20-22. See F. Armstrong, "Hay, W.," *Dictionary of Canadian Biography*, 391-393.

11. "... in the whole range of Canadian Ecclesiology, we shall scarce find a professedly Gothic church true to the type of its class in those respects. When we do happen to meet [one] with fair proportions and good outline form, a respectably pitched roof, we are almost certain to find the details exaggerated, perhaps borrowed from another edifice ten times its size. The building which, in other respects, would be tolerable, is simply marred by incongruity of proportions. Such is the case also with every feature of the building which is unfitted by form or dimensions for its proper destination. We frequently see, for example an erection perched on one end of the roof of a church, too large to be meant for a bell-cot, and too small for a steeple; but an evident apology for the latter. The roof not being a proper or secure support for a tower suffers in effect from the imposition." "Ecclesiastical Architecture," 20-22.

12. "Ecclesiastical Architecture," 20-22.

13. *Montreal Gazette,* 13 January 1860.

14. Ibid.

15. Ibid.

16. Ibid.

17. Ibid.

18. Land was obtained by Thomas Higginson from the estate of the Honourable Peter McGill. The church was officially opened in August 1846 by Rev. Francis Treymayne and the Rev. S. S. Strong of Bytown. The original Holy Trinity was a plain limestone church entered axially through the base of a frontal tower. The superstructure of the tower was never completed, and, as late as 1854, a dedicated group of parishioners was still trying to raise subscriptions for the construction of a spire. See Ottawa Anglican Diocesan Archives, Stormont Deanery Collection 6S-H2-5, Property files.

19. By the terms of his contract he was to "well and sufficiently erect and finish the following parts of Trinity Church at Hawkesbury, viz.: the chancel, porch and spire with new flooring including material and labour for nave of said church—agreeable to the several drawings, and specifications made by Messrs. Hopkins, Lawford and Nelson, Architects." Ottawa Archdiocesan Archives, (Anglican) Stormont Deanery Collection 6S-H2-5, Property files.

20. Additions to the church included a chancel rail, a chancel arch, four additional pews and a lightning rod. Higginson later billed the parish $18 for the construction of a reading desk and $32 for a new pulpit. See Ottawa Anglican Diocesan Archives, Stormont Deanery Collection 6S-H2-5, Property files.

21. The spire was described as rising "from the centre face of the tower, which is simply surmounted by a tooth moulding without any intervening parapet. It is octagonal shaped with sides that face the cardinal points sloping down to the eaves. . . . Many examples of this style of spire are to be found in north amptioshire [*sic*]." *Montreal Gazette*, 13 January 1860.

22. Excessive elevation was one of the features that William Hay had identified as a characteristic deformity of many Canadian churches.

23. Both of these churches are now lost.

24. The plans appear to have been acquired by James Rosamond from James Coleman. Both men were wealthy mill owners in Almonte and in Lynn, respectively. See Ottawa Anglican Diocesan Archives, Vestry Book of St. Paul, Almonte, entry for 23 April 1862, Box 6L-A1-6.

25. As he was designing these churches, Fuller was also supervising the construction of the Parliament Buildings in Ottawa, of which only the library remains. The High Victorian Gothic used on Parliament Hill was dramatically different from the archaeological Gothic Fuller chose for the construction of churches.

26. "The Bishop of Ontario's Confirmation Tour," *Canadian Churchman*, 18 June 1863.

27. *Canadian Churchman*, 19 September 1863.

28. The paper also noted that two local businessmen had made substantial contributions to the fulfillment of this project: "Its erection is mainly due to the liberality and zeal of James Rosamond Esq. who first in a most disinterested manner assumed the responsibility of signing the contract, and who had been untiring in his exertions to bring about the consummation now arrived . . ." *Canadian Churchman,* 13 July 1864. James Rosamond had been responsible for the selection of the church plans and, as chairman of the building committee, had played an active role in supervising the construction and progress on the church. See Vestry Book, 1 March 1864. Ottawa Anglican Diocesan Archives, Box 6L-A1-6.

29. "A new church in Ottawa is a matter of imperative necessity. Before the transference of some two hundred families of professed Church members with the Seat of Government from Quebec there is not sufficient accommodation for the local residents. Besides this the pews of the old Church (situated in the extreme west of the city) and the benches of a school house—used as a chapel were rented at high figures. . . ." *Canadian Churchman*, 3 January 1866.

30. According to Bedford-Jones St. Alban's was to be, "A church in which daily prayer and praise shall ascend to the Throne of God, and in which the Reformed Ritual of our ancient Anglican faith shall be conducted in full and strict accordance with the sanctions of the Book of Common Prayer—nothing more, but nothing less." Vestry Book, 1865, quoted by H. Carter, manuscript notes, n.d., in Ottawa Anglican Diocesan Archives, Box 6-O-1, S2-2, 19.

31. In a printed letter soliciting donations, the Rev. Thomas Bedford-Jones listed the members of the building committee and their credentials: The Hon. John Hamilton, M. L. C., Hawkesbury; Wm. F. Powell, M.P.P., Ottawa; Denis Godley, Governor's Secretary; G. W. Wicksteed, Q.C. Law Clerk, Legislative Assembly; John Langton, M.A., Auditor of Public Accounts of the Province; Frank Badgley, B.C.L., Assistant Law Clerk to the Legislative Assembly; Lt. Col. Bernard, A.D.C.; James S. Cartwright of Kingston; Thomas Cross, Civil Service; J. P. Featherstone, Civil Service; T. B. Fuller, Architect; Capt. F. Broughton, Staff Officer; John Graham of Ottawa; W. A. MacAgly of Ottawa; Major Ross, Accountant, Provincial See Dept.; J. G. Vansittart, Secretary of the Board of Railway Commissioners; H. A. Wicksteed, Accountant General, Post Office and Wm. J. Wills Agent for Immigration. Ottawa Anglican Diocesan Archives, Box 6-O-1, S2-13.

32. Vestry Book, 19 March 1864, Ottawa Anglican Diocesan Archives, Box 6-O-1, S2-2.

33. Land for the construction of St. Alban's had been purchased from the Besserer Estate during the winter months; however, once the snows melted, the site proved to be structurally unsuitable for construction of the church as originally planned. The southern side of the site was blue clay, but dipped dramatically into a sandy pit at the northern end of the site. Frustrated by the combined effect of these reversals, which led the church ever further from his original concept, Fuller relegated supervision and completion of the project to his assistant, King Arnoldi. Arnoldi's architectural ability is rec-

ognizable in the proficiency with which he salvaged so much of the medieval Gothic spirit while still accommodating dramatic design modifications forced by financial realities.

34. "St. Alban's Church building committee hereby beg to tender their best thanks to King Arnoldi . . . for the skill he has exhibited in the plans for St. Alban's Church and their successful execution under his superintendance; and they desire to avail themselves of this opportunity to express their high opinion of his taste and correct judgment in dealing with the details of a building which gives such general satisfaction when the limited means at his disposal are considered." Vestry Book, 28 September 1867, Ottawa Anglican Diocesan Archives, Box 6-O-1, S2-2.

35. J. M. Neale & B. Webb, *The Symbolism of Churches and Church Ornaments: A translation of the first book of the RATIONALE DIVINORUM OFFICIORUM written by William Durandus* (c. 1286). Translation and introductory essay by Rev. John Mason Neale and Rev. Benjamin Webb (Leeds: T. W. Green, 1843), c-ci.

36. Original land deeds and early site plans indicate a graveyard—this has since been moved. Ottawa Anglican Diocesan Archives, Box 6L-A1.

37. " . . . no corpse be ever allowed to be buried either in the church, or in the space in front of the west end, and that ten feet at least and twenty feet where possible all round the other three sides of the church be preserved . . . and that the ground at present free of graves be moved out into plots of twelve feet by nine feet. Nevertheless where a plot of said size is surrounded by graves it shall not be disturbed." Vestry Book for Christ Church, Huntley, 10 November 1854, Ottawa Anglican Diocesan Archives, Arnprior Deanery Collection, 6A-H-1. The only known example of intramural burial in the Ottawa Valley involves the interment of Mary Seaton (d. 1863) and George William Osborne (d. 1886), both in the nave of St. George (Anglican), Portage-du-Fort.

38. Archdiocesan Archives, Ottawa (Anglican), Clarendon Deanery Collection, 6-C-2; P2 - 1, 4.

39. Church builders had been instructed that "the foundation must be contrived as that the Head of the church may point due East, that is, to that point of the Heavens wherein the sun ariseth at the equinoxes; to signify that the Church Militant must behave Herself with moderation, both in prosperity and adversity." Neale and Webb, *Symbolism of Churches*, xx.

40. With the exception of the Church of St. James, Hull, all are still standing.

41. St. Paul, Almonte, Ontario (1863); St. Matthew, Charteris, Quebec (1864); St. Luke, Eardley, Quebec (1864); St. Alban, Ottawa, Ontario (1866); St. James, Hull, Quebec (1866); St. Bartholomew, Ottawa, Ontario (1868); St. James, Leslie, Quebec (1870); St. Paul, Shawville, Quebec (1872). All are representative of the changes that took place during this period. Each church is entered through a small porch projecting from the lateral wall of the nave. The side porches on some of the earlier churches such as St. Paul's Church, Almonte, and St. Alban's Church, Ottawa, tend to be comparatively smaller than those of slightly later churches such as Good Shepherd (1875), Plantagenet, and St. James (1876), Manotick.

42. This was due to a lack of funds in Almonte and a lack of a stable footing at St. Alban's Church, where the projected tower was to have stood to a height of 190 feet.

43. St. Luke, Eardley, St. Thomas, Bristol, St. Paul, Shawville, St. George, Fort Coulonge.

44. Durandus, "Of Bells," *Rationale*, Chapter IV, Sections 1-15, 87-97.

45. In section seven, Durandus explained that the wooden frame from which a bell was hung symbolized the wood of Christ's cross as it too was "suspended on high."

The wooden pegs were the prophets, while the iron clamps that joined the bell to the frame "denote charity, by which the Preacher being joined indissolubly unto the Cross, doth boast. . . ." The reader was told that the bell hammer represented the sanity of the preacher, while the rope itself was symbolic of the measure and humility of his life. In addition to several other symbolic entanglements the rope was to be made of three strands representing the historic, allegoric, and moral teachings of the Scriptures.

46. Poole, *Churches*, 40

47. This is pointed out in a number of nineteenth century publications including Neale and Webb's 1843 translation of Durandus' *Rationale Divinorum Officiorum*, 29; Poole's *Churches*, 1846, 34, and Garnier's *The parish church: a simple explanation of church symbolism* (London: Society for Promoting Christian knowledge, 1876), 30.

48. Neale and Webb, *Symbolism of Churches*, lxi.

49. Christ incarnate was considered more appropriately symbolized by couplets than by triplets, which were clearly emblematic of the Trinity and were to be found at the eastern end of the church.

50. "A beautiful font of Caen stone, imported express from Exeter, was presented by John Hamilton Esq., in 1857 and the close of the following year, a very costly solid silver communion service to the memory of George Hamilton (who died 21 May 1858) by members of the congregation and employees of Hamilton Bros. Such instances of Christian liberty are worthy of public notice because they are worthy of public imitation." *Montreal Gazette*, 13 January 1860.

51. Although the font was presented to the church in 1857, correspondence from Exeter indicates that an original font had arrived in 1856, but was damaged. Letter from Exeter, 31 December 1856. Archdiocesan Archives, Ottawa (Anglican), Box 6S-H2 7.

52. On Christmas Eve, a very acceptable and valuable gift was presented to the Rev. Fr. Jones by two British workmen of his congregation—Messrs. Painter & Taylor. It consisted of a "Fontlet." It seems that a few weeks previously, Dr. Jones had baptized infant children of both of these men, "whose trade was the higher branch of stonecutting, and had to use an unsightly bowl on the occasion, whereupon they set to work themselves to remedy the want." *Canadian Churchman*, 9 January 1866.

53. The locally carved font was described as "about two feet in height, elaborately carved, and composed of three descriptions of stone, the pediment being Arnprior marble, the pillar fine white marble and the actual font sandstone. This font is octagonal in shape, each side being a trefoil or quatrefoil and in four of the eight are devices exquisitely cut, the sacred monogram, a cross, a triangle with the symbol of the trinity and a monogram with the initials of the Rev. doctor's name. Around the beveled margin in old English Characters cut letters are inserted in the sandstone bearing the appropriate words, 'Suffer little children to come unto me.' These letters are coloured, the capitals being scarlet, the others a dark chocolate. The workmanship is exquisitely fine." *Canadian Churchman*, 9 January 1866.

54. Neale and Webb, "Introductory," lxxxi. On this subject, Poole noted "the octagon [is] the most appropriate form for the font, and the most beautiful as well as the most ecclesiastical; for the octagon is not only a very graceful form, and very favourable to the reception of sculpture on its several faces; but it is also in itself symbolical, according to the ancient methods of spiritualizing numbers, of the new birth in baptism: for the seven days' creation of the natural world are symbolized in the number seven; and the new creation by Christ Jesus, by the number eight. . . ." *Churches*, 50.

55. *Ecclesiologist*, Vol. IV, 33.

56. Students of church architecture were warned, "... Not to rush hastily into God's Presence. 'Keep thy foot when thou goest to the House of God' (Eccl. 5:1). We should compose the mind and hush the voice as we enter in: 'The Lord is in His holy Temple: let all the earth keep silence before Him' (Hab. 2:20)." T. P. Garnier, *The Parish Church*, 30-31.

57. St. Paul, Almonte, 1863; St. Luke, Eardley, 1864; St. Alban the Martyr, Ottawa, 1866; St. James, Hull, 1866; Emanuel Church, Ottawa, 1869; St. Bartholomew, Ottawa, 1869; St. Paul, Shawville, 1872; St. Thomas, Bristol Corners, 1875; St. Mary the Virgin, Blackburn Hamlet, 1880; St. John the Evangelist, Quyon, 1883; and St. Stephen, Greermont, 1883, are all surviving, well-documented examples.

58. "The Doctrine of the Holy Trinity has left, as might be expected, deeper traces in the structure of our churches than any other principle of our Faith ... we find the ideas carried out not only by the Nave and the two Aisles, but also by the triple division in length into Nave, Chancel, and Sanctum Sanctorum. . . . The Clerestory, the Triforium and Piers cannot fail to suggest it. . . . Again, the triple orders of moulding, which are so much more frequent that any other number may be supposed to refer to the same thing. The Altar steps, three, or some multiple of three certainly will do." Neale and Webb, *Symbolism of Churches*, lxxx.

59. St. Paul, Almonte, 1863; St. Luke, Eardley, 1864; St. Alban the Martyr, Ottawa, 1866; St. James, Hull, 1866; Emanuel Church, Ottawa, 1869; St. Bartholomew, Ottawa, 1869; St. Paul, Shawville, 1872; St. Thomas, Bristol Corners, 1875, all conform to this type.

60. *The Church*, 11 April 1850.

61. "The Window in the South East corner of the nave contains a representation of the 'raising of Lazarus' in the upper part, an angel is figured holding (a scroll) on which are figured the words 'Come Lord Jesus' and underneath the centre medallion the passage, 'I know that he will rise again,' is gracefully introduced. The opposite window contains a representation of 'the raising of Jairus' daughter.' A dove is stained at the top of the lancet, and at the bottom a white lily. In the tracery are scrolls containing the appropriate text—'weep not, she is not dead but sleepth.' In the west window the life-giving miracles are completed by the 'Resurrection of our Lord' in the centre of one lancet and the 'raising of the widow's son' in the centre of the other. In the upper and lower compartments of this window are stained the emblems of the four evangelists and in the quatrefoil at top that of the trinity. ... The drawings for them were procured from London and were executed in Montreal by Mr. Spence and will compare favourably with the windows manufactured in England. The remaining lights are filled with pattern glass stained by the same artist. The colours and patterns are varied and each lancet contains a short passage of scripture." *Montreal Gazette*, 13 January 1860.

62. "A flat ceiling is of all things the most destructive of that breath of tone which we may attain even in a small edifice; whereas the bare timbers of the roof ... assist it most materially. Go into any church, where the original open roof remains, and first observe the effect, as it appears at present, and then fancy it, for an instant, underdrawn and plastered, with half-a-dozen circular ornaments as centres of suspension for chandeliers, placed in geometrical order over the expanse: then ask yourself why a flat ceiled roof is so often seen in a (modern) Gothic church?" Poole, *Churches*, 67. Here the term "(modern) Gothic" refers not to the renewed interest in revived medieval style but to the productions of the Stuart and Georgian eras.

63. St. Andrew's Church in Vars, 1889, is a striking example.

64. "... though Christ is indeed the Foundation of the Church, yet these holy symbols should not be exposed to be trodden under foot." Neale and Webb, *Symbolism of Churches*, cxii.

65. The use of heraldic devices on the floor would "signify the worthlessness of worldly honours in the sight of God." Neale and Webb, *Symbolism of Churches*, cxii

66. Canadian readers were informed that "the practice of fixing doors to pews is much discontinued in England, as being supposed to be too exclusive for the House of God." *The Church*, 18 April 1850.

67. *The Church*, 18 April 1850.

68. In 1859, the visitation lectures of the Bishop of London were published over the course of his visit in the *Canadian Ecclesiastical Gazette*.

69. St. Alban's Vestry Book, 28 September, 1865, Ottawa Anglican Diocesan Archives, Box 6-O-1, S2-2. This also appeared verbatim in the *Canadian Churchman*, 3 January 1866.

70. *Canadian Churchman*, 3 January 1866.

71. Rev. Bedford-Jones set forth his case in a printed letter soliciting funds. "Under the circumstances, we are compelled to solicit external aid and we ask your help requesting you to observe: 1. That the church is to be ENTIRELY AND UNRESERVEDLY FREE, a principle which we believe to be that of the Gospel of Christ, and from which we trust the Church in this city will derive the greatest benefit. . . . 2. That there is no Parochial Endowment whatever. . . ." Ottawa Anglican Diocesan Archives, Box 6-O-1, S2-13.

72. "A number of low benches all looking the same way, and with an ornamental finial at the end of each seat, formed an avenue, along which the eye was irresistibly directed towards the altar." Poole, *Churches*, 69.

73. *The Church*, 18 April 1850.

74. *Canadian Churchman*, 30 September 1863. The vestry was not part of the original building programme, but a later addition.

75. The chancel was to correspond in width to the central nave; however, in the case of small or aisled churches, the chancel would never be less than eight feet wide and nine feet deep. *The Church*, 11 April 1850.

76. This can still be seen in Holy Trinity, Hawkesbury, and in St. Alban, Ottawa, although here, the chancel itself, while part of the original plan, was (for financial reasons) not part of the original building programme.

77. Church leaders provided very explicit specifications on this subject. It was recommended that the table be at least four feet long, two and a half feet wide, with a minimum height of three feet. A kneeling stool at least eighteen inches by ten inches with a one and a half inch slope and a maximum height of eight inches was to stand at either end of the table. The railing was to be installed in such a manner so as to allow for a kneeling place two feet four inches deep. *The Church*, 18 April 1850.

78. Frequently the discussion of this sort was also used not only to advance what one considered to be architecturally correct, but also to state one's position vis-à-vis other Christian denominations. In one instance, the reader is told: "even after the time of Constantine altars were for a long time generally of wood: thus, for instance, in the sacrilegious outrages of the Donatists in the fourth century, in which they acted nearly as wicked a part as the Presbyterians and independents, at the time of Oliver Cromwell,

some of the altars were burned; and we read of persons being beaten with broken fragments of others." Poole, *Churches*, 103.

79. *The Church*, 18 April 1850.

80. In this context it is essential that "worship" be understood in a Protestant—as opposed to Roman Catholic—interpretation of the term. The importance of this distinction is discussed in J. White, *Protestant Worship, Traditions in Transition* (Louisville, Kentucky: Westminster/John Knox Press, 1988), 15-24.

81. "The relative importance of preaching and praying, and Holy Communion, being forgotten, and preaching having usurped the place of all the rest, it has become difficult to satisfy the eyes and ears of the people, and at the same time to preserve a decent harmony of effect in the position and decoration of the pulpit. Hence plans of all degrees of clumsiness, and contrivances of all degrees of deformity, are continually emanating from clergymen, carpenters, gas-fitters, architects and congregations." Poole, *Churches*, 98.

82. There is a renewed interest among some Ecclesiologists of incorporating the form of an eagle into a lectern. If this was done, Ecclesiologists made it quite clear it was supposed to be a Christian eagle and not a heathen eagle. "But it must be remembered that the Eagle of the Church and of St. John is not the equal of the heathens and of Jupiter, with an eye of lightning, with the thunderbolt in his talons, and with a neck bending as if beneath the weight of Ganymede; but it is forward looking, and intent on the simple service of holding the book committed to its flattened back and outstretched wings." Poole, *Churches,* 96.

83. Revivalists were divided on the virtues of the various materials possible. "But wooden pulpits are, perhaps more manageable, as they are, certainly, more common. They are generally of a date posterior to the Reformation, and partake of the successive degradations in the taste of the several generations from Queen Elizabeth to the present day." Poole, *Churches*, 99.

84. This arrangement also allowed easy circulation during Communion and Confirmation services, as congregational congestion in this area was thought to detract from the dignity of the ceremony. *The Church*, 11 April 1850.

85. See J. Jebb, *The choral service of the United church of England and Ireland* (London: J. W. Parker, 1843).

86. Although the choir was usually composed exclusively of lay people, they were considered to be performing a specific act of worship and were justly placed in a distinct setting as ministers of the liturgy.

87. "The Church of the Holy Trinity, at West Hawkesbury, County of Prescott, C. W., has just been enriched by the presentation of a solid silver Communion Service, in the memory of the late George Hamilton Esquire, of the firm of Hamilton Brothers, the extensive Lumber Merchants of Ottawa. *Ecclesiastical Gazette,* December 1858, 93.

88. "SOLID SILVER MEMORIAL COMMUNION SERVICE—In consequence of the great number of articles which were presented at the Exhibition last week, we were prevented from giving that prominent notice, which it deserved, to a Solid Silver Memorial Communion Service, manufactured by our justly celebrated and enterprising fellow-citizen Mr. W. C. Morrison. We now call special attention to it because it is one of those services which are generally imported from London, under the false impression that such articles cannot be properly manufactured on this side of the Atlantic. . . . The three articles are taken from a service which is in St. George's Church in this city. The designs are by John Butterfields, the well-known church architect of City Road, London. The three

articles are to be presented to the Church of the Holy Trinity, Hawkesbury, C. W., in memory of the late George Hamilton, Esq., as the following Latin inscription (which each of the sacred vessels bears) will show: 'In memoriam Georgii Hamilton Hawkesburiensis, de civibus in vita optime merentis, D. D. D. Amici valde desiderantes. Obit 21o Mai A.S. MDCCCLVIII., ætatis suæ XXXIV.—In usum perpetuum SS. Trinitatis Ecclesiæ apud Hawksburienses in Canada Ulteriori. Johanne Strachan S.T.P.LL.D. Episcopo Torontonensi; Johanne Gilberto Armstrong A.B. Ecclesiæ Rectore; Joh. Hamilton : Joh. Gul : [*sic*] Higginson, Æedituis'." *The Toronto Colonist, Ecclesiastical Gazette*, December 1858, 94.

89. *Ecclesiastical Gazette*, December 1858, 94.

90. W. Butterfield, *Instrumenta Ecclesiastica, A Series of Working Designs for the Furniture, Fittings and Decorations of Churches and their Precincts* (London: John Van Voorst, 1847).

CHAPTER FIVE

MARKING IT AS A HOUSE OF GOD: From Survival Gothic to Neo-Gothic

The Anglicans were not the only Christians in the Ottawa Valley to be making greater use of the Gothic style in the construction of their new churches. During the middle years of the nineteenth century, most of the Christian congregations building in the Ottawa Valley included some reference to the Gothic style; this can be seen not only in the active revival of medieval prototypes, but also in the widespread use of Gothic elements on churches built by Baptists, Congregationalists (fig. 5.1), Methodists, Presbyterians, and Roman Catholics. While Roman Catholics explored this style more fully than many other Christian denominations and occasionally remarked on the intrinsically Christian nature of Gothic, there is little evidence to suggest a preoccupation with the revival of medieval prototypes and the advocacy of strict archaeological fidelity. As one Roman Catholic cleric noted, "l'Église n'a aucun style qui lui soit propre. Elle les admet tous selon les temps et les lieux. . . . Les églises ne sont pas faites pour plaire aux archéologues, mais pour honorer Dieu. . . ."[1] The rejection of servile devotion to medieval prototypes was not uniquely Roman Catholic.

Many Anglo-Protestants were not convinced that the revival of style and detailing that predated the Protestant Reformation was the wisest course of architectural action. Several denominations kept a watchful eye on the developments within the Church of England. From the 1840s onwards, the Protestant press devoted considerable space to the discussion of "Tractarianism," "Puseyism," "Revivalism,"

Fig. 5.1. Ottawa First Congregational Church (Congregationalist), 1862–1888.

This was the second church built by Ottawa's Congregationalist community. It replaced the church originally erected during the mid-1840s. "First" applies to the parish, not to the structure. The main body of the building reflects a continued use of survival Gothic. This is most notable in the continued use of a single axial entry and the large elongated windows of the lateral walls. The generous slope of the roof suggests attention to the contemporary discussion of medieval traits as does the geometrical tracery of the gable end window, the frontal wall buttresses, and the prominent string course that surrounds the building (Photo courtesy: National Archives of Canada).

and "Ritualism." Non-Anglicans often considered the revival of medieval Gothic to be a direct outcome of the Oxford Movement despite the refusal of the Oxonians themselves to acknowledge any exclusive supremacy of Gothic. Even before the formation of the Cambridge Camden Society, the *Canadian Christian Examiner and Presbyterian Magazine* had warned its readership that all was not as it should be in the English Church. In the early 1840s, the magazine had reprinted an article from the *Edinburgh Christian Instructor* in which the Church of England was denounced as a "Half-Reformed Church." The article was essentially a denunciation of the Oxford Movement and its influence on the Church of England, claiming:

"Nor have we any great cause to wonder at the Popery of the Church of England in her liturgy, rubrics, canons, vestments, rites, and in what may be termed her *traditional*, as distinguished from her *symbolical* theology."[2] The editors of the Canadian magazine had reinforced this opinion by noting that "Most of our readers are aware that a party in the Church of England, whose headquarters are at Oxford, are labouring to introduce Popery into the Church, as well as into the country at large under a mask of concern for religion."[3]

Although a significant number of non-Anglican editors and journalists were willing and able to discuss developments originating at Oxford and Cambridge with considerable understanding and skill, a great many more were not. It is worth noting, especially in light of the frequency with which the topic was discussed, that many correspondents were either unable or inclined not to distinguish between Oxonian theology and Camdanian Ecclesiology. This tendency appears to have been somewhat more common among individuals who were less comfortable with the use of revived medieval Gothic. This reservation did not necessarily extend to all forms of Gothic expression. There was no equivalent to the Oxford Movement or the

Fig. 5.2. Anglican, Methodist, and Presbyterian churches of Fallowfield.

St. Barnabas (Anglican), 1889, (left) reflects a strong influence of revivalist thought as seen in the architecturally distinct chancel, the bipartite western window, and the side entry. The restrained use of Gothic seen on the Presbyterian church of 1891 (centre) and Methodist church of 1888 (far right) was all some congregations needed to distinguish their church as a place of Christian worship (Photo courtesy: Lois Long and Lorne Davis).

Ecclesiologists within other Protestant confessions. Nor did a Pugin emerge from within their midst to champion the cause of fitting and soulful church building. Instead, with the obvious exclusion of the Church of England, the greater part of Anglo-Protestant church-building theory was generated in, and circulated more or less anonymously through, the denominational press. Despite these reservations and, in some instances, a general lack of direction, Gothic continued to be used extensively by both Protestants and Roman Catholics (fig. 5.2).

Methodist Concerns

Among those observing the Anglicans with particular vigilance were the Methodists. Previously associated with a less educated and less affluent segment of the population, the places of prayer used by various Methodist communities had, for many years, a degree of structural constancy in keeping with the temperance of their private homes. This had been a trait of Methodist church architecture. Many buildings afforded little more than modest shelter from the elements. Still, it would be a loss to dismiss Methodist churches simply as functional and of no historic interest or consequence. This has been done

Fig. 5.3. Prospect Church (Methodist), Prospect, 1847.

Many small rural Methodist churches continued to be solidly built and devoid of gratuitous embellishments, much as they had in the earlier years of the century. Occasionally, the slant of the roof accounted for a greater percentage of the total vertical elevation than it had in previous years, generally attributed to a stylistic (but not liturgical) influence effected by architectural revisions in the Anglican church (Photo: A. Erdmer).

all too often by architectural historians more intent on material style than spiritual design. As noted earlier, Methodists in the Ottawa Valley often associated their place of worship with a complexity of religious ideals that transcended the preoccupations and daily banalities of adequate shelter. The manner in which Methodists understood church building was closely linked to the Methodist perception of their own role in a complex interrelation of Divine favour and mortal duty. Just as God gave generously of spiritual and material blessing, so was it the duty of Christians to give generously to God. Part of this Christian duty was to build a place where God could be properly honoured (fig. 5.3). By the middle years of the nineteenth century, Methodists in Central Canada were becoming increasingly aware that they no longer were indigent colonists. Along with their material prosperity, they had greater access to prestigious social positions in developing towns and villages. As this happened, many Methodists became more interested in building places of worship that were larger and closer to the preoccupations of their own daily lives. As for itinerant preachers in shirt sleeves, many of their churches did not lend themselves especially well to the improved conditions of the many parishioners. The discrepancy between their comfortable homes and their stark churches was a rapidly escalating concern. This difference was not felt to reflect well on Methodism as a whole, and there was a growing eagerness that this distance should be reduced in the not too distant future.[4] While in many cases the construction of a church building clearly attested to a renewed interest in grace and spiritual progress, rules regulating this construction continued to be vague. Within the Methodist churches, there had been very little discussion of specific architectural needs. Questions concerning size, style, external presentation, and the creation of suitable sanctuaries were only now beginning to emerge, and determining the most appropriate construction for the manner in which Methodists experienced their religion presented some difficulties—a predicament Methodists in the Ottawa Valley had experienced first-hand. A report concerning recent advances on the Richmond Circuit noted that:

> Most of this time seemed like one continued Sabbath and the very atmosphere sacred. God was moving onward in the majesty of his love, and from day to day rolling upon us a sea of glory. The power of the Highest overshadowed us and the windows of heaven were opened and we had hardly room to receive the blessings that descended. Our house of worship was filled from day to day and often overflowing, though the attention of the people to religion was intense and long-continued, there was no trespass upon the rules of Christian decorum, all was solemn and peaceful.[5]

This description of the Richmond experience was typical of mid-nineteenth century Methodist discussion of the transcendence of God. The actions of the Almighty were frequently described in powerful meteorological terms. Any structure built by human hands would be ill-suited to accommodate the rank and eminence of such a theophany. The chronicle of this encounter between His earth-bound parishioners and the unsullied nobility of the divine illustrates how the Methodist church building served as a point of contact between two very different worlds. Of equal importance is the insistence on the behaviour of those gathered in the church. All was quiet and dignified. These remarks were clearly directed to the general public and denote an increasing desire among Methodists to distance themselves from public and vocal displays of extreme emotions. Methodist tolerance for this type of behaviour was diminishing quickly, as the preferred place of worship shifted from the outdoor camp meeting to indoor church services.[6]

Despite their modest demeanour, these church buildings were increasingly being depicted as a point for contact with the benefits of religion.[7] By frequenting the church building itself, an individual could gain access to other elements of faith. While some Methodists were presenting the church building as a unique point of entry through which many dimensions of spiritual grace could be accessed, others were drawing attention to the fact that none of this would be possible if the church building itself was unattractive. A church building devoid of visual merit was unlikely to entice the casual or lukewarm Christian to enter, and it was precisely such individuals who were in the greatest need. This was an occasion not to be missed; an obligation not to be taken lightly. It was part and parcel of a Christian's duty to God. Methodists in Central Canada, determined that none should be lost, moved quickly to fill the void. However, while some Methodists were emphatically insisting on the need for suitable places of worship, others were politely voicing some practical inquiries: "What is meant by a suitable place of worship?"[8] The *Christian Guardian* attempted to answer this question by volunteering that the question could not be properly answered without knowing the material means of the congregation.[9] This reply was not without an element of common sense, but did little to address questions of orientation, size, and stylistic propriety. The Methodist discussion began without the dogmatic assurance of Anglican writers, and many early suggestions were ambiguous:

> Whatever may be the dimension of the structure to be erected, or whatever materials to be used, perhaps there will be no second

> opinion as to the propriety of keeping in view, in all arrangements, both the durability and neatness of the edifice, while, at the same time, in perfect accordance with Methodist simplicity, extravagance and unnecessary ornament should be avoided.[10]

The question was not destined to remain that simple, however, and answers of much greater complexity were soon to be demanded. This was especially true as Methodists became increasingly aware of Anglican church-building activities. By the middle years of the nineteenth century, the matter of better-looking churches had in certain instances become a moral dilemma. Some were still reluctant to assign God to a place built by human hands, while others worried that, without church buildings, Methodism could not survive.[11] Still others feared that although churches should be built, it might be in some way sinful to build churches that were too elegant or stylish. Methodists sent their questions and opinions to their denominational journals. Replies or rebuttals were published and the debate raged back and forth with comparatively little guidance from Church officials.

Although the exigency for proper church buildings had been recognized for some time by the mid-1850s, the necessity for some very practical guidance was clear. It was no longer enough to simply build a place of worship; certain rules of architectural balance and proportion had to be observed.[12] In addition to calling for higher architectural standards, Methodists echoed the Anglican call for churches that were unequivocally identifiable as places of Christian prayer.[13] They were also prepared to acknowledge that, like their Anglican neighbours, Methodism was in need of a good and standardized set of reliable plans;[14] however, precise instructions continued to be vague. A church was to be neatly built with well-proportioned demonstrations and "fitted up in a way suited for the purposes for which it is designed."[15] To achieve this end, congregations were advised to hire architects who were familiar with Methodist worship, request that they provide clear plans, and remember to pay them.[16] While this advice itself might not have been detrimental to improved construction, it was far from providing potential church builders with an explicit set of blueprints.

By the 1860s, the position that advocated uncompromising austerity in the construction of Methodist churches was increasingly under attack. A lengthy article in the *Christian Guardian* used Biblical passages to justify financial expenditures on the material church. Readers were reminded that, while the Jews wandered in the desert, the "most costly tent" was used to house the tabernacle.[17] In

Jerusalem, the "most costly house" was the temple.[18] The word "costly," readers are informed, appears often in the Old Testament in connection with building the house of God: "costly stones," "costly stones and cedars." They are reminded that no one appears to have questioned the wisdom of Solomon in this undertaking, and that his father, David,[19] "refused to offer to the Lord what had cost him nothing."[20] It was also pointed out that when Mary washed the feet of Jesus with "costly ointment,"[21] Jesus himself had "commended the deed" and the only one to object was "a certain utilitarian."[22] There was a sharp protest against the equation of well-built churches with buildings that were architecturally trendy. It had been suggested that well-built churches might possess "a decent body but no soul."[23] The *Christian Guardian* replied to this charge with a searing tirade against "stinginess with the garb of piety,"[24] announcing that "this stigmatizing whatever is generous and bountiful and tasteful and costly in the offerings and preparations of Christianity as fashionable religion is worse than a fallacy: it is a mischievous delusion."[25] Still missing was any concrete direction on the subject of actually building a church. There were still no specific examples of what might constitute a just display of generosity. Methodists were still without direc-

Fig. 5.4. Presbyterian Church, 1891, and Methodist Church, 1888, Fallowfield.

Even in the latter decades of the nineteenth century, many Presbyterian and Methodist church builders continued to build much as they had during earlier years. Although brick is now used with greater regularity than stone once was, the external appearance of the church building reflects very little change (Photo: Courtesy of Bruce Elliot and Helen Wilson).

tion on the subject of orientation, proportion and the required dimensions of specific internal furnishings. Nor did anyone seem willing to suggest just where that crucial, but elusive, line between fine craftsmanship and fashionable frivolity might run (fig. 5.4).

In 1854, the Wesleyan Methodist minister in charge of the Clarendon and Portage-du-Fort missions, Rev. W. T. Hewitt, noted in his annual report that "Puseyism has made several attempts to raise its head, but the atmosphere is too evangelical for its growth, it is sickly, it is dying."[26] He was later appointed to a neighbouring region of western Quebec, near Thurso, an area with a strong Baptist community and in which Methodist progress had been slow. In 1858, Hewitt complained that there was still no church in the Lochaber Mission and that the local Baptist community was taking advantage of this weakness. "Immersionists," he declared solemnly, "have tried to sink the Wesleyan ship."[27] His remarks are in many ways reflective of the problems that faced Methodist church builders during the second half of the nineteenth century. They were charged with the delicate task of building a suitable place of worship, without appearing to succumb to Puseyism or to mean-spiritedness. Surviving evidence suggests that many Methodist church builders in the Ottawa Valley felt that Gothic was the style best suited for this task. In response to the needs of many remote or newly formed communities, the second half of the nineteenth century was marked by the construction of numerous small Methodist churches. Regardless of the building material used, these churches were often very similar in their architectural massing. They had simple rectangular ground plans and were most commonly entered by way of a single axial entry. Earlier churches were rarely fitted with towers, although these became more common during the final quarter of the nineteenth century. This most basic interpretation of Gothic had a number of advantages; it was simple yet dignified and easy to build, but was also, in architectonic terms at least, well beyond the social and stylistic confines of a log structure. For some time Methodist church builders continued to use variants of this basic plan for the construction of churches in towns and cities where a larger population required a correspondingly larger church.

One of the oldest and few surviving examples of this type of church is a small clapboard structure built along the 9th Line road of Fitzroy Township. Known today as Diamond Church (fig. 5.5 and fig. 5.6),[28] it was built by the Wesleyan Methodists of Fitzroy Township in 1862. The church was set back slightly from the roadway but was fronted to the property line. It was entered by way of a

Fig. 5.5. Diamond Church (Methodist), Fitzroy Township, 1862.

The only embellishment found on this façade was a delicate tracery in the upper portion of the arched entryway. The eave returns show faint traces of a distant classical ancestry. The side walls are opened by three gothic windows with plain glass. The interlacing of the glazing bars echoes the pattern above the front door (Photo: A. Erdmer).

Fig. 5.6. Diamond Church (Methodist), Fitzroy Township, 1862.

The western end that corresponds to the sanctuary remains blank. There is no architectural suggestion of privileged space. The axis of the church is perpendicular to the township road (Photo: A. Erdmer).

single axial doorway in the eastern façade. Inside, the church was a simple rectangle, forty-five feet long and thirty feet wide. The western end of the church was flat. There were no windows or architectural embellishments. The sanctuary was placed against the western wall of the church. It was understated with a floor that was raised only slightly above the ground level of the nave. There was a modest pulpit and unpretentious sittings for those ministering. The whole was surrounded by a low rail. While this arrangement continued to be used in some parishes through to the final years of the nineteenth century, changes within the Methodist community itself were occasioning a new openness to architectural evolution.

During the fourth quarter of the nineteenth century, there were profound transformations within the Methodist Church itself, marked most conspicuously by a significant shift towards greater unity among the various Methodist confessions. In 1874, the Conference of the Wesleyan Methodist Church in Canada, the Canada Conference of the Methodist New Connexion, and the Wesleyan Conference of Eastern British North America united to form the Methodist Church of Canada. A decade later, the Primitive Methodist Church in Canada, the Methodist Episcopal Church in Canada, and the Bible Christian Church joined forces with the Methodist Church of Canada. This new union was known simply as the Methodist Church. One of the most visible outcomes of this trend towards a greater unity was the expansion of congregation size. With their new augmented membership, the material resources of many Methodist congregations increased significantly. This new prosperity resulted not simply from the combined resources of the Methodist communities, but also from a growing affluence of church members as individuals. Differences that had for so long segmented Methodists and limited their church-building resources were being resolved. Many communities were free, perhaps for the first time, to indulge in more emphatic architectural enterprises. Methodist church builders in the Ottawa Valley did not lag behind their contemporaries in other parts of Ontario and Quebec.

By December 1881, Canadian Methodists, looking back on the past ten years, declared that between 1871 and 1881 their denomination had made unprecedented growth in the field of church building.[29] It was also noted, perhaps with an attempt at humour, that Methodists were not simply building larger and more architecturally imposing churches, they were building churches with equally imposing mortgages.[30] By this time, however, Methodist communities were no longer being rebuked for holding such debts. The

Fig. 5.7. Shawville Methodist Church (Methodist), Shawville, 1890.
Although the builders borrowed ideas introduced by Anglican revivalists, they did so only in terms of architectonic massings. This is especially evident in the generous slope of the roof, the lower lateral walls, and the asymmetrical tower. The stylistic use of Gothic was considered to Romish for some Protestants (Photo: V. Bennett).

Christian Guardian suggested that a church mortgage was nothing less than "a sublime exhibition of faith on the part of the church herself," and asked rhetorically: "And what would the church be, after all, without this faith?"[31] In this manner the building of churches continued to be presented as correlated to God's favour and as an outcome of good works, no matter how the flavour of the discussion had changed.

While the building of Methodist churches was on the rise throughout Central Canada, it was the Methodist church builders of the Ottawa Valley that were held up to all as a most laudable example for the rest of the country.[32] Amidst all the lively verbosity of this discussion, not a single word was devoted to stylistic preference. There is no discussion of the liturgical merits of one architectonic configuration over the other. Nor is there any mention of how these new church buildings should proclaim themselves to the world, other than perhaps by their increasing size. Despite the silence on the matter of style, the increased preoccupation with construction was not without justification. With unification, many newly formed communities sought to strengthen and affirm congregational unity through the construction of new, larger churches. In addition, the growing importance of Sunday school within the Methodist church, led to a demand for churches that were more than simple single-room rectangular boxes. Extra space was now needed either beneath, beside, or within the church building itself.

In rural communities, Gothic continued to be used for the construction of new church buildings, although by the final quarter of the nineteenth century, trace elements of Anglican influence can be identified (fig. 5.7). Despite this cautious adaptation of Anglican Gothic, there is no corresponding stylistic philosophy or theory. Externally, this influence is most evident in the new popularity of towers. Some were frontal and axial, but a great number were also placed asymmetrically on one corner of the façade. The gable end was frequently opened by a large Gothic window. Methodist church builders were not generally inclined to refer to this as the "western" end of the building nor were sanctuaries necessarily placed at the "eastern" end of the church. Physical orientation continued to be dictated by the secular site plan. The slope of the roof on many of these new churches tended to be somewhat steeper than the roof angle of many earlier buildings. Still, Methodist church builders in the Ottawa Valley never indulged in the dramatic angles as seen on some Anglican churches, such as the Good Shepherd, Plantagenet. Inside, galleries were becoming less common while coloured window glass was enjoying an unprecedented popularity.

In urban centres where the population and material resources of a congregation tended to be significantly larger, many Methodist church builders chose to move away from the Gothic parallelogram in favour of a new amphitheatre, or "Akron" plan. In many ways this plan reinforced and redefined the boundary between the majority of the congregation and those actively involved in the liturgy.[33] This is not to suggest that Methodists no longer prayed or sang as a congregation. The spatial dynamics of these new churches with their sloping floors and second-story balconies were much closer to those of contemporary concert halls than the traditional gathering places. The pulpit, communion table, organ, and choir all retreated to a new elevated prominence within a raised stage-like sanctuary. Of all the transformations that occurred over the course of the nineteenth century, the introduction of the amphitheatre-plan church represented the single most dramatic restructuring of Methodist cult space. It was, however, a spatial restructuring that had no stylistic alliance, which is not to say that Gothic elements did not appear in amphitheatre-plan churches. There were, in fact, a number of these churches built in the Ottawa Valley with Gothic style window heads, moulding and pinnacles. The use of Gothic, however, was entirely superficial. The stylistic versatility that characterized the early use of this new plan gradually led Methodist church builders away from the use of Gothic towards a preference for Romanesque-style windows and mouldings. It, like Gothic, could also be used interchangeably with

Fig. 5.8. Almonte (Methodist), Almonte, 1891.
Reflective of neither survival nor revival Gothic, the heavy, earthbound masses suggest little of the liturgical practices of those who gathered within. The reference to Gothic was of minimal relevance, as solid monumentality was of greater importance (Photo: V. Bennett).

any stylistic variation of the builders' choosing. It bore no relation to the liturgical arrangements of the church interior and made no statement of belief (fig. 5.8).

Baptists

During the nineteenth century, architectural terminology appeared with considerable regularity in Baptist literature. This discussion of religious architecture rarely related in any physical manner to architectonic manifestations. When Baptists refer to points of theology or doctrine in the same sentence as architectural terminology, it is far more likely that spiritual instruction, not the embodiment of principles of faith, is being discussed.[34] This attachment to the use of architectural symbolism is effectively illustrated by an incident that occurred in the Ottawa Valley during the mid-1860s. The affair involved several British military officers, all members of the Horse Guard, who had been stationed in Ottawa in connection with several engineering and surveying projects. A few of the officers, in particular Lord Cecil and Lieutenant Dunlop, had taken to preaching the gospel among soldiers and civilians. News of their ministrations does not appear to have sat particularly well with their senior officers who referred the matter to their superiors in London. Military authorities suggested that if the young officers intended to remain in the service of the Horse Guard, they would be well advised to refrain from public preaching. The men chose instead to resign their commissions, and the whole affair excited enormous discussion in the local Baptist community.

The various activities of Lord Cecil and Lieutenant Dunlop were monitored with considerable interest, especially when they resigned their commissions on the grounds that the "Lord said to David 'Because thou hast been a man of blood, thou shalt not build me a house'."[35] Notwithstanding the reason given by Lord Cecil and Lieutenant Dunlop for resigning their commissions, there is no evidence that either one of them was actively (or even remotely) involved in the advancement of church architecture.[36] Their activities continued to be a source of ongoing interest, and the men were depicted to some extent as martyrs for the Baptist cause.[37] Their "going down into the water" was duly noted, and, in several instances, their preaching was credited with the outbreak of revival.[38] Resignations and revivals notwithstanding, there is no evidence to suggest that these former men of blood ever made any effort to build a church or that the matter of church building was of any particular importance to them. Still, this does not suggest that the Baptists of Central Canada put no value on the building of churches. The Baptist press was full of notices announcing the opening of newly built churches (fig. 5.9).

There does not appear, however, to have been any fixed policy regarding the organization, building, or financing of churches. This lack of direction is well illustrated by a letter sent to the *Canadian Baptist* in January 1867. The correspondent explained that he was writing to the press because "the Canadian Baptist is the organ through which the principles of Baptists are made known to the world" and that he wished to publicize the problems his own community had encountered in the building of their chapel so that they

Fig. 5.9. Baptist Chapel (Baptist), Osgoode Township, 1870s.

This 1870s engraving clearly shows that Ottawa Valley Baptists were using Gothic to distinguish their churches as a place of Christian—if not specifically Baptist—worship (Source: Belden, *Carleton County, 1879*, p. 49).

might be avoided by other Baptists.[39] The editors refused to publish the location of the chapel in question, but did publish the rest of the letter on the grounds that "the principle involved in the following plan of chapel building and management is what mainly interests the public."[40] The letter was lengthy and somewhat convoluted; however, according to the evidence, it appears that arrangements to build a Baptist church were made based on the sale of forty shares. When the church building was completed, those who held full shares that were paid up were given first choice of the best seats. The complainant claimed that six pews were also reserved for a choir, one for the minister's family, and eight at the door for strangers. The whole affair had apparently been the source of considerable chagrin in the parish. So that this same fate might not trouble other parishes, the correspondent recommended that those planning to build Baptist churches might wish to consider the following:

> 1. That it is unwise for the parties to undertake the building of a chapel or place of worship as share-holders.
>
> 2. That it is not right for the share-holders, after the opening of the chapel and setting it apart as God's house, to make it a house of merchandise in taking possession of the pews as private property for themselves.[41]

Fig. 5.10. First Baptist (Baptist), Ottawa, 1877–1881.

Built in 1877, this church underwent major structural modifications after the ceiling collapsed in 1881. It is much more reflective of contemporary Gothic fashion than many of its rural counterparts, which may be attributed to its location in the national capital and suggests a desire to establish architectural parity with St. Andrew's Church of Scotland and the Anglican Cathedral. Builders added an asymmetrical tower, which, like the triplets, was more an indication of contemporary taste than of Baptist Ecclesiology (Source: *Canadian Illustrated News*, 9 November 1878, p. 300).

What little architectural advice there was appears to have been shared primarily through the Baptist press. The *Canadian Baptist* also took it upon itself to inform its readership on matters related to civil regulation.[42] Even after the founding of the Church Edifice Society in 1868, the *Canadian Baptist* continued to be a primary vehicle for the diffusion of architectural information. Readers were reminded of practical considerations and warned that the laws of Ontario should not be confused with the laws of Quebec. Baptists in Ontario, it seems, suffered from the erroneous belief that church property, in general, was not subject to tax. The *Canadian Baptist* pointed out that in Ontario, contrary to the situation in Quebec, "no church property except the building used for worship and the ground connected with it is exempt from municipal taxes."[43]

In 1870, the *Canadian Baptist* published what it claimed to be an "almost exhaustive list of topics [that] will be useful not only for Conventions, Institutes and teachers' meetings but for pastors, superintendents, speakers and writers on Sunday school subjects generally." The article listed the 142 different suggested topics. While the roster contained subjects ranging from "How can a Sunday school be made attractive without a loss of spiritual power?" to "Hints on the art of preaching to children" to "How to best praise God in singing."[44] There was not a word on church building, or even a suggestion that the merits of having one's own church building be discussed. Still, advertisements in the Baptist press suggest that this was not a subject without market. By the mid-1870s, the *Canadian Baptist* regularly published advertisements from commercial enterprises along with its religious articles and general news. Among those who advertised on a regular basis were several companies specializing in the production of church fittings and stained glass. The samples illustrated in many of the advertisements depicted windows with religious figural imagery. By the 1880s, the *Canadian Baptist* was carrying an ever increasing quantity of secular advertisements. A considerable variety of material, including hats, pianos, insecticides, corsets, and "Eggleston's elastic trusses for hernias," was advertised alongside stained glass and religious imagery. Throughout this time, however, there was no discussion by journalists or correspondents as to when or how such windows might be integrated into a church building. When architectonic progress was discussed in a public forum, it was done so with considerable verbal economy. Typically, a church opening was described as follows:

> This is the first and only Protestant place of worship in East Hawkesbury. The building is 36 x 24 feet; it is frame. The posts are grooved and filled in with sided timber; making a very solid and compact wall, and they intend to finish the outside with brick in the spring. Inside it is both neat and comfortable.[45]

Equally cryptic in terms of stylistic discussion was a report concerning Baptist activity in Ottawa where a fine, if somewhat austere, Gothic church had recently been completed. It was noted that, only a few years earlier, there had been no Baptist church and that the new church was clear of debt—information concerning size and style was not addressed.[46] After a visit to Almonte in 1868, the Baptist minister from Perth, Rev. William Caldwell, voiced his concern that Baptists were still meeting in the local schoolhouse while other Protestants

Fig. 5.11. Baptist Chapel (Baptist), Almonte, 1868.

Typical of Baptist chapels built throughout eastern Ontario and western Quebec, the Almonte chapel is a near perfect replica of the Baptist chapel built nearby in Phillipsville three years earlier. Originally, the principal sacrament, baptism, was not practised inside the church building, but on the shores of the river behind the church (Photo: A. Erdmer).

had suitable churches.[47] He expressed hope that the situation in Almonte would soon be rectified, but pointed out that it would "require a thousand or twelve hundred dollars to build anything commensurate with the growing wants of the place and in keeping with the already existing places of worship."[48] Caldwell's remarks suggest the existence of a certain degree of architectural competition despite claims that Baptists did not treat other Protestant confessions "as rivals but as friends" and that church-building efforts were singularly for and in recognition of God's greater glory. While overt architectural rivalry was denied, the idea of building a place of worship that was not on par with the other churches in town was clearly out of the question. To amend this want, the Baptists of Almonte built for themselves "a beautiful Gothic stone chapel" (fig. 5.11).[49]

By comparison to other local churches this was a modest affair, measuring only 30 by 40 feet. The occasion of its official opening was an important one, nonetheless, and ministers from the neighbouring village of Perth and the townships of Beckwith and McNab came to preach. Of the three sermons,[50] it was that of the Rev. E. Rainboth who spoke on Acts 7:49—"Heaven is my throne and the earth my footstool. What house will you build for me, says the Lord, or what is my place of rest?"—that best reflected the Baptist attitude towards church space.[51] Although Baptist communities were building churches with the hope of increased numerical strength, they were still clearly uncomfortable with any suggestion that God could be pinpointed to a single spot. Furthermore, it cannot be ignored that, for much of the nineteenth century, the single most important sacrament, that of baptism, was not performed inside built space. Even during the winter months, ice would be broken for adults to be baptized in running water.[52] Nor did Ottawa Valley Baptists confine their preaching activities to places built by human hands. Instead, it was common for religious services to be held at the same place where their primary sacrament was performed—at the water's edge. In 1871, one minister was described as preaching "to a large audience on the banks of the Madawaska River under some sturdy Elms that formed a leafy temple of worship."[53] Visible and tangible expression of Baptist belief was clearly not best expressed through architectural embodiment. In the meantime, however, Baptist churches continued to be neat, plain, and Gothic.

Presbyterians

Presbyterians continued to draw frequently on older building traditions, which, for many congregations, meant a continued use of Gothic. It did not mean, however, a dramatic reversal to early medieval Gothic. One historian of Scottish architecture noted tersely that Gothic continued to be used in church building, not because of revived ideals but because it had never really been abandoned (fig. 5.12).[54]

Presbyterian architecture in the Ottawa Valley offers little evidence to the contrary, especially prior to the final quarter of the nineteenth century. Gothic was used primarily to distinguish small, austere structures as a place of Christian worship. In this the external presentation of Presbyterian churches differed little from those of other Anglo-Protestants.

Surviving evidence of structural expression clearly indicates that, while Presbyterian church builders were using Gothic with considerable versatility, they did so with a frugality of form that was a faithful reflection of their Calvinistic heritage (fig. 5.13). Country churches continued to be small rectangular structures with axial entries and unembellished Gothic windows. Whether these churches were of wood, stone, or brick depended primarily on the means and resources of a community.

Fig. 5.12. St. Andrew (Presbyterian), Almonte, 1861.

Originally built by a congregation associated with the Church of Scotland, this church is an excellent example of the continued use of survival Gothic well into the second half of the nineteenth century. The spire is a late and somewhat unfortunate addition to an otherwise fine example of sober Scottish masonry (Photo: A. Erdmer).

When a larger building was needed to accommodate a more populous congregation, the ground plan was simply elongated, as illustrated in 1854 by the enlargement of the original stone church of St. Andrew, Ottawa (fig. 5.14).[55]

A continued commitment to Calvinistic austerity was also evident in the severity and understated bareness of the internal furnishings. Frequently, the pulpit by virtue of its size claimed visual supremacy; however, in keeping with Calvinistic teachings on the importance of sacramental unity, the Eucharistic table and facilities for baptism typically shared the same axial centrality. Occasionally

Fig. 5.13. Melville Auld Kirk (Presbyterian), Ashton, 1879.

When the Gaelic-speaking parishioners of Ashton rebuilt their church in 1879, they combined elements of Scottish survival Gothic, as seen in the strong axial tower and the accentuated quoins, with elements of Anglican revivalist Gothic seen in the sharp slope of the roof and the low lateral walls (Photo: A. Erdmer).

the central portion of the end wall of the sanctuary was defined by applied moulding that took the form of a large Gothic arch. This arrangement had no structural significance and was of minimal decorative value but served more importantly to draw the eye in towards the focal point of cult activity. Little else was added to this minimal embellishment without due cause and reflection. In 1853, Rev. M. Spence had to apply to the church committee and submit a statement for the minutes of the Kirk session before he was allowed to put a branch candlestick in the pulpit.[56]

During the third and fourth quarters of the nineteenth century, Ottawa Valley Presbyterians who, like their Methodist neighbours, had suffered from considerable fragmentation during earlier decades, gradually moved towards a greater confessional unity. In 1861, the Synod of the Free Presbyterian Church of Canada and the United Presbyterian Synod in Canada in Connection with the United Presbyterian Church in Scotland joined forces. Later, in 1875, synods of the Church of Scotland united with other Presbyterians to form the Presbyterian Church of Canada.[57] Many Presbyterian congregations now found themselves in a situation similar to that of certain Methodist communities. Their modest church building of earlier days was not always well adapted to the augmented numbers of a unified congregation. Unsegmented resources soon allowed for more emphatic statements of architectural purpose. Despite this, Presbyterian church builders did not indulge in flamboyant displays of architectural decor (fig. 5.15).

Fig. 5.14. St. Andrew (Presbyterian), Almonte, 1861.

The addition of a transept was to facilitate the placement of a larger portion of the congregation in greater proximity to the pulpit. There is nothing to suggest that builders were influenced either by the Anglican style or by contemporary fashion (Photo: A. Erdmer).

Fig. 5.15. St. Andrew (Presbyterian), Ottawa, 1872.

This forceful entry with its skilfully carved archivolts and elevated gable does not lead into the main body of the church, but opens onto a large landing. The sanctuary is located in the small transept, seen on the right. A second transept, hidden by the tower, allowed more parishioners to sit immediately in front of the pulpit (Photo: V. Bennett).

Fig. 5.16. Lochwinnoch Church (Presbyterian), Lochwinnoch, 1894.

This church reflects traces of Anglican influence, as seen in the large gable end window and the side entry. Inside, however, there is no central aisle. A central block of pews is set in front of an axial pulpit that stands against the end wall, beneath the tracery of a large Gothic arch. No other architectural features are associated with the sanctuary (Photo: V. Bennett).

The majority advanced, but with extreme caution, into a slightly expanded use of Gothic. This was usually most evident in the construction of asymmetrical entries surmounted by towers and elongated steeples. When the church was entered by way of a side door or vestibule in the tower base, the gable wall that stood opposite the sanctuary was often opened with a large Gothic window. There is little evidence to suggest that Presbyterian church builders sought to introduce a revived form of medieval Gothic, as did their Anglican neighbours. Likewise, discussion of architectural symbolism is almost nonexistent.

After having avoided any comprehensive or even systematic discussion of the subject for the better part of a century, the Pres-

Fig. 5.17. Presbyterian Church (Presbyterian), Pembroke, 1881.
Presbyterian church builders were now using cruciform ground plans with amphitheatre-type fittings. Here, a balcony swings out of a small transept and curves around the main body of the church. The window, installed in 1894, reflects a new tolerance for figural imagery although it remains strictly confined to the church windows (Photo: V. Bennett).

byterians of Central Canada decided, in 1890, that the time had come to address the question of church architecture. To this end the Presbyterian Church in Canada announced that it had decided to improve the quality of church architecture by publishing a pamphlet with designs and instructions for the building of their churches. [58] Despite the late date, Presbyterians had not come to this decision with undue haste, for despite minimal public discussion, Presbyterian church builders had been quietly adopting amphitheatre plan churches (fig. 5.17).

These buildings, like those built by many Methodist communities, were distinguished by their stylistic versatility. Similarly, the architectural shell offered few clues about the liturgical arrangements within. Neo-Romanesque or Gothic elements could be used interchangeably according to the taste of the builder. In contrast to the direction given by Anglican officials on the subject of church architecture, Presbyterian officials did not impose similar guidance. There were no prepared guidelines in which basic architectural criteria were set forth, nor was there any real discussion concerning size, proportion, or the requisite furnishings of a Presbyterian church. Instead, Presbyterian officials in Central Canada decided to acquire new church plans by holding a public architectural competition. The project was advertised most prominently not in the Presbyterian press, but in the professional journal, *Canadian Architect and Builder.*[59]

Details relating to the interests of the architectural profession were carefully attended to. Prizes of seventy-five, fifty, and twenty-five dollars were to be awarded to "the three best designs in order of merit irrespective of the class under which they may be sent in."[60] Organizers of the competition were also very particular in terms of how these plans were to be presented.[61] Each set of plans was to be accompanied by a description of the proposed design. Furthermore, in addition to justifying the choice of building material, competitors were also required to provide cost estimates of the church-building project. The committee reserved the right to correct the submitted cost estimates if they were thought to be unduly modest. All decisions set forth by the committee of experts were to be final. Interestingly and in decided contrast to Anglican procedure, this committee of experts was appointed not by officials of the Presbyterian Church, but by the Council of the Ontario Association of Architects and plans were to be submitted directly to the registrar of the Ontario Association of Architects in Toronto.

The Presbyterians did identify seven distinct categories of churches. Each category was identified in terms of its environmental setting, desired capacity, ancillary rooms, and finally heating needs. The two smallest churches were to serve a country parish and small village parish, respectively. The country church was to seat 150 to 200 worshippers, while a small village church was to accommodate 250 to 300. Both types of church were to be heated by stoves, and each was to have a single service room that doubled as a vestry and a library. Churches in larger villages were to accommodate 350 to 400 people but were to have a separate vestry and library. This category of church was to be heated with a furnace. In small town churches, that is, those needing a seating capacity of 350 to 400, there was to be a vestry and a school room. Large town churches were to accommodate 500 to 600 people while city churches were to provide seating for 600 to 1,000 people. Churches in these two categories were to have a vestry, a library, a school room, and a kitchen. Large city churches, that is, those seating 1,000 to 1,300 people, were also to have a vestry, library, and kitchen, but were to have facilities for more than one school room. In the last four categories of churches the architect was responsible for the integral design of an adequate heating system.[62]

While there was reasonable clarity as to just how the architectural illustrations should be drafted, no such precision was made concerning liturgical arrangements or architectural symbolism.[63] In further contrast to earlier Anglican experience, contest organizers did not appear to have been inundated with questions. More significantly, contest organizers appear to have been particularly evasive when replying to questions concerning liturgical arrangements.

Response to the competition was poor, and it was announced again in the early spring of 1891. When re-advertising the competition, a few liturgical concerns were addressed, but not in very helpful terms:

> As the competition is one which is for the purpose of securing good designs, both as to plan and exterior elevations, it was thought better not to hamper the competitors in any way. Each competitor will therefore place the choir in such a position as he may deem will give the best results architecturally and at the same time fulfill the wants of a Presbyterian congregation.
> It is hoped that many of the abler young men in the profession will take this opportunity to attempt to solve the problem of fulfilling the wants of a Presbyterian congregation and at the same time designing a thoroughly ecclesiastical building.[64]

Despite the reluctance of Presbyterian officials to disclose the architectural necessities of Presbyterian worship, they were very careful to stress that architectural authorship would be duly acknowledged and that design copyright would remain inviolate.[65] The call for submissions was reissued on several occasions, each time stressing professional standards but remaining very noncommittal concerning liturgical arrangements. There was neither mention of how the interior of the church was to be arranged, nor was there any mention of stylistic preference or the inclusion of any specific architectonic expression of Christian belief. Furthermore, and in contrast to the middle years of the century when the discussion of religious architecture aroused considerable public fascination, interest in the Presbyterian project was most conspicuous by its absence. In July 1892, the committee of experts who had been appointed to examine the plans of the Presbyterian Church Design Competition admitted that they did not have an adequate sampling of plans to publish the projected pamphlet.[66] Despite this the project was not without benefit, as several satisfactory designs were identified and the committee suggested that attempts could be made once again over the course of the forthcoming winter to secure a greater selection of plans.[67]

Roman Catholics

Roman Catholics made frequent use of Gothic during the second half of the nineteenth century; however, they did so in a manner that was distinctly different from the Anglican or Anglo-Protestant use of Gothic (figs. 5.18-5.20).

Of all the Christian denominations that made application of the Gothic style, it was the Roman Catholics who explored the decorative potential of Gothic most fully. In fact, Roman Catholic church builders in the Ottawa Valley placed such an emphasis on the decorative possibilities of Gothic that it must be seen as a distinctive characteristic of their use of Gothic. This is especially true of their treatment of internal features. Although early Catholic churches had boasted few embellishments, this stark plainness was not due to a quest for primitive simplicity or the espousal of Cistercian principles,

Fig. 5.18. St. Luc (Roman Catholic), Curran, 1863.

Not all Catholics were eager to try new forms of Gothic expression. This is especially evident in rural parishes such as St. Luc, where a very austere form of survival Gothic continued to be used well into the second half of the nineteenth century (Photo courtesy: Archdiocesan Archives Ottawa [R. C.]).

Fig. 5.19. St. Mary (Roman Catholic), Almonte, 1869.

Increasingly the façade of Roman Catholic churches acquired importance. Frontal monumentality was achieved through an emphasis on the central tower, drawing strongly on earlier Anglo-Irish prototypes (Photo: V. Bennett).

but rather to a general lack of material resources. Financial restrictions were such that completion of a church interior was often not an integral part of the original construction project for many parishes.[68] Still, Roman Catholic communities were on the whole no different from other contemporary Christian communities in the Ottawa Valley in that they had limited funds that could be dedicated to the visual expression of their belief. The interiors of many early churches were not finished until the third or fourth quarter of the nineteenth century; such was the case with Notre Dame Cathedral, Ottawa, where Mgr. Gigues halted all work on the interior in 1864, and Our Lady of the Visitation, South Gloucester (fig. 5.21).

Similar projects existed on a lesser scale in many other parishes; many large church-building projects begun in the second half of the nineteenth century such as St. Patrick's Church, Ottawa (fig. 5.20), St-Isidore-de-Prescott (fig. 5.22), and the church in St-Eugène, were extended through the better part of several decades.

The South Gloucester church and the Ottawa cathedral offer clear examples of the diversity with which Gothic was used to decorate Roman Catholic churches.[69] The Gothic interior of the South Gloucester church is distinguished by the use of light colours and slender marbled columns. The walls, vault fields, and spandrels of the intercolumnations of colonnades are painted a creamy yellow. The primary decor is non-figural, consisting essentially of a delicately gilt floral scrolling that clings to the corners of the spandrels and edges of

Fig. 5.20. St. Patrick (Roman Catholic), Ottawa, 1869.
Although modified to adapt to the Canadian climate, the architectonic massings of St. Patrick was very much in keeping with the Puginesque spirit of Gothic (Photo courtesy: Archdiocesan Archives Ottawa [R. C.]).

Fig. 5.21.
Our Lady of the Visitation (Roman Catholic), South Gloucester, c. 1870.
Although the vaults are of plaster and of no structural consequence, decorative Gothic has been used to accentuate vertical monumentality and draw attention to the liturgical focal point (Photo: Xavier Erdmer).

Fig. 5.22.
St. Isidore-de-Prescott (Roman Catholic), St. Isidore-de-Prescott, Photo 1897.

A heavier, but deliberate use of decorative Gothic can be seen in this late-nineteenth-century interior. Gothic styling was used to draw attention to the high altar. The success of these efforts is challenged by the presence of a practical, but very conspicuous stove pipe (Photo courtesy: Archdiocesan Archives Ottawa [R. C.]).

the vault fields. The Gothic arches of the nave's windows, the arch mouldings of the colonnades and the ribs of the vaults are all painted white to animate the upward momentum. This church presents a dramatic contrast to the deeply coloured walls and heavy Gothic embellishments that characterized the cathedral. At Notre Dame, the walls are muraled in deep and regal tones of red and cobalt blue. The mouldings of the colonnades are affixed with carved crockets, and the spandrels with floriated appliqué. The ribs of the vaults are polychrome and the vault fields are painted dark blue with a generous sprinkling of gold stars. The sanctuary contains a monumental reredos encompassing the entire sanctuary.[70] While this is unquestionably a masterpiece of nineteenth century architectural sculpturing, it is peopled with a collection of statues that step forth with emphatic gestures from the space defined by their Gothic pedestals and canopies in a decidedly flamboyant manner.

During the final quarter of the nineteenth century, the taste for ornamentation was ubiquitous in Roman Catholic churches in the Ottawa Valley, although the majority of them were finished with a decor that was somewhat less elaborate than the cathedral. Amid the considerable variety of structural embellishments used by Catholic church builders, the single most conspicuous trait was a careful spatial structuring that emphasized upward momentum, which was achieved most often through the addition of internal fittings that were strictly decorative. Most prominent among such additions were *faux* marbled columns, decorative tracery, and plaster vaults. These were not an integral part of the external shell and bore no structural value, and must be seen as defining characteristics of the Roman Catholic use of Gothic in the Ottawa Valley. Despite its limited structural relevance, this use of Gothic was not strictly decorative in that, while not affiliated with any deeper discourse of Christian expression, it was intended to invite the eye upwards and the heart to a contemplation of higher things. This somewhat superficial application of Gothic is again demonstrated through the manner in which the Roman Catholic church builders adapted Gothic to traditionally non Gothic architectural formulas. Certain Ottawa Valley parishes, such as Ste. Anne, Ottawa,[71] and St. Dominique, Luskville,[72] chose to continue an architectural tradition popular in Quebec since the days of the French regime. Other communities did not wish to abandon traditional structural configurations, but still desired to use Gothic, which was considered to be somewhat more fashionable. This posed no particular problem. Roman Catholic church builders, simply, and without any evidence of much discussion, replaced the round-headed arches with Gothic arches. St. Paul (1857), Plantagenet, and St. Luc

(1863), Curran (fig. 5.18), testify to this trend. Although Gothic had been popular among Roman Catholic church builders, it was not recognized by Roman Catholic authorities as the only way to build Catholic churches. In fact, nineteenth century writings on the subject suggest that style was only a subordinate consideration.[73]

By the final quarter of the nineteenth century, many Catholics were turning a new and revitalized Ultramontanism with increased commitment interest. This did not pass unnoticed by communities in the Ottawa Valley who turned their eyes not simply to Rome, but to Italian culture with a new interest.[74] This trend continues well beyond the nineteenth century. Among the many ways in which Ultramontanism marked contemporary Catholicism was through a dramatic reconfiguration of church architecture, especially manifest in the increasing abandonment of Gothic. Church builders still strived to retain external and internal monumentality, but their inspiration now came from the great basilicas of Rome. In Plantagenet, the

Fig. 5.23. St. Hughes (Roman Catholic), Sarsfield, 1867 and 1895.
Fewer illustrations offer a more striking demonstration of the architectonic revolution that occurred when the influence of Ultramontanist thought encouraged a general abandonment of Gothic in favour of an Italianate style. The original Gothic church is shown during the course of demolition, while the walls of the new church rise well above the roof of the earlier modest structure (Photo courtesy: Archdiocesan Archives Ottawa [R. C.]).

earlier Gothic church was eventually remodeled to be as un-Gothic as possible. While the exterior stone shell of the church has retained its Gothic windows—which would have been difficult and expensive to change—the interior window frames were re-plastered and replaced by round-headed windows. Inside, the unusual configuration of the spandrels of the colonnade suggest that pointed segments of the Gothic arches had simply been plastered over. At this same time, Catholic church builders were also raising structures with larger windows and brighter interiors. The lateral walls of Roman Catholic churches were rising to unprecedented heights, accompanied by a similar expansion of the windows in the lateral walls. A striking example of this can be seen in a photograph (c. 1895) depicting the original church of St. Hughes (1867), Sarsfield, and the new church under construction immediately beside it. Though incomplete, the walls of the new church rise well above the roof crest of the older building (fig. 5.23).[75]

Ideally, according to nineteenth century treatises on this subject, Catholic churches were to be distinctly placed, with favour given to a conspicuous or elevated sight. In doing so, the church could rise above the commerce of everyday life as symbolic of higher aspirations.[76] While the façades of most Catholic churches built in the Ottawa Valley during the first half of the nineteenth century had been in architectural equilibrium with their surroundings, this practice was not continued. Instead, during the final quarter of the nineteenth century, there was a marked move towards a new frontal monumentality. There is considerable continuity in the configuration of these façades despite some stylistic variation (fig. 5.24). The façades of these churches were powerful, dominant, and triumphant.

By the late nineteenth century, Roman Catholic churches were systematically raised by several steps above the surrounding site. Many churches featured a strong central tower set in relief of the main façade. Side entries were often opened in the façade of the church while the main entry was placed in the base of the tower. The main entry also enjoyed increased architectural emphasis as it marked the longitudinal axis of the church which culminated at the high altar. Above the entry was the tower, which rose well beyond the apex of the roof and was surmounted by a steeple or a slender spire. The uppermost reach of the physical church was marked with a cross. St. Paul (1877), Plantagenet; St. Laurent (1885), Carlsbad Springs; Our Lady of Malacky (1890), Mayo; St. Hughes (1894), Sarsfield, all offer good examples of this façade type. The configuration of the façade was, in turn, to anticipate the interior of the church.[77] As few nineteenth century interiors have

Fig. 5.24. Our Lady of Malaky (Roman Catholic), Mayo, 1897.

By the late nineteenth century, Roman Catholic church builders were achieving equally dramatic façades without any reference to Gothic. This stylistic change rarely affected the architectonic massing of the church façade itself (Photo: A. Erdmer).

survived the twentieth century without radical transformations, it is nevertheless possible to identify in some churches, such as St. Bernard, Fournier. There is a conspicuous constancy between the stylistic structure of the principal façade and the architectural features of the high altar. Thematic continuity between the site, the type of building chosen, and a new monumental treatment of the façade reflects one of the most significant architectonic developments in Roman Catholic church building in the Ottawa Valley. While Gothic is used in the construction of some of these façades, there is no evidence to suggest that this style was considered in any way uniquely suited to the embodiment of Roman Catholic belief. By the latter decades of the nineteenth century, Catholics in the Ottawa Valley chose to proclaim their faith not through Gothic style but my means of architectural monumentality.

Complacent Application and Challenges

In January 1872, the church-building committee of Christ Church (Anglican), Ottawa, looked around at the building activities in the capital of the new country and announced that "the time has fully arrived when the congregation of Christ Church should furnish themselves with a building harmonizing with the improvements taking place in the architecture of the city."[78] This marked a significant change from the discourse of only a few years earlier and was reflective more of attitudes from the earlier decades of the century rather than those recently advocated by Camdanian Ecclesiologists and other revivalists. It still was only after this declaration, which clearly denotes a certain preoccupation with one's secular image, that the committee noted that they were also in need of a building that was "more worthy of the high and sacred purpose to which it is devoted."[79] After several meetings in which neither the embodiment of Christian principle or the intrinsically Christian nature of Gothic were discussed, the building committee informed the parishioners of Christ Church that it had given the architect license to prepare plans according to his own discretion, on the sole condition that expenses did not overrun their ceiling of $25,000.[80] The committee had not specified that the church be built in the Gothic style, although it had chosen King Arnoldi, who had worked so hard to retain the "Early English" flavour of St. Alban's Church during the 1860s. By the 1870s, however, Arnoldi was no longer working in the "Early English" style Gothic, but in what was commonly referred to as "Decorated" or "Middle English" Gothic. In reality this form of Gothic was marked much more by High Victorian fashion than by a spirit of archaeological fidelity (fig. 5.25).

Fig. 5.25. Christ Church Cathedral (Anglican), Ottawa, 1872.

Although the architect King Arnoldi was well versed in medieval Gothic, Christ Church, is much more a product of Victorian taste than Camdanian Ecclesiology. The ornate iron finials that once topped the pinnacles and the large cross that once marked the apex of the gable end have been removed (Photo: V. Bennett).

While most Anglican church building remained solidly grounded in the architectural and liturgical arrangements of the revivalist movement, many architectonic configurations were gradually being taken for granted (fig. 5.26).

Much of the zeal and enthusiasm that marked the discussion of Gothic during the middle years of the century was disappearing from common parlance (fig. 5.27).

Fig. 5.26. St. Paul (Anglican), Shawville, 1872.
While the builders were clearly inspired by English Gothic, they lacked the stylistic agility seen at St. Paul's Church, Almonte (Fig. 4.7). The walls are low, the slope of the roof great, and the chancel is architecturally distinct. Early English triplets are used, but at the wrong end of the building. Window gables are used to break the roof line of the lateral wall. There is a static dryness that is not a factor at the Almonte church (Photo: V. Bennett).

During the final decades of the nineteenth century, Gothic was losing its unchallenged position as the preferred style for the architectonic expression of Christian belief. Some Anglicans were openly suggesting that the use of medieval Gothic was not necessarily indicative of architectural wisdom. In 1889, Sir Daniel Wilson, a founding member of the Royal Society of Canada and then president of the University of Toronto, published an article in the *Canadian Architect and Builder*, in which he severely criticized architects in the service of the Church of England for perpetuating medieval models. Architecturally, he argued, these churches were ill suited to the needs and realities of Anglican worship.[81] Soon afterwards, architectural professionals were stating that they were no longer content to simply theorize about the suitable arrangements of church buildings. An article that appeared in the *Canadian Architect and Builder*, in 1890, demonstrates that architectural professionals were prepared to jealously defend not only their ability, but their right to build proper churches:

> It is an undeniable fact that 90% of our churches are entirely devoid of any artistic quality, the greater number of the remaining 10% are not what they should be. . . . In the opinion of many, a building of simple parts is devoid of artistic merit, while the building of many parts is one of beauty. A building of simple well proportioned design looks so simple to the ignorant individual that he at once assumes that he could design one of equal merit and that consequently it does not amount to much. . . . What a blessing it would be if the unnecessary architectural features on our churches . . . were done without, and their cost devoted to other purposes of a legitimate character.[82]

This text is a significant reflection of the milieu into which the discussion of church building had passed. By the end of the nineteenth century, much of the discussion about church architecture had returned to questions of aesthetics and style. Inasmuch as Gothic was now involved, stylistic choice had shifted from the theologian to the architect.

Fig. 5.27. St. John the Evangelist (Anglican), Quyon, 1885.
Builders were unquestionably guided by Gothic revivalists, however, this is not a pure use of revivalist Gothic; instead it foreshadows a new use of Gothic that was to find a fuller expression during the opening decades of the twentieth century (Photo: V. Bennett).

Notes

1. X. B. de Montault, *Traité pratique de la construction, de l'ameublement et de la décoration des églises selon les règles économiques et les traditions romaines avec un appendice sur le costume ecclésiastique* (Paris: P. Louis Vivès, 1878), 24.

2. *Canadian Christian Examiner and Presbyterian Magazine,* March 1840, 90-91.

3. Ibid.

4. *Christian Guardian*, 10 March 1847, 82.

5. *Christian Guardian*, January 1848, n.p.

6. For further discussion of this phenomenon see V. Bennett, "Religious Regulation of Anglo-Protestant Cult Space in nineteenth century Canada," *Des dieux et des hommes en terre Canadienne,* ed. R. Lemieux, (Québec: Presses de l'Université Laval), forthcoming.

7. *Christian Guardian*, 10 March 1847, 82.

8. Ibid.

9. " . . . a just reply can be given only in view of the circumstances of those who make the inquiry. What may be suitable in one place may be unsuitable in another place; but in no case, we believe, should the house of God be *inferior* to the house of His servants; and well may that servant blush who leaves his own comfortable and richly-furnished dwelling to worship his master on the holy Sabbath, in a house that will bear no kind of comparison with the building he so recently left. Shall the servant be greater than the lord?" *Christian Guardian*, 10 March 1847, 82.

10. *Christian Guardian*, 10 March 1847, 82.

11. Ibid.

12. "I think that at the present a good deal of attention is being paid by our connexion [*sic*] to the matter of church building. . . . But sometimes mistakes occur. The buildings designed for a 'house of prayer' is as shapeless or ill shaped, nondescript kind of thing; without symmetry, without regular proportions; commenced and finished without a plan or design. . . . Some are inconveniently low, others needlessly high, . . . and in other respects built in defiance of all rules of Architecture, and when built, inconvenient and unhandsome, nor as durable as though the plan and work had been done according to the rules of the building Art." *Christian Guardian,* 19 March 1856, 94.

13. *Christian Guardian,* 19 March 1856, 94.

14. Ibid.

15. Ibid.

16. "Let a competent architect be employed. One sufficiently acquainted with our peculiar forms and usage to know how to construct the internal part of a church so as to be adapted to our use—let him furnish plans of churches of various sizes—with front and side views—plans of internal arrangement, with specifications and such directions as would be necessary for the guide of mechanics and as would be understood by our people; and let him be paid for his work from the chapel relief fund. Let such plans as may be approved of by a competent committee be adopted." *Christian Guardian,* 19 March 1856, 94.

17. Ex. 26: 1-37.

18. 1 Kings 5: 15-32; 1 Kings 6: 1-36.

19. 1 Chronicles 21: 23-25.

20. *Christian Guardian*, 21 February 1861, 33.

21. John 12: 3-6.

22. *Christian Guardian*, 21 February 1861, 33.

23. *Christian Guardian*, 21 February 1861, 33.

24. "We object to the covert idea implied in the association of 'fine churches' with fashionable religion. Our interrogation links these together and claims to be in the opposition against us. Begging his pardon, there is some religious caut [*sic*] in his phrase, it begs the question. By fashionable religion we suppose he means that which is formal merely, unspiritual having a decent body but no soul. Now it be really so, by any law of nature or grace that people can not worship devoutly in a handsome and costly church then we give it up. If they must abjure taste, comfort, good architectural proportions, neat furniture and all en [*sic*] crossing their thresholds and starting to the house of God, under pain of not worshipping him in spirit and truth, than away with paint and planed planks, don't even peel the poles; let us have dirt floors and things to match." *Christian Guardian*, 21 February 1861, 33.

25. *Christian Guardian*, 21 February 1861, 33.

26. Rev. W. T. Hewitt, *Annual Report of the Wesleyan Methodist Church in Canada in Connection with the English Conference 1854*, xxxviii.

27. Rev. W. T. Hewitt, *Annual Report of the Wesleyan Missionary Society in Canada in Connection with the English Conference, 1858*, n.p. City of Ottawa Archives, Box MM2.

28. At the time of its construction in 1862, the church was referred to as "Stevenson Church," and, during the 1870s, it appears in reports as the 9th Line Church of the Fitzroy Mission. The name Diamond appears to have been used for the first time in 1885, although the nearby settlement had been known as Diamond Village since 1859. The name itself comes from the village of Diamond in County Antrim, Ireland, the birthplace of some of the local settlers. O.A.C. United Church Records Collection, Box 9/Fir 26-(a).

29. "During the past decade, that is to say from 1871 to 1881, our denomination has exhibited a very extraordinary spirit of Church enterprise in the direction of building churches, parsonages, and colleges. The last published statistics of the church show an increase of church property, for the same period of eight hundred and eleven thousand, three hundred and fifty dollars . . . the figures adduced give ample evidence of real advancement, and, in our opinion, are well calculated to assure all who are engaged in the work of building up the Methodist Episcopal church in this Country." *Canada Christian Advocate*, 24 December 1881, n.p.

30. "Of course this denominational zeal and progressive spirit developed in the past few years have led us into debt. It could not be otherwise; and in this we are sharing the experience of every active and aggressive Church in the country. We ought to be thankful for this common experience. Thank God that no one denomination in this land can claim the monopoly on church debts. They are within the reach of us all. *Canada Christian Advocate*, 24 December 1881, n.p.

31. *Canada Christian Advocate*, 24 December 1881, n.p.

32. "One district alone, Ottawa, we are told has, during the past eight years, raised over one hundred thousand dollars for building and relieving churches within the bounds of the district. . . . If our church has accomplished anything for God in this country and made headway in face of difficulty and danger, it is due, humanly speaking, to the men who have believed in things and in God and evinced their faith by heroes deeds and personal consecration. The value of our church property has very nearly trebled in the past ten years, our people have greatly increased in wealth, and there is amongst us at present a spirit of enterprise and liberality unprecedented in the history of the denomina-

tions. We are in common with other sections of the Church of God, bearing the burdens and doing work for our common Lord. . . . " *Canada Christian Advocate*, 24 December 1881, n.p.

33. For a fuller discussion of Akron plan churches in Canadian context, see Janis R. Zubalik, "'Advancing the Material Interests of the Redeemer's Kingdom': The Erskine Presbyterian Church, Montreal, 1894"; M.A. thesis, Concordia University, 1986.

34. Typical of this was the exegesis of 1 Cor. 3:10-15, presented by Rev. J. Cooper to the Elgin C. Ministerial Conference in London under the heading "The Building, The Builder and His Works." In the lengthy discussion, the author suggested that the key to understanding the whole letter lay in line 9 where Paul's own use of symbolism shifts from the horticultural to the architectural. He then uses the text as a platform from which to reaffirm the Baptist position concerning church-state relations and infant baptism:

> What are we to understand by this building? What is its material? How is it erected? Does the Apostle refer to doctrines or to persons? Would he have us understand that he is speaking of the temple of truth, or of man? The general opinion is that he is speaking of doctrines and that his meaning may be stated as follows: The foundation being Christ, the gold, silver, and precious stones represent the true doctrines of the Gospel; that truth which has come from Christ, and which like the precious metals is indestructible . . . The wood, hay, and stubble on the other hand, represent false or unsound doctrines to which, when the true test shall be applied, they shall be like wood in the fire . . . According to this view, the passage is an exhortation to test the doctrines we preach.
>
> In the other view this temple is thought to be persons. Christ is the foundation; the aggregate of professed believers in Christ. Some believe in vain—dead while they live. The gold, silver, and precious stones represent those who are truly Christ's—good material on a good foundation. The wood, hay, and stubble, are false professors, attached to the Church, but not in Christ, and who lack that indestructible quality which renders the other fire-proof. The former is the popular view and sustained by the great bulk of commentators. We shall now endeavor to prove that the latter is the Apostle's meaning. . . .
>
> . . . They [the Corinthians] were thus the objects of his special care and his pious fear, for in losing them, he would lose his reward. To whom he says: "I have planted, Apollo watered, but God gave the increase," "ye are God's husbandry," that is his field or vineyard; we must observe that he is still speaking of persons, and that just as an efficient gardener can point to his garden and say "That is my work," so Paul's highest ambition was to convert souls and at last present everyone he taught perfect in Jesus. Then the figure is changed from the garden to a building. "Ye are God's building." This figure runs through the whole paragraph and is the key to its meaning. . . .
>
> To understand the Apostle speaking here of doctrines rather than of persons does not harmonize with his other teachings. This building, of which as a wise master-builder, Paul laid the foundation in the 10th verse, is the temple of God in the 17th verse. But this is not a temple of truth, but of persons. "Not strangers and foreigners but fellow citizens with the saints of the household of God; built on the foundation of the Apostles and Prophets, Jesus Christ himself being the chief cornerstone, in whom all the building fitly framed together grows into a holy temple in the Lord, in whom also ye are builded together for an habitation of God through the Spirit. Eph. 2. 19-22. Who can doubt that the conception here is identical with that in our paragraph. Saints are built on the foundations of the Apostles and Prophets. This is the genitive of agent or originating cause. The Apostles were not the foun-

dation, Rev. 21, 14; . . . Peter also tells us that believers coming to Christ as a living stone, are built up as living stones on him; the same word is applied to him and them, for when they come to him they become alive as he is; and they are built up a spiritual house, and offer up spiritual sacrifices acceptable to God through him." We know of no text where Paul speaks of the temple of truth, or the Holy Spirit dwelling in true doctrine; or in a correct system of theology.

To make this a temple of doctrines rather than of persons introduces confusion of thought. . . . As a wise master-builder Paul says he laid the foundation, and another (builder) buildeth thereon, but if he lay unsuitable material on that foundation his work shall be destroyed. Now, to say that the builder *teaches*, is to confuse figures which Paul does not. He says the builder *builds* a temple; and of believers themselves, he says, "Ye are my work"—ye are the living stones—the gold, silver and precious stones of which the temple of God is composed. That the building itself is the builder's work is certainly the truth which is here taught. In the capacity of a builder Paul's mission was twofold. First, he expounded the doctrine of Christ for the salvation of men. . . .

The view we are opposing extracts the spirit from the whole paragraph, and makes it tame and insipid. . . .

This is one of the many passages in Paul's writings that have been obscured by the systematic introduction of the world into the church. Lax practices in the church will lead to lax interpretation of Scripture. Every favorite *ism* must be brought under the wing of the holy book, and to everything that ecclesiastical authority has decreed to be expedient, it must lend its high sanction. Foremost in this wholesale corruption of the living temple stands the State Church. The country is cut into sections, and every man in the parish is expected to be a member of the parish church, whether he understands anything about conversion or not. And not only is this privilege thrown open to all adults but it is also thrown open to children. Infant baptism is the life blood of Church State ism [*sic*]. In the language of one party, baptism signifies and seals the child's grafting into Christ. Another calls it an outward and visible sign of an inward and spiritual grace and a third more plainly still declares that the baptized is no longer outside of the member saved, but has in the rite been made a member of the body of Christ and heir of the kingdom of heaven. The children of Episcopalians, Methodists, Presbyterians, and Congregationalists are taught often this manner in their Sabbath schools, and when children don't believe what they are taught, teachers are wont to regard it as a calamity. In some of these communions the doctrine is openly preached and spread, that a young person even though not converted, is safer in the church than in the world, just as a lamb is safer in the fold than in the woods. Let any one examine the commentaries written by Pedobaptists on this paragraph, and he will perceive that with scarcely an exception they will trip on this point, and very conveniently confine the loss of the unskillful builder to his unsound doctrine, without any regard to his corrupted membership. . . . (*Canadian Baptist,* 5 September 1867, 2).

35. "Ottawa Correspondence," *Canadian Baptist*, 23 July 1868, 1.

36. A Lieutenant Turner also appears to have been involved with this group, although it is not clear if he was actually preaching or if he, too, resigned his commission in the Horse Guards.

37. *Canadian Baptist*, 15 August 1868, 2.

38. "The Revival on the Ottawa," *Canadian Baptist,* 24 September 1868.

39. *Canadian Baptist,* January 1867, 2.

40. Ibid.

41. Ibid.

42. "Church doors Opening Outward—We would call the attention of the deacons and trustees of Baptist Churches to the requirements of law with the references to the doors of Churches 'opening outwards.' The Act goes into force very soon and neglect will render them libel to penalties. The Act goes into force almost immediately." *Canadian Baptist*, 15 August 1867, 3.

43. *Canadian Baptist*, 13 December 1888, 3.

44. *Canadian Baptist*, 23 June 1870, 2.

45. *Canadian Baptist*, 5 December 1867, 2.

46. "You will be interested to know what is going on in the Capital City of Ottawa. Well a merciful God has not overlooked the struggles and labours of love of his people here . . . A few years ago there was not a vestige of a Baptist Church in Ottawa City, it now members over 60 persons. Last year they cleared the chapel of debts. . . . The Protestant ministers of this city (Church of England excepted) met in the Baptist Chapel for united prayer on the first Monday of the month." *Canadian Baptist*, February 1868, 3.

47. "Nearly all the Evangelical denominations have flourishing interests here and beautiful places of worship. . . . " " The Cause in Almonte," *Canadian Baptist*, March 1868, 2.

48. "The Cause in Almonte," *Canadian Baptist*, March 1868, 2.

49. *Canadian Baptist*, 21 January 1869, 2.

50. Rev. Caldwell of Perth preached on John 4:24, and Rev. John Stewart of Beckwith on 2 Cor. 3:18.

51. This attitude is especially clear when read in the context of the preceding line, Acts VII-48: "Yet the most High does not dwell in houses made with hands."

52. It was not uncommon for Baptists to equate Baptism with descending into the grave with Christ. *Canadian Baptist,* March 1871, 2.

53. *Canadian Baptist*, 21 September 1871, 2. The Madawaska is a tributary of the Ottawa River.

54. This author betrays his own position on church building as being one somewhat hostile to the movements that occurred within the Church of England: "For an adequate study of Scottish post-Reformation church architecture, some appreciation of the factors which contributed to it is necessary . . . popular conceptions both of the Middle Ages and of the Reformed period are still largely the product of the Romantic Movement and of the dubious Ecclesiology to which it gave rise." G. Hay, *The Architecture of Scottish Post-Reformation Churches 1560-1843*, (Oxford: Clarendon Press, 1957), 38.

55. Minutes of the Temporal Committee meeting, 19 April 1854, Public Archives of Canada, MG-9 D7-35 vol. 23 Part 1.

56. Minutes of the Temporal Committee Meeting, (St. Andrew's Church of Scotland, Ottawa), 23 May 1853, Public Archives of Canada, MG D7-35 vol. 23, Part 1.

57. Traces of this once prevalent divisiveness can still be identified in some contemporary accounts of local parish history. In one instance, it is suggested that several psychological and theological differences keep the Church of Scotland synods from joining the initial move towards Presbyterian unity. Members of the Church of Scotland are identified as being much less temperance-minded, less evangelical, more lax in doctrine and as politically rigid conservatives, who "made pretensions of being a state establishment of religion" and regarded other Presbyterian bodies as "dissenters from the Scottish Religious Establishment." G. Lucas, *St. Paul's, Carp Ontario, 1824-1974*, 27.

58. *Canadian Architect and Builder*, December 1890, 134.

59. "It is proposed to have a competition of designs of churches as per the list of requirements given hereafter, and to publish those designs which may meet with the

approval of the experts. The plans and perspectives only, with possibly one elevation will be illustrated, as it is not desirable to give sufficient drawings to allow the design being made use of except through the author. The intention of the committee of the Presbyterian church which has this matter in hand, is that the author of a design which may be approved of by any congregation proposing to build shall be employed at the usual commission." *Canadian Architect and Builder*, December 1890, 134.

60. *Canadian Architect and Builder,* December 1890, 134. This does not appear to have been considered an overly generous purse even in the late 1800s. Organizers soon felt it necessary to justify the sum offered. "The Committee does not expect that all three prizes which it has decided to give are sufficient inducement to competitors to send in designs, and it has only proposed to give these prizes as a small acknowledgment on its part of the obligation under which the Committee will be placed to those who may send in designs." *Canadian Architect and Builder,* February 1891, 24.

61. "The drawings are to be prepared in black and white to a scale of 8 feet to the inch, plans and elevations in line only with windows blocked in or not as preferred by the designer. The perspective should be a thoroughly good drawing, and may be rendered thought fit; but a large amount of extraneous material should not be put in. The perspectives to be set up from a plan drawn four feet to an inch." It was also stipulated that the "experts will be instructed to favour the designs for small and inexpensive buildings in preference to those for large and costly ones. . . . Bad or inferior drawings will not be illustrated no matter how good the design may be, but an opportunity will be afforded the author to prepare or have prepared, suitable drawings. . . . The excellence of a plan will consist in the closeness with which the conditions have been fulfilled, the quality of the design and the inexpensiveness of erecting the building. No limit has been made as to the cost in any class, as it is desirable that the designers should not be hampered except in so far that he must bear in mind that a good design which is inexpensive is superior to an equally good or even better design which will cost more money." *Canadian Architect and Builder,* December 1890, 134.

62. *Canadian Architect and Builder,* December 1890, 134.

63. The following is a statement of the classes of buildings that are required to meet the wants of the average congregations in each of the classes in which it has been thought well to divide church buildings:

1st. Country Church to seat from 150 to 200 persons, with one room to be used as a vestry and library. Church to be heated with stoves.

2nd. Village church, capacity 250 to 300 persons, with one room to be used as a vestry and library. Church to be heated with stoves.

3rd. Large Village Church, seating 350 to 400, with vestry and library. To be furnace heated.

4th. Small town church seating 350 to 400 persons with vestry or school room.

5th. Large town church with seating capacity of from 500 to 600, with vestry, library, school room and kitchen.

6th. City church, seating from 600 to 1,000, with vestry, library, school room and kitchen.

7th. Large city church, seating from 1,000 to 1,300, with vestry, library school rooms and kitchen.

In the last four clauses the designer will himself settle the method of heating and arrange the same. All designs to be sent in on or before the 14th day of March 1891, addressed to the Registrar of the Ontario Association of Architects, Toronto. (*Canadian Architect and Builder,* December 1890, 134.)

64. *Canadian Architect and Builder,* February 1891, 24.

65. "The Council of the Ontario Association of Architects has undertaken to conduct the competition, because it believes that much benefit may result to the church architecture of the Province through the effort that is now being made by this denomination. There is no intention to publish any designs which may be submitted in a manner which will allow there being used by any congregation which desires to erect a church, without employing the author. Only the perspective and the plans will be shown, with the object of 1st, giving examples of what is considered good ecclesiastical architecture by competent judges; and 2nd, to afford congregations proposing to build such information as will enable them to select such information as will enable them to select an architect capable of designing a church such as they may want, with some artistic excellence. . . ." *Canadian Architect and Builder*, February 1891, 24.

66. *Canadian Architect and Builder,* July 1892, 71.

67. Ibid.

68. There is little surviving evidence of early interiors, which, for the most part, appear to have been plain, painted in equally plain colours, or simply whitewashed. The church of Our Lady of the Visitation, South Gloucester, was finished in 1849; however the interior decor was not finished until 1860, and box pews were not built until 1874.

69. For a complete analysis of the architecture and interior decor of Notre-Dame, see N. Pagé, *La Cathédrale Notre-Dame d'Ottawa,* (Ottawa: Les Presses de l'Université d'Ottawa, 1988).

70. This work is discussed in detail in Pagé, *La Cathédrale Notre-Dame,* 106-126.

71. C.I.H.B. Archives, File 061070026-00530. In keeping with these desires, the churches were entered by a principal axial entry that was flanked to either side by two lesser doors. All three doors stood beneath round-headed archways, the upper portion of which was usually filled with a window. Above the doors were windows, statue niches, or a combination of both. These façades were frequently pierced by an oculus just below the apex of the gable end. A bell turret or steeple was set back slightly in retreat of the façade. To accentuate the façade, acroterion were often added to either end of the gable base.

72. C.I.H.B. Archives, File 050046000-00052. Both Ste-Anne and St-Dominique are well preserved.

73. "Le style basilical est simple, majestueux, économique. . . . Le style byzantin n'est pas à dédaigner avec ses coupoles et sa richesse de décoration. . . . Le style roman est sévère, lourd, imposant, mais d'ordinaire il est sombre et a des nefs trop étroites. . . . Le style ogival, que l'on a dit l'apogée de l'art chrétien, a des grâces particulières dans son ornementation. Toutefois que sa nef, longue et serrée, se prête peu aux réunions ou l'on veut voir et entendre. . . . Le style de la renaissance inaugure le retour aux formes classiques. . . . Le style moderne accentue de plus en plus les traditions de l'antiquité grecque et romaine, mais pour les détails seulement car il crée de toutes pièces les vaisseaux les plus commodes pour l'exercice du culte." Barbier de Montault, *Traité Pratique,* 25.

74. For a fuller discussion of this phenomenon see Pierre Savard, "L'Italie dans la culture canadienne-française au XIXe siècle, in *Les Ultramontains canadiens-français,* ed. Nive Voisine et Jean Hamelin (Montreal: Boréal Express, 1985), 255-266.

75. Archives of the Archdiocese of Ottawa (Roman Catholic), Sarsfield Collection, file P.

76. Many nineteenth century guides to church-building stress this point; see, for example, Mgr. Devie, *Manuel de connaissances utiles aux ecclésiastiques sur divers objets d'art notament sur l'architecture des édifices religieux anciens et modernes, et sur les con-*

structions et la réparation d'églises, avec plans et dessins lithographiés (Lyon: L. Lesne, 1843), 300 and Barbier de Montault, *Traité pratique*, 12.

77. Barbier de Montault, *Traité pratique*, 43.

78. Christ Church Vestry Book, 30 January 1872, Archdiocesan Archives, Ottawa (Anglican), 6-O-3: C-4.

79. Archdiocesan Archives, Ottawa (Anglican), Ottawa Deanery Collection, Box 6-0-3: C-4, Christ Church Vestry Book, 30 January 1872.

80. Ibid.

81. "Large, commodious and frequently beautiful places of worship are being erected for other denominations, where the wants of the whole body of worshippers have been made the primary aim of the architect. . . . There is no reason that a modern church shall be less beautifully architecturally, or less distinctively expressive in form and structure as 'the house of God,' because of its being constructed in harmony with the manifest aim of the Book of Common Prayer. . . ." Sir Daniel Wilson, "Church Builders," *Canadian Architect and Builder*, 1889, 42-43.

82. "Notes on Church Architecture," *Canadian Architect and Builder,* 1890, 52-53.

CONCLUSION

AN ANALYSIS OF THE PROCESS

Throughout the nineteenth century, Gothic was continuously associated with a community space built for the collective practice of Christian worship. Surviving documentation distinctly indicates that Gothic was frequently used as an expression of Christian belief; however, as witnessed here, the use of Gothic, like the Christian communities that used it, was neither monolithic nor static. Furthermore, it is clear that before Gothic can be discussed, either in terms of an architectural style or as a symbolic expression of Christian belief, a number of complex factors, both peripheral and integral, must be addressed. Prior to any discussion of architectural style, it is necessary to situate the church building itself within the secular context and material cosmos of which it is both a part and a product. First, from a secular perspective and in terms of extra-stylistic considerations, it is necessary to determine what role the church building itself held within the broader context of the secular community, but without neglecting a discussion of the church building as a means through which religious thought is embodied. Second, it should be remembered that, regardless of an individual's devotion to or disregard for religion today, for much of the nineteenth century, the Christian church was usually the largest single public building in a town or village in the Ottawa Valley. In many instances, a church was the only building in which a greater portion of the population could gather and it was often the local church that offered early settlers the only reprieve from the labours and isolation of their farms. While this may not be an overwhelming preoccupation for late twentieth-century Canadians who live in a society of comfortable mobility—with easy access to numerous large-scale civic buildings, stadiums, and commercial complexes with sprawling roofs that cover several acres—one would be ill advised to dismiss the secular environment of these early churches with undue haste. In the context of the early nineteenth century, this can not be ignored.

In the earliest days of Ottawa Valley settlement, the church building was habitually used to accommodate the secular needs of a community. Most frequently, the church doubled as a schoolhouse or town hall. Despite this multiplicity of use, there was never any question of plurality of purpose. Initially, the secular use of a church building was not considered to have distracted significantly from its primary function. Instead, a greater emphasis and concern was placed on the church building as a sign that the settlement in which it stood held promise of survival. This attitude was prevalent even when the church buildings themselves were little more than log cabins or modest variations of domestic architecture. By virtue of their very presence, these churches also suggested commitment on the part of the religious community to which they belonged. They were, in their own way, a vote of confidence and a sign of belief in the inevitability of forthcoming prosperity.

Other times, communities were already well on their way to becoming villages or important centres of commercial activity. These centres of promising undertaking, which were usually linked to lumbering and milling operations or the construction of canals, were peopled by entrepreneurs, engineers, military personnel, and individuals skilled in a variety of trades. As more people were drawn to these areas, and stronger, more concentrated settlements soon began to emerge, a different type of church building began to appear. These churches were often more than the vernacular log structures of isolated communities. Furthermore, churches built in emergent towns often drew not only on a wider range of people, but occasionally were better funded. Many were built in stone. Their façades were often architecturally accentuated or emboldened by the addition of frontal towers. Many of these early church buildings were seen by the community of believers that they served to emphasize or underscore their own sense of permanence, not only in terms of denominational commitment, but also in secular society.

Marked as a House of God

Though stern and austere, the spiritual dimension of many churches built in the Ottawa Valley during the first half of the nineteenth century was not one that found its fullest expression through an atmosphere of sacred mystery and pious contemplation. While few of these buildings were imbibed with an aura of transcendent mystery, there is little data to propound that an atmosphere of spirituality was either strictly enforced or even cultivated. Church builders may have attempted to raise structures that were architecturally imposing; however, this was a statement directed towards the surrounding environment and to a large degree, a proclamation of social standing. It is important that architectural declarations of this era not be confused with the architectural monumentality that was to become popular in the later decades of the century. During the first half of the nineteenth century, structural monumentality must be understood to be as much of a socio-political statement as a socio-religious one.

Preserved material shows that when builders did not strive to achieve structural monumentality, there were few visible features to distinguish a church from much of the local domestic architecture. Frequently, it was only the pointed Gothic arches of the windows that identified a structure as a place of Christian prayer. As such, it is undeniable that on the strength of a simple Gothic reference, a building was distinguished from the secular structures of everyday life and marked as a Christian church. During the first half of the nineteenth century, Ottawa Valley church builders often sought to raise their buildings in the midst of human activity, or in a manner that was best adapted to local custom. Rarely were specific geographic features sought. Instead, they were aligned so as to be most convenient for those individuals who financed their construction. This was not always the most felicitous solution, but it was considered to be a positive reflection of the moral fabric and work ethic of the community and was rarely detrimental to the value of nearby land. In the same way that a centre of activity tended to attract church-building projects, the building of a church was often a pivotal point in determining the centre of future development. Often, construction was organized or generously supported by individuals who had a personal (and not infrequently financial) interest in seeing the area developed. This is not to suggest that church builders were motivated uniquely by a sense of personal gain, for religion in the nineteenth century was very much intertwined with everyday life.

The use of Gothic during the early years of the nineteenth century was neither technically complex, nor was it filled with symbolic refinement, or intended to be. It was nevertheless intended, unequivocally, as Christian. The preference for stylistic austerity precluded any Gothic that was overly ornate or flamboyant. The unscholarly and flamboyant use of Gothic that resulted in the theatrical displays associated with some late-eighteenth and early-nineteenth century productions was not common in the Ottawa Valley. At the same time, this early Gothic was rarely bound by archaeological precession or historically correct detailing. Instead, the Gothic used was an expression that drew on the tradition of the builders and craftsmen, and on the memory of merchants and military men. Strict canons of measure or proportion were neither rigorously aspired to, nor were they demanded; still many of the churches built in the Ottawa Valley during the 1820s and 1830s were well proportioned. Working largely from memory and with limited material and financial resources, early church builders in the Ottawa Valley were not in a position to indulge in architectural trivia or gracious embellishment. Theirs was an intensely succinct expression of Gothic. More often than not, the "Gothicness" of a structure was expressed primarily through the practice of pointed windows in a simple rectangular building. This early use of Gothic did not have the ideological implications that were later to be associated with Gothic church architecture. Characterized by its abstemious simplicity and an austere dignity, Gothic, as it first appeared in the Ottawa Valley, was not a Gothic of revival but one of survival.

During the late second and early third quarter of the nineteenth century, the building of churches took on a new significance. This coincided with an influx of settlers from such denominations as the Methodists, who had been active in the Ottawa Valley from an early date, but lacked numerical strength. By the late second quarter of the nineteenth century, both Episcopal and Wesleyan Methodists made strong inroads into the Ottawa Valley. The remarkable increase in the number of Methodist stations, as listed in missionary reports, was particularly evident from the early 1830s[1] to the mid-1850s.[2] As Episcopal and Wesleyan Methodists competed for membership, there emerged an increasingly urgent discussion of the need for church buildings. Once again, it should be remembered this frequently meant simply a log cabin. Despite the modesty of the constructions, discussion of this process presented a significant contrast from earlier days when camp meetings held precedent over the construction of permanent church buildings. Increasingly, Methodists were seeking to define the moral duties of church building.

Among the individual communities of the Ottawa Valley, documentation suggests that the reason for building a church varied. Some communities were concerned that they must build to establish a sense of permanence, others worried that only through building could they secure membership. Still others appear to have built as a direct result of revival inspiration. When revivals were involved, there were few better ways to demonstrate a community's devotion to God than through the construction of a separate place of worship. However, while Gothic was frequently used, the data currently available does not allow this phenomenon to be linked to or be a product of Gothic ideology. There is nothing to suggest that any specific stylistic allegiance was advocated.

During the middle years of the nineteenth century, there was a gradual shift in emphasis concerning the responsibility of church building. An increasing level of responsibility was now being placed on individual church members who were exhorted to build as a demonstration of commitment to Christian duty. Again this was not a specifically Gothic phenomenon, but Gothic makes a strong showing in the material evidence. The buildings themselves were gravid with immense but intangible symbolism. This resulted in a sophisticated and highly abstract understanding of the church building that went well beyond architectonic limits. In the Ottawa Valley, discussions of this sense of obligation to build a church offer an important insight into the adaptability and commitment of many nineteenth-century Christians. As the century progressed, various Christian denominations were called upon to give visual testimony of their gratitude to God. Preachers often reminded their congregations that the material benefits they now possessed were gifts from God. Public acknowledgment of these gifts was easier for some than others.

Many Christian traditions did not allow for unrestrained material expressions of belief. On this specific point, most Ottawa Valley Protestants were somewhat disadvantaged when compared to their Roman Catholic neighbours. Even after the considerable reforms imposed by the Council of Trent, Roman Catholics had retained a rich and varied tradition of visual and material expression. Most other Christian confessions present in the Ottawa Valley had traditionally refrained from this practice. Reformed Anglo-Protestants had gravitated to an interpretation of the Scriptures that was centred on reading and hearing the Word of God. In many instances, they denied the validity of most material expressions of religious belief such as devotional statuary, painted stations of the cross, and large-scale crosses or crucifixes. As a direct consequence, much of their outward expression of religious belief was unavoidably aniconic. This, in and of itself, had posed no particular problem, that is until it was suggested that increased material well-being was an expression of God's favour and should be acknowledged in an equally tangible manner. Findings suggest that, in response to this, many Protestant congregations who lived and worshipped in the Ottawa Valley during the nineteenth century, turned to the building of churches as the preferred manner in which to give material expression to their devotion and gratitude. Through church architecture, the material embodiment of Christian belief could be visually and tangibly manifest.

With the increasing sense of obligation to build churches came an increasing uncertainty as to how places of worship should best be built. This tendency was especially evident among Anglicans and present to a considerably lesser, but nonetheless important degree among Methodists. These transformations were motivated by different forces from both inside and outside various denominations. Methodists, for example were acquiring an unprecedented level of social acceptance. Parallel to this, they place a new importance upon the dignity and decorum of worship. Their services are moved from outside to inside. There was now a new preference for religious ceremonies to be held inside church buildings, and the popularity of the old style—outside at camp meetings—went into decline. Others, most notably the Anglicans, were finding that their traditional place of social primacy was being called into question. Many of these questions arose at a time when long-standing church-state relations were in a period of transition. At the same time, traditional Anglican church-building forms, which had for years been taken for granted, were no longer thought to fully respond to Anglican needs and concerns. The middle decades of the nineteenth century were, thus, a time when church buildings were physically, and in certain traditions, ecclesiastically transformed.

While the Anglicans of Central Canada may have considered the mid-nineteenth century to be a time of denominational hardship, documentation shows that this period was one of the most intense and dynamic in terms of thought concerning church building. Increasingly, the answer is in some form of Gothic dialect. However, while an increased number of Christian denominations may have been choosing Gothic for their church buildings, only within the Anglican church was the Gothic style presented as the unique vehicle for the architectonic expression of Christian principle. Furthermore, in the Anglican church, Gothic was given widespread and extensive Episcopal endorsement. It is perhaps no coincidence that ideas from

Oxford and Cambridge gained wider circulation in Central Canada at the very time that the Church of England in Canada was feeling short-changed by the civil government. While the Oxonians did not seek to actively occupy themselves with architectural concerns, as did the Camdanians, both were to have considerable influence on the attitudes many Anglicans held towards worship and the environment in which worship took place. Although the influence of both is popularly associated with the revival of medieval Gothic, both groups recommended a partition of church and state in favour of a renewed emphasis on their confessional history and clerical authority.

Throughout the middle years of the nineteenth century, Anglo-Protestant congregations that were not part of the Anglican Church discussed the subject of church building to varying degrees. The discussion of Gothic in the context of secular journals reflects a widespread interest, if not unqualified acceptance, in the use of revived medieval Gothic as an architectural style truly adapted to Christian needs. This gave rise to considerable discussion among other Protestant denominations. Questions and opinions on the matter of church building were often sent for publication to various confessional journals. Replies or rebuttals were published, and the debate raged back and forth with comparatively little guidance or concrete direction from church officials on the subjects of orientation, proportion, or the required dimensions of specific internal furnishings.

By the 1860s there was a tone of greater urgency among those seeking to define a Methodist church-building tradition. As discussed previously, the Methodist understanding of church building, as demonstrated through their own descriptions of revivals, building projects, and divine visitations, suggests that the traditionally curt dismissal of their architectural efforts is both unfortunate and uninformed. Coupled with a spiritually complex and highly abstract understanding of church space, Methodists began to place an increasing importance on the building of churches. In addition to this, they were also placing an increased importance on the manner in which churches were built. There is, however, no evidence to suggest that the question was addressed in a systematic manner by church authorities. There were still no specific examples of what might constitute a just display of generosity. Methodists were still without direction on the subject of orientation, proportion, and the required dimensions of specific internal furnishings. Throughout the middle decades of the nineteenth century, Methodists continued to be faced with the problem of building churches that reflected their commitment and, of course, their generosity, without pretentious displays of architectural caprice. Although Gothic continued to be used, Methodists did not enter into scholarly studies, produce architectural treatises, or publish the building guides or copy books that were characteristic of the Anglican revival of Gothic.

During the second half of the nineteenth century, Baptists gained significant numerical strength in the Ottawa Valley. While Baptist congregations built a number of small churches and several architecturally significant structures, including the large Gothic church that still stands in Ottawa at the corner of Elgin and Laurier, very little discussion was devoted to architectonic undertaking. In contrast, Baptists made extensive use of architectural symbolism, especially as a tool for exegetical analysis. However, there is little indication of any preoccupation with translating this symbolism into solid structure. While the architectonic interests may appear comparatively undervalued in the Baptist tradition, it must be remembered that while baptism is the keystone sacrament and the one in which their Christian belief and practice achieved its highest expression, it was often not experienced in built space. Nevertheless, Gothic elements appear in a number of their church buildings. As with the Methodists, however, there is no data to indicate that Baptists were active participants in the revival of medieval Gothic.

Presbyterians continued to use Gothic, having never really abandoned it since the days of the Reformation. Despite this long tradition, Presbyterians do not appear to have ever felt any great need to discuss the subject. Initially, Presbyterian church builders in Central Canada continued Scottish tradition. They built rectangular churches with large Gothic openings. The dimensions were simply adjusted to meet the needs of the congregation without much structural or stylistic compromise. Occasionally, centres of liturgical significance, such as the wall against which the pulpit stood, were decorated with trace moulding in the form of a Gothic arch. When the amphitheatre plan began to gain popularity, many Presbyterian parishes continued to incorporate decorative Gothic elements into the shell of their building. There was, however, rarely any affiliation between the Gothic exterior and the liturgical arrangements within. When the Presbyterians of Central Canada decided, in 1890, that the time had come to address the question of church architecture, they did not seek advice from their own clergy or even specifically from within their own denomination. In contrast to the Anglican Church, whose clergy played an important role in defining the religious symbolism and theological content of their church buildings, Presbyterian church officials were conspicuously absent from these discussions. Instead, the Presbyterian Church turned to the trade journals and public sector in the hopes of finding a suitable response to their church-building needs.

Although Roman Catholics usually declined to share church buildings or style with those of questionable theology, their reverence for the building itself was never so strict as to be impractical. Early chapels were often recycled to enjoy a second career as a rectory or a schoolhouse,[3] and the rectory-chapel was an excellent example of the results of planned obsolescence. While Roman Catholic bishops in the Ottawa Valley frequently took an active interest in the architectural details of a church building[4] and often suggested construction or architectural modifications in none too subtle terms,[5] they were remarkably mute on the matter of style. Gothic had not played a part in the French Catholic church-building tradition during the French Regime and its introduction to Central Canada was occasioned by a rather convoluted route. The first Roman Catholic church of consequence built in reasonable proximity to the Ottawa Valley was Notre-Dame of Montreal. In many ways, this church paved the way for the introduction of the Gothic style, being one of the earliest monumental neo-Gothic churches in North America. Notre-Dame, however, owed much more to the Gothic of the Commissioners Churches of Anglican England than to any serious attempt to introduce archaeologically inspired structures. This is not to suggest that the introduction of Gothic into the Catholic church-building programme is merely symptomatic of Anglo influence.

The construction of Montreal's St. Patrick by French expatriates offered a stronger case that the Gothic style was not only a viable option for the construction of Catholic churches, but also demonstrated that it could be done with a decidedly French flavour. Here again, the architects sought to create a powerful sense of frontal monumentality and inner vertical ascension. Similarly, it was through the efforts of French clergy that Gothic appears to have been first introduced to Catholic church building in the Ottawa Valley. The well-documented efforts to Gothicize the neoclassic grounding of Ottawa's Notre-Dame coincided with numerous other, less conspicuous, Gothic projects; however, all were equally silent on the subject of style. Characteristic of Catholic Gothic in the Ottawa Valley is the attempt that was made to create an atmosphere of inner monumentality and vertical ascension. This appeared from an early date in both French and Irish parish churches, but is much more reflective of continental Gothic. Catholic church builders in the Ottawa Valley showed a definite affinity for the great internal heights that were recommended by Pugin; however they achieved these heights in a decidedly un-Puginesque manner. This became gradually more obvious as the century progresses and the internal architecture of new and earlier churches was completed with iron columns, plastered vaults, and false ceilings.

During the third and fourth quarter of the nineteenth century, Roman Catholic churches in the Ottawa Valley displayed a new thematic continuity between the type of site chosen and the impressive and monumental treatment of a church's façade. Through the elevation of glorious and triumphant façades, Catholic church builders sought to translate the preaching of their clergy into architectural reality. There is, however, no documentation to indicate that the architectonic ideals of Roman Catholic belief were thought to be best expressed through the use of Gothic. On the contrary, by the later decades of the nineteenth century, Roman Catholic church builders were moving away from the use of Gothic in favour of a new Italianate influence.

The nineteenth century was a time when many denominations sought to redefine their own architectural needs. The understanding of church space as space apart gained widespread acceptance over the course of the nineteenth century among all denominations. As a result, there was, among some communities, not simply an identification of new architectural needs, but a new openness to architecture altogether. This is most notable in the widespread construction of churches of all kinds. While a greater openness to new architectural ideas is evident, it should be remembered that a certain degree of reservation and resistance to change persisted. Nevertheless, by the close of the nineteenth century, even the most conservative parish accepted architectural arrangements that would probably have shocked even the most *avant-gardistes* at the beginning of the century.

In light of the wholesale adoption of pre-Reform prototypes, one might logically expect to see Anglican and Roman Catholic architecture becoming progressively closer as the century unfolds. This is, however, not what happens, as Roman Catholics, inspired by the Ultramontanist movement, moved closer to Rome and Italianate architecture and increasingly farther from Gothic architecture. Baptists, Congregationalists, Methodists, and Presbyterians continued to use Gothic as a decorative element in the construction of their churches, although considerable modifications took place inside. Like the Roman Catholics, the churches they raised during the first half of the nineteenth century had been proportionately scaled to the other elements of their built environment. This tradition, however, was progressively abandoned during the later decades of the nineteenth century in favour of a new frontal monumentality. The façades of many Protestant churches built during the fourth quarter of the century were powerful, triumphant, dominant, and progressively less Gothic.

The revival of medieval Gothic and the continued use of Gothic, not simply as symbolic of a place of Christian worship, but as a unique embodiment of Christian principle, must be seen primarily as an Anglican phenomenon. Despite the fact that other Christian denominations made considerable use of Gothic features, their officials were generally not inclined to openly advocate the superiority of Gothic. Attention to the details of specific cult arrangements and the practice of these with dignity and precession was of far greater interest to many. No denomination other than the Anglicans entered the research and discussion of Gothic church building with such zeal and

Fig. 6.1. St. Stephen (Anglican), Greermount, 1886.
The drama and isolation of the setting have changed little since the time when parishioners hauled material to the site and camped on the grounds during construction. While clearly influenced by Camdanian Ecclesiology, this building is not a transplant from medieval England, but a striking example of Canadian adaptation and interpretation (Photo: A. Erdmer).

commitment. No other denomination approached architectural embodiment of Christian principles or the use of architectural symbolism with paralleled sobriety. Nor was the liturgy of any other denomination translated so intimately into the physical body of the church. Within the Anglican tradition, the introduction of revived medieval Gothic denoted a systematic rethinking of the visual, physical, and ritualistic atmosphere in which worship takes place (fig. 6.1).

Christian parish architecture in the nineteenth century Ottawa Valley presents an interesting and sometimes eclectic picture of Central Canada's past. While a number of denominations unquestionably took many cues from British or European prototypes and were, to some extent, influenced by contemporary taste, they showed great ingenuity for adapting the principles of their faith to difficult and varied circumstances. While the unqualified term "Gothic" is used much too frequently as a catchall term for buildings with windows that have pointed tops, surviving evidence clearly indicates that there is a deeper and indeed much more complex dimension to Gothic.

Notes

1. In 1833, activity in the Ottawa Valley was summarized as follows: "Clarendon Mission—This mission is about 100 miles north of Brockville, on the north side of the Ottawa river, opposite the Bonchère river, on the Upper Canada side. The mission embraces the Township of Clarendon and Bristol. There are six appointments for preaching besides several prayer meetings. There are four classes and 47 members in the society. A Temperance Society has been formed on the plan of entire abstinence—it now numbers 50. It is about six years since this settlement commenced. The emigrants are mostly from Ireland and Scotland, and a very enterprising and hospitable people." *8th Annual Report of the Missionary Society of the Wesleyan Methodist Church in British North America—1833*, 6-7. By 1836 there was a 'Bytown Circuit,' 'Hull Circuit Branch' and the 'Mississippi Circuit Branch.' No specific locations were given although the 'Ottawa Circuit Branch' did include St. Andrews, La Chute, Chatham Chapel and Hawkesbury. *11th Annual Report of the Missionary Society of the Wesleyan Methodist Church in Canada—1836*, 21-25.

2. By the mid-1850s the Methodist missionaries were working numerous circuits and substations within the Ottawa Valley. From 1854-1855, the Wesleyans were working the following areas: Carleton Place Circuit, including a station at Eighth-Line Branch, Bellamy Branch, Lanark Branch, Blair's Branch, Boyd's Branch, and the Pakenham Circuit, which included the Pakenham Branch and Fitzroy Branch. The Ottawa Circuit had a larger population and was devoted solely to the Ottawa Branch, as was the case of the Aylmer Circuit and Chelsea Branch. The Richmond Circuit included the Richmond Branch, North Gower Branch, and Beckwith Branch, Argue's Branch, and Shillington Branch. The St. Andrew's Mission included La Chute Branch, Chatham Branch, North Gower Branch, and St. Andrew's Branch. The L'Orignal Circuit took in L'Orignal Branch, Longueuil Branch, VanKleek Hill Branch, West Hawkesbury Branch,

and East Hawkesbury Branch. There was now a Lochaber Mission, which had expanded to include Lochaber Branch, Lochaber Gower Branch, Bay Branch, Upper Cumberland Branch, Lower Cumberland Branch, and Buckingham Branch. The Osgoode Mission included the Metcalfe Branch, Bowesville Branch, Long Island Branch, Gloucester Branch, Russell Branch and Cumberland Branch. The Gatineau Mission included the Wakefield Branch, Hull Branch, and Templeton Branch, while the Clarendon and Portage-du-Fort Mission included Clarendon Branch, Portage-du-Fort Branch, Clarendon Front Branch, and Quyon Branch. There was also a Westmeath Mission, Huntley Mission, and Grenville Mission, which included a Grenville Branch and an "Augmentation" Branch. *30th Annual Report of the Missionary Society of the Wesleyan Methodist Church in Canada in Connexion with the English Conference, 1854-55.*

3. Mgr. Duhamel, *Registre des visites épiscopales*, 1875, Episcopal visit to L'Ange-Gardien, Archives of the Archdiocese of Ottawa (Roman Catholic). Although it was not common practice, Catholics would occasionally purchase a church building from another denomination.

4. In the correspondence of Mgr. Gigues, there is a contract with detailed architectural specifications of the construction of an unnamed church: "Specifications d'une église à bâtir pour Mgr. l'évêque d'Ottawa," 1873, Archives of the Archdiocese of Ottawa (Roman Catholic), G1-1-14-1.

5. Mgr. Duhamel, *Registre des visites épiscopales*, Archives of the Archdiocese of Ottawa (Roman Catholic), contains numerous recommendations for improvements, modifications, new installations, and repairs.

APPENDIX I

ARCHITECTURAL INVENTORY

Architectural findings for all church buildings surveyed in this study were entered in a computerized architectural inventory. As noted in the introduction, data was gathered from denominational and public archives, missionary reports, a wide variety of nineteenth-century confessional and secular publications, as well as from surviving structures. Material has been organized in nine major categories:

1. General information
2. Site
3. Façade
4. Interior
5. Cult space
6. Annexes
7. Builders
8. Archival resources
9. Visual documentation

Classification of material within these categories is as follows:

1. General Information:

Each church building has been entered in alphabetical order according to the name of the town, village, or township in which it was built. The county and province in which the church was built is also noted. The place names used correspond to the site names currently used by the Cartographic Division of the Ministry of Energy, Mines and Resources on their 1:250,000 scale maps as revised in 1982. As many of these names do not conform to those popularly used during the nineteenth century, a cross-referenced index of nineteenth- and twentieth-century place names in the Ottawa valley has been provided in Appendix III.

There may be several entries for an individual parish or congregation. The number of entries will correspond to the number of separate structures raised during the nineteenth century. Also noted in this category is the denomination, date of construction, orientation, style, church name, model, and material. Provision has also been made in this category for noting of significant historical events (if any) associated with the history of the building.

As many church buildings remained in the planning stage for long periods of time, and many more were not completed the same year that construction began, the date of construction entered corresponds, as closely as possible, to the date on which construction began. Frequently a number of other dates are closely related to the construction of a church building and can provide valuable insight into the church-building history of a community (see Appendix II). This information is noted in the parenthesis that follow the date of construction. These supplementary entries were used to record the following information:

(2) Second church built by the congregation
(3) Third church built by the congregation
(a) Major alterations to the original structure
(b) Blessing of the edifice
(c) Circa
(d) Destruction (fire, etc.)
(f) Closure
(m) Moved (a building is physically transported to a new site)
(n) New location (the location of a new church differs from the location of an earlier structure)
(p.o.d.) Purchased from an other denomination
(r) Removal or dismantling of a building
(s) Secularization
(t.a.q.) *Terminus ante quem*
(t.p.q.) *Terminus post quem*

2. **Site:** Identifies the original environment in which the church was built.

3. **Façade:** Notes major features such as windows, doors, and structural elevations.

4. **Interior:** Notes the length, width, and height of the nave, seating capacity, supplemental seating, and ceiling treatment.

5. **Cult space:** Defines structural space and corresponding measurements, liturgical furnishings, floor level, and lighting.

6. **Annexes:** Notes the presence of vestries, sacristies, and meeting halls.

7. **Builders:** Notes, whenever possible, leading members of building

committees, architects, contractors, builders, masons, carpenters, painters, and plasterers.

8. **Archival resources:** Includes primary archival sources as well as the Canadian Inventory of Historic Buildings (CIHB) file number, when relevant.
9. **Visual documentation:** Computer scan of ground plan and/or photo when possible.

A completed sample form follows.

Town:	**OTTAWA**	*County:*	Ottawa C.:	*Province:*	O
Denomination:	**ANGLICAN**	*Date:*	1866	(1/t.1867)	
Orientation:	west-east	*Style:*	Gothic		
Church name:	St. Alban	*Model:*	Medieval Revival		
Event:	Chancel completed in 1877				
Material:	Stone				

Site: Suburban. Major modifications to original plans after blue clay and sand pits discovered in spring of 1866. Projected 190-foot tower abandoned due to unstable footing.

Façades & entries: Southern side porch with understated gable end.

Windows: Elongated Gothic couplets flank either side of central axis in western gable end.

Structural/ Decorative: Ridge crestings on apex of roof. Sanctecote above chancel arch; wrought iron finials mark apex of entry, vestry gables, eastern gable end and sanctecote.

Nave: Axial central aisle. All seating on benches—no pews.

Capacity: 600

Length:	78 feet	*Width:*	38 feet	*Height:*	

Windows: Pairs of small lancet windows grouped between stepped wall buttresses.

Seating+: In-chancel choir

Width:	22 feet	*Depth:*	

Ceiling: Un-ceiled wooden panels. Four seven-foot dormers cut into roof.

Sanctuary: Architecturally distinct, but continues roof line of nave.

Length: 40 feet *Width:* 22 feet *Level:* 3 steps above nave

Altar: Axial altar—stands a total of 7 steps above floor level of nave.

Chevet: Rectangular with flat eastern end axial light. Couplets in north and south walls.

Windows: Main lancet flanked by two of lesser height; replaced by "Trinity in Unity" motif with raised treffle.

Sacristy/ annexe(s): Vestry on southern side of chancel 16 by 16 feet.

Other spaces: Chapel and school room in basement.

Choir: Contained in sanctuary—seats 35.

Architect: Thomas Fuller, project finished by King Arnoldi.

Building Committee: Rev. Bedford Jones and committee of eighteen prominent citizens.

Builder/ contractor: Mr. Painter & Mr. Taylor (Original building project).

Mason: James Matthews (Chancel). W. McKay (paint)

Carpenter: Stewart & Gilmor (Chancel). J. Strachan (plaster)

Reference: A.D.A.A.—Ottawa

Address: Daly & King Edward

CIHB: 06-107-0002-00125

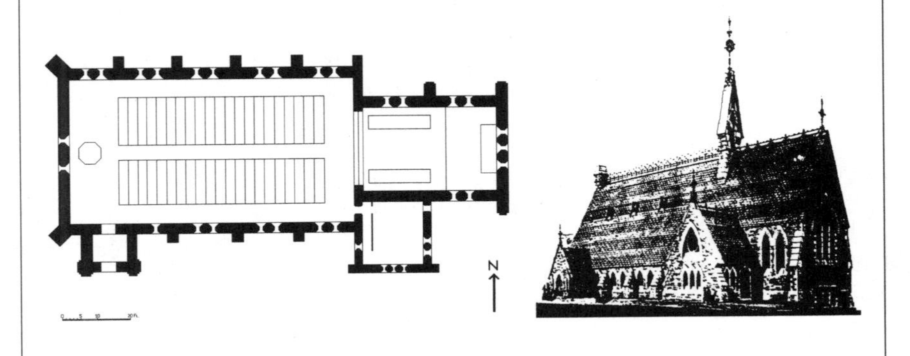

APPENDIX II

CHRONOLOGICAL LISTING OF CHURCHES

A. Churches built from 1820 to 1839

DATE	LOCATION	PROV.	DENOM.	NAME
1820	St-André Est	Quebec	Presbyterian	
1821	Montebello	Quebec	Catholic	N.-D.-de-Bonsecours
1821	St-André Est	Quebec	Anglican	Christ Church
1822	Franktown	Ontario	Anglican	St. James
1823	Richmond	Ontario	Anglican	St. John
1823	Hull	Quebec	Anglican	St. James
1824	Prospect	Ontario	Methodist	
1825	Vankleek Hill	Ontario	Presbyterian	
1825	Richmond	Ontario	Catholic	St. Peter
1826	Aylmer	Quebec	Presbyterian	
1826	Aylmer	Quebec	Methodist	
1827	Ottawa	Ontario	Methodist	
1827	Richmond	Ontario	Methodist	
1828	March	Ontario	Anglican	St. Mary
1828	Ottawa	Ontario	Presbyterian	St. Andrew
1829	Hawkesbury	Ontario	Presbyterian	St. Paul
1830	Grenville	Quebec	Presbyterian	
1831	Burrit's Rapids	Ontario	Anglican	Christ Church
1831	Ottawa	Ontario	Catholic	St-Jacques
1832	Fitzroy Harbour	Ontario	Presbyterian	
1832	Grenville	Quebec	Anglican	St. Matthew
1832	L'Orignal	Ontario	Presbyterian	St. Andrew
1832	Ottawa	Ontario	Anglican	Christ Church
1833	Carleton Place	Ontario	Methodist	
1833	Farrellton	Quebec	Catholic	St-Camille
1833	L'Orignal	Ontario	Catholic	St-Jean-Baptiste
1833	Monfort	Quebec	Catholic	N.-D.-du-Rosaire
1833	Fallowfield	Ontario	Catholic	St. Patrick
1834	Aylmer	Quebec	Congregational	
1834	Beckwith	Ontario	Presbyterian	

1834	Carleton Place	Ontario	Anglican	St. James
1835	Beckwith Twshp	Ontario	Presbyterian	St. Andrew
1836	Cushing	Quebec	Presbyterian	St. Mungo's
1837	Corkery	Ontario	Catholic	St. Michael
1837	Huntley	Ontario	Anglican	Christ Church
1838	Osgoode	Ontario	Methodist	
1838	Spring Hill	Ontario	Presbyterian	
1838	Gloucester	Ontario	Methodist	
1838	Osgoode	Ontario	Presbyterian	
1839	Templeton	Quebec	Catholic	Ste-Rose-de-Lima
1839	Pointe Gatineau	Quebec	Catholic	St-François-de-Sales
1839	South March	Ontario	Anglican	St. John

B. Churches built from 1840 to 1859

DATE	LOCATION	PROV.	DENOM.	NAME
1840	Johnston's Corners	Ontario	Presbyterian	
1840	Manotick	Ontario	Union	Union Church
1840	Osgoode	Ontario	Baptist	
1840	Osgoode	Ontario	Catholic	St. John the Evangelist
1840	Shawville	Quebec	Anglican	St. Paul
1840	Allumettes, Ile des	Quebec	Catholic	St-Alphonse-de-Liguori
1840	Calumet	Quebec	Catholic	Ste-Anne
1840	Metcalfe	Ontario	Catholic	St. Catherine
1840	Chelsea	Quebec	Catholic	St-Étienne
1840	Aylmer	Quebec	Catholic	St-Paul
1840	Buckingham	Quebec	Catholic	St-Grégoire-de-Naziance
1841	La Passe	Ontario	Catholic	N.-D.-du-Mt-Carmel
1841	Lac Sainte-Marie	Quebec	Catholic	Ste-Marie
1841	Ottawa	Ontario	Catholic	Notre-Dame
1842	Almonte	Ontario	Catholic	St. Mary
1842	Grenville	Quebec	Methodist	
1842	Shillington	Ontario	Methodist	
1843	Aylmer	Quebec	Anglican	Christ Church
1843	Grand Calumet	Quebec	Catholic	Ste-Anne
1843	Mt. St. Patrick	Ontario	Catholic	St. Patrick

1843	Osceola	Ontario	Catholic	St. Pius
1844	Cumberland	Ontario	Presbyterian	Carmel Church
1844	Ottawa	Ontario	Methodist	York St. Church
1844	Smith's settlement	Ontario	Presbyterian	
1844	Hawkesbury	Ontario	Anglican	Holy Trinity
1844	Pakenham	Ontario	Anglican	St. Mark
1844	South Gloucester	Ontario	Presbyterian	Free Kirk
1844	Wakefield	Quebec	Catholic	St-Joseph
1844	Douglas	Ontario	Catholic	St. Michael
1845	Eganville	Ontario	Catholic	St-Fidèle
1845	Hawkesbury	Ontario	Catholic	
1845	Hazeldean	Ontario	Anglican	
1845	Masham	Quebec	Catholic	Ste-Cécile
1845	Osgoode	Ontario	Presbyterian	
1845	Renfrew	Ontario	Catholic	St. Francis Xavier
1845	Spring Hill	Ontario	Presbyterian	
1845	St. André Est	Quebec	Methodist	
1845	Vankleek Hill	Ontario	Anglican	
1845	Ashton	Ontario	Anglican	Christ Church
1845	Hull	Quebec	Catholic	Chapelle-des-Chantiers
1845	Huntley 3rd Line	Ontario	Presbyterian	
1845	Ottawa	Ontario	Presbyterian	Knox Church
1845	Black's Corners	Ontario	Presbyterian	Knox Presbyterian
1845	Fitzroy Harbour	Ontario	Catholic	St. Michael
1845	Plantagenet	Ontario	Catholic	St. Paul
1846	Admaston Twshp.	Ontario	Methodist	Rosebank
1846	Goulburn 10th Line	Ontario	Methodist	Magee Wesleyan Chapel
1846	Nepean	Ontario	Union	
1846	South Gloucester	Ontario	Catholic	Our Lady of the Visitation
1847	Ottawa	Ontario	Congregational	1st Congregationalist
1847	Prospect	Ontario	Methodist	
1847	Pembroke	Ontario	Catholic	
1847	Renfrew	Ontario	Presbyterian	Canaan Church
1847	Grenville	Quebec	Methodist	
1848	Bearbrook	Ontario	Anglican	Trinity Church

1849	Aylwin	Quebec	Catholic	N.-D.-de-la-Visitation
1849	Franklin Corners	Ontario	Methodist	
1849	Huntley 3rd Line	Ontario	Methodist	3rd Line Wesleyan
1849	Lac des sables	Quebec	Catholic	
1849	Osgoode Twnshp	Ontario	Methodist	
1849	White Lake	Ontario	Presbyterian	
1849	Dwyer Hill	Ontario	Catholic	St. Sylvester
1849	Onslow	Quebec	Catholic	St. Brigitte
1849	Portage-du-Fort	Quebec	Catholic	Ste-Mélanie
1849	South Gloucester	Ontario	Catholic	Our Lady of the Visitation
1849	St-André-Avellin	Quebec	Catholic	St-André-Avellin
1849	Bristol	Quebec	Catholic	St-Édouard
1850	Bonchere	Ontario	Methodist	
1850	Carlsbad Springs	Ontario	Anglican	
1850	Kars	Ontario	Anglican	St. John
1850	Ottawa	Ontario	Anglican	St. John
1850	Portage du Fort	Quebec	Catholic	St-Jacques & Ste-Rosalie
1850	Nepean	Ontario	Catholic	St. Jude
1850	Osgoode Twnshp	Ontario	Methodist	
1851	Hazeldean	Ontario	Union	
1851	Thorbolton Twnshp	Ontario	Presbyterian	
1851	Perkins	Quebec	Catholic	St-Antoine-de-Padoue
1852	Buckingham	Quebec	Anglican	St. Stephen
1852	Pakenham	Ontario	Catholic	St-Pierre-Célestin
1852	Orleans	Ontario	Catholic	St-Joseph
1852	Ashton	Ontario	Presbyterian	Melville
1852	Eganville	Ontario	Catholic	St-Jacques
1853	Bell's Corners	Ontario	Union	Union Church
1853	L'Orignal	Ontario	Catholic	St-Jean-Baptiste
1853	Leitrim	Ontario	Anglican	St. James
1853	Ottawa	Ontario	Methodist	
1853	Pakenham	Ontario	Presbyterian	
1853	Richmond	Ontario	Presbyterian	St. Andrew
1853	Vankleek Hill	Ontario	Anglican	St. John
1853	Argenteuil	Quebec	Catholic	St-Philippe
1853	Grenville	Quebec	Catholic	N.-D.-des-Sept-Douleurs
1853	St-Eugène	Ontario	Catholic	St-Eugène

1853	Gatineau Mission	Quebec	Methodist	
1853	Osgoode Twnshp	Ontario	Methodist	
1854	Angers	Quebec	Catholic	L'Ange-Gardien
1854	North Gower	Ontario	Presbyterian	
1854	Prospect	Ontario	Anglican	St. Augustine
1854	Thorne Center	Quebec	Anglican	St. George
1854	Thurso	Quebec	Catholic	St-Jean-l'Évangéliste
1854	Aylmer	Quebec	Catholic	St. Paul /(N.-D.)
1854	Fort Coulonge	Quebec	Anglican	
1854	Chelsea	Quebec	Catholic	St-Étienne
1854	Metcalfe	Ontario	Methodist	
1855	Alfred	Ontario	Catholic	St-Anaclet
1855	Kenmore	Ontario	Baptist	
1855	Montebello	Quebec	Catholic	Chapelle L.J. Papineau
1855	Ottawa	Ontario	Presbyterian	Knox Church
1855	Buckingham	Quebec	Catholic	St-Grégoire-de-Naziance
1855	Osgoode Twnshp	Ontario	Methodist	
1856	Cumberland	Ontario	Catholic	St-Eugène
1856	Lowery	Ontario	Presbyterian	
1856	Russell	Ontario	Anglican	St. Mary
1856	Lowery	Ontario	Presbyterian	Lowery Congregation
1856	Metcalfe	Ontario	Anglican	Holy Trinity
1856	North Gower	Ontario	Anglican	Trinity Church
1856	Ottawa	Ontario	Anglican	St. John the Evangelist
1856	Ottawa	Ontario	Catholic	St. Joseph
1856	Pontiac	Quebec	Catholic	
1856	Portage du Fort	Quebec	Anglican	St. George
1856	Vinton	Quebec	Catholic	Ste-Élisabeth
1856	Embrun	Ontario	Catholic	St-Jacques
1856	Gatineau	Quebec	Methodist	
1857	Bromley	Ontario	Presbyterian	Barr's Church
1857	Chapleau	Quebec	Catholic	St-Alphonse
1857	Mayo	Quebec	Catholic	Our Lady of Malacky
1857	Vankleek Hill	Ontario	Presbyterian	
1857	Westmeath	Ontario	Methodist	

1857	Wright	Quebec	Catholic	N.-D.-de-la-Visitation
1857	Angers	Quebec	Catholic	L'Ange-Gardien
1857	Arnprior	Ontario	Catholic	St. John Chrysostome
1857	Aylwin	Quebec	Catholic	N.-D.-de-la-Visitation
1857	Quyon	Quebec	Anglican	St. John the Evangelist
1857	St-Eugène	Ontario	Catholic	St-Eugène
1857	Clarence	Ontario	Baptist	
1857	Plantagenet	Ontario	Catholic	St. Paul
1857	Cantley	Quebec	Catholic	Ste-Élisabeth
1858	Cambridge Ctr	Ontario	Catholic	St. Michael
1858	Clarence Creek	Ontario	Catholic	Ste-Félicité
1858	Dunrobin	Ontario	Methodist	
1858	Manotick	Ontario	Catholic	St. Bridgid
1858	Onslow	Quebec	Catholic	St. Brigitte
1858	Russell	Ontario	Presbyterian	St. Andrew
1858	Bearbrook	Ontario	Catholic	
1858	Fitzroy Harbour	Ontario	Presbyterian	St. Andrew
1858	Jock	Ontario	Catholic	St. Margaret & St. Peter
1858	Osgoode	Ontario	Catholic	St. John the Evangelist
1858	Fitzroy Harbour	Ontario	Presbyterian	
1858	Richmond	Ontario	Catholic	St. Peter
1859	Aylmer	Quebec	Methodist	
1859	Ferguson's Falls	Ontario	Catholic	St.Patrick
1859	Lemieux	Ontario	Catholic	St-Bernard
1859	Renfrew	Ontario	Methodist	
1859	Wakefield	Quebec	Catholic	St-Joseph
1859	Douglas	Ontario	Catholic	St. Michael
1859	Embrun	Ontario	Catholic	St-Jacques
1859	Fournier	Ontario	Catholic	St-Bernard
1859	Metcalfe	Ontario	Catholic	Ste-Catherine
1859	Papineauville	Quebec	Catholic	Ste-Angélique
1859	Richmond	Ontario	Anglican	St. John

C. Churches built from 1860 to 1879

DATE	LOCATION	PROV.	DENOM.	NAME
1860	Aylmer	Quebec	Presbyterian	
1860	Metcalfe	Ontario	Presbyterian	
1860	Morin Heights	Quebec	Anglican	Trinity Church
1860	Sebastopol	Ontario	Catholic	St-Benoît
1860	St-Eugène	Ontario	Catholic	St-Eugène
1860	Fitzroy Harbour	Ontario	Catholic	St. Michael
1860	Alfred	Ontario	Anglican	St. Peter
1860	Grand Calumet	Quebec	Catholic	Ste-Anne
1860	South March	Ontario	Catholic	St. Isidore
1860	Stanley Corners	Ontario	Anglican	St. Thomas
1860	Burdenell	Ontario	Catholic	St. Mary
1861	Almonte	Ontario	Presbyterian	St. Andrews
1861	Chute-à-Blondeau	Ontario	Catholic	St-Joachim
1861	Denbigh	Ontario	Lutheran	St. Paul
1861	Horton	Ontario	Anglican	St. Barnabas
1861	Ottawa	Ontario	Baptist	First Baptist Church
1861	Cumberland	Ontario	Catholic	St-Antoine-de-Padoue
1861	Burdenell	Ontario	Catholic	St. Mary
1862	Augsburg	Ontario	Lutheran	St. John
1862	Cumberland	Ontario	Anglican	St. Mark
1862	Cumberland	Ontario	Methodist	
1862	Cumberland	Ontario	Presbyterian	
1862	Grenville	Quebec	Catholic	N.-D.-des-Sept-Douleurs
1862	Navan	Ontario	Anglican	St. Mary
1862	Ottawa	Ontario	Congregational	1st Congregationalist
1862	Ripon	Quebec	Catholic	St-Casimir
1862	Vankleek Hill	Ontario	Catholic	St-Grégoire
1862	Chénéville	Quebec	Catholic	St-Félix-de-Valois
1862	Eardley	Quebec	Catholic	St-Dominique
1862	Luskville	Quebec	Catholic	St-Dominique
1862	Fitzroy Harbour	Ontario	Methodist	Diamond Church
1863	Almonte	Ontario	Methodist	
1863	Arnprior	Ontario	Presbyterian	
1863	Beachburg	Ontario	Methodist	

1863	Black River Falls	Quebec	Methodist	
1863	Bonnecher	Ontario	Lutheran	St. John
1863	Bouchette	Quebec	Catholic	St-Gabriel
1863	Corkery	Ontario	Catholic	St. Michael
1863	Fitzroy Harbour	Ontario	Anglican	St. George
1863	Almonte	Ontario	Anglican	St. Paul
1863	Angers	Quebec	Catholic	L'Ange-Gardien
1863	Curran	Ontario	Catholic	St-Luc
1863	Clarendon	Quebec	Anglican	St. Alexander
1863	Rankin	Ontario	Lutheran	Grace Lutheran
1864	Buckingham	Quebec	Presbyterian	St. Andrew
1864	Burdenell	Ontario	Methodist	
1864	Eardley	Quebec	Anglican	St. Luke
1864	Farrellton	Quebec	Catholic	St-Camille-de-Lellis
1864	Ottawa	Ontario	Anglican	St. George
1864	Pembroke	Ontario	Anglican	
1864	Tacote	Quebec	Methodist	
1864	Templeton	Quebec	Anglican	Christ Church
1864	Thurso	Quebec	Baptist	
1864	Wakefield	Quebec	Catholic	St-Camille-de-Lellis
1864	Charteris	Quebec	Anglican	St. Matthew
1864	Clontarf	Ontario	Catholic	
1864	Ottawa	Ontario	Methodist	Ottawa West Church
1864	Eganville	Ontario	Anglican	St. John the Evangelist
1864	Onslow Twnshp	Quebec	Methodist	
1865	Almonte	Ontario	Presbyterian	St. John
1865	Ottawa	Ontario	Anglican	All Saints
1865	Vankleek Hill	Ontario	Methodist	
1865	Westmeath Twnshp	Ontario	Methodist	
1865	Wilberforce	Ontario	Methodist	
1865	Harrington	Quebec	Methodist	
1865	Huntley 5th Line	Ontario	Methodist	Bethel Church
1866	Arnprior	Ontario	Methodist	
1866	Huntley 4th Line	Ontario	Methodist	
1866	North Wakefield	Quebec	Methodist	
1866	Poltimore	Quebec	Anglican	Christ Church
1866	Russell	Ontario	Methodist	St. Paul or Forester's Hall

1866	Thorne Centre	Quebec	Catholic	
1866	Alice	Ontario	Lutheran	St. Peter
1866	Arundel	Quebec	Methodist	
1866	Eardley Twnshp	Quebec	Methodist	Eardley Circuit
1866	Fallowfield	Ontario	Catholic	St. Patrick
1866	Ottawa	Ontario	Anglican	St. Alban
1866	North Wakefield	Quebec	Methodist	
1867	Arnprior	Ontario	Methodist	
1867	Aylwin	Quebec	Methodist	
1867	Beachburg	Ontario	Methodist	
1867	Bromley Charge	Ontario	Methodist	
1867	Eganville	Ontario	Methodist	
1867	Hull	Quebec	Anglican	St. James
1867	Leslie	Ontario	Methodist	
1867	Ripon	Quebec	Catholic	St-Casimir
1867	Sarsfield	Ontario	Catholic	St-Hugues
1867	Ottawa	Ontario	Methodist	York St. M. E. Church
1867	Perkins	Quebec	Lutheran	St. John
1868	Almonte	Ontario	Baptist	
1868	Grenville	Quebec	Methodist	
1868	Osceola	Ontario	Catholic	St. Pius
1868	Ottawa	Ontario	Presbyterian	Bank Street Church
1868	Roxboro	Ontario	Methodist	
1868	Roxboro	Ontario	Methodist	Raymond Church
1868	Caldwell	Quebec	Anglican	St. Luke
1868	Maniwaki	Quebec	Catholic	Notre-Dame
1868	Ottawa	Ontario	Anglican	St. Bartholomew
1868	Ottawa	Ontario	Presbyterian	Bank Street Church
1868	Burdenell	Ontario	Catholic	St. Mary
1868	Osgoode Twnshp	Ontario	Methodist	
1869	Clarence Creek	Ontario	Catholic	Ste-Félicité
1869	Denbigh Circuit	Ontario	Methodist	
1869	Mt. St. Patrick	Ontario	Catholic	St. Patrick
1869	Ottawa	Ontario	Catholic	St. Patrick
1869	Vinton	Quebec	Catholic	Ste-Élisabeth
1869	Almonte	Ontario	Catholic	St. Mary
1869	Arnprior	Ontario	Anglican	Emmanuel Church

1869	Carleton Place	Ontario	Presbyterian	Zion Presbyterian Church
1869	Martendale	Quebec	Catholic	St-Martin
1869	Hull	Quebec	Catholic	N.-D.-de-Grâce
1870	Ashton	Ontario	Methodist	
1870	Doyle Settlement	Ontario	Catholic	St. Ignatius
1870	Golden Lake	Ontario	Catholic	St-Jean-Baptiste
1870	Huntley 5th Line	Ontario	Methodist	
1870	Inkerman	Ontario	Methodist	
1870	Leslie	Quebec	Anglican	St. James
1870	Mille Isles	Quebec	Presbyterian	
1870	Ramsayville	Ontario	Presbyterian	
1870	Riceville	Ontario	Baptist	
1870	Sand Point	Ontario	Catholic	St-Alexandre
1870	Aylwin	Quebec	Anglican	St. John in the Wilderness
1870	Clayton	Ontario	Anglican	Grace Church
1870	Ottawa	Ontario	Catholic Apostolic	
1870	Riceville	Ontario	Methodist	
1870	Shrewsbury	Quebec	Unknown	
1870	North Gower	Ontario	Unknown	
1871	Admaston Twshp	Ontario	Presbyterian	
1871	Angers	Quebec	Catholic	L'Ange-Gardien
1871	Arnprior	Ontario	Catholic	St. John Chrysostome
1871	Collefield	Ontario	Methodist	
1871	Dunning	Quebec	Methodist	
1871	Masham	Quebec	Catholic	Ste-Cécile
1871	Ottawa	Ontario	Catholic	Chapel N.-D.-du-Sacré-Coeur
1871	Ottawa	Ontario	Presbyterian	Bank Street Church
1871	Renfrew	Ontario	Anglican	St. Paul
1871	Alfred	Ontario	Catholic	St-Victor
1871	Collefield	Ontario	Methodist	
1871	Orleans	Ontario	Catholic	St-Joseph
1871	Vanier	Ontario	Catholic	N.-D.-de-Lourdes
1872	Aylmer	Quebec	Methodist	
1872	Bell's Corners	Ontario	Methodist	
1872	Blanche	Quebec	Union	Mulgrave Protestant
1872	Calabogie	Ontario	Methodist	

1872	Carp	Ontario	Methodist	Wesleyan Methodist Church
1872	Hull	Quebec	Presbyterian	
1872	Huntley 3rd Line	Ontario	Methodist	3rd Line Wesleyan Church
1872	Kazabazua	Quebec	Methodist	
1872	Lavant	Ontario	Catholic	St-Declan
1872	North Onslow	Quebec	Methodist	
1872	Ottawa	Ontario	Catholic	Ste-Anne
1872	Pointe Gatineau	Quebec	Catholic	St-François-de-Sales
1872	Rockliffe	Ontario	Catholic	
1872	Cantley	Quebec	Catholic	Ste-Élisabeth
1872	Ottawa	Ontario	Anglican	Christ Church
1872	Ottawa	Ontario	Catholic	St-Jean-Baptiste
1872	Ottawa	Ontario	Presbyterian	St. Andrew
1872	Pembroke	Ontario	Catholic	St. Columba
1872	Shawville	Quebec	Anglican	St. Paul
1873	Alice	Ontario	Methodist	
1873	Antrim	Ontario	Anglican	St. John
1873	Lockesly	Ontario	Methodist	
1873	Ottawa	Ontario	Methodist	West End Methodist
1873	Quyon	Quebec	Methodist	
1873	Renfrew	Ontario	Methodist	
1873	Lac Sainte-Marie	Quebec	Catholic	Ste-Marie
1873	Laus	Quebec	Catholic	Notre-Dame
1873	Ottawa	Ontario	Anglican	St. John
1873	Pembroke	Ontario	Lutheran	Grace Church
1873	Quyon	Quebec	Catholic	
1873	Wendover	Ontario	Catholic	St-Benoît-Labre
1873	Renfrew	Ontario	Catholic	St. Francis Xavier
1873	Osgoode Twnshp	Ontario	Methodist	
1874	Augsburg	Ontario	Lutheran	Zion Church
1874	Breckenridge	Quebec	Anglican	St. Augustine
1874	Britannia	Ontario	Methodist	
1874	Cantley	Quebec	Methodist	
1874	Carp	Ontario	Presbyterian	St. Andrew
1874	Cobden	Ontario	Methodist	
1874	Danford	Quebec	Methodist	
1874	Draffus	Ontario	Methodist	

1874	Ottawa	Ontario	Presbyterian	New Edinburgh Church
1874	Sand Point	Ontario	Methodist	
1874	Stewartville	Ontario	Presbyterian	
1874	Stittsville	Ontario	Presbyterian	
1874	Templetown	Quebec	Methodist	
1874	Bearbrook	Ontario	Methodist	
1874	Ottawa	Ontario	Lutheran	St. Paul
1874	Hazeldean	Ontario	Anglican	St. Paul
1874	Ottawa	Ontario	Presbyterian	Knox Church
1875	Allumettes, Ile des	Quebec	Catholic	St-Alphonse-de-Liguori
1875	Boyds	Ontario	Unknown	
1875	Breckenridge	Quebec	Unknown	
1875	Bristol	Quebec	Catholic	Ste-Mélanie
1875	Caledonia Springs	Ontario	Methodist	
1875	Franktown	Ontario	Catholic	St. Elizabeth
1875	George's Lake	Ontario	Methodist	L'Orignal Circuit
1875	Hawkesbury	Ontario	Catholic	St-Alphonse-de-Liguori
1875	Kars	Ontario	Presbyterian	St. Andrew
1875	Kenmore	Ontario	Baptist	
1875	Leslie	Ontario	Catholic	St-Charles
1875	Lockesley	Ontario	Methodist	
1875	Low	Quebec	Catholic	St-Martin
1875	Masham	Quebec	Methodist	
1875	Mayo	Quebec	Catholic	Our Lady of Malacky
1875	Osgoode	Ontario	Catholic	St. John the Evangelist
1875	Ottawa	Ontario	Presbyterian	MacKay Presbyterian
1875	Plantagenet	Ontario	Anglican	Ch. of the Good Shepherd
1875	Chelsea	Quebec	Methodist	
1875	Chénéville	Quebec	Catholic	St-Félix-de-Valois
1875	Edwards	Quebec	Methodist	Alice Mission
1875	Ottawa	Ontario	Anglican	St. Paul (later St. Luke)
1875	Thurso	Quebec	Catholic	St-Jean-l'Évangéliste
1875	Bristol	Quebec	Anglican	St. Thomas
1875	Calumet	Quebec	Catholic	Ste-Anne

1875	Carlsbad Springs	Ontario	Catholic	St-Laurent
1876	Cantley	Quebec	Presbyterian	
1876	Eardley Twnshp	Quebec	Methodist	Aylmer circuit
1876	Hartwell	Quebec	Catholic	St-Félix-de-Valois
1876	Lachute	Quebec	Catholic	
1876	Manotick	Ontario	Anglican	St. James
1876	Nepean	Ontario	Presbyterian	
1876	Ottawa	Ontario	Methodist	Dominion Methodist
1876	Pakenham	Ontario	Anglican	St. Mark
1876	Shawville	Quebec	Methodist	
1876	Silver Creek	Quebec	Anglican	St. Thomas
1876	Vankleek Hill	Ontario	Catholic	St-Grégoire
1876	Wilno	Ontario	Catholic	
1876	Embrun	Ontario	Catholic	St-Jacques
1876	Emmet	Ontario	Catholic	St-Stanislas-d'Emmet
1876	Fort Coulonge	Quebec	Catholic	St-Pierre
1876	Lachute	Quebec	Catholic	
1876	Pakenham	Ontario	Anglican	St. Mark
1876	St-André-Avellin	Quebec	Catholic	St-André-Avellin
1876	Rockland	Ontario	Anglican	
1877	Beech Grove	Quebec	Methodist	Bethel
1877	Blair's	Ontario	Methodist	
1877	Mohr's Corners	Ontario	Methodist	
1877	Munster	Ontario	Methodist	
1877	Nolan's Corners	Ontario	Methodist	
1877	Ottawa	Ontario	Anglican	Holy Trinity Church
1877	Richmond	Ontario	Methodist	
1877	Wakefield	Quebec	Catholic	St-Pierre
1877	Bois Franc	Quebec	Catholic	St-Antoine-de-Padoue
1877	Chelsea	Quebec	Anglican	St. Mary Magdalen
1877	Lefaivre	Ontario	Catholic	St-Thomas
1877	Pointe Alexandre	Ontario	Catholic	
1877	Ottawa	Ontario	Baptist	First Baptist Church
1878	Rockland	Ontario	Methodist	
1878	Inlet	Quebec	Lutheran	St. Matthew's
1878	La Garde	Quebec	Catholic	N.-D.-de-la-Garde
1878	Renfrew	Ontario	Methodist	

1878	South March	Ontario	Methodist	
1878	St. Albert	Ontario	Catholic	St-Albert
1878	Wolfe	Ontario	Catholic	St-Faustin
1878	Fitzroy Harbour	Ontario	Baptist	
1878	Lachute	Quebec	Anglican	
1878	St. Isidore	Ontario	Catholic	St-Isidore
1879	Bell's Corners	Ontario	Anglican	Christ Church
1879	Bouchette	Quebec	Catholic	St-Gabriel
1879	Burrit's Rapids	Ontario	Methodist	
1879	Carp	Ontario	Methodist	St. Paul
1879	Cumberland	Ontario	Presbyterian	Carmel Church
1879	Dirleton	Ontario	Presbyterian	
1879	High Falls	Quebec	Lutheran	St. Paul
1879	Kenmore	Ontario	Presbyterian	
1879	La Salette	Quebec	Catholic	Notre-Dame-de-la-Salette
1879	Long Island Village	Ontario	Methodist	
1879	North Gower	Ontario	Methodist	
1879	Osgoode Twnshp	Ontario	Baptist	Baptist Chapel
1879	Ottawa	Ontario	Anglican	Trinity Church
1879	Bearbrook	Ontario	Presbyterian	Patterson Church
1879	Maniwaki	Quebec	Catholic	St-Cajétan
1879	North Gower	Ontario	Anglican	Holy Trinity Church

D. Churches built from 1880 to 1899

DATE	LOCATION	PROV.	DENOM.	NAME
1880	Bouchette	Quebec	Catholic	St-Gabriel
1880	Carleton Place	Ontario	Presbyterian	St. Andrew
1880	Heyworth	Quebec	Unknown	
1880	Johnston's Corners	Ontario	Presbyterian	
1880	Kazabazua	Quebec	Anglican	
1880	Kennedy's Corners	Ontario	Methodist	
1880	Kinburn	Ontario	Presbyterian	St. Andrew
1880	South Onslow	Quebec	Methodist	
1880	Admaston Twnshp	Ontario	Presbyterian	
1880	Blackburn	Ontario	Anglican	St. Mary the Virgin

1880	Calumet	Quebec	Anglican	Holy Trinity Church
1880	Cobden	Ontario	Presbyterian	St. Andrew
1880	Ottawa	Ontario	Catholic	St-Jean-Baptiste
1880	Becketts Landing	Ontario	Anglican	St. Paul
1880	Chelsea	Quebec	Catholic	St-Étienne
1881	Arnprior	Ontario	Baptist	
1881	Caledonia	Ontario	Catholic	
1881	Carleton Place	Ontario	Methodist	
1881	Fort William	Ontario	Catholic	St-Siméon
1881	Hawkesbury	Ontario	Congregational	
1881	L'Orignal	Ontario	Methodist	
1881	Micksburg	Ontario	Presbyterian	
1881	North Onslow	Quebec	Anglican	St. Matthew
1881	Pembroke	Ontario	Baptist	
1881	Pembroke	Ontario	Methodist	
1881	Pembroke	Ontario	Presbyterian	
1881	Ponsonby	Quebec	Catholic	Ste-Valérie
1881	Renfrew	Ontario	Methodist	
1881	Russell	Ontario	Methodist	St. Paul
1881	Vankleek Hill	Ontario	Congregational	
1881	Suffolk	Ontario	Catholic	St-Émile
1881	Bonfield	Ontario	Catholic	
1881	Osceola	Ontario	Presbyterian	St. Andrew
1881	Poltimore	Quebec	Lutheran	St. Paul
1881	St. Albert	Ontario	Catholic	St-Albert
1881	White Lake	Ontario	Presbyterian	St. Andrew
1881	Carleton Place	Ontario	Anglican	St. James
1881	Wright	Quebec	Anglican	St. James
1881	Carlsbad Springs	Ontario	Catholic	St-Laurent
1882	Stark's Corners	Quebec	Methodist	
1882	Lachute	Quebec	Methodist	
1882	Vankleek Hill	Ontario	Baptist	
1883	Beachburg	Ontario	Anglican	St. Augustine
1883	N.-D- de la Salette	Quebec	Catholic	Notre-Dame
1883	Ponsonby	Quebec	Catholic	Ste-Valérie
1883	St-Rémi-d'Amherst	Quebec	Catholic	St-Rémi
1883	Argenteuil	Quebec	Catholic	St-Philippe
1883	Greermont	Quebec	Anglican	St. Stephen
1883	Pembroke	Ontario	Lutheran	Christ Church
1883	Pembroke	Ontario	Lutheran	Zion

1883	Renfrew	Ontario	Presbyterian	Canaan Church
1883	St. Anne	Ontario	Catholic	St. Anne
1884	Cobden	Ontario	Methodist	Queen's Line Pastoral
1884	Pontmain	Quebec	Catholic	Notre-Dame
1884	Richmond	Ontario	Presbyterian	St. Andrew
1884	Casselman	Ontario	Catholic	Ste-Euphémie
1884	Cobden	Ontario	Anglican	St. Paul
1884	Kerr Line	Ontario	Presbyterian	
1884	Limoges	Quebec	Catholic	St-Viateur
1884	Luskville	Quebec	Catholic	St-Dominque
1885	Aldfield	Quebec	Catholic	Ste-Sophie
1885	Bourget	Ontario	Catholic	Sacré-Coeur-de-Jésus
1885	Grand Lac	Quebec	Catholic	
1885	Guigues	Quebec	Catholic	
1885	Huntley 6th Line	Ontario	Anglican	St. John the Evangelist
1885	Marathon Village	Ontario	Anglican	St. John
1885	North Onslow	Quebec	Anglican	St. Matthew
1885	Orleans	Ontario	Catholic	St-Joseph
1885	Russell	Ontario	Presbyterian	St. Andrew
1885	South March	Ontario	Catholic	St. Isidore
1885	Spring Hill	Ontario	Presbyterian	
1885	Appleton	Ontario	Methodist	
1885	Founier	Ontario	Catholic	St-Bernard
1885	Queen's Line	Ontario	Methodist	
1885	Quyon	Quebec	Anglican	St. John the Evangelist
1885	Rapides des Joachim	Quebec	Catholic	
1885	Rockland	Ontario	Catholic	Très-Sainte-Trinité
1885	Ottawa	Ontario	Anglican	St. John the Evangelist
1886	Beech Grove	Quebec	Presbyterian	
1886	Rockland	Ontario	Catholic	St. Thomas Aquinus
1886	Kilmaurs	Ontario	Presbyterian	
1886	Laus	Quebec	Catholic	Notre-Dame
1886	Leslie	Quebec	Anglican	St. James
1886	Nolan's Corners	Ontario	Anglican	St. Bede
1886	Russell	Ontario	Anglican	St. Mary
1886	Bonfield	Ontario	Catholic	

1886	Douglas	Ontario	Catholic	St. Michael
1886	Harwood Plains	Ontario	Catholic	St-Isidore
1886	La Passe	Ontario	Catholic	N.-D.-du-Mont-Carmel
1886	Osgoode	Ontario	Anglican	St. Paul
1886	Renfrew	Ontario	Baptist	
1886	St. André Avellin	Quebec	Catholic	St-André-Avellin
1886	Vanier	Ontario	Catholic	N.-D.-de-Lourdes
1886	Wentworth	Quebec	Catholic	St. Michael
1886	Middleville	Ontario	Baptist	Middleville Baptist
1886	Kinburn	Ontario	Methodist	
1887	Appleton	Ontario	Methodist	
1887	Duhamel	Quebec	Catholic	N.-D.-du-Mont-Carmel
1887	Fitzroy Harbour	Ontario	Presbyterian	
1887	Fitzroy Harbour	Ontario	Anglican	St. Paul
1887	Grenville	Quebec	Baptist	
1887	Jock	Ontario	Methodist	Victoria Church
1887	Munster	Ontario	Anglican	St. Stephen
1887	Ottawa	Ontario	Anglican	St. Margaret
1887	Palmer Rapids	Ontario	Lutheran	St. Stephen
1887	South Indian	Ontario	Presbyterian	
1887	Chute-à-Blondeau	Ontario	Catholic	St-Joachim
1887	Douglas	Ontario	Presbyterian	
1887	Eganville	Ontario	Lutheran	St. Luke
1887	Lévesqueville	Ontario	Catholic	St-Thomas
1887	Buckingham	Quebec	Catholic	St-Grégoire-de-Naziance
1888	Dwyer Hill	Ontario	Catholic	
1888	Fallowfield	Ontario	Methodist	
1888	Goulburn	Ontario	Catholic	St. Sylvester
1888	Onslow	Quebec	Catholic	Ste-Brigitte
1888	Ottawa	Ontario	Anglican	St. George
1888	Ottawa	Ontario	Congregational	1st Congregationalist
1888	Rockland	Ontario	Baptist	
1888	Russell Township	Ontario	Methodist	North Russell Church
1888	Vankleek Hill	Ontario	Methodist	
1888	Argenteuil	Quebec	Catholic	St-Philippe
1888	Bourget	Ontario	Catholic	Sacré-Coeur-de-Jésus

1888	Casselman	Ontario	Catholic	Ste-Euphémie
1888	Clarence Creek	Ontario	Catholic	Ste-Félicité
1888	Masson	Quebec	Catholic	N.-D.-des-Neiges
1888	Carleton Place	Ontario	Baptist	
1888	Ottawa	Ontario	Presbyterian	St. Paul
1889	Arnprior	Ontario	Lutheran	St. John
1889	Black Donald	Ontario	Catholic	St-Jean-Baptiste
1889	Darling	Ontario	Catholic	St. Declan
1889	Fallowfield	Ontario	Anglican	St. Barnabas
1889	Palmer Rapids	Ontario	Lutheran	First Lutheran
1889	Alcove	Quebec	unknown	
1889	Rockland	Ontario	Catholic	St. Thomas Aquinus
1889	Brightside	Ontario	Catholic	St. Declan
1889	Carp	Ontario	Anglican	St. James
1889	Cobden	Ontario	Catholic	
1889	Griffith	Ontario	Catholic	N.-D.-du-Rosaire
1889	Ottawa	Ontario	Anglican	All Saints
1889	Ottawa	Ontario	Anglican	St. Luke
1889	Ottawa	Ontario	Catholic	St. Bridgid
1889	Templeton	Quebec	Catholic	Ste-Rose-de-Lima
1889	Ottawa	Ontario	Episcopal	St. David
1889	Thurso	Quebec	Catholic	St-Jean-l'Évangéliste
1889	Vars	Ontario	Anglican	St. Andrew
1890	Breckenridge	Quebec	Unknown	
1890	Buckingham	Quebec	Baptist	Buckingham Baptist
1890	Buckingham	Quebec	Presbyterian	St. Andrew
1890	Curries	Ontario	Catholic	St. Joseph
1890	Greely	Ontario	Anglican	All Saints
1890	Martendale	Quebec	Catholic	
1890	Morin Heights	Quebec	Standard	Hornwright Church
1890	Ottawa	Ontario	Anglican	St. Barnabas
1890	Ottawa	Ontario	Anglican	St. Matthias
1890	Suffolk	Ontario	Catholic	St-Émile
1890	Bayswater	Ontario	Catholic	N.-D.-du-bon-Conseil
1890	Fort Coulonge	Quebec	Presbyterian	St. Andrew
1890	Haley's Station	Ontario	Anglican	
1890	Osceola	Ontario	Catholic	St. Pius

1890	Ottawa	Ontario	Anglican	St. John the Evangelist
1890	Ottawa	Ontario	Society of Friends	
1890	Poltimore	Quebec	Catholic	
1890	Mayo	Quebec	Catholic	Our Lady of Malacky
1891	Almonte	Ontario	Cameronian	
1891	Appleton	Ontario	Presbyterian	
1891	Arnprior	Ontario	Lutheran	
1891	Arundel	Quebec	Catholic	N.-D.-d'Arundel
1891	Arundel	Quebec	Presbyterian	
1891	Blankeney	Ontario	Presbyterian	
1891	Bristol les mines	Quebec	Baptist	
1891	Brownsburg	Quebec	Methodist	
1891	Brownsburg	Quebec	Presbyterian	
1891	Bryson	Quebec	Anglican	St. James
1891	Bryson	Quebec	Methodist	
1891	Bryson	Quebec	Presbyterian	St. Andrew
1891	Caldwell	Quebec	Methodist	
1891	Caledonia	Ontario	Methodist	
1891	Calumet	Quebec	Methodist	
1891	Cambria	Quebec	Anglican	
1891	Cambria	Quebec	Presbyterian	
1891	Castleford	Ontario	Baptist	
1891	Castleford	Ontario	Presbyterian	
1891	Chelsea	Quebec	Presbyterian	
1891	Chute-à-Blondeau	Ontario	Presbyterian	
1891	Clayton	Quebec	Methodist	
1891	Clayton	Ontario	Presbyterian	
1891	Curran	Ontario	Methodist	
1891	Denbigh	Ontario	Methodist	
1891	Eardley	Quebec	Methodist	
1891	Eganville	Ontario	Methodist	
1891	Eganville	Ontario	Presbyterian	
1891	Fallowfield	Ontario	Presbyterian	
1891	Hawkesbury	Ontario	Presbyterian	
1891	Kars	Ontario	Methodist	Kars Methodist Church
1891	Lac des quinze	Quebec	Catholic	
1891	Lemieux	Ontario	Catholic	St-Joseph
1891	Limoges	Ontario	Presbyterian	

1891	Low	Quebec	Methodist	
1891	Luskville	Quebec	Anglican	
1891	Luskville	Quebec	Presbyterian	
1891	Maniwaki	Quebec	Anglican	
1891	Manotick	Ontario	Methodist	
1891	Mohr's Corners	Ontario	Methodist	
1891	Namur	Quebec	Catholic	
1891	Namur	Quebec	Presbyterian	St. Paul
1891	Navan	Ontario	Anglican	St. Mary
1891	North Onslow	Quebec	Catholic	
1891	Palmer Rapids	Ontario	Methodist	
1891	Papineauville	Quebec	Anglican	
1891	Papineauville	Quebec	Baptist	
1891	Pembroke	Ontario	Anglican	
1891	Plantagenet	Ontario	Presbyterian	
1891	Portage du Fort	Quebec	Methodist	
1891	Portage du Fort	Quebec	Presbyterian	
1891	Quinville	Quebec	Catholic	St. Columban
1891	Quinville	Quebec	Presbyterian	
1891	Rankin	Ontario	Anglican	
1891	Rapides des Joachim	Quebec	Presbyterian	
1891	Sand Point	Ontario	Anglican	
1891	Sand Point	Ontario	Presbyterian	
1891	Sebastopol	Ontario	Catholic	
1891	Shawville	Quebec	Baptist	
1891	Snake River	Ontario	Anglican	
1891	Snake River	Ontario	Methodist	
1891	South Gloucester	Ontario	Methodist	
1891	Ste-Anne	Ontario	Presbyterian	Ste-Anne
1891	Thorne Centre	Quebec	Methodist	
1891	Thurso	Quebec	Presbyterian	
1891	Westmeath	Ontario	Presbyterian	
1891	Embrun	Ontario	Catholic	St-Jacques
1891	L'Orignal	Ontario	Anglican	Church of the Nativity
1891	Long Sault	Quebec	Catholic	N.-D.-de-Bonsecours
1891	Pembroke	Ontario	Lutheran	St. John
1891	Renfrew	Ontario	Lutheran	St. James
1891	Blanche Lake	Quebec	Anglican	St. Andrew
1892	Hawthorne	Ontario	Methodist	

1892	L'Orignal	Ontario	Methodist	Zion
1892	Ottawa	Ontario	Anglican	St. Stephen
1892	Pakenham	Ontario	Catholic	St-Pierre-Célestin
1892	Bromley	Ontario	Methodist	
1892	Ottawa	Ontario	Catholic	St. Joseph
1892	Hull	Quebec	Catholic	N.-D.-de-Grâce
1893	Lac des loups	Quebec	Catholic	St-François-d'Assise
1893	Munster	Ontario	Methodist	
1893	Ottawa	Ontario	Baptist	McPhail Memorial
1893	Ottawa	Ontario	Catholic	Sacré-Coeur
1893	Aylmer	Quebec	Catholic	St. Paul /(N.-D.)
1893	Curran	Ontario	Catholic	St-Luc
1893	Limoges	Ontario	Catholic	St-Viateur
1894	Ottawa	Ontario	Congregational	2nd Congregationalist
1894	Russell	Ontario	Baptist	Russell Baptist
1894	Sarsfield	Ontario	Catholic	St-Hugues
1894	Snake River	Ontario	Presbyterian	Scotland Church
1894	Clarke's Settlement	Quebec	Anglican	St. John
1894	Lochwinnoch	Ontario	Presbyterian	Lochwinnoch Presbyterian
1894	Montebello	Quebec	Catholic	N.-D.-de-Bonsecours
1894	Thorne Centre	Quebec	Anglican	St. George
1894	Britannia	Ontario	Catholic	St. Bonaventure
1895	Bristol les mines	Quebec	Anglican	St. Barnabas
1895	Eganville	Ontario	Catholic	St-Jacques
1895	N.-D.-de-Lumière	Quebec	Catholic	Notre-Dame
1895	Wendover	Ontario	Catholic	St-Benoît-Labre
1895	Wilno	Ontario	Catholic	
1895	Ottawa	Ontario	Lutheran	St. John
1895	Calabogie	Ontario	Catholic	Précieux Sang
1896	Ladysmith	Quebec	Lutheran	St. John
1896	Lake Louisa	Quebec	Anglican	
1896	Metcalfe	Ontario	Presbyterian	
1896	Mulgrave	Quebec	Baptist	Mulgrave Baptist
1896	Parkham	Quebec	Anglican	St. Alban
1896	Pointe au chêne	Ontario	Catholic	
1896	Tennyson	Ontario	Anglican	St. John the Evangelist
1896	Vankleek Hill	Ontario	Presbyterian	

1896	Vinton	Quebec	Catholic	Ste-Élisabeth
1896	Barry's Bay	Ontario	Catholic	
1896	Dunrobin	Ontario	Anglican	St. Paul
1896	Forrester's Falls	Ontario	Methodist	
1896	Hawkesbury	Ontario	Catholic	St-Alphonse-de-Liguori
1896	Thurso	Quebec	Catholic	St-Jean-l'Évangéliste
1897	Pakenham	Ontario	Presbyterian	St. Andrew
1897	Renfrew	Ontario	Methodist	Trinity Methodist Church
1897	Round Lake	Ontario	Catholic	
1897	Metcalfe	Ontario	Anglican	Holy Trinity
1897	Navan	Ontario	Presbyterian	Wilson Church
1897	New Killaloe	Ontario	Catholic	
1898	Admaston Twnshp	Ontario	Methodist	Byer's Chapel
1898	Bell's Corners	Ontario	Presbyterian	
1898	Limoges	Ontario	Catholic	St-Viateur
1898	Nepean	Ontario	Presbyterian	Elim Church
1898	Ottawa	Ontario	Anglican	St. Matthew
1898	Antrim	Ontario	Anglican	St. John
1898	Casselman	Ontario	Catholic	Ste-Euphémie
1898	Kilroy Crescent	Quebec	Unknown	
1899	Admaston Twnshp	Ontario	Holiness Mvnt	Beulah Chapel
1899	Ashton	Ontario	Methodist	
1899	Edwards	Ontario	Anglican	
1899	Radford	Quebec	Anglican	Holy Trinity
1899	St. Declan	Ontario	Catholic	St. Declan
1899	Wyman/Billerica	Quebec	Methodist	
1899	Burnstown	Ontario	Presbyterian	
1899	Charteris	Quebec	Anglican	St. Mathew
1899	Balsam Hill	Ontario	unknown	Beulah Chapel
1899	Westmeath	Ontario	Anglican	St. Mary
1899	Buckingham	Quebec	Anglican	St. Stephen

APPENDIX III

NINETEENTH-CENTURY PLACE NAMES

ALMONTE, Ont.	Ramsay Village, Ont. Shipman's Falls, Ont. Shipman's Mills, Ont. Shipman's Village, Ont.
ALTA VISTA, Ont.	Ellwood, Ont. now part of **OTTAWA** known as Alta Vista.
APPLETON, Ont.	Appleton Falls, Ont.
ARCHEVILLE, Ont.	now part of **OTTAWA**, Ont.
ARGENTEUIL, Que.	see **CHATHAM**, Que.
ASHTON, Ont.	Goulbourn, Ont. Mount Pleasant, Ont. Summers Corners, Ont. (also Sumners Corners)
Bellamy's Mills, Ont.	see Clayton, Ont.
BILLING'S BRIDGE, Ont.	Farmer's Bridge, Ont. Gateville, Ont. now part of **OTTAWA** known as Billing's Bridge.
BLACKBURN, Ont.	Daggville, Ont. Gloucester, Ont. now part of Gloucester known as Blackburn.
BLAKENEY, Ont.	Rose Bank, Ont.
Bonsecours, Que.	see **MONTEBELLO**, Que.
BOURGET, Ont.	The Brook, Ont.
BRISTOL, Que.	Bristol Corners, Que. Bristol Mills, Que. Inkerman, Que.
BRITANNIA, Ont.	now part of **OTTAWA** known as Britannia.
Brook, The	see **BOURGET**, Ont.
Bytown, Ont.	see **OTTAWA**, Ont.
Cambridge, Ont.	see **ST-ALBERT** Ont.
CARLETON PLACE, Ont.	Carleton Junction Station, Ont. Carleton Place Junction, Ont. Morphy's Falls, Ont. (also Murphy's Falls) Morphy's Mills, Ont.
CARLSBAD SPRINGS, Ont.	Eastman Springs, Ont.
Castor, Ont.	see **RUSSELL**, Ont.
CHARTERIS, Que.	North Clarendon, Que.
Chatham, Que.	see **ARGENTEUIL**, Que.
Chaudières, Que.	see **HULL**, Que.

Chenail Écarté, Ont.	see **Hawkesbury**, Ont.
Clarence, Ont.	Clarence Creek, Ont. New England, Ont.
Clarendon Centre, Que.	see **Shawville**, Que.
Clarlington, Ont.	now part of **Ottawa** known as Carlingwood.
Clayton, Ont.	Bellamy's Mills, Ont.
Daggville, Ont.	see **Blackburn**, Ont.
Dawson, Ont.	see **Prescott Road**, Ont.
Des Chats, Ont.	see **Fitzroy Harbour**, Ont.
Duncanville, Ont.	see **Russell**, Ont.
Dwyer Hill, Ont.	Goulbourn, Ont.
Eastman's Springs, Ont.	see **Carlsbad Springs**, Ont.
Eastview, Ont.	see **Vanier**, Ont.
Ellwood, Ont.	see **Alta Vista**, Ont.
Embrun, Ont.	Rivière-du-Castor, Ont.
Fallowfield, Ont.	Nepean (Mission de), Ont.
Farmer's Bridge, Ont.	see **Billing's Bridge**, Ont.
Fitzroy Harbour, Ont.	Des Chats, Ont. The Cats, Ont.
Fraserville, Que.	see **Thurso**, Que.
Galetta, Ont.	Hubble's Falls, Ont.
Gateville, Ont.	see **Billing's Bridge**, Ont.
Gloucester, Ont.	see **Blackburn**, Ont.
Gloucester, Ont.	see **South Gloucester**, Ont.
Gloucester-Nord, Ont.	see **Orleans**, Ont.
Goulbourn, Ont.	see **Ashton**, Ont.
Goulbourn, Ont.	see **Dwyer Hill**, Ont.
Gower Point, Ont.	see **Lapasse**, Ont.
Grand Chantier, Ont.	see **Ste-Anne-de-Prescott**, Ont.
Hamilton Mills, Ont.	see **Hawkesbury**, Ont.
Harvey Mills, Ont.	see **Pakenham**, Ont.
Hattville, Ont	see **Plantagenet**, Ont.
Hawkesbury, Ont.	Chenail Écarté, Ont. Hamilton Mills, Ont.
Hawthorne, Ont.	now part of **Ottawa** known as Hawthorne.
Hintonberg, Ont.	now part of **Ottawa**, Ont.
Hubble's Falls, Ont.	see **Galetta**, Ont.
Hull, Que.	Chaudières, Que.
Inkerman, Que.	see **Bristol**, Que.
Janeville, Ont.	see **Vanier**, Ont.

Kars, Ont.	Lindsay's Warf, Ont. Wellington Village, Ont.
L'Orignal, Ont.	Longueil, Ont. Nouvelle Longueil, Ont. Treadwell, Ont.
La Blanche, Que.	see **Perkins**, Que.
La Côte, Ont.	see **Vankleek Hill**, Ont.
Lapasse, Ont.	Gower Point, Ont. Westmeath, Ont.
Leitrim, Ont.	Cowansville, Ont. now part of **Ottawa** known as Leitrim, Ont.
Lemieux, Ont.	Petit Moose Creek, Ont.
Limoges, Ont.	Limoges Station, Ont. South Indian, Ont. (South Indian Station, Ont.)
Lindsay's Warf, Ont.	**Kars**, Ont.
Lochaber, Que.	**Thurso**, Que.
Longueil, Ont.	see **L'Orignal**, Ont.
Lowrie, Ont.	Lowry, Ont. North Huntley, Ont.
Maniwaki, Que.	River Desert, Que.
March-Sud, Ont.	**South March**, Ont.
Masham, Que.	La Pêche, Que. Sainte-Cécile-de-Masham, Que.
Merivale, Ont.	now part of **Ottawa** known as Merivale, Ont.
Miller's Corners, Ont.	see **North Gower**, Ont.
Montebello, Que.	Bonsecours, Que.
Morphy's Falls, Ont.	see **Carleton Place**, Ont.
Mount Pleasant, Ont.	see **Ashton**, Ont.
Muddy Branch, Que.	see **Argenteuil**, Que.
Nepean (Mission de), Ont.	see **Fallowfield**, Ont.
New England, Ont.	see **Clarence**, Ont.
North Gower, Ont.	Miller's Corners, Ont. Stephensville, Ont.
North Clarendon, Que.	see **Charteris**, Que.
North Huntley, Ont.	see **Lowry**, Ont.
Nouvelle Longueil, Ont.	see **L'Orignal**, Ont.
Orleans, Ont.	Gloucester-Nord, Ont. Saint-Joseph, Ont. Saint-Joseph-d'Orléans, Ont.
Osceola, Ont.	Snake River, Ont.
Ottawa, Ont.	Bytown, Ont. (now includes several small villages) Alta Vista (a.k.a. Ellwood) Archeville Billings Bridge

OTTAWA, Ont.	Britannia Carlington Hawthorne Hintonbery Merivale Rochesterville Westboro
OUTAOUAIS, Rivière des	Grand Rivier,
PAKENHAM, Ont.	Harvey Mills, Ont.
Pélissier, Que.	see **WAKEFIELD**, Que.
PERKINS, Que.	La Blanche, Que. Perkins' Mills, Que.
Petit Moose Creek, Ont.	see **LEMIEUX**, Ont.
PLANTAGENET, Ont.	Hattville, Ont. Plantagenet Mills, Ont.
PRESCOTT ROAD, Ont.	Dawson, Ont.
PRESCOTT, Ont.	Scotch River, Ont.
Ramsay Village, Ont.	see **ALMONTE**, Ont. This is not to be confused with **RAMSAYVILLE**, located just south of **OTTAWA**.
Rivière-du-Castor, Ont.	see **EMBRUN**, Ont.
Rochesterville, Ont.	now part of **OTTAWA**, Ont.
Rose Bank, Ont.	see **BLAKENEY**, Ont.
RUSSELL, Ont.	Castor, Ont. Duncanville, Ont. Russell Station, Ont.
Scotch River, Ont.	see **ST-ISIDORE-DE-PRESCOTT**, Ont.
Scotch-Saint-Isidore, Ont.	see **ST-ISIDORE-DE-PRESCOTT**, Ont.
SHAWVILLE, Que.	Clarendon Center, Que.
Shipman's Falls, Ont.	see **ALMONTE**, Ont.
Shipman's Mills, Ont.	see **ALMONTE**, Ont.
Shipman's Village, Ont.	see **ALMONTE**, Ont.
Snake River, Ont.	see **OSCEOLA**, Ont.
SOUTH GLOUCESTER, Ont.	Gloucester, Ont.
SOUTH MARCH, Ont.	Lewisville, Ont. March-Sud, Ont.
South Indian, Ont.	see **LIMOGES**, Ont.
ST-ALBERT, Ont.	Cambridge, Ont.
ST-ISIDORE-DE-PRESCOTT, Ont.	Scotch-Saint-Isidore, Ont.
St-Joseph, Ont.	see **ORLEANS**, Ont.
St-Joseph, Que.	see **FARRELTON**, Que.
St-Joseph-d'Orléans, Ont.	see **ORLEANS**, Ont.
ST-PHILIPPE-D'ARGENTEUIL	Muddy Branch, Que.

STE-ANNE-DE-PRESCOTT, Ont.	Grand Chantier, Ont.
Ste-Cécile-de-Masham, Que.	see **MASHAM**, Que.
Stephensville, Ont.	see **NORTH GOWER**, Ont.
Summers Corners, Ont.	see **AHTON**, Ont.
The Cats, Ont.	see **FITZROY HARBOUR**, Ont.
THURSO, Que.	Fraserville, Que. Lochaber, Que.
Treadwell, Ont.	see **L'ORIGNAL**, Ont.
VANIER, Ont.	Eastview, Ont. Janeville, Ont.
VANKLEEK HILL, Ont.	La Côte, Ont.
VINTON, Que.	Franktown, Que.
WAKEFIELD, Que.	Pélissier, Que.
Wellington, Ont.	see **KARS**, Ont.
Westboro, Ont.	now part of **OTTAWA**, Ont.
Westmeath, Ont.	see **LAPASSE**, Ont.
WOODROFFE, Ont.	now part of **OTTAWA** known as Woodroffe.

BIBLIOGRAPHY

1. PRIMARY SOURCES

Manuscript Collections

Anglican Diocesan Archives, Ottawa, Ontario
- Arnprior Deanery Collection
- Carleton Deanery Collection
- Clarendon Deanery Collection
- Lanark Deanery Collection
- Ottawa Deanery Collection
- Pembroke Deanery Collection
- Prescott and Russell Deanery Collection
- Stormont Deanery Collection

Archdiocesan Archives (Roman Catholic), Ottawa, Ontario
- *Mandements des évêques d'Ottawa*, 1848-1878, Vol. 1
- Mgr. Duhamel, *Registre des visites épiscopales I* (1875-1889)
- Parish Collections
- Photograph Collection

Archives Deschatelets (O.M.I.), Ottawa, Ontario
- Parish and Mission Collection

Archives of the Diocese of Ontario (Anglican), Kingston, Ontario
- Merrickville Parish Collection

City of Ottawa Archives, Ottawa, Ontario
- United Church of Canada Records Collection

Public Archives of Canada (P.A.C.)
- Church Records and Registeries Collection
- Hamnett K. Pinhey Papers
- Topley Collection
- Cartographic and Architectural Division Collection

Queen's University Archives, Kingston, Ontario (Q.U.A.)
- Presbyterian Church of Canada in Connection with the Church of Scotland Collection

Printed Reports

Abstract of the Minutes of the Synod of the Presbyterian Church of Canada, Session 5, 1835.

Abstract of the Minutes of the Synod of the Presbyterian Church, Kingston, 1832.

An Account of the Proceedings of the Committees on Union Appointed by The Synod of the Presbyterian Church in Canada and the Synod of the Missionary (Now the United Presbyterian) Church in Canada, Synod of the United Presbyterian Church, W.M. Sutherland, London, C.W. 1849.

Annual Report of the Canada Conference Missionary Society (Methodist), 1830.

Annual Report of the Congregational Church, Ottawa, 1870-1874, 1876-1889.

Annual Report of the Missionary Society of the Methodist Church of Canada, 1875, 1876, 1877, 1878, 1879, 1880.

Annual Report of the Missionary Society of the Methodist Episcopal Church in Canada, 1855-1856.

Annual Report of the Missionary Society of the Methodist Episcopal Church in Canada, 1867, 1868, 1869, 1870, 1874, 1877, 1878, 1880, 1882, 1883.

Annual Report of the Missionary Society of the Wesleyan Methodist Church in British North America, 1833.

Annual Report of the Missionary Society of the Wesleyan Methodist Church in Canada, 1835, 1836, 1839, 1840-1841, 1841-1842, 1843, 1844, 1845, 1846, 1847.

Annual Report of the Missionary Society of the Wesleyan Methodist Church in Canada in Connexion with the English Conference, 1848, 1849, 1850, 1850-1851, 1852, 1853, 1854, 1855, 1856, 1865, 1866, 1871, 1872, 1874.

Circular to the Ministers in Connection with the Established Church of Scotland in Upper Canada, August 1830.

Extracts from the Minutes of the Synod of the Presbyterian Church of Canada in Connexion with the Established Church of Scotland, York, 1833.

Report of the Cambridge Camden Society for MDCCCXLI, Cambridge, 1841.

Report of the Committee for Missions of the Synod of the Presbyterian Church in Canada, Kingston, 1831.

Rules and Regulations for Proprietors of the Church in Bytown U.C. in Communion with the Established Church of Scotland, 1833.

The Principal Acts of the General Assembly of the Church of Scotland, Edinburgh, 1835.

Newspapers and Journals

Anglo-American Magazine, Toronto, 1852-1855.

Bytown Gazette, 1836-1837, 1840, 1843.

Canada Christian Advocate, 1845-1848, 1870-1882.

Canadian Architect and Builder, 1888-1899.

Canadian Baptist, 1859-1871, 1888-1889.

Canadian Christian Examiner and Presbyterian Magazine, 1839-1840.

Canadian Church Magazine and Mission News, 1891-1893.

Canadian Churchman, 1853-1864.

Canadian Ecclesiastical Gazette, 1850-1862.

Canadian Presbyter, 1857-1858.

Christian Guardian, 1829-1851, 1856-1869, 1872-1884.

Christian Messenger, 1854-1859.

Church Builder, 1866-1878.

Congregational Record, 1885-1889.

Dominion Churchman, 1876, 1877-1879, 1881-1882, 1885, 1886, 1888.

Ecclesiastical Gazette, 1850-1851.

Ecclesiologist, 1846-1848.

Evangelical Churchman, 1880.

Mélanges Religieux : Recueil Périodique, 1841.

Montreal Gazette, 1860.

Orange Lily and Protestant Vindicator, Bytown, 1849-1850.

Ottawa Church of England Magazine, 1891-1893.

Ottawa Daily Citizen. 1871- 1876, 1879, 1880-1883.

Ottawa Times, 1866.

Ottawa Tribune, 1854-1855, 1861-1862.

Presbyterian Review, 1885.

Rideau Record, 1901.

The Church, 1837-1856.

The Journal, 1887-1890.

Young Churchman, 1851.

Books and Articles

Bangs, Nathan. *History of the Methodist Episcopal Church*. Vols. 1 and 2. New York: Lane and Stanford, 1844.

Barbezieux, Alexis de. *Histoire de la Province Ecclésiastique d'Ottawa et de la Colonisation dans la Vallée de l'Ottawa*. 2 vols. Ottawa: La companie d'imprimerie d'Ottawa, 1897.

Barbier de Montault, X. *Traité pratique de la construction de l'ameublement et de la décoration des églises selon les règles canoniques et les traditions romaines avec un appendice sur le costume ecclésiastique*. Paris: P. Louis Vivès, 1878.

Bedford-Jones, Thomas. "How St. Alban's Church, Ottawa, Had Its Beginning Under the First Rector." *Journal of the Canadian Catholic Historical Society* 3, 3 (May 1957): 1-23.

Belden, H. *Historical Atlas of Carleton County, Ontario—Illustrated 1879*. Toronto: H. Belden and Co., 1879. Reprinted Port Elgin: Ross Cummings, 1971.

—. *Historical Atlas of Prescott and Russell, Stormont, Dundas and Glengarry Counties, Ontario*. Toronto: H. Belden and Co., 1881.

—. *Historical Atlas of Lanark and Renfrew Counties, Ontario—Illustrating 1880-1881*. Prescott: D.P. Putman,1882.

Bethune, A.N. "A charge addressed to the clergy of the Archdeanery of York." *The Church* 13, 14 (1 November 1849).

Bettridge, William. *A Brief History of the Church in Upper Canada: Containing the Acts of Parliament, Imperial and Provincial, Royal Instructions, Proceedings of Deputation, Correspondence with the government, Clergy Reserves Question . . .* London: W.E. Painter, 1838.

Bloxam, Mathew. *The Principles of Gothic Ecclesiastical Architecture with an Explanation of the Technical Terms and a Centenary of Ancient Terms*. 8th ed. London: David Bogue, 1846.

Bordeaux, R. *Traité de la réparation des églises; principes d'archéologie pratique*. 2e éd. Evreux: A. Hérissey, 1862.

Bouger, L. *Liturgical Piety*. Notre Dame, 1955.

Butterfield, William. *Instrumenta Ecclesiastica, A Series of Working Designs for the Furniture, Fittings and Decorations of Churches and Their Precincts.* London: John Van Voorst, 1847.

Carre, William H. *Art Work on the Ottawa*, s.l. W. Carre, 1898.

Carrol, John. *Case and His Contemporaires: or Biographical History of Methodism in Canada From its Introduction into the Province till the Death of the Rev. William Case in 1855*. Toronto: Wesleyan Conference Office, 1871.

Devie, Mgr. Alexandre-Raymond. *Manuel de connaissances utiles aux ecclésiastiques sur divers objets d'art notamment sur l'architecture des édifices religieux anciens et modernes, et sur les constructions et réparations d'églises avec plans et dessins lithographiés*. Lyon: L. Lesne, 1843.

Durandus, Guilielmus. *The Symbolism of Churches and Church Ornaments: A translation of the first book of the RATIONALE DIVINORUM OFFICIORUM* (c. 1286). Translation and introductory essay by Rev. John Mason Neale and Rev. Benjamin Webb. Leeds: T.W. Green, 1843.

"Ecclesiastical Architecture: Village Churches." *Anglo-American Magazine*. 1854, 4:20.

Ecclesiological Late Cambridge Camden Society. *Hierurgia Anglicana or Documents and Extracts Illustrative of the Ritual of the Church in England after the Reformation*. London: J.G.F. and J. Rivington, 1848.

Ecclesiological Late Cambridge Camden Society. *A Handbook of English Ecclesiology*. London: Joseph Masters, 1847.

Garnier, Thomas, P. *The parish church: a simple explanation of church symbolism*. London: Society for Promoting Christian Knowledge, 1876.

Gourlay, J. L. *History of the Ottawa Valley: A Collection of facts events and reminiscences for over half a century*, Ottawa: s.n., 1896.

Gregg, William. *History of the Presbyterian Church in the Dominion of Canada: from the earliest times to 1834 with a chronological table of events to the present time and map*. Toronto: Presbyterian Printing and Publishing Co., 1885.

Gregg, William. *Short History of the Presbyterian Church in the Dominion of Canada*. Toronto: Poole, 1900.

Grimthorpe, E. B. *Lectures on church building*. London: Bell and Daldy, 1856.

Hay, William. "Architecture for the Meridian of Canada." *Anglo-American Magazine*. 2, 3 (March 1856): 253-255.

Jebb, J. *The choral service of the United church of England and Ireland*. London: J.W. Parker, 1843.

Hay, William. "The Late Mr. Pugin and the Revival of Christian Architecture." *Anglo-American Magazine* 2 (1853): 70.

Lamond, Robert. *A narrative of the rise and progress of emigration from the counties of Lanark and Renfrew to new settlement in Upper Canada to new settlements on government grants: Comprising the proceedings of the Glasgow Committee for directing the affairs and embarcation of the societies with a map of the townships, designs for cottages and a plan of the ship Earl of Buckinghamshire, also, interesting letters from the settlements*. Glasgow: Chalmers and Collins, 1821. Reprinted by Ottawa: Canadian Heritage Publications, 1978.

Naylor, W. H. *The Church in Clarendon*. St John's: E.R. Smith Co., 1919.

"Notes on a Trip to the West." *Canadian Architect and Builder*. November 1888, 1:5.

Poole, George, A. *Churches: their structure, arrangement and decoration*. London: J. Burns, 1846.

Pugin, A. W. *Apology*. London: J. Weale, 1843.

—. *Contrasts: Or A Parallel Between the Noble Edifices of the Fourteenth and Fifteenth Centuries, and Similar Buildings of the Present Day; Shewing the Present Decay of Taste: Accompanied by Appropriate Text*. London: Printed for the author and published by him, 1836. Reprinted by New York: Leicester University Press, 1973.

—. *Glossary of Ecclesiastical Ornament and Costume*. London: H. G. Bohn, 1844.

—. *On the present state of Ecclesiastical Architecture in England*. London: Charles Dolman, 1845.

—. *True Principles of Pointed or Christian Architecture*. London: J. Weale, 1841.

Rae, J. "How ought the Clergy Reserve question be settled?" *The Canadian Christian Examiner and Presbyterian Magazine* 3, 9 (September 1839): 269.

Roger, C. *Ottawa Past and Present*. Ottawa: Times Printing and Publishing, 1871.

Russell, J. F., ed. *A Hand-Book of English Ecclesiology*. London: Joseph Masters, 1848.

Sanderson, W. "Alice, Ontario." *Annual Report of the Missionary Society of the Wesleyan Methodist Church in Canada in Connexion with the English Conference*, 1872, lxxii.

Thomas, C. *History of the Counties of Argenteuil Que. and Prescott Ont. from the earliest settlement to the present*. Montréal: John Lovell and Son, 1896.

Vasari, Giorgo. *Vasari on Technique. Being the Introduction to the Three Arts of Design, Architecture, Sculpture and Painting, Prefixed to the Lives of the Most Excellent Painters, Sculptors and Architects*. ed. B. Brown, New York: Dover Publications 1960.

"What Is Popery?" *Canadian Christian Examiner and Presbyterian Magazine*. October 1839, Vol. 3, no. 10, p. 293.

Wilson, Daniel. "Church Builders." *Canadian Architect and Builder,* 2 April 1889, 42-43.

Wren, C. *Parentalia: or Memoirs of the Family of the Wrens; viz of Matthew Bishop of Ely, Christopher, Dean of Windsor, etc., but chiefly of Sir C. Wren; in which is contained, besides his works, a great number of original Papers and Records. . . . Compiled by his son Christopher. . . . published by S. Wren, with the care of J. Ames.* London: T. Osborne and R. Dodsley, 1750.

Canadian Inventory of Historic Buildings

Admaston, Ontario. n.n. (Presbyterian). File 06-0098000-00214.
Alcove, Quebec. Alcove United Church (United). File 05-0081000-00057.
Angers, Quebec. Ange-Gardien (Catholic). File 05-7120040-00295.
Anse-Saint-Georges, Quebec. n.n. (Catholic). File 05-0002000-00063.
Antrim, Ontario. St. John (Anglican). File 06-0089000-00017.
Argenteuil, Quebec. St-Philippe (Catholic). File 05-5200002-00276.
Ashton, Ontario. Christ Church (Anglican). File 06-0041000-00024.
Ashton, Ontario. Christ Church (United). File 06-0041000-00807.
Ashton, Ontario. Melville (Presbyterian). File 06-0041000-00016.
Aylmer, Quebec. n.n. (Presbyterian). File 05-3730004-00000.
Aylmer, Quebec. n.n. (Wesleyan Methodist). File 05-3730019-00034.
Aylmer, Quebec. Christ Church (Anglican). File 05-3730004-00103.
Aylmer, Quebec. n.n. (Methodist). File 05-3730001-00166.
Aylmer, Quebec. n.n. (Presbyterian). File 05-373004-00073.
Aylmer, Quebec. Notre-Dame (Catholic). File 05-3730006-00061.
Aylmer, Quebec. St-Médard (Catholic). File 05-0043000-00183.
Aylmer, Quebec. Unidentified. File 05-3730019-00031.
Aylwin, Quebec. St. John in the Wilderness (Anglican). File 05-0121000-00059.
Bagot, Ontario. Unidentified. File 06-0098000-00183.
Balsam Hill, Ontario. Beulah Chapel (Holiness Movement). File 06-0098000-00217.
Bearbrook, Ontario. Trinity Church (Anglican). File 06-0093000-00266.
Beckett's Landing, Ontario. St. Paul (Anglican). File 06-0078000-00410.
Bell's Corners, Ontario. Christ Church (Anglican). File 06-0083000-00491.
Black's Corners, Ontario. n.n. (Presbyterian). File 06-0041000-00098.
Blackburn, Ontario. St. Mary-the-Virgin (Anglican). File 06-0083000-00628.
Blanche, Quebec. Notre-Dame-de-Lumière (Catholic). File 05-0110000-00161.
Bois-Franc, Quebec. St-Antoine-de-Padoue (Catholic). File 05-0153000-00100.
Bois-Franc, Quebec. Unidentified. File 05-0153000-00001.
Bouchette, Quebec. St-Gabriel (Catholic). File 05-0145000-00006.
Boyds, Ontario. Unidentified. File 06-0041000-00163.
Breckenridge, Quebec. St. Augustine (Anglican). File 05-0043000-00048.
Breckenridge, Quebec. Unidentified. File 05-0043000-00043.
Breckenridge, Quebec. Unidentified. File 05-0043000-00047.
Bromley, Ontario. n.n. (Methodist). File 06-0097000-00197.
Brownsburg, Quebec. Brownsburg Church (United). File 05-5170001-00207.
Bryson, Quebec. n.n (Anglican). File 05-0047000-00005.
Bryson, Quebec. St. Andrew (United). File 05-0047-000-00001.
Bryson, Quebec. St. James (Anglican). File 05-0047000-00005.
Buckingham, Quebec. Ange-Gardien (Catholic). File 05-7120040-00295.

Buckingham, Quebec. Buckingham Baptist Church (Baptist). File 05-7120019-00117.
Buckingham, Quebec. St-Grégoire-de-Naziance (Catholic). File 05-7120009-00150.
Buckingham, Quebec. St. Andrew (Presbyterian). File 05-7120002-00570.
Buckingham, Quebec. St. Stephen (Anglican). File 05-7120029-00400.
Burdenell, Ontario. St. Mary (Catholic). File 06-0072000-00001.
Burnstown, Ontario. n.n. (Presbyterian). File 06-0098000-00079.
Calumet, Quebec. Holy Trinity (Anglican). File 05-4670002-00176.
Cantley, Quebec. Ste-Elizabeth (Catholic). File 05-0081000-00195.
Carlsbad Spring, Ontario. n.n. (Anglican). File 06-0093000-00149.
Carlsbad Spring, Ontario. St-Laurent (Catholic). File 06-0093000-00183.
Carp, Ontario. St. Andrew (Presbyterian). File 06-0089000-00065.
Carp, Ontario. St. James (Anglican). File 06-0089000-00074.
Chéneville, Quebec. Unidentified. File 05-750001-00110.
Corkery, Ontario. St. Michael (Catholic). File 06-0089000-00289.
Cumberland, Ontario. Carmel Church (Presbyterian). File 06-0117000-00010.
Cumberland, Ontario. St. Mark (Anglican). File 06-0117000-00016.
Cushing, Quebec. Unidentified. File 05-00003000-00532.
Cushing, Quebec. Unidentified. File 05-0003000-00499.
Cushing, Quebec. St. Mungo (Presbyterian). File 05-0068000-00349.
Douglas, Ontario. n.n. (Presbyterian). File 06-0097000-00256.
Duhamel, Quebec. N.-D.-du-Mont-Carmel (Catholic). File 05-0150000-00001.
Dunrobin, Ontario. n.n. (Methodist). File 06-0089000-00005.
Eardley, Quebec. Eardley United Church (United). File 05-0046000-00049.
Eardley, Quebec. St. Luke (Anglican). File 05-0046000-00048.
Ellard, Quebec. n.n. (Anglican). File 05-0138000-00047.
Fallowfield, Ontario. n.n. (Methodist). File 06-0083000-00506.
Fallowfield, Ontario. St. Patrick (Catholic). File 06-0083000-00280.
Farm Point, Quebec. St-Clément (Catholic). File 05-0081000-00175.
Farrellton, Quebec. St-Camilius (Catholic). File 05-0081000-00138.
Fassett, Quebec. St-Fidèle-de-Fasset (Catholic). File 05-7390004-00066.
Fassett, Quebec. Unidentified. File 05-7390004-00081.
Ferguson's Falls, Ontario. St. Patrick (Unidentified). File 06-0004100-00178.
Fitzroy Harbour Ontario. St. George (Anglican). File 06-0089000-00012.
Fitzroy Harbour, Ontario. St. Michael (Catholic). File 06-0089000-00010.
Forrester's Falls, Ontario. n.n. (Methodist). File 06-0097000-00098.
Forrester's Falls, Ontario. n.n. (United). File 06-0097000-00072.
Fort Coulonge, Quebec. St. Andrew (Presbyterian). File 05-0044000-00014.
Galetta, Ontario. St. Augustine (United). File 06-0089000-00774.
Galetta, Ontario. Unidentified. File 06-0089000-00772.
Gloucester, Ontario. N.-D.-de-la-Présentation (Catholic). File 06-0083000-00101.
Gracefield, Quebec. N.-D.-de-la-Visitation (Catholic). File 05-7370001-00014.
Greely, Ontario. All Saints (Anglican). File 06-0083000-00637.
Grenville, Quebec. n.n. (Presbyterian). File 06-0034000-00046.
Grenville, Quebec. St. Matthew (Anglican). File 05-0034000-00040.
Harwood Plains, Ontario. St-Isidore (Catholic). File 06-0083000-00038.
Heyworth, Quebec. Heyworth United Church (United). File 05-0081000-00003.
Horton, Ontario. Garden of Eden (Christian). File 06-0097000-00014.
Hull, Quebec. Cusham Memorial (Presbyterian). File 05-3700021-00020.
Hull, Quebec. St. James (Anglican). File 05-3700015-00062.
Huntley, Ontario. Christ Church (Anglican). File 06-0083000-00204.
Huntley, Ontario. St. John (Anglican). File 06-0089000-01111.

Kars, Ontario. n.n. (Methodist). File 06-0078000-01758.
Kars, Ontario. St. Andrew (Presbyterian). File 06-0078000-00068.
Kars, Ontario. St. John (Anglican). File 06-0078000-00380.
Kazabazua, Quebec. n.n. (Anglican). File 05-0121000-00047.
Kazabazua, Quebec. Kazabazua United Church (United). File 05-0121000-00040.
Kenmore, Ontario. Kenmore United Church (United). File 06-0116000-00122.
Kerr Line, Ontario. n.n. (Presbyterian). File 06-0097000-00076.
Kilmaurs, Ontario. n.n. (Presbyterian). File 06-0089000-00003.
Kilroy Crescent, Quebec. Mountain View Church (United). File 05-0043000-00073.
Kinburn, Ontario. n.n. (Methodist). File 06-0089000-00032.
Kinburn, Ontario. St. Andrew (Presbyterian). File 06-0089000-00024.
L'Orignal, Ontario. St-Jean-Baptiste (Catholic). File 06-0004000-00032.
L'Orignal, Ontario. St. Andrew (Presbyterian). File 06-0040000-00021.
Lac Ste. Marie, Quebec. St-Nom-de-Marie (Catholic). File 05-0120000-00058.
Lachute, Quebec. Lachute United Church (United). File 05-1070013-00459.
Lascelles, Quebec. Holy Trinity (Anglican). File 05-0081000-00264.
Leitrim, Ontario. St. James (Anglican). File 06-0089000-00092.
Lochwinnoch, Ontario. Lochwinnoch (Presbyterian). File 06-0098000-00017.
Low, Quebec. Low United Church (United). File 05-0120000-00028.
Luskville, Quebec. St-Dominique (Catholic). File 05-0046000-00052.
Maniwaki, Quebec. "Église indienne" (n.d.). File 05-6170012-00304.
Maniwaki, Quebec. n.n. (Anglican). File 05-6170002-00199.
Maniwaki, Quebec. Assomption (Catholic). File 05-6170016-00331.
Maniwaki, Quebec. Maniwaki United Church (United). File 05-6170011-00183.
Manotick, Ontario. Old Methodist (Methodist). File 06-0078000-01752.
Manotick, Ontario. St. James (Anglican). File 06-0078000-01750.
Marathon Village, Ontario. St. John (Anglican). File 06-0089000-01111.
Martindale, Quebec. n.n. (Catholic). File 05-0120000-00042.
Mattawa, Ontario. St. Alban (Anglican). File 06-3740006-00002.
Mattawa, Ontario. St. Andrew's in the Pines (United). File 06-3740006-00001.
Mayo, Quebec. Our Lady of Malacky (Catholic). File 05-0110000-00152.
Messines, Quebec. St-Raphaël (Catholic). File 05-0138000-00052.
Metcalfe, Ontario. Holy Trinity (Anglican). File 06-0116000-00141.
Metcalfe, Ontario. Metcalfe United Church (United). File 06-0116000-00148.
Middleville Ontario. Middleville Baptist Church (Baptist). File 06-0041000-01018.
Middleville, Ontario. Trinity Church (United). File 06-0041000-01011.
Mille Isles, Quebec. n.n. (Presbyterian). File 05-0085000-00034.
Moncerf, Quebec. Ste-Philomène (Catholic). File 05-0155000-00004.
Montebello, Quebec. L.-J. Papineau Chapel (Catholic). File 05-0034000-00065.
Montebello, Quebec. Notre-Dame-de-Bonsecours (Catholic). File 05-7480001-00001.
Morin Heights, Quebec. Hornwright Church (Standard Ch.). File 05-5190003-00038.
Morin Heights, Quebec. Trinity Church (Anglican). File 05-5190003-00037.
Munster, Ontario. n.n. (Methodist). File 06-0078000-01813.
Munster, Ontario. St. Stephen (Anglican). File 06-0078000-00137.
N.-D.-de-la-Paix, Quebec. N.-D.-de-la-Paix (Catholic). File 05-754-0001-00001.
Namur, Quebec. St. Paul (Presbyterian). File 05-7520002-01000.
Navan, Ontario. St. Mary (Anglican). File 06-0093000-00196.
Nepean, Ontario. n.n. (Presbyterian). File 06-0083000-00540.
Nepean, Ontario. Christ Church (Anglican). File 06-0083000-00491.
Nepean, Ontario. Elim Church (Presbyterian). File 06-0083000-00485.

Nepean, Ontario. Merivale United Church (United). File 06-0083000-00540.
Nolans Corners, Ontario. St. Bede (Anglican). File 06-0080000-00298.
North Gower, Ontario. Holy Trinity (Anglican). File 06-0078000-01798.
North Gower, Ontario. North Gower Church (United). File 06-0078000-00343.
N.-D.-de-la-Salette, Quebec. Notre-Dame (Catholic). File 05-0120000-00087.
Old Chelsea, Quebec. St-Étienne (Catholic). File 05-0081000-00123.
Osceola, Ontario. St. Pius (Catholic). File 06-0097000-00237.
Osgoode, Ontario. St. Bridget (Catholic). File 06-0078000-00038.
Osgoode, Ontario. St. John the Evangelist (Catholic). File 06-0078000-00038.
Ottawa, Ontario. n.n. (Society of Friends). File 06-1070158-00091.
Ottawa, Ontario. Chinese Church. File 06-1070034-00312.
Ottawa, Ontario. Christ Church (Anglican). File 06-1070107-00439.
Ottawa, Ontario. Dominion Chalmers U. Church (United). File 06-1070028-00355.
Ottawa, Ontario. First Baptist Church (Baptist). File 06-1070106-00140.
Ottawa, Ontario. Free Methodist Church (Methodist). File 06-1070159-00160.
Ottawa, Ontario. Glebe Presbyterian (Presbyterian). File 06-1070156-00650.
Ottawa, Ontario. Grace Church (Anglican). File 06-1070030-00073.
Ottawa, Ontario. Holy Trinity (Anglican). File 06-1070025-00115.
Ottawa, Ontario. Knox Presbyterian Church (Presbyterian). File 06-107—34-00120.
Ottawa, Ontario. McPhail Memorial Church (Baptist). File 06-1070064-00249.
Ottawa, Ontario. Notre-Dame-du-Sacré-Coeur (Catholic). File 06-1070047-00143.
Ottawa, Ontario. Sacré-Coeur (Catholic). File 06-1070029-00585.
Ottawa, Ontario. Ste-Anne (Catholic). File 06-1070026-00530.
Ottawa, Ontario. St-François d'Assise (Catholic). File 06-107-115-01026.
Ottawa, Ontario. St. Bartholomew (Anglican). File 06-107-008-00125.
Ottawa, Ontario. St. Brigid (Catholic). File 06-1070026-00314.
Ottawa, Ontario. St. David (Reformed Epicopal). File 06-1070092-00013.
Ottawa, Ontario. St. George (Anglican). File 06-1070037-00152.
Ottawa, Ontario. St. James (United). File 06-1070071-00265.
Ottawa, Ontario. St. John (Lutheran). File 06-1070092-00250.
Ottawa, Ontario. St. John the Evangelist (Anglican). File 06-1070042-00154.
Ottawa, Ontario. St. Matthew (Unidentified). File 06-1070071-00217.
Ottawa, Ontario. St. Patrick (Catholic). File 06-1070138-00058.
Ottawa, Ontario. St. Paul (Lutheran). File 06-1070017-00210.
Ottawa, Ontario. St. Paul (Methodist). File 06-1070148-00001.
Ottawa, Ontario. St. Paul (Presbyterian). File 06-1070002-00102.
Ottawa, Ontario. Ukrainian Church (Orthodox). File 06-1070232-01000.
Ottawa, Ontario. Unidentified. File 06-1070062-00507.
Ottawa, Ontario. Unidentified. File 06-1070080-00250.
Ottawa, Ontario. Unidentified. File 06-1070230-00175.
Ottawa, Ontario. Westboro Baptist Church (Baptist). File 06-1070119-00307.
Pakenham, Ontario. St. Andrew (Presbyterian). File 06-0089000-01471.
Pakenham, Ontario. St. Mark (Anglican). File 06-0089000-01478.
Pakenham, Ontario. St. Peter Celestine (Catholic). File 06-0089000-01483.
Papineauville, Quebec. n.n. (Anglican). File 05-7530005-00137.
Papineauville, Quebec. Ste-Angélique (Catholic). File 05-7530001-00294.
Perkins, Quebec. Old Perkins United Church (United). File 05-0105000-00102.
Perkins, Quebec. St-Antoine-de-Padoue (Catholic). File 05-0105000-00100.
Pierce's Corners, Ontario. Unidentified. File 06-0078000-00403.
Pinhey Point, Ontario. New St. Mary (Anglican). File 06-083000-00328.
Plaisance, Quebec. Cœur-très-pur-de-Marie (Catholic). File 05-747001-00281.
Poltimore, Quebec. n.n. (Catholic). File 05-0120000-00082.

Poltimore, Quebec. Christ Church (Anglican). File 05-0120000-00075.
Portage-du-Fort, Quebec. Pentecostal Church (Presbyterian).
File 05-0047000-00049.
Portage-du-Fort, Quebec. St-Jacques and Ste-Rosalie (Catholic).
File 05-0047000-00045.
Portage-du-Fort, Quebec. St. George (Anglican). File 05-0047000-00041.
Portage-du-Fort, Quebec. St. James (Catholic). File 05-0047000-00045.
Poupore, Quebec. n.n. (Anglican). File 05-0105000-00084.
Prospect, Ontario. n.n. (United). File 06-0078000-00267.
Prospect, Ontario. St. Augustine (Anglican). File 06-0078000-00257.
Queen's Line, Ontario. n.n. (Methodist). File 06-0097000-00072.
Quinnville, Quebec. St. Columban (Catholic). File 05-0105000-00126.
Quyon, Quebec. n.n. (Methodist). File 05-0046000-00193.
Quyon, Quebec. St. John the Evangelist (Anglican). File 05-0046000-00001.
Ramsayville, Ontario. Bethany United Church (United). File 06-0083000-00603.
Riceville, Ontario. n.n. (Baptist). File 06-0085000-00084.
Riceville, Ontario. n.n. (Methodist). File 06-0085000-00085.
Richmond, Ontario. St. John (Anglican). File 06-0078000-01737.
Richmond, Ontario. St. Peter (Catholic). File 06-0078000-00231.
Rockhurst, Quebec. Wakefield United Church (United). File 05-0081000-00048.
Rupert, Quebec. Rupert United Church (United). File 05-0081000-00077.
Sarsfield, Ontario. St. Hugues (Catholic). File 06-0093000-00215.
Shawville, Quebec. n.n. (Baptist). File 05-0046000-00324.
Shawville, Quebec. n.n. (Methodist). File 05-0046000-00331.
Shawville, Quebec. St. Paul (Anglican). File 05-0046000-00332.
Shrewsbury, Quebec. Unidentified. File 05-0085000-00048.
Silver Creek, Quebec. St. Thomas (Anglican). File 05-0110000-00170.
Spring Hill, Ontario. Spring Hill Chapel (Presbyterian). File 06-0116000-00138.
Springtown, Ontario. St-Gabriel (Catholic). File 06-0098000-00232.
St-André Avellin, Quebec. St-André (Catholic). File 05-7490002-00070.
St-André Est, Quebec. n.n. (Congregational). File 05-4970008-00020.
St-André Est, Quebec. n.n. (Presbyterian). File 05-4970003-00007.
St-André Est, Quebec. Christ Church (Anglican). File 05-4970008-00012.
St-André Est, Quebec. Unidentified. File 05-4970006-00003.
St-Philippe d'Argenteuil, Quebec. St-Philippe (Catholic). File 05-5200002-00276.
Stark's Corners, Quebec. n.n. (Methodist). File 05-0047000-00074.
Ste-Cécile de Masham, Quebec. Ste-Cécile (Catholic). File 05-0046000-00304.
Stewartville, Ontario. n.n. (Presbyterian). File 06-0089000-00179.
Val des Bois, Quebec. n.n. (Catholic). File 05-0120000-00097.
Vars, Ontario. Knox United Church (United). File 06-0117000-00064.
Vars, Ontario. St. Andrew (Anglican). File 06-0093000-00270.
Vinton, Quebec. Ste-Elizabeth (Catholic). File 05-0044000-00002.
White Lake, Ontario. St. Andrew (Presbyterian). File 06-0089000-00210.
Wilson's Corners, Quebec. St. Andrew (United). File 05-0081000-00100.
Woodlawn, Ontario. Epworth Church (Unidentified). File 06-0089000-00050.
Woodlawn, Ontario. St. Thomas (Anglican). File 06-0089000-00608.
Wright, Quebec. St. James (Anglican). File 05-0138000-00080.

2. SECONDARY SOURCES

Adell, J., M. Coleman, L. Maitland, and M. Trépanier, "Mid-Nineteenth Century Cathedrals." Ottawa: Historic Sites and Monuments Board of Canada, 1989.

Airhart, Phyllis D. "Ordering a New Nation and Reordering Protestantism 1867-1914." In *The Canadian Protestant Experience 1790-1990*. ed. G. Rawlyk, 98-138. Burlington: Welch Publishing, 1990.

Akenson, Donald H. *The Irish in Ontario: A Study of Rural History*. Kingston and Montreal: McGill-Queens University Press, 1984.

Allen, W. O. B., and E. McClure, *The History of the Society for Promoting Christian Knowledge 1698-1891*. New York: B. Franklin, 1970.

Anon. *Album des églises de la province de Québec*. Vol. 1-7, Montréal: Compagnie canadienne nationale de publication, 1928.

Aubert, M., ed. *Petites monographies des grands édifices de la France*. Paris: Henri Laurens, n.d.

Bédard, Hélène, *Maisons et églises au Québec XVIIe, XVIIIe, XIXe siècles*. Québec: M.A.C., 1969.

Bennett, V. "Early Catholic Architecture in the Ottawa Valley: An initial investigation of nineteenth century parish churches," *Canadian Catholic Historical Studies*, vol. 60 (1993-1994): 17-42.

—. "Religious regulation of Anglo Protestant Cult Space in nineteenth century Canada", *Les dieux et des hommes en terre canadienne*. ed. Raymond Lemieux. Québec: Presses de l'Université Laval. Forthcoming.

Bergevin, H. *Églises protestantes*. Montréal: Libre Expression, 1981.

Bertal Henney, William, ed. *Leaders of the Canadian Church*. Toronto: Ryerson Press, 1918.

Bibby, Reginald. *Fragmented Gods: The Poverty and Potential of Religion in Canada*. Toronto: Irwin Publishing, 1987.

Bielier, A. *Liturgie et architecture, le temple des chrétiens; Esquisses des rapports entre la théologie du culte et la conception architecturale des églises chrétiennes des origines à nos jours*. Genève: Léon et Fidès, 1961.

Black, Robert M. "Anglicans and French Canadian Evangelism 1839-1848." *Journal of the Canadian Church Historical Society* 26, 1 (1984): 18-33.

—. "Different Visions: The multiplication of Protestant Missions to French-Canadian Roman Catholics, 1834-1855." *Canadian Protestant and Catholic Missions 1820s-1960s, Historical Essays in Honor of John Webster Grant*. Vol. 3. Toronto: Studies in Religion, 1988.

Bond, Courtney. *City on the Ottawa*, Ottawa: Queen's Printer, 1961.

Bonelli, R. *Il Duomo di Orvieto e l'Archittettura Italiana del Duecento Trecento*. Edizioni dell'angelo: Città di Castello, 1952.

Bony, Jean. *French Gothic Architecture of the 12th and 13th Centuries*. Berkeley: University of California Press, 1983.

Brault, L. *Histoire de la Pointe-Gatineau, 1807-1947*. Montréal: École industrielle des Sourds-Muets, 1948.

—. *Histoire des comtés unis de Prescott et de Russell.* L'Orignal: Conseil des comtés unis, 1965.

—. *Hull, 1800-1950*. Ottawa: Les Éditions de l'Université d'Ottawa, 1950.

—. *Ottawa, capitale du Canada: de ses origines à nos jours*. Ottawa: Les Éditions de l'Université d'Ottawa, 1942.

—. *Ottawa Old and New*. Ottawa: Ottawa Historical Information Institute, 1946.

Brooke, C. *Monasteries of the World: The Rise and Development of Monastic Tradition*. New York: Crescent Books, 1982.

Brosseau, Mathilde. *Le Style néo-gothique dans l'architecture au Canada*. Ottawa: Centre d'édition du Gouvernement du Canada, 1980.

Brown, B. ed. *Vasari on Technique*. New York: Dover, 1960.

Buggy, Susan. "Researching Canadian Buildings: Some Historical Sources." *Histoire sociale/Social History*, 10, 20 (November 1977): 409-426.

Burish, Alice Biehler. *Olden Days: A History of German Settlement in the Township of Mulgrave-Derry, Quebec, 1850-1890*. Quyon: Chesley House Publications, 1990.

Burt, A. L. *Guy Carleton, Lord Dorchester, 1724-1808*. Ottawa: Canadian Historical Association, 1985.

Camber, Robert, and John Somerville, eds. *Rules and Forms of Procedure in the Church Courts of the Presbyterian Church in Canada.* Toronto: Westminster Co., 1914.

Carrière, Gaston. *Histoire documentaire de la Congrégation des missionnaires Oblats de Marie-Immaculée au Canada*. Ottawa: Les Éditions de l'Université d'Ottawa, 1957-1975.

Carrington, Philip. *The Anglican Church in Canada*. Toronto: Collins, 1963.

Cartwright, D. G. "Ecclesiastical Territorial Organization and Institutional Conflict in Eastern and Northern Ontario, 1840-1910." *Historical Papers/Communications historiques.* Ottawa and London: Société historique du Canada, 1978.

Chadwick, O. *The Mind of the Oxford Movement*. London: Black, 1960.

Champneys, Arthur C. *Irish Ecclesiastical Architecture with some notice of similar or related works in England, Scotland and elsewhere*. London: G. Bell and Sons Ltd.; Dublin: Hodges, Figgis and Co. Ltd., 1910. Reprinted by Shannon: Irish University Press, 1970.

Chinard, Gilbert. *Les réfugiés huguenots en Amérique*, Paris: Société d'édition les Belles Lettres, 1925.

Choquette, Robert. "French Catholicism in the New World." *The Encyclopedia of the American Religious Experience*. New York: Scribner's and Sons, 1988.

—. *L'Église catholique dans l'Ontario français du dix-neuvième siècle*. Ottawa: Les Éditions de l'Université d'Ottawa, 1984.

—. *Language and Religion. A History of English-French Conflict in Ontario.* Ottawa: University of Ottawa Press, 1975.

Christensen, C. *Art and the Reformation in Germany*. Athens: Ohio University Press, 1979.

Christie, N. "'In these times of Democratic Rage and Delusion': Popular Religion and the Challenge to the Established Order, 1760-1815." ed. G. Rawlyk, 9-47. *The Canadian Protestant Experience 1790-1990*. Burlington: Welch Publishing, 1990.

Church, R. W. *The Oxford Movement, Twelve Years 1833-1845*. Hamden, CT: Archon Books, 1966.

Clark, Kenneth. *The Gothic Revival: An Essay in the History of Taste*. New York: Harper and Row, 1962.

Clark, S. D. *Church and Sect in Canada*. Toronto: University of Toronto Press, 1948.

Clarke, Basil F. L. *Church Builders of the Nineteenth Century: A Study of the Gothic Revival in England*. London: Society for Promoting Christian Knowledge, 1938.

Clasen, K. H. *Handbuch des deutschen Kunstdenkmäler*. 5 vols., Berlin: n.p., 1927.

Clerk, Natalie. *Palladian Style in Canadian Architecture: Studies in Archaeology, Architecture and History*. Ottawa: Parks Canada, Minister of the Environment, 1984.

Clifford, N. K. "His Dominion: A Vision in Crisis," *S.R.* 2, 4 (1973).

Cooper, John I. *The Blessed Communion, The Origins and History of the Diocese of Montreal*. Montreal: Archives Committee of the Diocese of Montreal, 1960.

Cronmiller, C. R. *History of the Lutheran Church in Canada*. Toronto: Evangelical Lutheran Synod of Canada, 1961.

Danylewycz, Marta. *Taking the Veil: An Alternative to Marriage, Motherhood and Spinsterhood in Quebec, 1840-1920*. Toronto: McClelland and Stewart, 1987.

Decker, H. *L'Italie gothique*. Paris: Braun et Cie, 1964.

Dehil, G. *Geschichte der deutschen Kunst*. Berlin: W. de Gruyter, 1930-1934.

Devie, A.-R. *Manuel de connaissances utiles aux ecclésiastiques sur divers objets d'art notamment sur l'architecture des édifices religieux anciens et modernes, et sur les constructions et réparations d'églises—Avec plans et dessins lithographiés*. Lyon: L. Lesne, 1843.

Dorland, A.G. *A History of the Society of Friends (Quakers) in Canada*. Toronto: Macmillan, 1927.

—. *The Quakers in Canada:* A History. Toronto: Ryerson Press, 1968.

Duclos, R. P. *Histoire du protestantisme français au Canada et aux États-Unis*. Montréal: Librairie Évangélique, 1913.

Eire, Carlos. *War against the Idols: The Reformation of Worship from Erasmus to Calvin*. Cambridge: Cambridge University Press, 1991.

Elliot, Bruce S. "Ritualism and the Beginnings of the Reformed Episcopal Movement in Ottawa." *Journal of the Canadian Church Historical Society* 27, 1(April 1985): 18-47.

—. "The Northern Tipperary Protestants in the Canadas: A Study of Migration, 1815-1880." Ph.D. thesis, Carleton University, 1984.

—. *The City Beyond: A History of Nepean, Birthplace of Canada's Capital 1792-1990*. Nepean: City of Nepean, 1991.

Emery, George. "The Origins of Canadian Methodist Involvement in the Social Gospel Movement, 1890-1914." *The Bulletin* 19, 26 (1977).

Epp, Frank H. *Mennonites in Canada, 1786-1920, The History of a Separate People*. Toronto: Macmillan, 1974.

Fahey, Curtis. "A Troubled Zion: The Anglican Experience in Upper Canada 1791-1854." Ph.D. dissertation, Carleton University, 1981.

—. *In His Name: The Anglican Experience in Upper Canada 1791-1854*. Ottawa: Carleton University Press, 1991.

Fee, Norman. *Knox Presbyterian Church, A History of the Congregation*. Ottawa: Mortimer Ltd., 1944.

Fitch, E. R., *The Baptists of Canada: A History of their Progresses and Achievements*. Toronto: Standard, 1911.

Fitchen, John. *The Construction of Gothic Cathedrals*. Chicago: The University of Chicago Press, 1961.

Focillon, Henri. *The Art of the West in the Middle Ages*. ed. Jean Bony. London and New York: Phaidon Press, 1963.

Fontaney, Pierre. *Le renouveau gothique en Angleterre: Idéologie et architecture*. Bordeaux: Presses Universitaires de Bordeaux, 1988.

Foucart, Bruno. *Viollet-le-Duc*. Paris: Éditions de la Réunion des musées nationaux, 1980.

Frankl, Paul. *Gothic Architecture*. Baltimore: Pelican, 1962.

—. *Principles of Architectural History. The Four Phases of Architectural Style, 1420-1900*, ed. James O'Gorman, James, ed. Cambridge: MIT Press, 1968.

Fraser, Brian J. *The Social Uplifters: Presbyterian Progressives and the Social Gospel in Canada 1875-1915*. Vol. 20. Waterloo, Ont.: Wilfrid Laurier University Press, 1988.

French, Goldwin. *Parsons and Politics, The Role of the Wesleyan Methodists in Upper Canada and the Maritimes from 1780-1855*. Toronto: Ryerson Press, 1962.

Gall, E. *Die Gotische Baukunst in Frankreich und Deutschland*. Braunschweig: Klinkhardt, 1955.

Gauvreau, Michael. "Protestantism Transformed: Personal Piety and the Evangelical Social Vision, 1815-1867." In *The Canadian Protestant Experience 1790-1990*, ed. G. Rawlyk, 49-97. Burlington: Welch Publishing, 1990.

—. *The Evangelical Century: College and Creed in English Canada From the Great Revival to the Great Depression*. Kingston and Montreal: McGill-Queen's University Press, 1991.

Gaya Nuño, J. A. *Historia del Arte Español*. Madrid: Plus Ultra, 1968.

Gloag, John. *Victorian Taste: Some Social Aspects of Architecture Industrial Design, From 1820-1900*. London: David and Charles Reprints, 1972.

Gowans, Alan. *Building Canada, An Architectural History of Canadian Life*. Toronto: Oxford University Press, 1966.

—. *Church Architecture in New France*. Toronto: University Press, 1955.

Graham, Elizabeth. *Medicine Man to Missionary: Missionary Agents of Change Among the Indians of Southern Ontario, 1784-1867*. Toronto: Peter Martin Assoc., 1975.

Grant, John W. "Canadian Confederation and the Protestant Churches." *Church History*, Vol. 38, 3:327-337.

—. "Confederation and the Protestant Churches." Paper delivered at a joint session of The American Society of Church History and The American Catholic Historical Association, Toronto, December 29, 1967.

—. "Kanada." *Evangelisches Kirchenlexikon:* International theologische Enzyklopädie. eds. Britta Hübener and Dietrich Voorgang. Göttingen: Vandenhoeck und Ruprecht, 1986.

—. "Presbyterian Home Missions and Canadian Nationhood." *Atti del 7º Convegno Internazionale di Studi Canadesi.* Biblioteca Della Ricerca, Cultura Straniera, 18-22 maggio 1988, 30.

—. *A Profusion of Spires: Religion in Nineteenth-Century Ontario.* Toronto: University of Toronto Press, 1988.

—. *Moon of Wintertime: Missionaries and the Indians of Canada in Encounter since 1534.* Toronto: University of Toronto Press, 1984.

—. *The Church in the Canadian Era.* Burlington: Welch Publishing Company, 1988.

Grodecki, L. *Gothic Architecture.* New York: Abrams, 1976.

Handy, Robert. *A History of the Churches in the United States and Canada.* New York: Oxford University Press, 1977.

Harris, Cyril. *Illustrated Dictionary of Historic Architecture.* New York: Dover, 1983.

Hay, George. *The Architecture of Scottish Post-reformation Churches 1560-1843.* Oxford: Clarendon Press, 1957.

Headon, Christopher F. "Developments in Canadian Anglican Worship in Eastern and Central Canada, 1840-1868." *Journal of the Canadian Church Historical Society,* vol. 17 (1975): 26-37.

—. "Women and Organized Religion in mid and late nineteenth century Canada." *Journal of the Canadian Church Historical Society,* 20, 1-2 (1978): 3-18.

Hessel, Peter. *Destination: Ottawa Valley.* Ottawa: Runge Press Ltd., 1984.

Heydon, N. *Looking Back: Pioneers of Bytown and March, Nicholas Sparks and Hamnett Kirkes Pinhey—Their Antecedents and Their Descendants.* Ottawa: Nemo Publications, 1980.

Hill, H. *History of Christ Church, Ottawa.* Ottawa: Runge Press Ltd., 1932.

Holmes, David. "The Anglican Tradition and the Episcopal Church." *E.A.R.E.*

Hubbard, R. H. "Canadian Gothic." *Architectural Review,* August 1954, 102-8.

—. *Cathedral in the Capital: A Short History of Christ Church Cathedral Ottawa.* Ottawa: Cathedral Centenary Committee, 1972.

Hughson, J. and C. C. Bond. *Hurling Down the Pine.* Old Chelsea: Historical Society of the Gatineau, 1964.

Humphreys, Barbara A. "The Architectural Heritage of the Rideau Corridor." *Canadian Historic Sites: Occasional Papers in Archaeology and History.* Ottawa: National Historic Parks and Sites, Indian and Northern Affairs, 1974.

Humphries, Doris, and Campbell Humphries. *Horton, the Story of a Township.* Renfrew: Juniper Books, 1986.

Ivirson, Stuart, and Fred Rosser. *The Baptists in Upper and Lower Canada Before 1820*. Toronto: University of Toronto Press, 1963.

Jaenen, Cornelius. *Friend and Foe: Aspects of French-Amerindian Culture Contact in the Sixteenth and Seventeenth Centuries*. Toronto: McClelland and Stewart, 1976.

—. *The Role of the Church in New France*. Toronto: McGraw-Hill Ryerson Ltd., 1976.

James, Peter D. "Righteousness Exalteth the Nation: The Toronto Banner and the Nineteenth Century Evangelical Crusade in Upper Canada." M.A. thesis, Carleton University, 1981.

Jantzen, H. *Kunst der Gothik*. Hamburg: Rowohlt, 1957.

Jefferson, R., and Leonard L. Johnson. *Faith of Our Fathers: The Story of the Diocese of Ottawa*. Ottawa: The Anglican Book Society, 1956.

Johnston, Grace. *Bowesville: A Place to Remember*. Gloucester: Gloucester Historical Society, 1988.

Kenyon, J. "The Influence of the Oxford Movement upon the Church of England in Upper Canada," *Ontario History*, vol. 51 (1959).

Kewley, A. E. "The Begining of the Camp Meeting Movement in Upper Canada," *Canadian Journal of Theology*, 10, 3 (1964): 192-202.

Kleinsteuber, R. Wayne. *More Than a Memory: The Renewal of Methodism in Canada*. Toronto: Light and Life Press, 1984.

Lapointe, Pierre-Louis. "Old Fort William (Quebec)," *Association of Preservation Technology Bulletin*, 8, 1(1976): 43-58.

Lee-Whiting, Brenda. *Harvest of Stones: The German Settlement in Renfrew County*. Toronto: University of Toronto Press, 1985.

—. *On Stony Ground*. Renfrew: Juniper Books, 1986.

Legrange, M.-S. *Code pour l'analyse des monuments civils*. Paris: Éditions du Centre national de la recherche scientifique, 1975.

Legros, H. and Soeur Paul-Émile. *Le Diocèse d'Ottawa, 1847-1948*. Ottawa: Le Droit, 1949.

Legros, H. *1830-1966, Sainte-Cécile-de-La-Pêche, Masham, Comté de Gatineau, Province de Québec*. Hull: n.p., 1967.

Lemieux, Lucien. *Histoire du catholicisme québécois: Les XVIIIe et XIXe siècle*. Montréal: Boréal, 1989.

Lerner, L. and M. F. Williamson. *Art and Architecture in Canada/Art et Architecture au Canada: Bibliographic Guide to the Literature to 1981/Bibliographie et guide de la documentation jusqu'en 1981*. Toronto: University of Toronto Press, 1991.

Little, Bryan. *Catholic Churches Since 1623: A Study of Roman Catholic Churches in England and Wales from Penal Times to the Present Decade*. London: Robert Hale, 1966.

Lockwood, Glenn, J. "Eastern Upper Canadian Perceptions of Irish Immigrants 1824-1868." Ph.D. dissertation, University of Ottawa, 1988.

—. *Beckwith: Irish and Scottish Identities in a Canadian Community*. Beckwith: Corporation of the Township of Beckwith, 1991.

—. *Montague: A Social History of an Irish Ontario Township*. Smiths Falls: Corporation of the Township of Montague, 1980.

Lortie, Jeanne d'Arc. *Lettres d'Elisabeth Bruyère, Vol. I, 1839-1849*. Montréal: Éditions Paulines, 1989.

Lower, J. Arthur. *Western Canada, An Outline History*. Vancouver and Toronto: Douglas and McIntyre, 1983.

Lucas, Calvin Glenn. "Presbyterianism in Carleton County to 1867." M.A. thesis, Carleton University, 1973.

MacFarlane, Kate. "Architectural Competition." Unpublished manuscript.

MacPhail, John G. *St. Andrew's Church—Ottawa: The First Hundred Years, 1828-1928*. Ottawa: Dodson-Merrill Press Ltd., 1931.

MacRae, Marion and A. Adamson. *Hallowed Walls: Church Architecture of Upper Canada*. Toronto: Clarke, Irwin and Co., 1975.

Magney, W. H. "The Methodist Church and the National Gospel." *The Bulletin*, no. 20 (1968): 3-95.

Maitland, L. *A Guide to Canadian Architectural Styles*. Peterborough: Broadview Press, 1992.

Maitland, Leslie, J. Hucker, and S. Ricketts. *Neoclassical Architecture in Canada: Studies in Archaeology Architecture and History*. Ottawa: Parks Canada, Minister of the Environment, 1984.

Mâle, E. *L'Art religieux de la fin du Moyen Âge en France*. Paris: Colin, 1931.

Masters, D. C. *Protestant Church Colleges in Canada: A History. Études sur l'histoire de l'enseignement supérieur au Canada/Studies in the History of Higher Education in Canada*. Toronto: University of Toronto Press, 1966.

May, E. G. and W. Millen. *The History of the Parish of Hull, Being the Record of the First Hundred Years 1823-1923*. Dadson-Merrill Press, Ottawa, 1923.

McGowan, M. and D. Marshall. *Prophets, Priests and Prodigals: Readings in Canadian Religious History, 1608 to Present*. Toronto: McGraw-Hill Ryerson, 1992.

Mealing, S. R. "The Enthusiasms of John Graves Simcoe." *Canadian Historical Association Report*, 1958.

Menozzi, Danièle. *Les Images: L'Église et les arts visuels*. Paris: Les Éditions du cerf, 1991.

Ministre des Affaires Culturelles du Québec. *Le Patrimoine du Pontiac.* Le groupe pour la sauvegarde du patrimoine du Pontiac, Les Cahiers du Patrimoine, no. 14, 1981.

Moir, John. *Church and State in Canada 1627-1867*. Toronto: McClelland and Stewart Ltd., 1967.

—. *Enduring Witness: A History of the Presbyterian Church in Canada*. Toronto: Eagle Press, 1987.

—. *The Church in the British Era*. Toronto: McGraw-Hill Ryerson, 1972.

Morisset, G. *L'Architecture en Nouvelle-France, Québec.* Québec: Charrier et Dugal, 1949.

—. *Les églises et le trésor de Lotbinière, Québec*. Québec: Charrier et Dugal, 1953.

—. *Les églises et le trésor de Varennes, Québec*. Québec: Médium, 1943.

Morton, W. L., ed. *The Shield of Achilles: Aspects of Canada in the Victorian Age/Le Bouclier d'Achille: Regards sur l'ère victorienne*. Toronto and Montreal: McClelland and Stewart, 1968.

Nivelle, N. *Code pour l'analyse des monuments religieux*. Paris: Éditions du Centre national de la recherche scientifique, 1975.

Noppen, Luc et al. *Québec, trois siècles d'architecture*. Québec: Libre Expression, 1979.

Noppen, Luc and Lucie K. Morisset. *La Présence anglicane à Québec*. Siller: Les éditions du Septentrion, 1995.

Noppen, Luc. *Au Musée des beaux-arts du Canada "Une des plus belles chapelles du pays."* Ottawa: Musée des beaux-arts du Canada, 1988.

—. *Les Églises du Québec 1600-1850*. Québec: Éditeur Officiel du Québec/Fides, 1977.

—. *Notre-Dame de Québec*. Québec: Éditions du Pélican, 1974.

O'Gallagher, Marianna. *Saint Patrick's, Quebec: The Building of a Church and of a Parish 1827-1833*. Quebec: Carraig Books, 1981.

Pagé, Norman. "La chapelle du Musée des beaux-arts du Canada et son contexte d'origine." *Cultures du Canada français*. Ottawa: Les Presses de l'Université d'Ottawa, 1989.

—. *La Cathédrale Notre-Dame d'Ottawa*. Ottawa: Les Presses de l'Université d'Ottawa, 1988.

Panofsky, E. *Gothic Architecture and Scholasticism*. New York: Meridian, 1951.

—. *Gothic Architecture and Scholasticism: An Inquiry into the Analogy of the Arts, Philosophy and Religion in the Middle Ages*. New York: Meridian Books, 1957.

Peers, Michael et al. "The Canadian Apostolic Genealogy: The Bicentennial of the Anglican Episcopate in Canada 1787-1987." *Journal of the Canadian Church Historical Society* 29, 2 (1987): 71, ff.

Penton, James. *Apocalypse Delayed: A Story of the Jehovah's Witnesses*. Toronto: University of Toronto Press. 1985.

—. *Jehovah's Witnesses in Canada: Champions of Freedom and Speech and Worship*. Toronto: Macmillan, 1976.

Petzsch, Helmut. *Architecture in Scotland*. London: Longman Group, 1971.

Pierson, W. *Technology and the Picturesque, the Corporate and the Early Gothic Styles*. Oxford and New York: Oxford University Press, 1986.

Pitman, Walter. *The Baptists and Public Affairs in the Province of Canada, 1848-1867*. New York: Arno Press, 1980.

Port, M. H. *Six Hundred New Churches*. London: S.P.C.K., 1961.

Prévost, Robert. *Montréal la folle entreprise : Chronique d'une ville*. Montréal: Stanké, 1991.

Quiring, Walter and Helen Bartel. *Mennonites in Canada: A Pictorial Review*. Altona: D.W. Friesen and Sons, 1961.

Rawlyk, George A., ed. *The Canadian Protestant Experience 1760 to 1990*. Burlington: Welch Publishing Company, 1990.

Reid, Richard M., ed. *The Upper Ottawa Valley to 1855*. Ottawa: Carleton University Press, 1989.

Renfree, Harry A. *Heritage and Horizon: The Baptist Story in Canada*. Mississauga: Canadian Baptist Federation, 1988.

Roger, C. *Ottawa Past and Present*. Ottawa: Times Printing and Publishing, 1871.

Roy, P. G. *Les vieilles églises de la province de Québec, 1647-1800*. Québec: Imprimeur du Roy, 1925.

Ruddel, David-T. *Le protestantisme français au Québec, 1840-1919: "images" et témoignages*. Ottawa: Musée national de l'homme, 1983.

Sanderson, J. E. *Methodism in Canada*. Toronto: William Briggs, 1910.

Schmidt, M. *Manuel de l'architecture des monuments ou Traité d'application pratique de l'archéologie chrétienne à la construction, à l'entretien, à la restauration et à la décoration des églises*. Paris: Roret, 1845.

Schwermann, Rev. Albert H. *The Beginnings of the Lutheran Church—Canada*. Edmonton: Lutheran Church—Canada, 1971.

Sider, E. Morris. *The Brethren in Christ in Canada: Two Hundred Years of Tradition and Change*. Canadian Conference, Brethren in Christ Church, Evangelical Press, 1988.

Simson, O. Von. *The Gothic Cathedral, The Origins of Gothic Architecture and the Medieval Concept of Order.* New York: Bollingen Foundation, 1956.

Smith, E., G. Hutton, and O. Cook. *English Parish Churches*. London: Thames and Hudson, 1989.

Smith, H.G. et al. *A Short History of the Presbyterian Church in Canada*. Toronto: Presbyterian Press, 1965.

—. *Enkindled by the Word: Essays on Presbyterianism in Canada*. Toronto: Presbyterian Press, 1965.

Spragg, Shirley. "St. Paul's Chapel of the Mohawks, Mohawk Road, Brantford Ontario." *Journal of the Canadian Church Historical Society*, 27, 2 (1988): 119-20.

Stanton, Phoebe B. *The Gothic Revival and American Church Architecture: An Episode in Taste 1840-1856*. Baltimore: John Hopkin's Press, 1968.

Steinhart, J. et al. *Conservation of Heritage Buildings in The National Capital Region; Legal and Economic Methods of Conserving Buildings of Historical Architectural or Cultural Importance*. Ottawa: n.p., 1971.

Stoddard, W. S. *Art and Architecture in Medieval France*. New York: Harper and Row, 1972.

Summerson, John. *Architecture in Britain 1530-1830*. Middlesex: Penguin Books, 1977.

—. *Georgian London*. Middlesex: Penguin Books, 1978.

Swan, W. *The Gothic Cathedral*. New York: Park Lane, 1984.

Sylvain, Philippe, and Nive Voisine. *Histoire du catholicisme québécois Vol. II, tome 2, Réveil et consolidation,1840-1898*. Montréal: Éditions du Boréal, 1991.

Tafuri, Manfredo. *Theories and History of Architecture*. New York: Harper and Row, 1980.

Thurlby, Malcolm. "Nineteenth Century Churches in Ontario: A Study of Meaning and Style," in *Historic Kingston*. vol. 35. Kingston: Kingston Historical Society, 1987.

Toker, F.K.B.S. *L'Église de Notre-Dame de Montréal, son architecture, son passé*. Ville LaSalle: Éditions Hurtubise H.M.H., 1981.

—. *The Church of Notre-Dame in Montreal.* Montreal and Kingston: McGill-Queen's University Press, 1970

Torres Balbás, L. *Ars Hispaniae : Historia universal del arte hispanica, Vol. vii Architectura Gótica*. Madrid: Plus—Ultra, 1947-1977.

Traquair, R. *The Old Architecture of Quebec.* Toronto: Macmillan, 1947

Tremblay, D. "Caractères et tendances de l'architecture religieuse dans le Québec." *Journal of the Royal Architectural Institute of Canada*, no. 323 (June 1952): 228-230

Turnor, Reginald. *Nineteenth Century Architecture in Britain*. London: B.T. Batsford Ltd., 1950.

Van Die, Marguerite. *An Evangelical Mind: Nathanel Burwash and the Methodist Tradition in Canada, 1839-1918*. Kingston and Montreal: McGill-Queen's University Press, 1989.

Van Kirk, Sylvia. *Many Tender Ties. Women in Fur-Trade Society in Western Canada 1670-1870*. Winnipeg: Watson and Dyer Publishing Ltd., 1980.

Vaudry, Richard W. *The Free Church in Victorian Canada 1844-1861*. Waterloo: Wilfrid Laurier University Press, 1989.

Voisine, Nive and Jean Hamelin. *Les Ultramontains canadiens-français*. Montréal: Boréal Express, 1985.

Voyer, L. *Églises disparues*. Québec: Libre Expression, 1981.

Watkin, David. *The Rise of Architectural History*. London: The Architectural Press, 1980.

Westfall, William. *Two Worlds: The Protestant Culture of Nineteenth-Century Ontario*. Kingston and Montreal: McGill-Queen's University Press, 1989.

White, J. *Art and Architecture in Italy, 1250-1400*. Hammondsworth: Penguin Books, 1966.

White, James F. *Protestant Worship and Church Architecture: Theological and Historical Considerations*. New York: Oxford University Press, 1964.

—. *Protestant Worship: Tradition in Transition*. Louisville, Ky: Westminster/John Knox Press, 1989.

—. *The Cambridge Movement: The Ecclesiologists and the Gothic Revival.* Cambridge: Cambridge University Press, 1962.

Whitton, Charlotte. "Most Venerable in the Capital, The Church of St. Alban the Martyr, Ottawa," *Journal of the Canadian Church Historical Society* 11, 2 (June 1969): 36-42.

Wilson, Alan. *The Clergy Reserves of Upper Canada: A Canadian Mortmain.* Toronto: University of Toronto Press, 1968.

Woelfle, John. *History of Lutheranism in Ontario*. n.p., 1938.

Yates, Nigel. *Buildings, Faith and Worship: The Liturgical Arrangement of Anglican Churches 1600-1900*. Oxford: Clarendon Press, 1991.

Zubalik, Janis R. "'Advancing the Material Interests of the Redeemer's Kingdom': The Erskine Presbyterian Church, Montreal, 1894"; M.A. Thesis, Concordia University, 1986.

LIST OF ILLUSTRATIONS

INDEX

The paper used in this publication meets the minimum requirements
of American National Standard for Information Sciences -
Permanence of Paper for Printed Library Materials, ANSI Z39.48-1992.

Québec, Canada
1998